Re-envisaging West Asia

Re-envisaging West Asia

Looking Beyond The Arab Uprisings

Editor
Priya Singh

Maulana Abul Kalam Azad Institute of Asian Studies

SHIPRA

ISBN: 978-81-7541-870-7

First Published in India in 2016

Re-envisaging West Asia: Looking Beyond The Arab Uprisings

Published by:
SHIPRA PUBLICATIONS
LG 18-19, Pankaj Central Market, I.P. Ext.
Patparganj, Delhi-110092, India
Tel: 91-11-2223 5152, 2223 6152
E-mail: info@shiprapublication.com
www.shiprapublication.com

Contents

Introduction

Re-conceptualising West Asia

Priya Singh

Robert Kaplan in analyzing the breakdown of the Arab world today, with lawlessness in parts of North Africa, the Arabian Peninsula, and the Levant, refers to it as the end of imperialism. According to him, the recent capture of Palmyra by the 'Islamic State' merely strengthens this argument as Palmyra exemplifies how the region in history has been defined by trade routes rather than fixed borders. Therefore, its capture simply establishes the fact that the world is once again returning to that fluid reality of constantly changing and indefinite borders. For Kaplan, the region is observing the collapse of three imperial systems.

First, Middle Eastern chaos demonstrates that the region has still not found a solution to the collapse of the Ottoman Empire after World War I. For hundreds of years, Sunnis and Shiites, Arabs and Jews, Muslims and Christians, in Greater Syria and Mesopotamia had few territorial disputes. All fell under the rule of an imperial sovereign in Istanbul, who protected them from each other. That system collapsed in 1918, unleashing the demon of national, ethnic, and sectarian disputes over who controls which territory at what border precisely. Second, the implosion of Iraq in the wake of the toppling of Saddam Hussein, the implosion of Syria in the wake of the Arab Spring, and the rise of the Islamic State has brought to an end the borders erected by European imperialism, British and French, in the Levant. Third, the demonstrably hands-off approach to these developments by President Barack Obama manifests the end of America's great power role in organizing and stabilizing the region.[1]

In the aftermath of the Arab uprisings, there have been constant attempts at rethinking or reimagining the region. However, it should be remembered, this is not the first time that a re-envisaging of the region labelled as West Asia or the Middle East and North Africa (MENA) is taking place. The construction and deconstruction of the region has been a recurrent feature among experts besides being intertwined in various debates and controversies. Morten Valbjorn, in attempting to explicate the ambiguity and vagueness of the construct described the Middle East as being shrouded in a "'geo-epistemological fog' which.... renders any attempt to demarcate its boundaries and define the theatre and cast of players nearly impossible."[2] Valbjorn refers to Said and McAlister to state that the expression 'Middle East' has in fact been regarded by some as fictitious in the sense that it refers to an 'imaginary region' created through discursive practices closely connected to the (re)construction of a distinctive western self-identity and style of controlling other parts of the world and using Gallie's terminology, characterises the region as constituting the category of 'essentially contested concepts,' as a result of which it would be futile to attempt at a universally approved understanding of what the Middle East actually is.[3] West Asia/MENA has essentially represented an ideational construct maintained by geographical, intellectual, and ideological representations. The geographical boundaries of the region have shifted over the past century to mirror the strategic interests of the major hegemonic power in the region, which, initially was Britain and later the United States. The region as a concept is a comparatively modern and an unsteady construction. Since the term was initially conceived at the beginning of the 20th century, it has been applied to diverse sets of nations and territories.[4] Likewise there is no unanimity regarding a generally accepted universalist approach to the study of Middle Eastern politics as it is looked upon in a certain way by exponents of international relations and in a different and distinctive manner by regional specialists. The rise of linguistic nationalisms further confounded the situation with the reiteration of the belief that the Middle East was much more than simply a geographical expression with its inhabitants responding to and articulating different loyalties and values as well as incorporating and accommodating Arab, Persian and Ottoman cultural influences and variants of Islam.

Reading the Arab Uprisings

Coming back to the present, the Arab uprisings, which began with the self-immolation of Mohammed Bouazizi in Tunisia in 2010, according to Marc Lynch, inducted a period of contentious politics, which has restructured the landscape of regional politics and defied the theories that have dominated the literature on the comparative politics of the Middle East. For the last several decades the political science literature on the region focused on the resilience of engrained authoritarianism, the comparative weakness of civil society and the seeming restricted effect of the dissemination of new norms and notions through new information and communications technology. The initial reactions to the uprisings perhaps exaggerated their uniqueness and possibility and whether the surge in confrontational political action will actually usher in lasting political change remains extremely unclear. It is also difficult to quantify and explain the political changes that have ensued. The overwhelming pace of the Arab Spring has now given way to a persistent, distrait and increasingly violent set of intertwined conflicts for control. The Arab uprisings of 2011 entail a vigorous model of political contention that takes into consideration the interface of various actors incorporating multiple levels of analysis. The interconnected political and media space in which these revolutions spread-out were possibly one of the most distinguishing characteristics of this period, entrenched in the long-lasting evolution of the pan-Arab media such as Al-Jazeera and the merging of global activist networks in the years leading up to the protests. However, those shared themes played out in separate political arenas, each with a distinctive accepted history, ethnic and sectarian composition and political balance of forces. The vigour of these protests was ultimately grounded in the face of the power and resolve of those regimes that did not capitulate to the original ferociousness, exposing significant alignments in the nature of regime resilience and the significance of diverse forms of endurance. The new upsurge of confrontational politics should be perceived as a limited but grave challenge to much of the conformist literature on the comparative politics of the Middle East. The uprisings undermined not only the regimes themselves but also the conclusions of a refined literature that evolved over the preceding decade to explicate the resilience of authoritarian Arab states. However, it is too early to conclude that the literature's emphasis on resilient authoritarianism was injudicious. Hybrid authoritarianism has proven more resistant than perceived in the initial days of 2011. Actually, the viciousness of the pushback against popular mobilization across the region following the fall of Hosni Mubarak, the descent of multiple cases into civil wars rather than smooth transitions, and the continuing power of the old guard in both Egypt and Tunisia all suggest the enduring applicability of authoritarian structures. Sustained attention on the resilience and power of state institutions may help Middle East specialists avoid errors in other regions by not yielding to enthusiasm for the democrats and keeping a close eye on the autocrats. At the same time, this continued focus on the real power of states and authoritarian regimes may blind observers to the evident changes in the tone and matter of politics across the region. Most Arab autocrats may have persisted thus far but almost all are proposing previously inconceivable concessions, and their societies are more prepared than at any time in the recent past. The dramatic and rapid upsurge of popular mobilization did not come out of nowhere, as some people may have imagined. Indeed, for most part of the decade of 2000s, popular protests had increasingly characterized Arab politics; a fact either ignored or missed out by the specialists on the region. [5]

Lynch concludes on the note that the political science of the Middle East by some means overlooked the accumulating force of the Arab uprisings. There were varied sources of disgruntlement across the Arab world and increasing manifestation of public protest across multiple segments in countries such as Egypt. Surveys conducted by groups such as the Arab Barometer findings exposed the complexities of this discontent as well as the general aspiration for greater representative, unbiased and accessible political systems. Studies of the new media setting, comprising the ever-growing viewership of the Al-Jazeera and the enhanced political impact of the Internet, predicted the cohesive nature of the region wide mobilization and the impacts of successful protests. The emphasis of the literature on authoritarian resilience did lead to overemphasizing the Arab regimes' capacity to encounter the increasing widespread challenges. Yet, notwithstanding all their faults, these regimes had managed to effectively suppress, embrace, or dissuade wave after wave of political protest, and there were very little signs in the decade's declining years that their subsistence policies had lost their effectiveness. Those policies continued to preserve governments in a majority of the Arab states, with the rulers being overthrown in only four countries (Tunisia, Egypt, Yemen, and Libya) and with two others (Bahrain and Syria) enduring only through the brute use of extreme violence. The military coup on July 3, 2013, justified the continual focus on the institutions and political forces of those old authoritarian regimes. Though the protestors through the region embraced a shared semantic and charted an analogous cursive, the political undercurrents that followed did not. The 'Arab uprising' archetypal of swift, unrelenting, and mostly peaceful mobilization compelling the president to resign in reality transpired only twice (in Tunisia and Egypt). In Bahrain, Libya, Syria and Yemen, extended violence or state failure overtook the wave of nonviolent protests. Many of the more affluent Gulf States repelled the protest movements through a mixture of subjugation and collaboration while learning from the blunders of other regimes and taking measures to back each other's existence policies. No Arab uprising has so far led to a genuine democratic transition, even as many countries in the region face an obstinate mobilization and political instability. The authoritarian retention, accompanied by Syria's slide towards extreme violence and the existential difficulties of the Egyptian and Tunisian transitions, provides a sobering remedial to the initial eagerness for far-reaching radical change. At some level, this retention justifies the last decade's close inquiry of the practices and constructs nourishing these authoritarian systems, and it ascertains the trouble of moving past such profoundly deep-seated political and societal structures. At the same time, one has to concede that the essential fabric of the polity has been fundamentally and irreversibly transformed. The operational, environmental changes have proven problematic for virtually all actors to navigate without difficulty. Islamist movements, for example, have struggled to adjust ideologically or tactically to their new political opportunities. Contending political movements have likewise struggled with the evolution from protest movements to political parties, with several of the bases of their strength during the uprisings becoming flaws in the electoral and institutional political battles that ensued. A range of indigenous reasons, from urban geography to civil-military relations to political economy, provide explanation for the unravelling of the political struggles.[6]

Regional demonstration effects had a potent effect on the prospects and performance of protest movements. Tunisia and Egypt stimulated the public protests as they unexpectedly assumed that they could make it, whereas a year later Syria's shocks probably dissuaded others from pushing for a revolution that could have evidently led to something worse. The regional impacts were not only incidental demonstration effects. The Arab uprisings have shaped and reintroduced the Arab cold war defined by competitive proxy involvements and new forms of regional association and encounter. Qatar's attempts at supporting the Muslim Brotherhood's movements across the region, mediations against the Libyan and Syrian regimes, and the use of Al-Jazeera to form and influence regional public opinion were one of the most apparent of such attempts. The objective behind Saudi Arabia's moves to back friendly monarchical regimes monetarily, politically, and even militarily (in case of Bahrain) was to protect and consolidate its conventional alliance structure. This continuing rationale of proxy wars and competitive mobilization within states that (possibly for the time being) lack actual domestic control has fashioned the consequences of numerous important waves of popular mobilization in the region's history. The passion in the early months of 2011 has long since given way to an extended, tenacious political tussle. It is far too soon to propose any decisive deductions about the eventual results of the Arab uprisings. However, absolutism is seldom as steady as it seems during the days of ordinary politics, but likewise seldom as transient as it might appear during revolutionary moments. The undercurrents of the initial days of mass mobilization rarely wholly foresee the consequences of the tough institutional and political battles to follow. Consequently, political scientists need to be equipped to elucidate both those political struggles and those moments when widespread mobilization gushes to overturn the system.[7]

According to Fawaz A. Gerges, a rupture has occurred in the Arab Middle East that has deeply stirred the totalitarian establishment. It has initiated a new semantic and a new era of combative politics and uprisings. It has also revived academic interest in ground level politics, with a focus on the labour force, masses, societal movements, public space and resistance, the decline of hegemony, the crisis of authority and the part of agency in general, which constitutes a refreshing change from the past obsession with elitist politics. However, Gerges contends that the revolutionary moment is still unravelling. Revolutionary moments in contrast to revolutions that instantaneously reverse a society's social, economic and political arrangement, all within a comparatively short period, will take time and space to create a revolutionary outcome. In the process, they might be abandoned, appropriated, incorporated, entrenched, or face hindrances. Therefore, Gerges opines that it is critical to distinguish between two processes: restructuring the circumstances and situations that led to the overthrow of the Zine El Abidine Ben Ali regime in Tunisia and of the Hosni Mubarak regime in Egypt; and investigating the evolution from political absolutism in various countries and the prospects of maintaining the cohesion and unity of the multitudes of protestors as the struggle turns to constructing a governing coalition, a new system for assigning power. The change from a revolutionary moment to a constitutional moment is replete with uncertainties, pressures, and opposing notions of the political. Despite the unpredictability and risks about democratic change, what has ensued in the Arab world is a defining moment. The agenda of political and economic opportunities had abruptly expanded. It is critical to be aware of the importance of this revolutionary episode in the modern history of the Middle East and the ingenious notions and pronunciations of resistance that devastated the system of dominance, predominantly the popular origins of these uprisings amongst the urban and rural poor. Irrespective of what the consequences will be, this trailblazing moment has spun the wheels of history in an evolving and progressive trajectory. For Gerges, considering the fragility of institutions in the Arab world and the structural socio-economic and political predicament there, the social and political tumult that has swamped the region after the Arab uprisings is likely and to be anticipated, a part and parcel of the excruciating birth pangs of a new world.[8]

For Gerges, the distinguishing feature of the uprisings was that the Arabs cutting across national boundaries presented a cohesive front in their disapproval of injustice and political authoritarianism. Taking possession of public space, symbols of liberation from colonial rule, Arabs from dissimilar political persuasions, thoughts, and predispositions 'performed the nation' as united citizens, in the pursuit of political liberation and civil and economic empowerment. Within this sparkle, original stories are articulated and new histories of resistance, optimism and resolve are expressed. Notwithstanding significant dissimilarities and specificities of the various uprisings, a uniting strand runs through all of them: a call for dignity, empowerment, political citizenship, social equity and justice, and reclaiming the state from premiers for life, as well as from their relatives and crony capitalists who appropriated it and instead electing representative governments. The distinguishing feature of the all-encompassing popular uprisings in 2011 was the vigorous participation by urban and rural workers and the poor in general. The uprisings were not really consistent and harmonious. There also existed a struggle for control inside the public squares within the protests, most conspicuously between religious conservatives and liberal-leaning groups. Gerges finds this struggle for domination not really unanticipated as the institutionalization of multiplicity/diversity and the 'parliamentarization' of politics is a long drawn process. The authoritarian governments did their best to extend the gulf and distrust between political groups. The enactment of the nation by the protestors comprised people with diverse philosophies and notions of the political and the social, a wide-ranging alliance whose members may possibly also intensely doubt each other. Therefore, multiplicity cannot be wished away. As such, the test confronting the post-authoritarian order is to institutionalize multiplicity or diversity, institute a far-reaching electoral alliance and re-establish political conviction. The revolutionary moment should not be mistaken with the unfolding consequences and the fierce political and social struggles. Gerges warns that instead of declaring the end of the supposed Arab Spring, experts should stress on interpreting the bases of susceptibilities confronting the evolution in distinct Arab societies and the drivers behind the political ideological encounters between dominant groups.[9]

While predicting the future in terms of the shape that the political, social and economic structures would assume in the aftermath of the Arab uprisings would be problematic, the revolts have nevertheless, shattered two myths about the Arab region: the resilience of authoritarian Arab regimes since the 1970s and the ineffectiveness of agency. The absence of democracy in the Middle East was not dealt with by probing the root causes behind the deficit or the manifold sources of dissatisfaction; instead the focus was on the permanence of political authoritarianism. As a consequence, high politics was overemphasized and low politics was understated; the role of autonomous action, as well as the vulnerabilities and weaknesses of political authoritarianism were overlooked. Besides, some scholars based their analysis on a "political culture approach to Middle Eastern politics,"which ascribed the absence of democracy and the prevalence of absolutism to Arab exceptionalism and the inheritance of Islam. Thus, Elie Kedourie argued that "the idea of democracy is quite alien to the mind-set of Islam,"[10] and Bernard Lewis opined that the "political history of Islam is one of almost unrelieved autocracy."[11] Ernest Gellner and Samuel Huntington also put forth similar opinions. The 'micro-politics' of social struggles and contentious politics, the 'quiet encroachment' and the routine policies of resistance and 'low key politics,' the unseen movements and 'non-movements,' that fashioned actors and their approaches as they poured into *mayadeen al-tahrir* were overlooked. And today a chorus of opinions has already pronounced the Arab Spring as either over or has already turned into a gloomy winter and that the region has long appeared like an 'infertile soil for democracy' with the military and the Islamists appropriating the uprisings. Gerges concludes that there is a tangible tension and dissimilarity between the more agency-centred, voluntaristic accounts of transitions from authoritarian rule (or revolution) and the more structuralist, institutionalist, or class-based inquiry. The happenings in the Arab world since 2010 do not indicate the end of history or the instantaneous dawning of a new representative and democratic era. It is a revolutionary moment; the beginning of a progression towards democratic evolution, not the end of democratic consolidation. The trials that jeopardize parliamentarization and democratic change in Arab countries should not be used as indication to highlight the prevailing narrative about the resilience of authoritarianism in the Arab region.[12]

Ahmed Ezz Eldin, has summed up the legacy of the Arab Spring, five years from its outbreak in the following sentences:

> It has been almost five years since the Arab Spring started. Yet, the spring turned into a cold dark winter. Political instability, civil wars,

millions of refugees, terrorism, failed states, and more brutal dictatorships are only some of the poor outcomes. The political disappointment of the Arab youth has drawn many of them into supporting extremist ideas and joining terrorist organizations. Dictators are being celebrated as heroes of 'liberation and political stability' instead of war criminals. The democracy-enthusiast Western governments have surrendered to the realities of Middle Eastern politics and retained their old strategies of supporting the region's dictatorships. What is worse, the bloodiness of the outcomes turned the masses towards supporting their dictatorships even more than before. Yet, the picture might not be all that bleak. Tunisia managed to successfully transition to democracy with minor bloodshed. The remaining lesson for the rest of the countries is that the idolization of revolutions might be deceptive. For revolutions to lead to better lives, they have to be undertaken with the complete understanding of the domestic and international political structures. Otherwise, they lead to worse outcomes: civil war and stronger dictatorships. The lesson from the Arab Revolutions is clear; as Louis de Saint-Just put it, "those who make revolutions by half do nothing but dig their own graves." It might be true that it could be decades before the Arab World revolts again. However, when it happens, the masses have a historical experience to learn from. This might be the only positive legacy of the Arab Spring.[13]

The Themes

In the 1950s and 1960s, a generation rose in protest against the Arab governments that were supposedly operating on the directive of the colonial powers. A generation later, many of these radical leaders and their successors had themselves become autocrats in the eyes of the people, leading them to revolt a second time. While there are reservations about the likelihood of the evolution of a truly revolutionary notion of freedom as one explores the threats and opportunities in an ever-changing political landscape, nevertheless the second Arab Uprisings of 2010 has set forth a plethora of queries pertaining to the region. With a view to engaging upon some of these dynamic questions of concern, the Maulana Abul Kalam Azad Institute of Asian Studies had organised an international seminar entitled 'Rethinking West Asia: Moving Beyond the Revolutions' in March 2014. This volume is a product of the discussions that took place in the seminar.

In the first essay of the volume, "In the Presence of Absence: The Arab Uprisings," Deen Sharp observes that in 2011, protesters in the streets and squares of the Arab urban-scape united to call for an end to the absence of 'bread, freedom and social justice.' The outbreak of protests throughout the Arab region made what appeared as improbable metamorphose into the 'ambitious possible.' The cohesive presence of the protestors removed from power Ben Ali in Tunisia, Hosni Mubarak in Egypt, Ali Abdalla Saleh in Yemen and, with the assistance of NATO, Muammar Qaddafi in Libya. Sharp contends that at present, however, the ambitious possible once again appears impossible as the authoritarian regimes in the region have once again supposedly crushed any hope of reform or revolution. As a consequence, for many, the Arab uprisings have come to an end and publications have already emerged focusing on what is termed as *After the Arab Spring*. For Sharp, a well-founded examination of the Arab uprisings, however, remains elusive and without this understanding it seems premature to declare their end. Academics have produced a rich and vast literature trying to grapple with the trajectories and structure of the Arab uprisings. Among other variables, they have consistently focused on the chants heard throughout the protests of "bread, freedom and social justice," and have claimed that it was the inability to live a dignified life that compelled the people of the Arab world to protest. In this paper, Sharp attempts to elaborate and consolidate on this literature that alludes to the inability to live a dignified life as a crucial vector for the social protest movement and to deliberate over the protest movement on the basis of the concept of absence.

In the essay, "The Arab Spring and the Palestinians: From the War in Syria to Operation Protective Edge," Harel Chorev contends that in contrast with the situation in Tunisia, Egypt or Syria, the Arab uprisings did not considerably affect the relations of the Palestinian people with its two regional leaderships, the Palestinian Authority (PA) that governs in the West Bank and the Hamas movement that rules the Gaza Strip. The Arab Spring did not manifest itself in the Palestinian arena in the way it did in other countries of the region. Chorev observes that numerous efforts in the Palestinian public sphere to duplicate and employ the characteristic symbols of the Arab Spring, such as Rage Days (*yawm al-gha?ab*), or establishing movements carrying names as *Tahrir* or *Tamarud-Gaza* (named after the Egyptian *Tamarud* which was one of the prominent movements calling for the resignation of President Mohammad Morsi), failed to gain ground. For Chorev, the Palestinian context was specific and dissimilar by almost any measure, most importantly by the absence of independence and full sovereignty; yet, the regional turmoil deeply influenced and affected the Palestinians in three vital spheres; on the geopolitical context of the two leading Palestinian players, the PA and Hamas, as well as their relationships with each other and their relations with Israel.

Priya Singh's essay, "Israel-Palestine: Revisiting the Bi-National State," attempts to revisit the notion of bi-nationalism in the context of Israel-Palestine. The bi-national idea, which is a vehemently disputed notion, is not new to the region. It was initially backed by the Jewish groups during the British Mandate period and involves the sharing of political powers equally between the Jewish and Arab communities in Israel/Palestine, irrespective of their comparative sizes. With the creation of a Jewish state of Israel in 1948, the bi-national idea appeared preordained to political oblivion. However, in recent times with the virtual collapse of the peace process, the eruption of the second Palestinian Intifada, the de facto Israeli reoccupation of the West Bank and Gaza, and especially the changes in the Jewish-Palestinian demography, this apparently disregarded notion seemed to have made a political comeback with most advocates of bi-nationalism being from the Palestinian side, with only a few on the Israeli side. The essay traces the origin of the notion of the bi-national state, recounts the debates on the issue from the Israeli and Palestinian perspectives and touches upon the institutional structures and informal means employed in recent times to publicize the idea of bi-nationalism. The author contends that this could be the opportune time to revisit and revitalise this alternative as state boundaries in West Asia are being redrawn and the region itself is being reimagined.

In "Islamic Geographies of Resistance: The Islamic Factor in Regional Geopolitical Strategy of Iran," Deepika Saraswat remarks that historically, the Middle East has experienced ravages of British, French, Russian colonialism, and American imperialism and that resistance to these predacious forces has been mounted in various forms. As the region encountered the incursion of colonial manipulation and domination, Islam evolved as an ideology of resistance in a dialogical conversation and in opposition to the European colonial modernity. The author contends that the ferocity and belligerency typical of the region cannot be explicated by referring to some intrinsic traits of Islam, but by understanding the multifaceted power struggle of the region encompassing regional and extra-regional great powers. The first section of the paper concisely interrogates the nation-state concept in revolutionary Iran and argues that the dualism innate in the notion of 'Islamic republic' is the reason why the language of politics and geopolitical discourse in Iran is abounding in Islamic frames. The later sections examine the use of religious frames in geopolitical strategy of the Islamic Republic of Iran in the twenty-first century. Saraswat claims that the Islamic revolution in Iran and the subsequent Islamic republic created a revolutionary identity of resistance which often moves beyond into the realm of a Universalist discourse of resistance. Thus, for Saraswat, the Islamic republic at least initially condemned nationalism as a western concept and incorporated a non-territorial universalist discourse of Islamic identity distinct from and in opposition to the West in general and America in particular and in that it has endeavoured to combine its security needs and ambition for regional power status with a radical Islamic ideology of resistance.

In the essay, "Of Islam and Other Things: The Drivers and Rhetoric in Iranian Politics," Kingshuk Chatterjee observes that at least in the initial stages of the so-called Arab Spring there were questions regarding the redundancy of Islam—or to be precise, Political Islam in the politics of the Middle East and the advent of Post-Islamism. However, the experience of the Ikhwan al-Muslimin and al-Nahda in power, and the implication of the civil wars in Libya and Syria, has apparently provided a reason to defer the final verdict on the demise of Political Islam. Chatterjee contends that in the wake of this twist in the debate on Political Islam and Post-Islamism, it would possibly be worth enquiring as to whether at all there was any major gap between the two. In the process of enquiry, the paper delves into issues such as what actually constitutes an agenda Islamic, whether it inevitably has anything to do with Islam, the religion, or even the cultural space and do social values, economic practices, political institutions have to attain a particular form or institutional apparatus for it to qualify as Islamic? These queries are dealt with by engaging with the considerations of what drives the formulation of agenda of the Islamic Republic of Iran, in present times as well as ever since the Islamic Revolution of 1979. The paper also examines the question of how such constructions that are 'packaged' by rhetorical usage is in reality linked to considerations that make them Islamic.

Sujata Ashwarya Cheema's essay, "The Iranian Nuclear Issue: Contending Narratives, Emerging Dynamics and the Road Ahead," contends that the polemic over the Iranian nuclear programme arises from proliferation concerns of the international community. The United States and its allies are of the opinion that Iran kept various aspects of its nuclear programme, particularly the uranium cnrichment programme, 'concealed' for many years, suggestive of an intent to produce fissile material for nuclear bomb. In addition, the contention is that Iran wants to control the entire fuel cycle, i.e. the process by which uranium ore is mined, processed, enriched, used, and reprocessed and disposed, which the western powers assert, establishes Iran's firm determination to obtain nuclear weapons. Cheema states that the opinion that Iran has been camouflaging its aim to develop a military nuclear programme has dictated international politics on the Iranian nuclear issue for more than a decade now. Iran, in contrast, contends that its nuclear programme is entirely peaceful and for civilian purposes, including production of electric power and medical isotopes. Cheema concludes on the note and with the prescription that a balance-of-power strategy in the region would, in effect, address Iran's ambition to be accepted as a regional power with a rightful role. The author underlines that a resolution of the Iranian nuclear impasse could also serve as the beginning of Iran's cooperation with major powers in the crises in Syria and Iraq, though she cautions that Iran may not embrace the new reality in the post-deal scenario in a way that benefits the West, but nevertheless it would definitely herald a relationship that is devoid of animosity and prepared for cooperative engagements.

In "The Rise of Contentious Politics in Turkey after the Arab Spring," Alper Y. Dede observes that abrupt popular uprisings and the subsequent changes of bureaucratic-authoritarian regimes across the Middle East, popularly termed as the Arab Spring, stunned the world as many analysts studying the region had not expected the sudden collapse of these status-quo oriented, bureaucratic-authoritarian regimes through mass protests. Dede asserts that in addition to the overwhelming socio-economic and political factors, the Arab Spring would in all probability have been impossible without two noteworthy factors, which he describes as the availability of modern means of communication and the presence of a sizeable cluster of exceedingly exasperated well-educated young people. Traditionally, the writings on the region concerning projections of political and social change revolved around the dominant concept of long-term gradual change. Dede observes that the Arab Spring proved that these historical analyses were erroneous in a fundamental way because they failed to diagnose the likelihood of sudden mass uprisings as a means of political change across the region. The Arab Spring yielded different conclusions in different countries. In other words, the progression of the Arab Spring did not turn out adequately for all countries that had experienced large-scale mass protests for overthrowing authoritarian regimes. Dede claims that the Arab Spring certainly had a spill over effect and comparable protests erupted across the Middle East including Turkey where large scale protests erupted in the summer of 2013 as people objected to the government's plan to demolish the Gezi Park. Dede's essay examines *three points* about the protests; the impact of the Arab Spring on contentious politics in Turkey; the social and political factors that contributed to the rapid spread of the protests across the country, and the response of the government to the protests and the persistent nature of the protest.

In the essay, "The Changing Dynamics of Turkey's Relations with Israel: The Arab Spring and its Aftermath," Mujib Alam traces the ups and downs in the Turkey-Israel relationship. Turkey's relations with Israel nose-dived in the mid-2000s after a series of critical events that took place at the bilateral levels between these two countries. The downward spiral in the relations seemed dramatic, keeping in mind the close relations that had developed between the two countries in the 1990s and continued even during the early years of the AK Party (*Adalet ve Kalkýnma* or Justice and Development), the ruling party in Turkey since November 2002. Several factors, either direct or indirect—at regional, domestic and individual levels—contributed to the development of the strained relationship between Turkey and Israel. Alam observes that the 'Arab Spring' which began since mid-

December 2010 has produced remarkable repercussions in one form or the other throughout the West Asian and North African region. In addition to initiating colossal changes in the domestic affairs of some countries, the Arab Spring has impacted and shaped, positively or negatively, bilateral and multilateral relations between/among the countries of the region. Turkey's relations with Israel should be viewed against this background. The developments arising out of the Arab Spring in the region and specifically in neighbouring Syria has created a different regional context and has perpetrated new challenges upon both Turkey and Israel. In his paper, Alam argues that because of the changing security scenario that has emerged out of the Arab uprisings and other reasons particularly economic ones, Turkey's relation with Israel has not reached the point of irreconcilability and in the future it will improve though not to the level that existed in the 1990s.

Joseph Alagha's essay, "Hizbullah's Axis and Turkey," claims that the Lebanese Shi'ite political party Hizbullah brands itself as an Islamic *jihadi* movement with its primary concern being the safeguarding of its identity in the wake of the Arab Uprisings, which has resulted in dramatic developments and chaos that can be regarded as establishing fault lines in the Middle East and North Africa (MENA). Alagha observes that as the so-called 'Arab Spring' or the Arab Uprisings turned into a Sunni-Shi'a conflict and a ripple effect of failing states, the Lebanese Hizbullah extended its regional involvement in Syria, Iraq, and Yemen, therefore joining the Iranian axis (with Russia and China) against the Turkish, Gulf Cooperation Council (GCC), and the US, UK, French axis. Alagha elaborates upon the history of the Hizbullah and the repeated and explicit accusation levelled by its Secretary, General Sayyid Hasan Nasrallah, blaming Turkey of connivance in the Syrian civil war by being on the side of the rebels and the militant Sunni Islamists. The Hizbullah considers the "Islamic State in Iraq and the Levant" (ISIL) as the creation of Turkey, with assistance from the United States, France and the United Kingdom. Continuing with this line of thinking, the Hizbullah contends that Turkey is the major consumer of ISIL's oil, which is contrary to the UN's resolutions and after a year of claiming its Caliphate by military conquest on 9 June 2014, the ISIL has actually gained ground, controlling 50 per cent of Syria and 40 per cent of Iraq, in spite of the continuous airstrikes by the coalition forces.

Alagha asserts that the 15 October 2014 US-led 'Operation Inherent Resolve' did not restrain the ISIL and its expansionist policy leading one to question as to whether the International Community has failed in controlling transnational *jihadi* networks.

In "The Divergent Trajectories of Arab Dignity Revolts: Egypt and Tunisia," Mustapha Kamel Al-Sayyid contends that Arab Dignity revolutions which started in Tunisia in December 2010 and in Egypt few weeks later, promised a fundamental change in the political systems of the Arab countries from authoritarian rule to democratic governments. However, these hopes and aspirations were dashed in most of the countries where the protests had taken place with Tunisia being the only exception, which succeeded in drafting and approving a constitution that explicitly provides for civil and political rights. Al-Sayyid points out that the case of Tunisia is in obvious contrast to that of Egypt, the other Arab country to overthrow an authoritarian leader, which finds itself swamped in a lingering conflict between the Military supported government and supporters and sympathisers of the country's Islamist movement. The vivid contrast according to Al-Sayyid stimulated a broad debate among political scientists and analysts of the region. The divergent trajectory of the uprisings in Tunisia and Egypt were sought to be explained in terms of the different political cultures, where the former was viewed as being more accommodating towards democratic institutions while the latter was perceived as marked by authoritarian traditions. Another explanation was in what was considered to be a fundamental difference between the principal Islamist movement in the respective country, the Ennahda Party in Tunisia and the Muslim Brotherhood (Brethren) in Egypt. The essay has used the rational actor's model to comprehend the different trajectories of the two countries, in the process pointing out the commonalities between the two countries, contrasting the divergent outcomes of the two revolutions and concluding by offering what could be an explanation of these deviating paths.

Paul Rivlin's essay, "The Tunisian Spring and the Egyptian Winter," also deals with the contrasting Tunisian and Egyptian chapters of the Arab Uprisings. Rivlin narrates the story of the Arab Uprisings at the beginning of 2011 when the leaders of Tunisia and Egypt were ousted from power, each after a prolonged stay in office as a consequence of massive public protests calling for democracy.

Rivlin observes that the fact that this happened in two Arab states, within one month, indicated that there must be substantial aspects in common between the two countries, which indeed there were. However, three years later, Rivlin contends the differences between them have emerged as after many complications and doubts, Tunisia has experienced an Arab Spring while Egypt has experienced what can only be called an Arab winter. The essay studies the similarities and dissimilarities between the two countries and some of the repercussions for the rest of the Arab world.

In her essay, "Contentious Politics, Economic Crisis and Regime Change in Egypt," Nadine Sika argues that the economic factors, which steered the mass mobilization and protests preceding the January 2011 uprising and during Egypt's transitional period, are still prevalent and are even more unrelenting with the coming of the Sisi regime. Though, unlike the Mubarak and Morsi regimes, this regime has greater legitimacy in addition to its ability to co-opt and repress its opposition. Sika contends that social debate among different sections of society, particularly workers, Islamists and human rights activists will continue; nevertheless she feels that the regime is expected to endure. During Mubarak's tenure in office, the survival of the regime, particularly through the 2000s decade, was based on subjugation and appropriation, much more than legitimation. The initiation of potent structural modification programmes in the 1990s along with neoliberal economic policies in the 2000s seriously affected the regime's legitimacy. Street strife by different protest groups increased since the early 2000s, which ultimately led to the overthrow of the Mubarak regime in February 2011. Since Mubarak's ousting, Egypt has been subjected to four different rulers, ranging from the Supreme Council of the Armed Forces, to Mohamed Morsi, to Adli Mansour to Abdel Fattah el-Sisi. Sika observes that in the meantime there have been different waves of disagreement with high and low levels of public mobilization, which climaxed in the ousting of Mohamed Morsi from office. She concludes with the observation that with the emergence of the Sisi regime in 2014 the question remains as to whether social contention will decrease or will remain the rule rather than the exception.

Konrad Pêdziwiatr in the essay, "Political Islam in Egypt after Morsi," describes the swearing in of Mohammad Morsi on 30 June

2012 as the first fully democratically elected president of Egypt as almost an unreal phenomenon. For Pêdziwiatr it was an incredible moment for Egyptian Islamism depicting its most remarkable success ever. Political Islam emerged as one of the big winners of the political transformation initiated by the Arab Spring, not only in Egypt but also in the wider region of the Middle East and North Africa. Its activists and members who till then had a fairly restricted access to the political scene took full advantage of the change in political opportunity and began to play a key role not only in politics at the local, but also national and regional levels. In the Egyptian context, this was accurate till 3 July 2013 when the army relying on alleged wide-ranging social disgruntlement and with approval of some opposition groups (e.g. *Tamarod*) and important figures of social and religious authority including the Grand Imam of al-Azhar (*Ahmed el-Tayeb*), the Coptic Pope (*Tawadros II*), and Mohamed El-Baradei removed President Mohammad Morsi from power, arrested the leaders of the Muslim Brotherhood and installed as new interim leader the head of the Supreme Constitutional Court, Adly Mansour. Pêdziwiatr argues that from that moment the thesis of "failure" or even the "end" of political Islam in the country, in fact more broadly in the region, has been gaining increasing popularity. The article analyses the validity of this sort of assertions. It sheds light on the crucial successes and failures of political Islam in Egypt after the Arab Spring, the corollaries of the political amputation of the Muslim Brotherhood and the plausible scenarios for the future.

Nikolay A. Kozhanov's essay, "Russia and the Middle East after the Arab Spring," analyses the Russian reaction to the events constituting the Arab Spring and its repercussions. The Russian government had, at the outset, tried to keep aside from the intra-Arab conflict and restricted its reaction to the events in Egypt, Libya, Tunisia, and Yemen by statements on the necessity of the peaceful settlement of conflicts but almost abruptly realised that the new Middle East was no longer as responsive to Moscow as it had been in the past. By 2012, the old regimes had already collapsed, and the new authorities had not yet defined their attitude to Russia as its neutral posturing prevented them from attributing to Moscow either the status of a friend or an enemy. When the authorities of the Russian Federation altered their policies and began clearly articulating their preferences, the new approach also appeared to bring provocative consequences. For instance, the Russian support of the regime of Bashar Assad stunned the majority of the Arab street: the knowledge that Moscow was backing the old dictatorial regime substantially contradicted with the image of the Russians as supporters of liberation movements in the Middle East that emerged during the 1960s and 1970s. Consequently, this led to the freezing of Russian relations with the bulk of the Arab world. Kozhanov thus views the events of the Arab Spring and their aftermath as a serious test for Russian foreign policy on the Middle East. In his opinion, it necessitated the need to restore, at least, part of the Russian influence in the Middle East, which had been lost after the fall of the Soviet Union. Conversely, the Arab Spring also provided an answer to the countries of the region regarding the place of modern Russia within the system of the international relations of the Middle East.

Contemporary Drifts

A lot has been written about the undoing of the Skyes-Picot system in the Middle East. The violent fragmentation of Iraq and Syria appeared to have finally torn apart the borders shaped by the British and French governments in the aftermath of World War I. It was not simply the emergence and consolidation of the so-called 'Islamic State' traversing and expunging the Syrian-Iraqi border. The unparalleled, co-ordinated widespread mobilization across borders during the early Arab uprisings of 2011 gave a compelling form to the ideals of transnational Arab political community usurping the confines of nation-states. As the uprisings turned gloomier and most of the democratic transitions failed, new contenders to the nation-states in the Middle East emerged: the Islamic state; the growing de facto independence of Kurds across Iraq and Syria, with corollaries spreading into Turkey and Iran; the rise of sub-regional identities passed by heavily armed militias in weakening states such as Yemen and Libya; extraordinary forced displacement moving millions of people within and across borders; and rampant sectarianism dividing Sunnis and Shiites. These developments did not have an exceptional influence on national identities. Some states have collapsed, creating space for new subnational identities to contest national unity but most have reverted into a more aggressive form of totalitarianism. Egypt's military coup, for example, has been sustained by an almost coercive advancement of extreme nationalism. Many Gulf States have used sectarianism to consolidate support for their regimes in ways that could have a long-term influence on popular notions of national identity. Encounters over the appropriate role of Islam in public life have reshaped political discourse from Egypt to Turkey and Tunisia. Likewise Kurds envisage novel political potentials in very dissimilar settings, through the historical experience of Turkey and Iraq.[14] Scholars and policy makers have offered a number of explanations for the crisis in the Middle East and North Africa/West Asia that arose with the Arab uprisings of 2010, which has swept the region, overthrown leaders in four countries, Tunisia, Egypt, Libya and Yemen; encouraged Saudi-led military intrusions in Bahrain and Yemen, kindled insurrections and confrontations in Syria, Iraq and Libya; and ignited the rise of the 'Islamic State' (IS) in Syria and Iraq, and the enlargement of its territorial reach to the Gulf and Africa.[15] A cluster of reasons have been recognised behind the collapse of the traditional system in the Middle East and North Africa, ranging from the desire for more freedom and social justice[16] to the instability of post-colonial regional states as a consequence of the failure of the despots to engage in nation-building, which in turn gave rise to ethnic, tribal and sectarian strife;[17] to intrinsic faults in colonial border arrangements at the time of the demise of the Ottoman Empire, such as the Skyes-Picot Agreement and the Treaty of Sevres.[18]

The Arab uprisings of 2010 took the region by surprise. The resultant state of lawlessness has become a source of religious fanaticism and militancy in the region and beyond. The Syrian crisis has added another dimension to the already existing chaos. The position of the Western powers has by and large been in favour of the ouster of Bashir Assad. Widespread reports suggest that the regional powers such as Saudi Arabia, Qatar and the UAE have been financing the Syrian opposition primarily to counter Iran's influence in the Shia belt extending to Iraq, Syria and Lebanon. After Iran's nuclear deal with the P5+1 nations, the Gulf countries perceive Iran's influence intensifying, and have counteracted using extremist Sunni forces as a deterrent. Israel's hostility towards Iran, and the backing the Hezbollah gets from Iran through Syria, gives it an objective motive to focus on the forces responsible for the mayhem. Israel is believed to have reached some kind of an understanding with Saudi Arabia, Qatar and UAE in countering Iran. Meanwhile Turkey's Ottoman era ambitions have surfaced with the Recep Tayyip Erdogan government, which supposedly aims at installing a government in Damascus, which is indebted and therefore favourably inclined towards it. It looks at the Kurds and not the 'Islamic State' as its foremost adversary. The origins and growth of the 'Islamic State' is also ambiguous. It is believed that the Gulf States had initially supported the 'Islamic State' but later feel endangered by its fanatic ideology. Turkey has been accused of supporting Turkmen groups in northern Iraq with contacts to al-Qaida. It is also alleged that oil from northern Syria, the region controlled by the 'Islamic State' is being smuggled to Turkey, providing the group financial resources for its extremist agenda. The US has so far been unwilling to go all out against the 'Islamic State.' Russia, on the other hand, has taken the decision to intervene in Syria, with its president Vladimir Putin, accusing some G-20 members of financially supporting the 'Islamic State' at the G-20 meeting in Turkey. Russia-Turkey relations have nose-dived since the downing of a Russian bomber by the Turkish air force and the killing of the Russian pilot by Turkmen rebels led by a nationalist Turk. After the recent terrorist attacks in Paris, (The attacks in Paris on the night of November 13, 2015 by gunmen and suicide bombers hit a concert hall, a major stadium, restaurants and bars, almost simultaneously and left 130 people dead and hundreds wounded. The Islamic State claimed responsibility for the blasts.) France's president, Francois Hollande, has been trying to forge a broad coalition to fight against the 'Islamic State' that would include Russia. Turkey views this as a setback to its all-inclusive strategy in Syria.[19]

If the situation in the region looked grim, developments in the recent past have only made things worse. Saudi Arabia's decision to execute a prominent Shia nonconformist cleric Nimr al-Nimr has set in motion a series of events that could have disastrous consequences for the region, among other things, inflaming sectarian tensions across West Asia/MENA. This comes a couple of weeks after Saudi Arabia announced the formation of an Islamic military coalition to fight terrorism that intentionally barred Iran and its allies Syria and Iraq. Besides, Saudi Arabia has been indulging on Arab allies; it has committed $22 billion to Morocco, $8 billion to Egypt. It is evident that the Shia-Sunni cracks are out in the open. Saudi Arabia blames Iran for trying to reconstruct the Persian Empire. Whether it's the Saudi military interference in Yemen (where Saudi Arabia faults Tehran for aiding Shia Houthi rebels) or the conflict in Syria (where the Assad regime backed by Iran and Russia continues to fight Sunni rebels) there's no contradicting the fact that a huge conflict is in motion between two titans representative of Islam's two most prominent sects. Though, regional expert, Marc Lynch, has cautioned that "the idea of an unending, primordial conflict between Sunnis and Shiites explains little about the ebbs and flows of regional politics. This is not a resurgence of a 1,400 year old conflict,"[20] Lynch expounds the Saudi aggressiveness in terms of the prevailing political reality, including the Saudi fear that it is weakening regionally after the Iran deal, and that its ruthless intrusion in Yemen has slackened. However, the significant point to remember is that this rivalry could very well provide the 'Islamic State' terror group an opportunity to flourish. The anarchy in West Asia/MENA appears unlikely to end sometime in the near future.[21]

---

* The Editor wishes to thank all the contributors to the volume.

** She also wishes to thank Rita Banerjee, in particular for her assistance with copy editing the volume.

References

1. Robert D. Kaplan, "The Ruins of Empire in the Middle East: Imperialism may have fallen out of fashion, but history shows that the only other option is the kind of chaos we see today," *Foreign Policy*, May 25, 2015.
2. Morten Valbjorn, "Introduction: Studying International Relations of the Middle East," in Morten Valbjorn and Fred H. Lawson (Edited), *International Relations of the Middle East*, Los Angeles, London, New Delhi, Singapore, Washington D.C.: SAGE reference, Volume I, p.xxi
3. Valbjorn and Lawson, *International Relations of the Middle East*, p. xxiii; Edward Said, *Orientalism: Western Conceptions of the Orient*, London: Routledge and Keegan Paul, 1978; Melani McAlister, *Epic Encounters: Culture, Media and U.S. Interests in the Middle East, 1945-2000*, Berkeley: University of California Press, 2001; Walter Bryce Gallie, "Essentially Contested Concepts," *Proceedings of the Aristotelian Society,* 56, pp. 167-220. All cited in Valbjorn, *op. cit*, p. xxiii.

4. "Where is the Middle East?," The Carolina Center for the Study of the Muslims and Middle East Civilizations, *See*: http://mideast.unc.edu/where/
5. Marc Lynch, Introduction in Marc Lynch, (Edited) *The Arab Uprisings Explained: New Contentious Politics in the Middle East,* New York: Columbia University Press, 2014, pp. 1-23.
6. Marc Lynch, Conclusion in Marc Lynch, (Edited) *The Arab Uprisings Explained: New Contentious Politics in the Middle East,* New York: Columbia University Press, 2014, pp. 313-315.
7. Lynch, *The Arab Uprisings Explained*, pp. 3-9.
8. Fawaz A. Gerges, (Edited) *The New Middle East: Protest and Revolution in the Arab World,* New York: Cambridge University Press, 2014, pp. 1-2
9. Gerges, *The New Middle East*, pp. 3-9.
10. Gerges, *The New Middle East*, p. 22.
11. Gerges, *The New Middle East*, p. 22.
12. Gerges, *The New Middle East*, pp. 20-26, p. 33.
13. Ahmed Ezz Eldin, "*The ending was determined by money and blood relations*," The Tale of the Arab Revolutions- Your Middle East*: http://www.yourmiddleeast.com/opinion/the-tale-of-the-arab-revolutions_37950*
14. Mark Lynch, Introduction in *Rethinking Nation and Nationalism*, Project on Middle East Political Science, POMEPS STUDIES, 14, June 2, 2015, pp. 3-5.
15. James Dorsey, MIDDLE EAST INSIGHTS NO. 135, 5 January 2016, MEI, National University of Singapore, p. 1.
16. Sheri Berman, "The Promise of the Arab Spring," Foreign Affairs, January/February 2013, cited in James Dorsey, MIDDLE EAST INSIGHTS NO. 135, p. 2.
17. Center for International and Regional Studies, "Fragile Politics, Weak States in the Greater Middle East (Doha: Georgetown University School of foreign Service in Doha, 2014)/ Bassam Tibi, The Simultaneity of the Unsimultaneous: Old Tribes and Imposed Nation-state in the Modern Middle East," in tribes and State Formation in the Middle East, edited by Philip S. Khoury and Joseph Kostiner, 127-151, Berkeley University of California Press, 1990, cited in James Dorsey, *op.cit*, p. 2.
18. Nick Danforth, "Forget Sykes-Picot. It's the Treaty of Sevres that Explains the Modern Middle East," Foreign Policy, August 10, 2015, cited in Dorsey, *op.cit*, p. 2.
19. Kanwal Sibal, "Lines in the Sand," *The Telegraph*, Kolkata, December 24, 2015.
20. Cited in James North, "Sophisticated Orientalism in the *New York Times*," *MONDOWEISS*, January 4, 2016.
21. Rudroneel Ghosh, "Saudi Arabia escalates conflict with Iran, wagers regional stability to preserve internal stability," in Talking Turkey, *Times of India*, January 9, 2016.

1

In the Presence of Absence

The Arab Uprisings

Deen Sharp

Introduction

In 2011, protesters in the streets and squares of the Arab urban-scape united to demand an end to the absence of "bread, freedom and social justice." The eruption of protests throughout the Arab region made what seemed impossible transmogrify into the "ambitious possible."[1] The protesters' united presence removed from power Ben Ali in Tunisia, Hosni Mubarak in Egypt, Ali Abdalla Saleh in Yemen and, with the assistance of NATO, Muammar Qaddafi in Libya. Now, however, the ambitious possible once again appears impossible. The iron fists of authoritarian regimes in the region have once again seemingly crushed any hope of reform or revolution. For many, the Arab uprisings are at an end. Indeed, publications have already emerged on *After the Arab Spring*.[2]

A firm understanding of the Arab uprisings, however, remains elusive and without this comprehension it appears premature to declare their end. What are the Arab uprisings? We still do not know and what we do know remains limited. Scholars, among others, however, have produced a rich and vast literature trying to grapple with the vectors and composition of the Arab uprisings.[3] In attempting to comprehend the Arab uprisings, academics have focused on the transformation in media technologies and in particular social media and the rise of Facebook and Twitter.[4] A furious debate raged between scholars as to the importance of social media in the uprising and produced a literature that emphasised the physical, as well as the virtual, spaces of the protest movement.[5]

The literature on the changes in communication technology principally focused on *how* people organized to produce some of the largest protests the world has ever witnessed. This debate only partially addressed the question of *why*. To answer why the Arab uprisings emerged many academics have focused on political economy with critical scholars keen to assert that the uprisings are a rejection of global neoliberal capitalism.[6] Academics have been attentive to the chants heard throughout the protests of "bread, freedom and social justice" and argue that it was the inability to live a dignified life that drove the peoples of the Arab world to protest.[7] In this paper, I want to build on this literature that cites the inability to live a dignified life as a central vector for the social protest movement and to think through the protest movement with the concept of absence.

Absence

Absence, according to the Merriam-Webster dictionary, is a state or condition in which something expected or wanted is not present or does not exist.[8] The Arab uprisings were first and foremost about a response to absence and principally an absence of justice, politics, freedom, dignity and bread. In attempting to explain the Arab uprisings as an absence, however, the richness and complexity of the term 'absence' itself becomes visible. Absence, as is apparent in its dictionary definition, gravitates around, rather than resists, presence. This is particularly significant, in the context of the Arab uprisings in which citizens of the Arab world established a mass presence through protests in public space in defiance of real and perceived absences. To think through the complexities of absence, in order to gain a firmer understanding of the Arab uprisings, this paper utilizes the work of Mahmoud Darwish and the concepts and ideas pursued by Darwish in his seminal text *In the Presence of Absence* (*Fi Hadrat al-Ghiyab*).

Absence is an important concept for Darwish and the way he thought about absence provides entry points into thinking about the Arab uprisings. For Darwish absence is not the opposite of presence. He attempts to push beyond polarities in his writing and this results, for instance, in comprehensions of life that do not render it the opposite of death and beginnings that are not framed in oppositions to ends.

Embracing the three-dimensional thinking of Darwish enables us to gain an equally rich comprehension of what the Arab uprisings are. This further enables an understanding of the Arab uprisings as not a beginning of the struggle to achieve "bread, freedom and social justice" but an intensification of this battle. The Arab uprisings never really began and will never fully end.

The social protest movement that intensified in 2011 should be understood as part of a prolonged and episodic endeavour to establish the ability to live a dignified life. The struggles against confronting the, often brutal, reality of power is one that is constantly made and remade: "The path is the search for the right path."[9]

Absence and the Arab Uprisings

Absence is powerful and it reverberates through landscapes, bodies and memories. The veins of the Arab uprisings are filled with absence. Governments in the region are made distinctive by their absence of legitimacy; the presence of elections has not displaced the absence of a democratic process. The presence of the police, the judiciary, and large structures in the urban landscape devoted to the rule of law only accentuate their absence. The presence of vast wealth for a few illuminates the absence of bread for so many. Many asked: Why do they not revolt?[10]

The self-immolation of Mohamed Bouazizi in the small Tunisian hinterland city of Sidi Bouzid was driven by absence. On 17 December 2010, policewoman Fedia Hamdi and another municipal official confiscated Mohamed Bouazizi's fruit cart for selling goods without a permit and presented him with a substantial fine that he did not have the ability to pay. When Bouazizi attempted to retrieve his cart from the police station, he was turned away. Requesting the audience of the local governor, he was again denied. At 1 p.m. in front of the gate of the municipal building, in the middle of the street, Bouazizi doused himself in gasoline and struck a match, setting himself alight.

The protests that followed Bouazizi's protest suicide resulted in a chain of revolts that established the Arab uprisings. The absence that led to Bouazizi's self-immolation was an absence felt by many across the Arab region and was met by a presence, a presence that filled the streets and squares of the Arab world. In Egypt, protests that erupted in the wake of Bouazizi's self-immolation were fuelled further by the images of another young man, Alexandrian Khaled Said's death, murdered by the police.

Amro Ali, a neighbour of Said in the Egyptian coastal city of Alexandria, noted how Khaled was being pursued by two police officers for the possession of cannabis. "Khaled shoved one of the officers back making some references to the law and his dignity," Ali wrote. "The spited officers grabbed Khaled from his long hair and the beating began, first in the Internet café and continued into the doorway of the adjacent building."[11] When Said's family visited Khaled's body in the morgue his brother took a photo of his corpse on his mobile phone and released it onto the Internet.

The image of Khaled Said shows a face broken up and reassembled into a cubist nightmare. Human Rights Watch noted, "Photos of Said's battered and deformed face published on the internet show a fractured skull, dislocated jaw, broken nose, and numerous other signs of trauma."[12] The government investigation into Said's death concluded that he died of asphyxiation after swallowing a packet of drugs. The absence of justice for the brutal murder of Said was further compounded by the continued presence of the police officers who murdered Said but were not relieved of their duties or questioned by prosecutors.[13] The absences of Khaled Said resonated with the Egyptian populous, as they chanted, "We are all Khaled Said."[14]

In Syria, Libya, Yemen, and Bahrain and across the region, protestors gathered and with them stories similar to the predicament of Bouazizi and Said rose to the surface. Protesters illuminated previously invisible geographies of torture and murder, the revolt made present the absence of the ability to live a dignified life.

Mahmoud Darwish on the Presence of Absence

Absence in Arabic is *ghiyab* and, as in English, means to not be present. In *In the Presence of Absence,* Mahmoud Darwish writes, "Paradise was born from the hell of absence"[15] and the "Past was born from the hell of absence."[16] The paradise and the past that Darwish refers to could be understood as the image of Palestine once it was ripped away in the *Nakba* ("the Catastrophe") of 1948. It was in 1948 when Israel was established and Israeli troops expelled

700,000 Palestinians producing the "hell of absence" for Palestinians. For the Israelis the paradise and past born from the hell of absence derives from the holocaust, one of contemporary history's most terrifying productions of absence.

Mahmoud Darwish was born in the village of Al-Birweh in Palestine in 1941 that was razed to the ground by Israeli forces in 1948. Following the forced exile of Palestinians by the Israelis in 1948, the Palestinian struggle has been focused on not being absent, to fill their absence from Palestine with a presence. Darwish writes, "They forced you from the field. As for your shadow, it neither followed you nor deceived you. It froze there and became a stone. Then it grew green like a sesame plant, green during the day and blue at night."[17] Darwish lived with his family in exile for many years and later returned to his homeland not as a Palestinian citizen, or an Israeli, but as a "present absentee."[18]

As a present absentee, it is no surprise that Darwish engaged deeply with the ideas of presence and absence and produced new ways in which to engage these concepts. Darwish wrote in *In the Presence of Absence* with the knowledge of his imminent death, and indeed, he died two years after completing the text. But Darwish also died *literally* more than once during his life. In 1984, Darwish suffered a heart attack and doctors noted that he was clinically dead for one and a half minutes before he was brought back to life.[19]

> You asked: Where was I then? You were told that death had kidnapped you for a minute and a half and that an electric shock had brought you back to life. You thought: Was death that beautiful and comforting? No, this is not death. It is another form of life. It is a healthy sleep, a sleep for utter pleasure. You realized what you had never realized before. Death does not pain the dead, it pains the living.[20]

In the text Darwish constantly references life and death, like presence and absence, in a manner that does not place them as opposites but in a more multidimensional frame, as he noted, "You avoided defining a thing by its opposite, because the opposite of wrong is not always right."[21] Instead Darwish explores concepts and ideas that gesture towards the nebulous terrain of absence. In exploring absence, Darwish delves into shadows, exile, longing, death, metaphor, pain, silence, imagination, imprisonment, nothingness, airports, myths and memory.

Darwish's journey through and within the idea of absence forcefully articulates the power of imagination. Without the imagination there is no absence, no homeland, no place, no poetry and no presence.

> The imagination soars, visible like clouds over hills with villages strapped to their sides as they cling to their genesis. … The villages buried under the earth send their memories to the surviving villages, whose inhabitants make the pilgrimage each spring to patches where the grass sprouts from the past: we were born right here, at the edge of this well, just as mallow, wild chicory, and rue are born. And I was born here just as imagination is gradually born from everything else. So how will you nurse your imagination back to health and once again fly on your horse?[22]

In the context of the Arab uprisings Darwish articulates how the self-immolation of Bouazizi and the brutal police murder of Khaled Said generated the power that they did. It is the power of the imagination that can create an absence; an absence cannot exist without a presence. The absence of justice for Bouazizi and Said would not be visible without the protests that made present this absence. Death pains the living, scars are memories that never cease working and the future is the encroaching past.

Darwish was imprisoned at various times by the Israelis and he writes in *In the Presence of Absence* how poetry enabled him to reclaim his freedom, to make the invisible visible, the absent present. "Prison deprives one of the sight of a tree and the sea. Freedom is the imagination capable of recalling them both in prison, making the invisible visible."[23] For Darwish, absence is not powerlessness, the end or death.

> You, not I, are the loser. He who lived on depriving others of lights drowns in the darkness of his own shadow. You will never be free of me unless my freedom is generous to a fault. Then it would teach you peace and guide you home. You, not I, are afraid of what this cell is doing to me. Dreaming is my profession while yours is pointless eavesdropping on an unfriendly conversation between my freedom and me.[24]

What is it?

The Arab uprisings articulated that what exists is insufficient, the protests illuminated the absence of the region through chanting their presence: Bread, Freedom and Social Justice. The Arab uprisings are an intensification of the simultaneous struggle in the illumination of absence and its removal. The Arab uprisings are the articulation of an imagination that the region need not exist as it currently is. The Arab uprisings are the idea and imagination that what exists is only partial and that another world is—the ambitious—possible. Imagination, however, is never singular and the competing ideas and struggles are always at work.

> The road rises and falls, undulates, zigzags, extends, and branches off into countless roads that meet back at the beginning. How many times must we start from the beginning? We survived much death. We defeated forgetfulness and you said to me: We survive, but do not triumph. I said to you: Survival is the prey's potential triumph over the hunter. Steadfastness is survival and survival is the beginning of existence.[25]

Absence provides one entry point into a greater understanding of the Arab uprisings. However, even this concept is limited and is not able to grasp the complexity of this ongoing social protest movement. Attempts to understand the Arab uprisings continue and questions as to the nature of this social protest movement remain: "What is it? Were we to know, our plans would have changed, for what we do not know exists and what we do know is limited and bound to change."[26]

References

1. Mahmoud Darwish, *In the Presence of Absence,* New York: Archipelago Books, 2011 [2006], p. 156.
2. John Bradley, *After the Arab Spring: How Islamists Hijacked The Middle East Revolts*, New York City: Palgrave Macmillan, 2012.
3. There are several bibliographies listing the vast literature on the Arab uprisings and include: The Project on Middle East Political Science (http://pomeps.org/category/academicworks/arabuprisings/) and Connected in Cairo (http://connectedincairo.com/resources/bibliography-of-the-egyptian-uprisings/). Of note are several books on the Arab uprisings, which include: Paul Amar and Vijay Prashad, *Dispatches from the Arab Spring: Understanding the New Middle East*, Minneapolis: University of Minnesota Press, 2013; Hamid Dabashi, *The Arab Spring: The End of Postcolonialism*, London,? New York?: Zed Books, 2012;

James L. Gelvin, *The Arab Uprisings: What Everyone Needs to Know*, New York: Oxford University Press, 2012; Bassam Haddad, Rosie Bsheer, Ziad Abu-Rish, and Roger Owen, *The Dawn of the Arab Uprisings: End of an Old Order?* London, New York: Pluto Press, 2012; Raphael Israeli, *From Arab Spring to Islamic Winter*, New Brunswick (USA), London: Transaction Publishers, 2013; David W. Lesch and Mark L. Haas, *The Arab Spring: Change and Resistance in the Middle East*, Boulder, CO: Westview Press. 2012; Marc Lynch, *The Arab Uprising: The Unfinished Revolutions of the New Middle East*, 1st edition, New York: Public Affairs, 2012; Lin Noueihed and Alex Warren, *The Battle for the Arab Spring: Revolution, Counter-Revolution and the Making of a New Era*, New Haven: Yale University Press, 2012; Kenneth M. Pollack, Daniel L. Byman, Akram Al-Turk, Pavel Baev, Michael S. Doran, Khaled Elgindy, Stephen R. Grand, *et al.*, *The Arab Awakening: America and the Transformation of the Middle East*, 1st edition, Washington, DC: Brookings Institution Press, 2011; Tariq Ramadan, *Islam and the Arab Awakening*, Oxford, New York: Oxford University Press, 2012; Jeannie Sowers and Chris Toensing, *The Journey to Tahrir: Revolution Protest, and Social Change in Egypt*, 1st edition, London, New York: Verso, 2012.

4. Sean Aday, Henry Farrell, Deen Freelon, Marc Lynch, John Sides, and Michael Dewar, "Watching From Afar: Media Consumption Patterns Around the Arab Spring," *American Behavioural Scientist*, 15 March 2013; Maximillian Hänska Ahy, "Networked Communication and the Arab Spring: Linking Broadcast and Social Media," *New Media & Society*, 5 June 2014; Miriyam Aouragh and Anne Alexander, "The Egyptian Experience: Sense and Nonsense of the Internet Revolution," *International Journal of Communication* 5, 2011; Walter Armbrust, "A History of New Media in the Arab Middle East," *Journal for Cultural Research* 16, nos. 2-3, 2012; Ginger A. Johnson, Hasan Nuseibeh and Brant Tudor, "140 Characters or Less: How Is the Twitter Mediascape Influencing the Egyptian Revolution?" *Middle East Journal of Culture and Communication* 6, no. 1, 2013: 126-48; Michael Teague, "New Media and the Arab Spring," *Al Jadid Magazine*, 8 May, 2011; Jillian York, "The Dangers of Social Media Revolt," *Al Jazeera*, 9 March 2011.
5. Jillian Schwedler, "Spatial Dynamics of the Arab Uprisings," *PS: Political Science & Politics* 46, no. 2, 2013: 230-34; Deen Sharp, "Beware of Small Cities," *Jadliyya e-zine,* 6 September 2012, http://www.jadaliyya.com/pages/index/7223/beware-of-small-cities. Accessed on 29 June; Helga Tawil-Souri, "Egypt's Uprising and the Shifting Spatialities of Politics," *Cinema Journal* 52, no. 1, 2012; Helga Tawil-Souri, "It's Still About the Power of Place," *Middle East Journal of Culture and Communication* 5, 2012: 86-95.
6. M. Abdelrahman, "A Hierarchy of Struggles? The 'economic' and the 'political' in Egypt's Revolution," *Review of African Political Economy* 39, no. 134, 2012: 614-28; Walter Armbrust, "The Revolution Against

Neoliberalism," *Jadaliyya e-zine*, 23 February 2011; Omar S. Dahi and Yasser Munif, "Revolts in Syria: Tracking the Convergence Between Authoritarianism and Neoliberalism," *Journal of Asian and African Studies* 47, no. 4, 2012: 323-32; Pete Moore, "The Arab 99 Percent: Understanding Political Economies of the 2011 Arab Uprisings," *APSA 2012 Annual Meeting Paper*, 2012.

7. Salwa Ismail, "Egypt's Dignity Revolution," *Counter Punch*, 10 February 2011. http://www.counterpunch.org/2011/02/10/egypt-s-dignity-revolution/; Nadia Marzouki, "The Call for Dignity, or a Particular Universalism," *Middle East Law and Governance* 3, nos. 1-2, 2011: 148-58; Amira Mittermaier, "Bread, Freedom, Social Justice: The Egyptian Uprising and a Sufi Khidima," *Cultural Anthropology* 29, no. 1, 2014: 54-79; Diane Singerman, "Youth, Gender, and Dignity in the Egyptian Uprising," *Journal of Middle East Women's Studies* 9, no. 3, 2013: 1-27.
8. http://www.merriam-webster.com/dictionary/absence. Accessed on June 2014.
9. Darwish, *In the Presence of Absence*, p. 73.
10. Alaa Al Aswany, *Limatha la Yathour El Masriyoon*, Cairo: Dar Al-Shorouq, 2010.
11. Amro Ali, "Saeeds of Revolution: De-Mythologizing Khaled Saeed," 5 June 2012. http://www.jadaliyya.com/pages/index/5845/saeeds-of-revolution_de-mythologizing-khaled-saeed. Accessed on June 2014.
12. Human Rights Watch, "Egypt: Prosecute Police in Beating Death," 2010. http://www.hrw.org/news/2010/06/24/egypt-prosecute-police-beating-death. Accessed on July 2014.
13. Human Rights Watch, "Egypt: Prosecute Police in Beating Death."
14. The Facebook group "We are all Khaled Said" was a central portal through which the image of Said's mutilated face was circulated.
15. Darwish, *In the Presence of Absence*, p. 124.
16. Darwish, *In the Presence of Absence*, p. 45.
17. Darwish, *In the Presence of Absence*, p. 19.
18. Darwish, *In the Presence of Absence*, p. 7.
19. Tetz Rooke, "In the Presence of Absence: Mahmoud Darwish's Testament," *Journal of Arabic and Islamic Studies* 8, 2008: 13.
20. Darwish, *In the Presence of Absence*, p. 101.
21. Darwish, *In the Presence of Absence*, p. 42.
22. Darwish, *In the Presence of Absence*, p. 139.
23. Darwish, *In the Presence of Absence*, pp. 61-62.
24. Darwish, *In the Presence of Absence*, p. 60.
25. Darwish, *In the Presence of Absence*, p. 67.
26. Darwish, *In the Presence of Absence*. p. 159.

2

The Arab Spring and the Palestinians

From the War in Syria to Operation Protective Edge

Harel Chorev

Unlike Tunisia, Egypt or Syria, the Arab Spring did not significantly affect the relations of the Palestinian public with its two regional leaderships, the Palestinian Authority (PA) that governs in the West Bank and the Hamas movement who rule the Gaza Strip. Several attempts in the Palestinian public sphere to copy and use typical symbols of the Arab Spring, such as Rage Days (*yawm al-gha?ab*), or establishing movements carrying names as *Tahrir* or *Tamarud-Gaza* (named after the Egyptian *Tamarud* which was one of the prominent movements calling for the resignation of President Mohammad Morsi), failed to take root. Indeed, the Palestinian context was too particular and different by almost any yardstick, first and foremost by the lack of independence and full sovereignty.

Having said that, the regional turmoil profoundly impacted the Palestinians in three crucial circles discussed in this article: first, the geopolitical realm in which the PA and Hamas are operating; second, at the relations of the PA and Hamas; and third, their relations, especially of Hamas, with Israel.

The Geopolitical Arena

Up until the overthrow of the Egyptian President Mohammad Morsi (June-July 2013), it seemed that the Palestinian Authority was the main loser of the Arab Spring's geopolitical shifts in the deeply divided Palestinian arena. Mubarak's sympathetic rule was toppled and was replaced by the parent movement of Hamas, the Muslim Brotherhood. Encouraged by the new support in its most important hinterland, Hamas committed a strategic estrangement from its allies in the Axis of Resistance (*Mihwar al-Mukawama*) that included Iran, Syria, and sub-state actors—Hezbollah and the Palestinian Islamic Jihad. The main reason for this shift was the bloody civil war in Syria, another outcome of the Arab Spring.

During a speech he gave on 16 May 2013, Secretary-General of Hezbollah, Hassan Nasrallah declared that "One day, the Palestinian organizations will admit that no one helped them as much as the regime of Bashar al-Assad."[1] Nasrallah words reflected criticism of Hamas, which several months before had broken off its long-standing alliance with the Syrian regime in favour of the Syrian opposition. In so doing, Hamas exacerbated a deepening crisis between the members of what until then had proudly constituted the "Resistance Axis" (*Mihwar al-Muqawama*). During the last two decades, the Resistance Axis has essentially constituted a political and military alliance. Consisting of Shiites and Sunnis, Arab and Persian, the Resistance Axis was not characterized by ethnic, religious or even ideological homogeneity. Rather, it constituted both an identity framework and a concrete alliance. The latter were based on confrontation with Israel, strong opposition to pro-western Arab regimes such as Mubarak's Egypt and Saudi Arabia, and the promotion of an Islamic-based political order. Syria was exception regarding these goals, but still an important member of the Axis for its own practical considerations, especially its military inferiority compared to Israel, as well as Syria's long-standing ambition to preserve its influence in Lebanon.[2]

Alongside common objectives, the Axis members shared important operational dimensions, such as an asymmetrical warfare doctrine, financing ties, training, and armament for the sub-state actors under Iranian sponsorship and Syrian facilitation. Hamas' abandonment of the Axis in the summer of 2012 was a direct result of the turmoil unleashed by the Arab Spring events, as well as three broader developments that preceded it. Most important was the civil war in Syria, which presented Hamas with a stark choice: to turn its back on the Syrian regime, and thus follow the path taken by most Arab governments, or to maintain a united front with the rest of the Resistance Axis members in support of the Assad regime. During the first year of the crisis, Hamas tried to find a middle ground that would allow it to avoid the negative consequences of choosing either of the two options. Therefore, it avoided taking a clear public stance as much as possible. Furthermore, the movement had even suppressed several attempts to organize public protests against Assad in the Gaza strip. On the other hand, Hamas spokesmen refused to express support for the Syrian regime, and even hinted at dissatisfaction with its actions. Nevertheless, the steady intensification of the crisis led to sharp public criticism of Hamas' neutrality, and its leaders eventually adopted a clear public stance against Assad. The subsequent fallout came quickly, as Iran reduced its economic support. In August 2012, Musa Abu Marzuq, deputy of Hamas's political bureau head Khalid Mash'al, acknowledged that the movement's relations with Iran had reached a low point due to the Syrian quagmire.[3] The Assad regime, for its part, began harassing Hamas representatives, starting with the arrest of Mash'al's daughter. Soon after, the movement closed its Damascus offices and Hamas officials departed from Syria in November 2012 to Egypt (Abu Marzuq) and Qatar (Mash'al). Hamas' geopolitical shift constituted a blow to the Resistance Axis, which has already lost popularity among the Arab public in light of its support for the Assad regime. One of the Axis' main assets up until the crisis was its inclusive pan-Islamic image, incorporating Sunnis and Shi'as, Persians and Arabs. Once Hamas, as a Palestinian and Sunni movement, began to drift away, the Axis' primary Shi'a colours were put on full display. This has further sharpened sectarian tensions in the region, which were increasingly manifesting themselves even before the Arab Spring erupted.

The second development that pushed Hamas to estrangement from the Resistance Axis was the rise of governments led by movements identified with the Muslim Brotherhood, Hamas' parent movement. This actually began as early as 2002 with the AKP party's rise to power in Turkey. AKP's leader, Recep Tayyip Erdoğan, has often expressed his solidarity with the Muslim Brotherhood, including its Palestinian offshoot, Hamas. In the wake of the political upheavals of the Arab Spring, the Brotherhood rose to power in Egypt, as did the like-minded *al-Nahda* party in Tunisia. Qatar also joined the ranks of this emerging pro-Brotherhood Sunni camp. Qatar was once considered amiable to the Resistance Axis and contributed to its popularity via sympathetic Al-Jazeera broadcasts. However, as the Syrian crisis unfolded, Qatar was initially slow to break with its image as a Resistance sympathizer, which *inter alia* cost Al-Jazeera viewers. But ultimately, like Hamas, Qatar fell in line with the rest of the Sunni world.

For a while Hamas had enjoyed new sources of economic and political support that it earned by distancing itself from the Resistance Axis. As an alternative income to the Iranian financial support, Hamas Government, which has an annual budget of $750-$900 million, could rely on taxes it collected on goods entering the Gaza Strip legally or illegally through more than 1,650 smuggling tunnels which crossed the border to Egypt.[4] Hamas gained approximately $500 million per annum from taxation of these tunnels alone.[5] Hamas could also rely on $400 million granted to it by the former Qatari Emir, Sheikh Hamad bin Khalifa Al Thani, during his visit to Gaza Strip in October 2012.[6] Politically, Hamas has already benefited from affiliation with this camp. The three-year Turkish-Israeli crisis provided Hamas with significant political gains that the Resistance Axis had never been able to match with the uplift of some of the restraints that Israel imposed on Gaza Strip. The visit to the Gaza Strip in May 2013 by the Brotherhood's spiritual leader, Sheikh Yusuf al-Qaradawi, who is known for his bitter opposition to Hezbollah and Iran, was another signal of Hamas' desire to get closer to its parent movement at the expense of the "Resistance."[7]

The third development that contributed to Hamas' move away from the Resistance camp is related to the process of its institutionalization in recent years. The movement's preparations to take over the Gaza Strip led to significant internal changes even before the takeover actually occurred. Most important of these was the change in the structure of Hamas' military wing. Alongside guerrilla and terrorist activities, Hamas established conventional security forces (*Al-Murabitun*) and adopted conventional military practices. These consisted of amassing of a massive rocket arsenal as a strategic arm in coping with Israel military superiority and building improved command and control systems. Following the Gaza Strip takeover in June 2007, Hamas has turned into a semi-sovereign authority with civil apparatus of about 43,000 employees and another 20,000 military personnel.

One concrete outcome of the Arab Spring for Hamas was the strengthening of its ties with Egypt. Egypt borders the Gaza Strip region and serves as its economic and logistic hinterland. Under President Mubarak, who was hostile toward Hamas, the ties between the latter and Egypt did not extend to the political sphere. With the rise to power of the Muslim Brotherhood in Egypt, Hamas' chances for assistance and rebuilding have increased. Nevertheless, despite the natural affinity between Hamas and Morsi's government, Hamas did not receive unconditional Egyptian support for its actions, particularly regarding its conduct vis-à-vis Israel and jihadi organizations that operate in the Gaza Strip. The security coordination between Egypt and Israel continued under Morsi, and the Egyptian Army has taken several tough measures such as flooding Gazan smuggling tunnels with sewage.[8] Such steps against what is an economic and military lifeline for the Gaza Strip made it clear to Hamas that even Morsi's Egypt expect it to demonstrate political responsibility. Additionally, there have been calls from within the Egyptian Government for Hamas, especially since Israel's military Pillars of Defence operation in November 2012, to reduce the military dimension of its struggle and adopt a strategy based on diplomatic channels that would yield greater benefits. In view of the military abilities that Hamas has presented during Operation Protective Edge in July-August 2014, it is clear that the Egyptian advice was not taken.

In July 2013, President Morsi was toppled by the Egyptian army supported by the masses. Morsi was jailed and replaced by General Abd al-Fattah al-Sisi. The latter viewed Hamas as a partner in all ways of the Egyptian Muslim Brotherhood as well as a collaborator of Islamist terror in the Sinai that had claimed the lives of Egyptian soldiers in several incidents. In early 2014, an Egyptian court ruled that Hamas is a terrorist movement, a declaration subsequently led the Egyptian government to freeze the assets of movement. Several senior Egyptian officials even openly declared their wish to topple the Hamas regime in Gaza.[9]

The Internal Arena: Hamas' Attempts to Prompt a Third Intifada

While the geopolitical ramifications of the Arab Spring on the Palestinian major players were crucial, it did not significantly impacted the intra Palestinian arena, despite Hamas' continuing efforts to exploit the Arab Spring to undermine the PA's control over the West Bank.

Following Hamas' takeover of the Gaza strip in 2007, the Palestinian Authority took immediate and affective steps to destroy the movement's organizational infrastructures in the West Bank. Hamas, for its part, has tried since the outbreak of the Arab Spring in early 2011 to use its terms and symbols to undermine the PA by organizing Days of Rage in the West Bank asserting that the *Haram al-Sharif* is in danger. Hamas' spokesmen have also frequently called for a third *intifada*. These efforts had three aims. The first was to divert attention of Gaza Strip residents away from their worsening economic predicament. Since the 2007 Hamas takeover, the Gaza Strip is suffering a severe economic crisis which stands in contrast to the relative prosperity in the West Bank under the PA. By the end of 2013, GDP per capita in the Gaza Strip was $1,600—an income of about five dollars a day—compared to $3,100-3200 in the West Bank. The unemployment rate in Gaza Strip was 41 per cent, while in the West Bank it was 26 per cent. The poverty rate in Gaza was 39 per cent and the deep poverty rate was 21 per cent.[10] This situation probably worsened in 2014, inter alia, as a result of a rapid population growth of three per cent, namely 50,000 additional Gazans every year.[11] Indeed, the $400 million Qatari assistance enabled Hamas to maintain its systems, but just barely, especially in light of the priority given to vast investments in military infrastructure of rockets and attack tunnels. Gazans had to make do with only a few hours of electricity a day. Against this background, Hamas hoped that destabilizing the West Bank will prove that there is unrest in the West Bank as well due to the pressure from Israel, and not necessarily because of the Hamas's shortcomings in the Gaza Strip.

Second, by encouraging a third *intifada* Hamas tried to thwart the peace negotiations conducted between Israel and the PA between August 2013 and March 2014. The basic ethos of Hamas has not significantly changed and remains bent on undermining any permanent political arrangement with Israel. Nevertheless, since its takeover of the Gaza Strip in June 2007 Hamas has more to lose in comparison to the 1990s when it was responsible for most of the guerrilla and terrorist attacks against Israel. From 2007, the movement's main interest is in preserving its quasi-sovereign control over the Gaza Strip. This interest became even more conspicuous in the wake of the developments in Hamas' geostrategic position, which directly affected the economy and security environment in the Gaza Strip.

Third, and most importantly, Hamas hoped that a third *intifada* will lead to the collapse of its rival, the Fatah controlled PA, either by the popular unrest or by the hands of Israel.[12] These attempts, however, were obvious to the PA.[13] Therefore it is interesting to note what has happened to the once sacred terms in the Palestinian narrative, such as *intifada*. On a contemporary context, whenever the term *intifada* was mentioned, in the media or elsewhere, the PA leadership saw it as a reflection of Hamas' efforts to destabilize the West Bank. Therefore, the PA and its president Mahmoud Abbas (Abu Mazen) openly rejected the option of a third *intifada*. Consequently, the PA's effective security cooperation with Israel continued, with the understanding that escalating attacks will not serve either the Palestinians' relations with Israel and the international community, or the PA's standing in the internal Palestinian political arena.[14]

In this relatively silent struggle between Hamas and the PA, the latter's security agencies were and still are key players. Since the end of the second *intifada*, in which many Palestinian security personnel took an active part, these agencies have been thoroughly reorganized under US guidance and training (under the supervision of Lt. General Keith Dayton), and produce professional commanders, such as Majed Faraj,[15] whom many—including Israel—regard as the next generation of Palestinian political leadership. These organizations are playing a key role in dismantling Hamas' organizational infrastructure in the West Bank as well as in thwarting the movement's attempts to prompt a new *intifada*. Unlike in the second *intifada* these agencies show no signs of instability or independence from the political echelon of the PA.

As for the West Bank society, up until July 2014 the PA's policy against a new *intifada* was generally backed. Despite the scepticism typical of both Israelis and Palestinians about the prospects of the peace negotiations, the very fact that they were taking place had a calming effect on the Palestinian public until the early 2014. Also important is the traumatic memory of *Intifadat al-Aqsa* (2000-2005) which is still vivid to many, and acts as a deterrent, as does the regional instability in the wake of the Arab Spring. Economic stability in the West Bank, and even some improvement during the 2013, especially since President Obama's visit in March, presumably also played a role in maintaining a certain level of calm.

Some circles in the West Bank society suggest that this calm is part of a broad socio-cultural phenomenon, and not necessarily a positive one. According to these circles, this phenomenon reflects the apparent materialism and indifference of what they call the "self-absorbed generation" (*al-Jil al-Ma?lahaji*). This term has become common recently and is used by some Palestinians to criticize the youth who are viewed as focusing on self-advancement rather than on national goals. This critique does not necessarily refer exclusively to the absence of a third *intifada*, but is being voiced in the broader context of the idea that the younger generation is ambivalent about pursuing collective goals for the benefit of Palestinian society as a whole. In other words, this phenomenon ostensibly reflects a quite opposite spirit to the rebellious generation who carried out at least the first stage of the Arab Spring revolutions.

Implications of Operation Protective Edge

In the spring of 2014, Hamas found itself in the most difficult crisis of its history. The movement was isolated geopolitically; the Qatari assistance—at least the formal $400 million assistances granted for civil purposes—ran out and Egypt destroyed the majority of the smuggling tunnels (approximately 1650 tunnels according to the Egyptian army).[16] Consequently, Hamas was soon to be left without ability to finance and maintain critical infrastructure, such as electricity and water,[17] or to pay the salaries of its 63,000 employees. These circumstances represented the primary motivation, on Hamas' part, to seek the reconciliation agreement with the Palestinian Authority, which it signed in late April from a position of extreme disadvantage. Hamas had to accept most of the PA's demands and in exchange expected that the PA, first and foremost, would alleviate its financial predicament and pay Hamas workers' salaries.[18]

Against this background, it appears that the kidnapping and murder of three Israeli teenagers who were students at a religious seminary in the West Bank on June 12 was an unwanted event for Hamas' political leadership who initially denied involvement in the abduction. Two months later Israel's General Security Service (Shin Bet) announced that the murderers, Amer Abu Aisha and Marwan Qawasmeh—both killed on an Israeli attempt to arrest them on 23 September—and their commander, Hossam Qawasmeh, who was arrested several weeks earlier, received funding through Hossam's brother, who lives in Gaza.[19] One can view this as evidence of Hamas' attempts to intentionally drag Israel to a confrontation. However, familiarity with the modus operandi of Iz al-Din al-Qassam, the military wing of Hamas, suggests that this is not necessarily the case. The information given by the Shin Bet reveals that the initiative for the abduction came "from the field," namely by the three who carried out the operation. According to the Shin Bet, the operation's details were known only to the three (all from Hebron) and to Hossam's brother, their contact in Gaza, for reasons of compartmentalization. The funding, NIS 220,000 given by Hamas-Gaza to the kidnapers, was given without concrete idea of the purpose of the planned action.[20] That being said, Hamas' record is filled with examples in which local operatives carried out operations in its name, without prior coordination. In most of these cases, Hamas leadership adopted such operations because they fit within its concept of struggle and its underground character, which didn't require a broad range of political considerations. Yet, since its takeover on Gaza Strip Hamas is calculating costs and benefits differently and thus cannot behave as it did previously.

Therefore, and although Hamas did not claim responsibility for the abduction of the three youths, it found itself almost immediately paying a heavy price for it. Although it was officially declared that there was no evidence tying Hamas to the operation,[21] PA President Mahmud Abbas viewed the abductions as likely to be orchestrated by Hamas. This has threatened to destroy the gains that he had reaped in the international arena: first and foremost, the emerging consensus in international opinion that the failure of the Israeli-Palestinian peace negotiations was Israel's fault. Abbas' forthright and unconditional public condemnation of the abductions led to an immediate *de facto* end to the reconciliation agreement. The salaries that were promised to Hamas personnel, who had not been paid since May 2014, remained in the coffers and the PA security organizations have resumed their actions against Hamas in the West Bank.[22]

These developments left the Hamas leadership without a clear strategy in the immediate aftermath of the abductions. As a result, it spoke with contradictory voices. On the one hand, Hamas' spokesmen such as Sami Abu Zuhari denied the movement's involvement in the kidnappings.[23] On the other, senior members, such as Khalid Mash'al, Isma'il Haniyeh, Fauzi Barhum, and Mushir al-Masri, praised the abductors, distorted uncomfortable facts such as the young age of the victims (Mash'al referred to them as "soldiers," Haniyeh called them "settlers"). As part of this confused response, Mash'al noted that the armed wing of Hamas was not subservient to the political wing, and thus left the door open for Hamas to assume responsibility for the operation.[24] By so doing, Mash'al left open the possibility for Hamas to take responsibility in the future, as indeed happened approximately one month later.[25]

As the PA's seriousness about terminating the reconciliation agreement became clearer, a hawkish and unified strategy began to coalesce within Hamas, towards both the PA and Israel. As Hamas was left with no other option to survive its deep economic crisis, the only option that remained on the table was to drag Israel, and preferably the PA too, to a military confrontation that will finalize with new arrangements that allow Hamas to get out of the quagmire. This has paved the way to another violent clash between Hamas and Israel, stronger than ever before.

On 23 June, the thirteenth day following the abduction of the three teens, Hamas Prime Minister Haniyeh announced that the "Third Intifada" had already begun in the West Bank.[26] This statement demonstrated the depths of polarization and crisis in the Palestinian political arena, as it stood in sharp contrast to the PA's firm opposition to any talk about a new *intifada*, and confirmed its suspicions that Hamas is moving to undermine the stability in the West Bank. As mentioned, the PA has been aware of such attempts for some time, and over the course of about seven months has not been content with simply strengthening its security apparatus, but also has reinforced its grip on the street. To that end, the PA has called into service its informal apparatus, first and foremost, the Tanzim organization of Fatah acting as its informal long-arm in the "streets." For their part,

Hamas spokesmen confirmed this polarization. Musa Abu Marzuq, deputy of Hamas' political bureau, argued on 2 July that Abbas effectively had given up the Gaza Strip, and that if it was offered to him, he wouldn't want it.[27]

While intra-Palestinian polarization deepened, a sixteen year old Palestinian youth from the Jerusalem neighbourhood of Shu'afat was murdered on 2 July by three Israeli extremists in revenge for the killing of the three Israeli youth.[28] The riots that broke out in response in Arab communities within Israel were viewed as an opportunity by Hamas who tried to use the riots as a means to advance its ambition of prompt popular resistance and instability in the West Bank. Arguably, Hamas hoped that a more active Palestinian "street" in the West Bank and Israel would redirect Palestinian animus towards Israel and the PA and would be used as leverage in the hands of Hamas in view of the crisis between it and the PA. Indeed, in July, Israel arrested 93 Hamas members on suspicion of trying to organize a third *intifada* in the West Bank.[29] At the same time, Hamas has also attempted to pour more fuel on the fire by firing rockets on Israeli cities and allowing other organizations to do so as well.[30] For its part, Israel's reactions to these developments, especially its killings of operatives in the Gaza Strip, also contributed to the escalation.

Hamas' intention to drag Israel into a confrontation was the principal reason why the Israeli and Egyptian attempts to bring about a cease-fire during the two weeks prior to Operation Protective Edge have failed. A prevailing analysis at the beginning of hostilities attributed this failure to the alleged independence of the military wing of Hamas, without consideration for the authority of the political wing.[31] However, Hamas' well-coordinated military conduct through the 50 days (51 according to Hamas counting) of Operation Protective Edge proves that these estimations were quite exaggerated. The autonomy Hamas' military wing enjoyed has suffered a blow, following the Israeli strike on its commander Ahmed Ja'abari in November 2012. Ja'abari's direct ties to Khalid Mash'al, and the Iranian financial pipeline that he controlled, enabled such independence. But following the Hamas estrangement from the Axis of Resistance and Iran over the last two years, as well as Ja'abari's death, it is doubtful that this was the situation at the eve of Operation Protective Edge. Furthermore, the political leadership's declarations before and during the operation did not reveal internal divisions, but rather the opposite and were extremely militant, especially from the moment it became clear that the reconciliation with the PA had crumbled.

Evidence to Hamas' desire to take advantage of the continuing turmoil and to escalate its relations with Israel was seen on 4 July, four days before Protective Edge, when spokesmen, such as Osama Hamdan, began to demand that, in exchange for a cease-fire, Israel would have to stop not only its targeted killings, but also remove the blockade on the Gaza Strip.[32] On 7 July Hamas added an additional demand: Israel must set free prisoners released as part of the October 2011 Gilad Shalit deal (an Israeli soldier held captive by Hamas from 2006 to 2011) and then rearrested after the abduction and assassination of the three Israeli youth. Hamas also demanded that Egypt should open the Rafah crossing.[33] It seems that Hamas was fully aware that the chances that Israel or Egypt will acquiesce to these demands were extremely low. In other words, Hamas has opened itself to a potential military confrontation with its eyes wide open. One of the most conspicuous evidence to this strategic intention was revealed by an Israeli operation on 5 July against a tunnel which was to be used to execute a strategic attack against Israel shortly after the operation took place. Following the Israeli operation seven Hamas militants were directly or indirectly killed in the tunnel, apparently while trying to execute their own operation for which the tunnel was constructed.[34] This event reinforces the assessment that Hamas intended to drag Israel into war.

Dragging Israel to a military confrontation was indeed a radical solution. However, Hamas had probably no option left after the PA has averted from paying the salaries of Hamas employees and the financial crisis has reached its peak. Paradoxically, an Israeli operation seemed less threatening than the possibility of internal collapse of the Hamas regime and offered a chance for a meaningful change in its difficult geopolitical, economic, and intra-Palestinian position. Consequently, the Israeli formula "quiet will be answered by quiet" expressed a deep misunderstanding of Hamas' intentions. Israel did not understand that in contrast to the tactical character of previous rounds of violence, the current confrontation with Hamas reflected strategic aims that were focused on Hamas' superior interest to preserve its control over its quasi-state in the Gaza Strip.[35]

This analysis was confirmed three days after Operation Protective Edge has begun by Prime Minister Haniyeh who argued that the war was the result of Hamas' desire to end the Israeli "siege."[36] Hamas correctly estimated that despite severe casualties and damages that an Israeli Operation will probably cause, it will not threaten its control over the Strip for three reasons: the Israeli concerns of suffering numerous casualties in ground operation; the absence of an alternative to Hamas affective governing; and from Israeli perspective, the even-worse alternatives to "the devil you know" of other radical groups, especially Islamist, active in the Gaza Strip. Indeed, during the 50 days of Protective Edge Israeli spokespersons gave every reason to conclude that these assumptions were informed.[37]

Having said that, Hamas' strategic assumption that another round of violence will allow it to break out of its crisis is yet to be proven, but it is already clear that the price the movement and the Gaza Strip had to pay was extremely heavy. There is a profound difference in the military perceptions of Israel and Hamas which reflect on their sense of "victory." Israeli perception of the conflict is based on conventional military terms: Iron Dome intercepted most of the rockets that Hamas and other organizations launched; the IDF demolished dozens of attack tunnels and killed approximately a thousand operatives, including senior commanders in Iz al-Din al-Qassam Brigades, such as Raid al-Attar and Mohammad Abu Shimala. Israel can also point out that Hamas's perception of Israeli society as weak and not cohesive was proven wrong during the operation. On the other hand, Hamas was able to meet its main struggle principle, demonstrating "steadfastness" in face of the Israeli military pounding, mainly through the consistent firing into Israel. Hamas also succeeded in killing Israeli soldiers and civilians. Through its use of civilians as human shields,[38] Hamas has also forced Israel to contend with a high death toll among civilians in the Gaza Strip, which Hamas used as a battering ram in the Palestinian and international arena. Hamas also demonstrated the ability to disrupt the daily life in Israel and for two days even hampered the routine of flights to Israel's Ben-Gurion International Airport.

Besides the differences in military perceptions, there is also a difference in the definition of political achievements each party pursues. Israel is seeking for deterrence that would prevent firing to its territory and last as long as possible. Israel has never stated the desire to overthrow the Hamas regime, and therefore, the latter's survival was not a failure from Israel's point of view. Only time will tell if Israel actually achieved that goal. At the same time, the required political achievement for Hamas was to preserve its control over the Gaza Strip. Although Hamas managed to deliver the message that the blockade of the Gaza Strip was the main reason for the confrontation, it has yet to secure its removal. Hamas has already secured one important achievement, which is raising funds for the reconstruction of the Gaza Strip. First attempts to raise money from traditional donors, such as Japan and Saudi Arabia, failed as these donors expressed their concerns that their assistance is likely to be burned in the next round of violence. This deadlock led the international community to initiate the Cairo summit (12 October 2014) in which $5.4 billion were raised for the reconstruction of the Gaza Strip.[39]

Given the above, neither Israel nor Hamas can claim for now that they achieved their strategic goals. It will take time to conclude whether Hamas ensured the survival of its regime, and whether Israel succeeded in creating long-term deterrence against Hamas and the other organization in the Gaza Strip. Since these are two different goals, it is not inconceivable that in the future the two sides can rightly claim that they won since they achieved their strategic goals.

Conclusion

The Arab Spring did not manifest itself in the Palestinian arena in the way it did in other countries of the region. It did, however, profoundly impact on the geopolitical context of the two leading Palestinian players, the PA and Hamas, as well as their relationships with each other and their relations with Israel. The civil war in Syria and the rise to power of the Muslim Brotherhood in Egypt—two salient outcomes of the Arab Spring—lead Hamas to a strategic manoeuvre that generated a chain reaction. Hamas pulled away from its allies in the Resistance Axis and turned to Egypt, Qatar and Turkey as its main political and economic support. At the same time, the movement continued with its efforts to exploit the symbols and terminology of the regional upheaval to undermine the position of the PA in the West

Bank, efforts that were recognized and treated accordingly by the PA and its security apparatus.

The turning point in these poisoned inner-Palestinian relationships began only after Hamas has performed its strategic move of estrangement from the Resistance Axis, which turned out to be a mistake in light of the overthrow of President Morsi in July 2013. Only few months later the Hamas found itself in the most severe geopolitical and economic crisis in its history, a development that posed a real threat on the movement's ability to maintain its rule in the Gaza Strip. Hamas' solution, although from a clearly inferior position, was to sign the reconciliation agreement with the PA in order to receive the latter's assistance in paying the salaries of Hamas' employees. However, the abduction of the three Israeli youths on 12 June damaged again the delicate fabric of relations with the PA and the salaries were not transferred.

Consequently, Hamas' last resort was to drag Israel to another round of violence, which Hamas has hoped will allow it to "re-open the game" and to ensure, first and foremost, its economic survival. A month and a half after the conclusion of Operation Protective Edge the uplift of the blockade is not yet been agreed. Having said that, there is a strong understanding in Israel that the blockade policy did not achieve its goals. Hamas continues to expand its arsenal of rockets and mortars, while proving autonomous abilities to manufacture its armament by itself. Indeed, the Israeli monitoring and limitations on supplies of materials to the Gaza Strip, did not prevent Hamas from constructing an impressive web of control and command, logistic and attack tunnels.

A removal of the blockade will probably calm the tension between Hamas and Israel. Unlike the Islamic Jihad, Hamas is not an avant-garde organization which has no intensions of becoming a social movement or becoming politically established. Instead, Hamas, like other offshoots of the Muslim Brotherhood, always aspired to establish itself as a social-mass movement and a ruling party. Therefore, the movement's impulse to preserve its rule was and remains central. Nevertheless, one should not expect that removing the blockade will prevent future confrontations between Hamas and Israel. Hamas is still highly committed, primarily for religious reasons and ideology, to "resistance"—a continuation of the struggle against the State of

Israel until its final annihilation. The military wing of Iz al-Din al-Qassam announced as early as six weeks after the conclusion of Protective Edge of its intensions to recruit new operatives, and more importantly, to reconstruct its power and infrastructures that were destroyed during the operation.[40] This announcement was quickly backed up by Hamas' political leadership. Former prime-minister, Isma'il Haniyeh and Khalid Mash'al, head of the movement's political bureau, declared that the recent war was only a first step to the final liberation war against Israel.[41]

In the Palestinian arena, Operation Protective Edge has strengthened Hamas' popularity at the expense of the PA. Nonetheless, past experience demonstrates that these fluctuations are volatile and difficult to maintain over time.[42] For now, reconstruction of the Gaza Strip is a common denominator for both Hamas and the PA. However, the basic disagreements stay, not only on the issue of how to deal with Israel, but also, and not less important, of who will dominate the Palestinian arena.

References

1. *Al-Manar channel*, 16 May 2012.
2. Michael Milstein, "The Challenge of Muqawama (Resistance) to Israel," *Strategic Assessment* 12, no. 4, February 201).
3. Interview with Khalid Mashal. www.mepanorama.net/234994/.
4. Agence France-Presse (Cairo), 27 July 2014.
5. Paul Rivlin, "The Economy and the War in Gaza," *Iqtisadi* 4, no. 8, August 2014: 4.
6. *New York Times*, 23 October 2012.
7. *Al-Arabia* Channel, 9 May 2013.
8. *Haaretz*, 23 February 2013.
9. www.al-monitor.com/pulse/originals/2014/01/egypt-israel-gaza-hamas-tamarod-movement.html#.
10. Eran Yashiv, "The Economics of the Gaza Situation: A Crucial Element in the Conflict and the Resolution," *Insight*, no. 585, Institute for National Security Studies, 6 August 2014.
11. Rivlin, "The Economy and the War in Gaza," 2014: 4.
12. www.ynetnews.com/articles/0,7340,L-4560000,00.html. Accessed on 19 August 2014.
13. Interview with PA former minister Ashraf al-Ajrami (Tel Aviv), 26 May 2014.

14. Interview with PA former minister Ashraf al-Ajrami (Tel Aviv), 26 May 2014.
15. On Faraj *see* www.maannews.net/eng/ViewDetails.aspx?ID=226151.
16. *AFP* (Cairo), 27 July 2014.
17. Reuters, 9 October 2013.
18. Interview with PA former minister Ashraf al-Ajrami (Tel Aviv), 26 May 2014.
19. *The Telegraph* (London), 6 August 2014.
20. *Haaretz*, September 4, 2014.
21. *Al-Quds*, June 21, 2014.
22. *Haaretz* (English edition), 16 June 2014.
23. *Al-Monitor*, 16 June 2014.
24. *Al-Jazeera*, 22 June 2014.
25. www.timesofisrael.com/top-hamas-sheikh-admits-to-june-kidnapping-of-israeli-teens/.
26. www.vetogate.com/1083685. Accessed on 23 June 2014.
27. *Al-Jazeera*, 2 July 2014.
28. *The Guardian*, 14 July 2014.
29. *The Jerusalem Post*, 18 August 2014.
30. Harel Chorev, "The Road to Operation Protective Edge: Gaps in Strategic Perceptions," *Israel Journal of Foreign Affairs* 8, no. 3, 2014: 1-5.
31. See for example, Israel's Channel One, an interview with Col. (Ret.) Dr. Shmuel Gordon, 11 July 2014.
32. http://alresalah.ps/ar/index.php?act=post&id=97045.
33. www.ynet.co.il/articles/0,7340,L-4538211,00.html. Accessed on 7 July 2014.
34. *Haaretz*, 7 July 2014.
35. Harel Chorev, ?Hamas: Charting a New Strategic Course of Action," *Tel Aviv Notes* 8, no. 1, Special edition, 10 July 2014: 4.
36. *Al-Quds*, 12 July 2014; see also www.palinfo.com/site/pic/newsdetails.aspx?ItemId=158786.
37. For example: *Al-Monitor*, 11 July 2014.
38. Speech by Fathi Hmad, Hamas' Minister of the Interior: www.youtube.com/watch?v=RTu-AUE9ycs.
39. *Maan News Agency*, 12 October 2014.
40. *Maan News Agency*, 9 October 2014.
41. *Maan News Agency*, 9 October 2014; see also www.ynet.co.il/articles/0,7340,L-4565367,00.html.
42. www.washingtonpost.com/blogs/worldviews/wp/2014/09/02/poll-hamas-popularity-surges-after-war-with-israel/; compare to www.washington post.com/blogs/worldviews/wp/2014/09/02/poll-hamas-popularity-surges-after-war-with-israel/

3

Israel-Palestine

Revisiting the Bi-National State

Priya Singh

The Concept and Categories of Bi-Nationalism

> "One day, in the near or further future, all this will be one binational state. It's just a question of how we get there. Either we Palestinians will get the independent state our leaders are currently calling for, alongside Israel—which will almost inevitably lead to a Europe-style reintegration between Israel and Palestine some years hence. Or else, disaggregation into two states will prove impossible, and we'll leave out that stage, going straight to the binational state."
> Sari Nuseibeh[1]

> "If there are not two states, there will be one. If there is one, it will be Arab. If Arab it is, there is no telling the fate of our children and theirs. …we must distinguish the permanent from the transitory. Our alliance with America is transitory. It is incumbent upon us to constantly invest in perpetuating it. On the other hand, our presence next to the Palestinians and in the midst of the Arab world is permanent features of our reality and should inform our choices."
> *Amoz Oz*[2]

The bi-national idea, an intensely contested one, is not new to the region nor is it a Palestinian creation. The Jewish groups during the British Mandate era first advocated bi-nationalism, that is, the sharing of political powers equally between the Jewish and Arab communities in Israel/Palestine, their comparative sizes notwithstanding. With Israel's establishment as a Jewish state in 1948, the bi-national idea seemed predestined to political extinction. However, with the virtual collapse of the peace process, the eruption of the second Palestinian Intifada, the de facto Israeli reoccupation of the West Bank and Gaza, and especially the changes in the Jewish-Palestinian demography, this seemingly overlooked notion appeared to have made a political comeback. This time, however, most advocates of bi-nationalism were from the Palestinian side, with a few on the Israeli side.[3] In the gradual course of time, some outside observers too, began advocating bi-nationalism as a solution. Tamar Hermann has analysed bi-nationalism along two lines of appraisal: "1) the time line, i.e. between the pre-state and the present day arguments for the bi-national idea on the Jewish side, b) the ethno-national line, i.e. between the rationales and programmes of today's Palestinian, Israeli and external bi-nationalists."[4] Historian Susan Lee Hattis observed that the future of Palestine after the British Mandate could have been any one of the four scenarios: "1) Palestine could become a predominantly Arab state; 2) Palestine could become a predominantly Jewish state; 3) Palestine could be partitioned into an Arab and a Jewish state; or 4) Palestine could be a bi-national state." [5] According to Ian Lustick, "Bi-national refers to a country in which two and only two national cultures are afforded pride of place, with juridically entrenched rights for control of shares of the state's resources, positions of authority, symbols, etc."[6] In the context of Israel-Palestine, Lustick elaborates, "Bi-national or other single-state solutions seek to secure what is needed by abandoning what is strongly desired; Jews and Arabs are to share the land, resources, recognition, and immigration opportunities afforded by a single state ruling the whole land, but at the cost of having to forever encounter each other in micro and macro struggles to achieve a distribution of those resources which each side feels is as much as it can get of what it deserves."[7] Tamar Hermann has expanded on the forms that bi-nationalism can take. She observes that the first three are only de facto bi-national though they do not reflect a bi-national reasoning however the other two are both de facto and de jure bi-national models.

1. "Unitary state with dominant national collectivity, allowing the other national collectivity that resides in the territory no collective political rights whatsoever and subjecting it to a

discriminatory set of laws and regulations, aimed specifically at controlling the 'dominated' group.

2. A political system that grants the non-dominant national/ ethnic group a certain amount of cultural autonomy and perhaps even equal individual human and civil rights, but no collective political rights, which are reserved for the dominant group only.
3. A classical liberal democracy, cohabited by two national groups and functioning on the principle of 'one person, one vote.' Neither of the two national groups is granted collective political rights, since the only individual identity recognised here is the civic one. In this model the linkage between the state and its citizens is direct, and it is not 'filtered' through ethnic or religious institutions or loyalties.
4. A parity based bi-national framework in which not only are the members of the two national groups granted equal human and civil rights, but the two groups as such are entitled to equal collective political rights whatever their respective numerical sizes.
5. Consociational democracy is today the most refined bi-national arrangement. It recognizes collective ethno-national rights and, by some cantonal or other arrangement agreed upon by the elites of the two national collectivities, guarantees that both groups get a fair share of the political powers."[8]

Hermann has examined four different proposals of bi-nationalism in the Israeli-Palestinian context. These are what she calls the 'old school' and 'new school' of Jewish bi-nationalism, contemporary Palestinian bi-nationalism and the variant of bi-nationalism espoused by observers from outside. Hermann has elaborated upon the four schools of bi-nationalism. a) 'Old School' of Jewish bi-nationalism, which envisioned a system based on parity. It did not view the bi-national arrangement as the best one but as the only one that would impede deterioration into a vicious strife. This group was ostracised by fellow Jews and their appeasing posture did not elicit a favourable response from the Arabs. It was generally perceived as politically inappropriate. b) The 'New School' of Jewish bi-nationalism was more pragmatic than the 'old school.' It was pessimistic about the viability of Israel as a Jewish entity in the context of the regional reality. It was vehemently against Israel's expansionist, occupationist and nationalistic drives, which they believed would lead to the state's collapse under demographic and other related pressures. It did not constitute a coherent group with well-articulated notions about the structure of bi-nationalism to be pursued. The majority of the Jewish public did not approve of this school as it did not guarantee the physical safety of the majority of the Jews in Palestine nor ensured the preservation of their collective identity and its articulation. c) Another category of bi-nationalists are the Palestinian supporters of bi-nationalism. This group is mainly composed of intellectuals with a pragmatic outlook primarily concerned with furthering Palestinian national interests. They hope for a change in the regional context which would facilitate the translation of the Palestinian demographic advantage into a political one in the future. The lack of support for this group from the Palestinian mainstream was due to their refusal to opt for an artificial Jewish-Palestinian civil identity and in the process relinquish their unique historical identity with the Arab and Islamic worlds. d) The fourth group of advocates of bi-nationalism consisted of external/outside observers, who predominantly belonged to liberal Western democracies and as such were unable to grasp and take into account the craving on both sides to preserve their national identity. The Jews particularly felt that what was being offered was essentially a PLO version of secular, liberal democracy with no concrete apparatus to guarantee either side collective rights particularly Israel's right to remain as a Jewish state and the physical security of the Israeli Jews in a hostile regional setting.[9] Burak Erdenir observes "The bi-national idea in the Israel/ Palestine case, unlike other cases had not been the outcome of an evolution; it has rather been a proposal of those who wished to change the status quo in their favour. In fact, the idea of bi-nationalism has emerged in times of change in power relations. The Jewish advocates supported the idea at the time of the Mandate, while the Arab advocates brought this issue recently with the expectation of change in power relations for their own advantage."[10] Erdenir, like Tamar Hermann has also classified the idea of bi-nationalism into four categories based on four different advocacies: a) The Old school of Jewish bi-nationalism, b) The New school of Jewish bi-nationalism,

c) Contemporary Palestinian bi-nationalism, and d) Outsiders' bi-nationalism.[11]

The Debates

According to Hani A. Farris, several Palestinians as well as others are of the opinion that the international community should recognise the conditions Israel has created in the occupied territories, which render the two-state solution impossible. As such, there is an urgent need to explore the only option left for a final negotiated settlement which would offer peace with justice for all concerned, that is, Israeli Jews and Palestinians. The latter consists of Palestinian citizens of Israel, Palestinians in the West Bank and Gaza, 1948 Palestinians and their descendants in the shatat (Diaspora). They visualise the two communities becoming citizens of a single democratic, secular and multicultural state in all of historic Palestine. Farris goes on to state that the notion has been outrightly rejected by a number of Jews and Palestinians alike as the general tendency among people is to conceptualise in either/or dualities or bi-polar relationships, rather than in a continuum or a dialectical interaction. In this sense, the one-state idea is seen as the antithesis of the two-state idea. Farris contends that the one-state idea is not the converse of the two-state solution and if Israel were to remove the Jewish settlers, withdraw to 1967 borders, allow the establishment of a sovereign Palestinian state and address the Palestinian rights of return, a majority of the Palestinians would endorse such a settlement. However, the reality is different and the inability of the peace process to produce the desired consequences has resulted in an impasse as the Palestinians continue to remain stateless and under occupation. This in effect compelled the likes of Edward Said to call for a bi-national Israeli-Palestinian state. A number of Jewish intellectuals also came out in support of the one-state solution. Tony Judt, for example, commented that Israel had become an 'anachronism' and 'dysfunctional' and that the time was now ripe to convert Israel from a Jewish state into a bi-national one. Both were severely criticised but the idea of the one-state solution gained ground among intellectuals and across religious and ethnic lines. [12]

In December 2001/January 2002, *Boston Review* convened a special forum "Fitting the Pieces Together," to debate the issue of bi-nationalism. In the forum, Lama Abu-Odeh in her lead article, "The Case for Binationalism," argued that serious misgivings about the ability of a two-state model to fulfil Palestinian national aspirations indicated that the time had come to reconsider the idea of bi-nationalism in a single state. Abu-Odeh called for a secular, binational, liberal-constitutional state in all of Mandate Palestine. In her view, the absence of 'post-colonizer' liberal elite in Israel signified that any two-state settlement would not offer much to the Palestinians. A change to bi-nationalism would point to a shift from an appeal to rights of national self-determination to an appeal to constitutional liberalism based on equal citizenship in the state of Israel. The move would entail a juridical strategy: a binationalist Palestinian legal posture modelled on the position of Palestinian Israeli citizens, who contend that liberalism should undermine Zionism. Abu-Odeh argued that binationalism offered Palestinians and Israeli Jews an opportunity to expand the territorial scope of their national aspirations to include all of Mandate Palestine as shared space. Abu-Odeh outlined a number of political approaches that was a prerequisite to enable Palestinians to make the shift from a struggle based on national independence to one based on civil rights. She concluded by outlining the appropriate constitutional boundaries of a binational state. She recommended a federal structure, wherein the boundaries of the administrative units or states would correspond to areas of predominant Jewish or Palestinian settlement. The states would be autonomous within their spheres of jurisdiction, which would include control over culture and education. Freedom of movement throughout the federation would be safeguarded. Inter-jurisdictional relocation of resources would be essential to guarantee equal citizenship.[13]

In the same forum, Helena Cobban in her response to Abu-Odeh, in an article, "Ends and Means," observes that Abu-Odeh makes a number of interesting observations in her essay. However, according to Coban she is not conclusive in her contention that shifting from the still-existing two-state formulation of Palestinian political goals to a binational variation of the one-state formulation would be in the interest of the Palestinians. Coban sought to explore two flaws that she perceives in her argument: her claim that "Oslo proved the

[Palestinian] nationalist goal unattainable," and the misperception that she appears entrapped in, between ends (one-state or two-state) and means (non-violent or violent). Instead of apportioning the entire blame on the Israeli military and political class for not allowing the Palestinian nationalist project to succeed, Cobban's conclusion was that strategic recklessness and a deep averseness to make critical decisions reigned on both sides during and in the post-Oslo period. Cobban also contends that contrary to Abu-Odeh's perception of the relationship between means and ends in which it is assumed that struggles for national independence are inevitably at all times pursued through violent means, while civil-rights struggles are essentially pursued through non-violent civil disobedience, the history of the twentieth century provides for a plethora of evidence to refute that assumption, citing the non-violent nature of the Indian civil disobedience movement against British rule as a case in point. Cobban suggests that a clever pursuit of non-violent means is not only the appropriate but also the most effective strategy and particularly so in the context of the Palestinians' struggle for freedom from the grip of Israeli military occupation. The development of a vigorous non-violent approach would allow the productive utilisation of the energies of all segments of the Palestinian population and the Palestinians inside as well as outside the occupied territories. It would also go a long way in giving Jewish Israelis the hope that that peaceful coexistence with a neighbouring Palestinian state is actually conceivable. It would also compel an Israel that is still aware of its liberal self-perception from resorting to disproportionate amounts of counter-violence. More importantly it would transfer the conflict from the arena of arms, where the Palestinians would never triumph over a nuclear-equipped Israel, to the arena of morals and rights, where the Palestinians could definitely make a conclusive example for having accepted national parity with Israel. Therefore, Cobban concedes that Abu-Odeh is fairly right to maintain that adopting completely non-violent means of struggle would be extremely advantageous for the Palestinians. However, she is erroneous in presuming that employing such methods unescapably involves altering the goal from national independence to the establishment of a bi-national state. Cobban argues that though there are a number of respected Palestinian social activists in the occupied territories who have been advocating, and experimenting with, the use of non-violent methods for several years but most of them have been doing so within the dominant political paradigm of aiming for national independence. Moreover, they are already finding it difficult amidst the dominantly militant Palestinian culture, to make their case effectively to their fellow citizens. Cobban is of the opinion that advocating the goal of a bi-national state to Israelis in the present juncture would be inappropriate. The history of the post-Oslo years, as subsequently combined with the protracted period of Intifada violence, has prompted a strong aversion for an intimate enduring entanglement. The aspiration for some sort of "separation" is profound on both sides as is the repulsion at any suggestion that might seek to weaken or even repudiate the 'national' content of that for which they have grieved through these years. Cobban concludes on the note that as Sari Nuseibeh and others have predicted somewhere down the line an independent Israel and an independent Palestine might seek to combine/share some of their powers into a joint political venture of some kind. However, she is categorical in stating that there seems no way of realizing any joint entity without crisscrossing a period of departure in the process.[14]

According to As'ad Ghanem, the concept of bi-nationalism evolved during the period of British Mandate. It was always an exclusive idea, developed and restricted among a small group of Jewish and Palestinian community leaders but it remained in the agenda till Israel became independent in the aftermath of which it became virtually extinct. In recent years the Bi-National State (BNS) alternative has once again appeared as a part of the political discourse among Israelis and Palestinians. The reasons behind the reappearance of the BNS were a series of issues, such as the failure of the peace process, the Israeli refusal to withdraw to the 1967 cease fire lines, the second Intifada of October 2000 and the unabated and forceful policy of occupation, which persuaded many in the academic community and in the domain of public affairs to revisit the One State (OS) solution. In the context of the Israeli-Palestinian conflict, bi-nationalism has by and large been synonymous with the notion of a democratic state consisting of all people living within the borders of Mandatory Palestine/ Eretz-Israel. For Ghanem, the BNS may have been only a moral alternative in the past but has since then evolved into a real alternative. In this context, he cites the example of the 'Future Vision of the Palestinian Arabs in Israel,' a document published by a group of Palestinian politicians and intellectuals in Israel in 2006 that drew worldwide attention and prompted a wide range of responses from the all groups, Jews, Arabs and others. The demand was for a consociational BNS to replace what was termed as a so-called liberal democracy akin to 'the tyranny of the majority.' Chaim Hanegbi and Oren Yiftachel, two prominent leftists also recommended the adoption of the BNS after the creation of a Palestinian state beside Israel. The Jewish critique of the proposal was due to it being perceived as undermining Israel's basic foundation as a 'Jewish and democratic' state. Ghanem explicitly spells out the unwillingness or lack of commitment among the majority of the Israeli citizens and policy makers in surrendering the Jewish nature of the state, to endure the consequences for an acceptable resolution of the Palestinian-Israeli conflict, including the return to 1967 borders, the evacuation of all Jewish settlements, the division of Jerusalem, and the return of Palestinian refugees.[15]

Burak Erdiner does not consider the bi-national idea as appropriate or a realistic solution to the Israel-Palestine conflict. In his opinion, it arose during periods of change in power relations and a lot remains unanswered in terms of its achievability. Erdiner contends that the Jewish believers of the bi-national notion were certain about the considerable Jewish immigration during the Mandate era, while the existing Palestinian supporters have been nurturing the notion with the anticipation that the higher birth rates of Palestinians will transmute the demographics and ultimately the power relations, to their benefit. Bi-nationalism may offer both sides with what is estimated as an earnest solution in the context of peace, territory, resources, recognition and immigration; however, it carries the price of facing each other in micro and macro tussles. The bi-national notion, therefore, does not provide adequate answers to many questions regarding the likelihood of people peacefully co-existing and having day to day encounters considering they have countless prejudices against each other founded on dissimilar narratives. Likewise, it is difficult to visualise Israelis reallocating their national wealth and transferring resources 'from the rich Jewish units to the poor Palestinians?'[16] In a similar vein, Tamar Hermann, while analysing the four different justifications for bi-nationalism, commented that notwithstanding the dissimilarities in their perspective, substance and style, and of course inspirations and repercussions, the four advocates—the 'old school' and the 'new school' of Jewish binationalism, contemporary Palestinian bi-nationalism, and bi-nationalist advocacy coming from outside observers—suggest certain parallels which diminish their likelihood of becoming a mainstream preference or alternative: "a) in all cases bi-nationalism is not the most desirable option, b) they all gained momentum on both sides in periods of instability, due to transformations in power relations between them or when the conflict reaches a point where the violence seems to become unbearable, c) all these bi-nationalisms present a rather uneasy mixture of moralistic arguments and pragmatic ones, d) in all cases the people who embrace the bi-national model are intellectuals. This gives their recommendations a touch of 'ivory tower' over rationalisation, further reducing their public appeal."[17]

According to Nasser Abufarha, the Palestinians and the Israelis live in a common shared landscape, which they both call home. This is a reality that any feasible resolution cannot ignore. Therefore any solution should not be based on a division of this landscape, but rather on the ways to share it. This actuality necessitates that both people reconsider their present programmes and the choices they make. For Abufarha, the Palestinian case is unique and can be set apart from other colonial contexts. Hence, a reassessment of the nationalist liberation programme is required. Israel as a colony is not sustained by a conventional/traditional metropole as in the case of France in Algeria or Britain in India. It is rather maintained by a vague, non-territorial metropole, which is the Jewish nation. These circumstances have engendered a new identity, Israeli, that is territorially linked and entrenched in the colony, not the metropole. This poses a new challenge to the Palestinian nationalist programme in the sense that would it be possible for the Palestinians to be committed to their national rights and at the same time remain dedicated to moral justice. These commitments would entail that the Palestinian nationalists seek ways and means to address Palestinian nationalist rights without endangering those of the Sabra Israelis. Abufarha states that nationalisms are not a single entity but it can very well be a colonizing tool, as in the case of Zionism, or, it can be a liberating tool. The Palestinian interpretation of nationalism should be based on liberating Palestine from colonial control and not essentially liberating it from the Israelis. Such programmes demand that the Palestinians incorporate into their nationalist platforms ways to accommodate for Israeli individual and collective rights as well as national rights for the new Israeli identity in Palestine. It is this interpretation and historical perspective that makes the bi-national programme the most receptive to Palestinian and Israeli rights. It also makes this programme for those who adopt it as an advanced Palestinian liberation programme that is grounded in moral justice. On the one hand, the bi-national programme is committed to Palestinian national rights; on the other, it remains committed to the social and moral responsibility towards the Israeli identity that currently shares the same space with the Palestinians. Bi-nationalism needs to be conceived as a path rather than a recommendation. The two-state option can become an episode on the way to bi-nationalism. The Israeli leftist intellectual Oren Yiftachel and the Palestinian leftist academic Said Zeedani have articulated in favour of adopting a phased method.[18]

Dov Waxman and Ilan Peleg accept that Zionism is a European colonialist enterprise and that Israel is the product of a settlement process initiated by the Zionist-Jewish elite in Europe and the West and realized by colonial countries contributing to it. In this version, Israel is portrayed as an offshoot of a colonial-settler project that was carried out in congruence with world imperialism and with the complicity of the Arab reactionary powers. Waxman and Peleg, consider the Vision Documents of 2006 as basically right in their representation of present-day Israel, both in terms of the existence of two nations (Jewish and Palestine) within the pre-1967 borders of Israel, and in terms of the complete control of the Jewish majority over the Palestinian minority. After a long period of denial, the bi-national truth within Israel should eventually be accepted by Israel's Jewish majority and by the state itself. Nonetheless while the Jewish majority and the State of Israel ought to recognize the bi-national character of Israeli society, this does not essentially imply that Israel must become a bi-national state. Waxman and Peleg contend that both the overt and implicit demand for the establishment of a bi-national state is unjustified. There now exists a degree of international unanimity on the necessity for the institution of a Palestinian state in the West Bank and Gaza Strip. Once a Palestinian state is created, a new political and historical actuality would materialise in Israel/ Palestine. If Israel were to be converted into a bi-national state, the Palestinian people would actually possess one and one-half state, while the Jews would have just half a state. Therefore, the demand for establishing a bi-national state in Israel (in conjunction with a Palestinian state in the West Bank and Gaza) is both unfair and politically inimical. Simply advocating the idea of bi-nationalism is viewed by most Israeli Jews as particularly confrontational, a stance that would create a political backlash, which would forestall the adoption of more reasonable and judicious solutions to the issue. Hence, instead of advancing Jewish-Palestinian cooperation and reconciliation, the call for bi-nationalism in Israel in the present scenario is a formula for persistent and intensifying inter-communal conflict. To end with, Waxman and Peleg assert that bi-national states have largely been unsteady and predisposed to conflict and strain among the constituent national groups. Moreover, bi-nationalism is above all unattractive when one of the groups is much bigger than the other (as Jews are within Israel's pre-1967 borders).[19]

Dubi Kanengisser observes that the preponderance of the debate on bi-nationalism, especially on the Israeli side has been conducted by academics and intellectuals. The popular media with the exception of *Haaretz*, has not encouraged such debate. However, in recent times an alternative has been found in the form of online forums and blogs, which offer the much needed space to engage in such opinions and counter-opinions. Eminent Israeli voices from the world of letters, such as Amoz Oz, Gideon Levy and Raz-Krakotzin[20] have either vocalised in favour of or against the notion of a bi-national state in such forums. It was in the 1980s that the notion of a bi-national state was revived by the historian, journalist and political activist, Meron Benvenisti. According to both Benvenisti and Kanengisser, Israelis and Palestinians are living currently in a bi-national reality and if the two communities want to accomplish a degree of comparative peace/ tranquillity in Israel/Palestine, bi-nationalist thinking needs to be articulated explicitly. Kanengisser cites the likes of Chaims Gans, Raz-Krakotzin, Yehuda Shenhav and others to underline the inescapability of the bi-national solution despite the lack of trust among the two communities as emphasized upon by the Israeli historian Benny Morris. Kanengisser contends that as long as the two sides are bound by the '1967 paradigm,' which construes the problem as purely an issue of the 1967 occupation without counting the problems of Israel's Arabs and the refugees, no understanding can be attained and there can be no responsiveness. It is only when this paradigm gives way to the '1948 paradigm' that all concrete impediments in the way of bi-nationalism can be removed or at least mellowed. [21]

Disseminating Bi-nationalism

On the basis of the claims made by the proponents and opponents of bi-nationalism, it can be inferred that there are genuine concerns about the feasibility of the bi-national option. On the one hand, the Israelis feel that it involves the risk of an attenuation of the Jewish identity of the state of Israel. There are misgivings among the Israelis about the practicability of the conjunction of a Jewish identity, which is more akin to the Western character with a Palestinian one that retains a Mediterranean personality. Moreover, there always remains a fear among the Jews that a bi-national state would no longer provide a safe haven for the world Jewry, in instances of persecution. On the other hand, the Palestinians feel that the majority of the Israelis would not back the bi-national option and as such they should look for a more attainable alternative to the two-state solution, at least in the short term. Besides, the superior Israeli economy would perpetuate the Palestinian susceptibility to economic control and political manipulation by the Israelis.[22] Despite these reservations, the quest for exploring the bi-national option remains among academics, members of the civil society and even a section of the practitioners of politics among both the communities. The aim is to find a more equitable resolution of the conflict and the vision strives for a comprehensive and enduring closure.

Since the turn of the last millennium, several efforts have been made to set up a platform to facilitate an organised attempt at debating and propagating the idea of bi-nationalism in Israel-Palestine. The efforts gathered momentum with the convening of the first international conference at Madrid during 2-6 July 2007, entitled 'Israel-Palestine: One Country, One State.' A second international conference on the one-state was held in London during 17-18 November 2007, entitled 'Challenging the Boundaries: A Single State in Palestine/Israel.' During 28-29 March 2009, the Boston Conference on 'One State for Palestine/ Israel: A Country for all its Citizens,' was convened. A fourth international conference, entitled 'Israel/Palestine: Mapping Models of Statehood and Paths to Peace,' was held during 22-24 June 2009 at York University in Toronto. The first Haifa conference entitled 'Haifa Conference for the Right of Return and the Secular Democratic State in Palestine,' was held on 20-21 June 2008. Invigorated by the success of the conference and the interest it stimulated, a follow-up to it was held in Haifa again on 28-30 May 2010. Various themes were explored and debated upon in these conferences, these included: 'Reimagining the Conflict,' 'Rethinking the Geography and the Nation,' 'Israel and International law,' 'Future Paths' and 'Translating Ideas into Action.' Both Palestinian and Israeli grass-roots activists and some non-governmental organisation (NGO) representatives participated as speakers and discussants. There were practical discussions on strategies, logistics, methods, policies and organisational means required for the implementation of the one-state.[23]

The Toronto Conference was not merely a one-state conference, it was rather an appraisal and examination of the effectiveness of alternative state models for resolving the conflict. The two states option was considered alongside the one-state solution. The conference included advocates of the one-state and two-state solutions as well as others. Many Zionist Israelis were present, as such the mood was quite electric and at times the arguments were animated, resulting in a degree of polarisation at the culmination of the deliberations. The conference enabled to break the prevalent sense of fear often connected with any questioning of conformist Zionist rationale and in the process unfastened new viewpoints. The Haifa Conference in particular conferred on the one-state paradigm a new facet. The notion had moved beyond the confines of academics and had struck roots in the ranks of the Palestinian community inside Israel. It was perceived as part of the on-going political awakening process they had been feeling and presented them with a platform to facilitate their ideas and help unite their ranks. Leaders of the major parties active among Palestinians in Israel, namely the Democratic Front for Peace and Equality (*Hadash*), the National Democratic

Alliance (*Balad*) and *Abnaa El Balad*, participated in the conference. The Haifa conference also stood out for incorporating Palestinian grassroots activists and youth, backed by a sizeable number of Jewish activists, articulating their views about the future. This introduced an aspect of realism to the theoretical debates which the intellectuals of the one-state movement had been engaged in so far.[24]

The reality today is that while the two-state solution continues to be the accepted choice for most in Israel-Palestine, there have been concerted attempts to bring together and project other models as possible alternatives, the most visible of the options is the bi-national option, which has been espoused by both communities at different points in time. As the differing viewpoints incorporated in the aforementioned section on the debates related to bi-nationalism reveal, the road ahead for the BNS certainly appears to be a long and winding one. Yet, there is a discernible attempt by sections of society within both the communities to popularise and promote the concept as a viable solution to the Israel-Palestine conflict. It seems appropriate to revisit and revitalise this alternative at this juncture, when state boundaries in West Asia are being redrawn and the region itself is being reimagined.

References

1. Cited from Lama Abu-Odeh, "The Case for Binationalism," *Boston Review*, December 2001. /January 2002
2. Amoz Oz, "For its survival, Israel must abandon the one-state option." *LA Times*, Op-Ed, March 7, 2015.
3. Meron Benvenisti, "The Inevitable Bi-national Regime," *Haaretz* (Opinion) January 22, 2010.
4. Tamar Hermann, "The Bi-national idea in Israel/Palestine: Past and Present," *Nations and Nationalism* II (3), 2005, p. 382.
5. Susan Lee Hattis, *The Bi-National Idea in Palestine during the Mandatory Times*, (Haifa Shikmona Publishing Company, 1970, p. 19) cited in Burak Erdenir, "The Idea of a Bi-national State in the Israeli-Palestinian Conflict," *Turkish Policy Quarterly*, Volume 7, No. 4, p. 26
6. Cited from Ian Lustick, "The Case for Binationalism," *Boston Review*, December 1 2001/January 2002
7. Cited from Ian Lustick, "The Case for Binationalism," *Boston Review*, December 1 2001/January 2002

8. Tamar Hermann, "The Bi-national idea in Israel/Palestine: Past and Present," *Nations and Nationalism* II (3), 2005, 383-384
9. Tamar Hermann, "The Bi-national idea in Israel/Palestine: Past and Present," *Nations and Nationalism* II (3), 2005, pp. 381-401
10. Cited from Burak Erdenir, "The Idea of a Bi-national State in the Israeli-Palestinian Conflict," *Turkish Policy Quarterly*, Volume 7, No. 4, p. 27
11. Burak Erdenir, "The Idea of a Bi-national State in the Israeli-Palestinian Conflict," *Turkish Policy Quarterly*, Volume 7, No. 4, p. 27
12. Hana A. Faris, "Introduction: The Failure of the Two-State Solution and Delimiting the One-State Idea," pp. 1-6 in Hana A. Faris (Ed), *The Failure of the Two-State Solution: The Prospects of One State in the Israel-Palestine Conflict.* New York: IB Taurus, 2013.
13. Lama Abu-Odeh, "The Case for Binationalism," *Boston Review*, December 2001. /January 2002
14. Helena Cobban, "Ends and Means," *Boston Review*, December 2001. / January 2002
15. As'ad Ghanem, "The Bi-National State Solution," *Israel Studies*, Vol. 14, No. 2, pp. 120-133
16. Burak Erdenir, "The Idea of a Bi-national State in the Israeli-Palestinian Conflict," p. 31.
17. Tamar Hermann, "The Bi-national idea in Israel/Palestine: Past and Present," p. 381.
18. Nasser Abufarha, "Bi-Nationalism in Palestine-Israel: A Palestinian Historical Choice, Not a Last Resort," *Development Affairs Journal*, July 2005, No. 31, Arab Thought Forum, Jerusalem.
19. Dov Waxman and Ilan Peleg, "Neither Ethnocracy Nor Bi-Nationalism: In Search of the Middle Ground," *Israel Studies*, Volume 23, Issue 2, Winter 2008:55-73
20. *See* Amoz Oz, "For its survival, Israel must abandon the one-state option." *LA Times*, Op-Ed, March 7, 2015; Gideon Levy "Israeli Binationalism is old news," *Haaretz*, October 5, 2014; Amnon Raz-Krakotzkin, "Lost in Exile, debating Israeli and Palestinian identities": http://www.resetdoc.org/story/00000022408/format/html , 6 June 2014
21. Dubi Kanengisser, "Binationalism in Israel/Palestine: Unbearable, Desirable, Inevitable?" (Presentation at the Association for Israel Studies, 26th Annual Conference 10-12 May 2010, Toronto, Ontario, Canada)
22. Nasser Abufarha, "Bi-Nationalism in Palestine-Israel: A Palestinian Historical Choice, Not a Last Resort." *op. cit.*
23. Hana A. Faris, "Introduction: The Failure of the Two-State Solution and Delimiting the One-State Idea," pp. 6-8.
24. Hana A. Faris, *op. cit.*, pp. 7-8.

4

Islamic Geographies of Resistance

The Islamic Factor in Regional Geopolitical Strategy of Iran

Deepika Saraswat

Introduction

Historically, the region called Middle East has experienced depredations of British, French, Russian colonialism, and American imperialism and resistance to these predatory forces has been mounted in various forms. As the region experienced the onslaught of colonial exploitation and imperialism, Islam developed as an ideology of resistance in a dialogical conversation and in confrontation with the European colonial modernity. The paper argues that the violence and militancy characteristic of the region cannot be explained by referring to some inherent attributes of Islam, but by understanding the complex power struggle of the region involving regional and extra-regional great powers.

In the Middle East one sees that secular struggles in domestic and regional/international politics are framed within Islamic discourse. That is to say that religion is not the cause of the discord but the medium through which politics is mobilized and resistance channelized. The Islamic revolution in Iran and subsequent survival of Islamic Republic in the face of all kinds of odds has only contributed to the use of Islam as an ideology of mass mobilization in domestic politics as well as a transnational ideology legitimating otherwise geopolitical struggles. The first section of the paper briefly explores the nation state concept in revolutionary Iran and argues that the duality inherent in the notion of 'Islamic Republic' is the reason why the language of politics and geopolitical discourse in Iran is replete with Islamic frames.

The later sections analyse the use of religious frames in geopolitical strategy of the Islamic Republic of Iran in the twenty-first century which began with an event of cataclysmic proportion, that is, 11 September attacks on World Trade Center and Pentagon, followed by American portrayal of Iran as part of 'axis of evil' comprising states allegedly developing weapons of mass destruction, which they could provide to their terrorist allies. The paper argues that the Islamic revolution in Iran and the subsequent Islamic Republic constitute a revolutionary identity of resistance which often transcends into a Universalist discourse of resistance. The Islamic republic at least in the first decade of its existence denounced nationalism as a western concept and embraced a non-territorial Universalist discourse of Islamic identity defined against the West in general and America in particular and in that it has tried to blend its security needs and drive for regional power status with a radical Islamic ideology of resistance.

The Duality of Nation State in 'Islamic Republic of Iran'

Critical geopolitics argue that the political language of the state is overall dedicated to gain legitimacy for the state and it presents complex reality in simple terms, using binaries easily understood in the society. In revolutionary Iran, foreign policy discourse has been driven by consolidating and creating legitimacy for the Islamic Republic and therefore its specific understanding and representation of regional geopolitics found expression in Islamic terms.

Understanding Islamic Republic's foreign policy within a strictly realist paradigm would only present a partial picture as Iran's strategic preferences are also guided by ideological preferences of an Islamic regime. Strategic preferences are systemic, cultural and institutionalized. They have depth and longitude that go beyond current politics.[1] The geopolitical strategy of Iran in the region is crafted with reference to two imperatives. Of foremost importance is constructing and sustaining the image of an 'Islamic republic.' The religious ideological foundation and character of the state has to be corroborated and sustained through its domestic as well as foreign policy and practice. The second factor is Iran's drive for regional power status which will further provide legitimacy to the theocratic regime.

The Islamic revolution transmuted the Iranian state in terms of the constituent institutions of the state and as new political elites sought to reconfigure the identity of the nation state in relation to the international society. The core ideals of the revolution were enshrined in the new constitution, therefore institutionalizing the ideology of the revolution. According to the IRI's constitution, Iranian foreign policy is crafted according to four fundamental principles: first, rejection of all forms of external domination; second, preservation of Iran's independence and territorial integrity; third, defence of the rights of all Muslims without allying with hegemonic powers; and fourth, the maintenance of peaceful relations with all non-belligerent states.[2] These principles are the basis of legitimacy of any government and have been broadly adhered to by most of them.

Even when governments followed a more pragmatic approach to further the cause of economic reconstruction and development, Mahmoud Sariolghalam (2013) argues that philosophical rivalries inherited from the anti imperialist literature of 1950s dictated almost all matters of governance. Nationalist and liberal leaning factions were gradually pushed aside.[3]

The revolutionary school of thought considered Islam an all-encompassing ideology. From their perspective there was no need to extend a helping hand to foreigners. In the end, Iran had achieved no result by cooperating with the British, Russians, or Americans. The international landscape is based on oppression, corruption and anti-Islamic sentiment.[4]

The revolutionary school of thought is best represented by the supreme leader and conservative factions but there are other factions with different visions of international politics and Iran's place in it. Pragmatists who were dominant during the presidency of Rafsanjani and Mohammad Khatami and are dominant again in the current government of Hassan Rouhani prioritize national economic development. They presume that Iran's national security stems from its economic interdependence with the international community and as such their priorities imply a conciliatory attitude towards the West.

The paper argues that these conflicting visions of international politics and Iran's place in it are result of dualism inherent in nation state concept of Iran. There is a dualism in Iran of nation state concepts intermingled with Islamic forms.[5] The duality is indicated in the very title of Islamic "republic" (*jomhuri*). The 'notion' of republic clearly implies a limited, political-territorial construct of nation (*millat*) of Iran and means that sovereignty lies with people (*millat*). "Republic" represents a link with the French revolution and all the revolutions of the twentieth century, in the region and outside, which have toppled a monarchy.[6] Conforming to the republican notion of state, Iran has a written constitution, drafted after wide ranging and heated debates by an elected Assembly of Experts. It also has an elected president and a parliament.[7] It is this elected executive that often gives precedence to real politic calculations driven by national interests over ideological matters, but the language of foreign policy is invariably tempered by Islamic ideological symbols.

The 'Islamic' in 'Islamic Republic of Iran' is attributed to Khomeini's doctrinal innovation of *vilayat-I-faqih* (the jurisconsult's trusteeship, or rule by the leading *faaqih*). Ayatollah Khomeini argued that only clerical rule in accordance with Shiite law can create just government in the absence of the imams.[8] Khomeini articulated in favour of the rule of jurists on the ground of Islamic principle of sovereignty of God and a government that would implement Islamic law, the *Shari'a*. Any sovereignty except the sovereignty of God is against the wellbeing of the people and is tyranny [jaur], and except for the laws of God, all laws are void and useless (*Khomeini: The Revealing of Secrets)*.[9] Therefore, *ulama* and especially jurists' participation in government stems from the advice they are able to give from their knowledge of the *Shari'a*. Vanessa Martin observes that Khomeini's argument against legislation (and implicitly western style constitutionalism) is effectively three-pronged: it introduces defective law; it is not suited to Iran; and it will bring to Iran all the evils of Europe. Khomeini believed a law that did not accepted spiritual supervision and did not subscribed to God's ordained law was inherently based on flawed judgement and leads to unjust or self-interested government.[10]

Iranian constitution makes the *faaqih* the central figure in the political order, enshrines the dominance of clerical community over the institutions of the state, entrenches Islamic jurisprudence as the foundation for the country's laws and legal system and limits individual freedoms to what was considered permissible under the Shi'ite Islam.[11] It is this religious-political institution that embodies the 'Islamic' component of the state and espouses a notion of political community by "declaring the unity and brotherhood of all Muslims in one *umma.*" But this apparent contradiction between a republican territorial political nation state and an Islamic non-territorial notion of community is moderated by the fact that Iranian Islam, being Shi'i reinforces Iranian nationalism, confronting as it does a predominantly Sunni Arab world and Turkey.

In keeping with the Islamic belief of 'unity and brotherhood of all Muslims in one *umma,*' revolutionary Iran has often distinguished between states and society while crafting its foreign policy in the region. In addition to that, ideological worldview of the Islamic republic distinguishes between oppressor (*Mustakbirin*)—dictators and monarchs—and the oppressed (*mostazafin*) people. The populist emphasis of the revolution and its championing of the *mostazafin* were translated into handouts and various forms of military and financial assistance to militias and dissident groups in the region.[12] Iran's support to the oppressed people's struggle is the most crucial component of its geopolitical strategy in the region, a point that is explored in some detail in the following sections.

Anti-Imperial Struggle: Fighting the Global Arrogance

Anti-imperial struggle is one of the core principles of the foreign policy of the Islamic Republic of Iran. Ayatollah Khomeini called the United States the *Great Satan*, while current supreme leader Ali Khameni frequently uses another Islamic term 'the global arrogance' (*Istekbar-e-Jahani*) for America. "Arrogance is a Quranic term. An arrogant individual, an arrogant government and an arrogant group of people mean those individuals and those governments which intend to interfere in the affairs of other human beings and other nations." For all purposes, the United States of America has been defined as the global arrogance and fourth of November, the day when in year 1979, Iranian students took over the US embassy in Tehran, labeled as 'den of espionage' by revolutionary leadership is now designated as the "National Day of Fighting against Global Arrogance."

Moreover vicious misrepresentation of Islamic republic from its very inception further entrenched the resistance identity of the state. Nayef Al-Rodham argues that if social context precludes a stable and positive group identity, for instance, because of being negatively defined by other people are more likely to generate a *resistance identity*, with boundaries that appear impermeable and safe, or by engaging in identity construction that can lead to xenophobia, rigid ethnocentrism, or forms of ideological radicalism.[13] The negative representation in the western media has gone hand in hand with and legitimized US led sanctions and its other hostile policies. This negative representation and campaign of fear reached its crescendo with President Bush characterising Iran as part of the 'Axis – of – Evil,' imposition of 'crippling sanctions' and threats of pre-emptive war, which in turn fed into ideological radicalism in Iranian political circles as seen during the belligerent presidency of Mahmoud Ahmadinejad.

In his *Nouruz* message last year, Supreme leader Ali Khameini articulated the vision of what he calls resistance economy. Resistance economy means an economic plan that utilizes Iran's intellectual potential as well as domestic production capacity to reduce the country's vulnerability to sanctions and external factors.[14] The Supreme Leader emphasized that resistance economy seeks to advance national economy without compromising politically with the arrogant power of America. He asserted Iran will not acquiesce to western dictates in the course of nuclear negotiations in exchange for relief from economic sanctions. He argues that the arena of economy, because of America's hostile policies, is an arena of struggle, arena of war, war of a specific kind and therefore Iran should pursue a resistance economy, whose key features include changing the banking structure to facilitate domestic investment, creation of knowledge based economy, support for small business, and encouraging Iranians to purchase domestic products, among others.[15]

In addition to the United States, ideological mobilization against 'Zionist' regime of Israel is one of the guiding principles of Iranian foreign policy. The state of Israel, a creation of British colonialism in the region and whose security is underwritten by the United States continues to be seen as a symbol of humiliation by Arabs and Muslims in the region. The cause of Palestinian state resonates strongly in the regional political imagination and active support for the same is seen an important criterion of claims to regional leadership. The Palestinian cause has been appropriated by the Iranian Government as a way to claim regional leadership and play a central role as the defender of Muslim rights. For instance, religious leaders in Iran consider holy sites such as the *Al-Aqsa* mosque as Islamic *waqf* (religious endowment) whose sovereignty should be shared by all Muslims, not only Palestinians.[16] Arshin Adib-Moghaddam, notes that in an effort to institutionalize the pro-Palestinian sentiments of his Islamic followers and the Iranian left, Ayatollah Khomeini designated the last Friday of Ramadan to the liberation of Jerusalem (so called Quds Day). "The road to Jerusalem Passes through Baghdad," was a prominent slogan of the millions of volunteers of the newly established Islamic Revolutionary Guards Corps and their Basij militia during the devastating Iran-Iraq war.[17]

Regional Geopolitical Strategy of Iran or the Shi'i Crescent

The Islamic Republic's prioritizing of strategic independence—a core aspect of its legitimacy—has shaped the way it has conducted its international affairs. It has, for instance, aimed to maximize its security through developing its own sphere of influence in the region. At its establishment, the Islamic Republic had no strategic depth, with its revisionist status putting it at odds with practically all of its neighbours and ensuring an all-but-nonexistent buffer zone with all potential enemies.[18] Given the revisionist nature of revolutionary Iran and the fact revolutionary leadership saw Iran's revolution as a model and catalyst for Islamic revolutions throughout the region, Iran embarked on a geopolitical strategy based on cultivating strategic partnership with dissident and non-state elements in the region, by supplying them with material and ideological assistance. The Iranians projected themselves and these non-state groups as an archipelago of resistance against an axis of dominance led by the Saudis. That the US was backing the Saudi alliance actually strengthened the Iranian narrative that it was the vanguard of anti-imperialist struggle in West Asia.[19] Hence, Iran's geopolitical strategy of creating a sphere of influence by cultivating strategic ties with dissident and militant groups across the region was able to combine the ideological goals of exporting the revolutions and fighting imperial America and colonial Israel with practical geopolitics.

Right from beginning, Islamic republic has supported Lebanese Shi'i campaign against the United States and the Israeli presence in Lebanon. Shiite militia Hezbollah—or the party of God—emerged in Lebanon in early 1980s and became the region's leading radical Islamic movement, determined to drive Israeli troops from the Lebanon, and inspired by the success of Iranian revolution, the party also dreamt of transforming Lebanon's multi-confessional state into an Iranian style Islamic state.[20] Hezbollah is now a powerful regional militia with strong strategic linkages with Iran and Syria and also with militant sections of Palestinian movement. Syria was the vital strategic linchpin connecting Iran to Hezbollah. It provided strategic depth and transfer of arms, which explained the heavy effort by Iran and Hezbollah to preserve Assad regime.[21] Lebanese Hezbollah began to take on a more direct combat role in Syria as the Assad regime began losing control over Syrian territory in 2012 and with the rise of Islamic State (called *Daesh* in Iran) Iran's IRGC (Islamic Revolution Guardian Corps) ground force is fighting alongside Hezbollah.

Supreme Council for Islamic Revolution in Iraq and the Islamic Dawa Party outlawed under Saddam Hussein, who called them traitors, sought refuge in Iran during the 1980s and 1990s and operated from there. Post Saddam Iraq has been another theatre of geopolitical competition between Iran, who exercises influence through Shi'i parties and Saudi Arabia and Gulf States who extended support to Sunni Islamists and former Baathists and emboldened Wahhabi forces as a means to counter Iranian influence. The evolution of Shiite Islamic politics promises to have major geopolitical impact across the Arab world and outside. The watershed event is the transformation of a once downtrodden and marginalized community into a vibrant Shiite political community bidding for power in Iraq.[22] The Saudi threat perception of regional networks of Shi'i dominance extending from Iran, Iraq into Syria and Lebanon is one of the reasons why Sunni Islamists in Iraq and Syria have joined ranks against Shi'i political forces.

While Iran has constructed a geopolitical strategy based on extending ideological and material support to non state actors and

Shiite minorities, Saudi Arabia for its part fears the removal of predictable, allied Arab regimes and the increased agency of Islamist political movements that challenged the Saudi Wahhabi interpretation of Islam.[23] For instance when protests touched off in Bahrain, a Shia majority country ruled by a Sunni royal family, the Saudis saw the Iranian hand and later on in March 2011, Saudi Arabia and the United Arab Emirates sent troops to Bahrain to brutally remove protesters from Manama's Pearl Square.[24] It was in the light of increasing regional footprint of Iran that the thesis of Shi'i Crescent has been advanced by its opponents; therefore giving a sectarian colour to what is in fact a geopolitical competition between Iran and Saudi Arabia. The sectarian Sunni-Shi'i axis is being increasingly portrayed as the geopolitical fault line in the region. Since the starting of Syrian civil war in 2011, while Iran supported Syrian President Bashar al-Assad, Saudi Arabia and its GCC (Gulf Cooperation Council) allies actively funded and weaponized Syrian rebel groups which played a major role in destabilizing parts of the country. It is from this chaos that Abu Bakr al-Baghdadi rebuilt his dilapidated terror machinery into the IS of today.[25] Islamic State now governing a large territory stretching from Northern Syria to gates of Baghdad, started from control over tiny "emirates" in northern Syria that rebels had liberated from the Assad regime. They could expand their domain in Iraq by their partnership with Sunni militias that are hostile to the government of hard line Shi'i Prime Minister Nouri-al-Maliki and on the tacit consent of country's disaffected Sunnis.

The latest theatre of geopolitical competition along sectarian axis is Yemen, considered by Saudis to be within their sphere of influence. In March, Saudi-led intervention launched an air campaign, 'Operation Decisive Storm', in reaction to the entry of the Houthis (a Shi'a offshoot) into Aden, where former president Abd Rabbuh Mansur Hadi had taken refuge. In this situation of regional geopolitical rivalry between Iran and Saudi Arabia and its sectarian nature, spectre of civil wars along sectarian lines have taken the shape of proxy wars and region is further exposed to humanitarian crisis that often provides the pretext for imperialist intervention in this part of the world.

The strategy to counter the Islamic State or *Daesh* which has recasted the political geography of the region along sectarian lines and resurgent Kurdistan movement on its western border forms the new fulcrum of Iran's regional geopolitical strategy. Fighting the Islamic State has put the United States and Iran on the same side, corroborating the argument that it is strategic imperatives, not religion, that dictates the terms of engagement between the two countries in the Middle East. Given the ongoing talks on nuclear deal with P5 +1 – US, UK, China, France, Russia and Germany and a pragmatic leadership in Iran, Iran is expected to play a more constructive and stabilizing role in the region, the most important being joint action against Sunni extremists in Syria and Iraq, a prospect raised by foreign minister, Javad Zarif, during the final stages of nuclear negotiations.

Conclusion

Thus the paper concludes that in order to understand Iran's geopolitical discourse one has to look into the ideological and cultural foundations of the Islamic republic, power distribution between and nature of its elected and unelected institutions, nature of opposition groups who challenge and contest the regime's hegemony over religion and politics, etc.

The regional geopolitical strategy of Iran is driven by its quest for carving a sphere of influence in the region in the context of geopolitical rivalry with Saudi Arabia and Israel, but given the Islamic foundation and make-up of the state, the language of geopolitical discourse is given to use Islamic symbols.

Notes

1. Arshin Adib-Moghaddam, "Iran in world politics after Rouhani," 2014. http://studies.aljazeera.net/en/dossiers/2014/03/2014331104216470679.html/. Accessed 25 June 2015.
2. Anoushiravan Ehteshami and Mahjoob Zweiri, *Iran's Foreign Policy: From Khatami to Ahmadinejad*, Eastbourne: Sussex Academic Press, 2011.
3. Mahmood Sariolghalam, "Transition in the Middle East: New Arab Realities and Iran," *Middle East Policy* 2008: 121-34.
4. Sariolghalam, "Transition in the Middle East."
5. Sami Zubaida, "Is Iran an Islamic State?" in *Political Islam: Essays from the Middle East Report*, Joel Beinin and Joe Stark (eds.), New York: I.B. Tauris 199).

6. Zubaida, "Is Iran an Islamic State?"
7. Zubaida, "Is Iran an Islamic State?"
8. Juan Cole, "Iran and Islam," http://iranprimer.usip.org/resource/iran-and-islam/. Accessed 25 June 2015.
9. Vanessa Martin, *Creating an Islamic State: Khomeini and the Making of New Iran*, New York: I.B. Tauris, 2003.
10. Martin, *Creating an Islamic State*.
11. Mazlum Uyar, "The Concept of Sovereignty and the Position of the 'Ulama in Both Constitutions of Iran," *EKEV AKEDEMI DERGISI*, Spring 2007, http://ktp.isam.org.tr/pdfdrg/D01777%5C2007_31/2007_31_UYARM.pdf /. Accessed 20 June 2015
12. Uyar, "The Concept of Sovereignty."
13. Nayef Al-Rhodhan, "The Geopolitics of Culture: Five Substrates," *Harvard International Review*, 24 June 2014, http://hir.harvard.edu/archives/6191/. Accessed 25 June 2015.
14. Tahir Mustafa, "Islamic Iran's Resistance Economy and Culture," April 2014, http://www.crescent-online.net/2014/04/islamic-irans-resistance-economy-and-culture-tahir-mustafa-4375-articles.html. Accessed on 23 June 2015.
15. Mustafa, "Islamic Iran's Resistance Economy and Culture."
16. Arshin Adib-Moghaddam, "Iran in world politics after Rouhani."
17. Adib-Moghaddam, "Iran in world politics after Rouhani."
18. Sina Tooshi, "Deciphering Iran's Strategic Vision," http://www.lobelog.com/deciphering-irans-strategic-vision/. Accessed on 24 June 2015.
19. Stanly Johny, "The hot Saudi Iran Cold War," 15 June 2015, http://www.thehindu.com/opinion/lead/the-hot-saudiiran-cold-war/article7315490.ece/. Accessed on 29 June 2015.
20. Kathryn Westcott, "Who are Hezbollah?" 4 April 2002, http://news.bbc.co.uk/2/hi/middle_east/1908671.stm/. Accessed on 5 July 2015.
21. Nicholas Blanford, "Iran and Region IV: Lebanon's Hezbollah," 28 January 2015, http://iranprimer.usip.org/blog/2015/jan/28/iran-region-iv-lebanons-hezbollah/. Accessed on 5 July 2015.
22. Graham E. Fuller, "Islamist Politics in Iraq after Saddam Hussein," *Special Report: United Institute of Peace*, August 2003, http://www.usip.org/publications/islamist-politics-in-iraq-after-saddam-hussein/. Accessed on 20 June 2015.
23. Nick Grinstead and Iba Abdo, "Yemen: under fire, desperate for peace," 16 June 2015, https://www.opendemocracy.net/opensecurity/nick-grinstead-iba-abdo/yemen-under-fire-desperate-for-peace/. Accessed on 27 June 2015.
24. *See* Johny, "The Hot Saudi Iran Cold War."
25. Johny, "The Hot Saudi Iran Cold War."

References

Acharya, Amitav. "State Sovereignty after 9/11: Disorganised Hypocrisy," *Political Studies* 55, 2007: 274-96.

Adib-Moghaddam, Arshin. (2014) "Iran in world politics after Rouhani." 2014. http://studies.aljazeera.net/en/dossiers/2014/03/20143311042164 70679.html. Accessed 25 June 2015.

Al-Rhodhan, Nayef. (2014) "The Geopolitics of Culture: Five Substrates." 2014. http://hir.harvard.edu/archives/6191. Accessed 25 June 2015.

Alloul, Jaafar. "The Shi'i Crescent Theory: Sectarian Identity or Geopolitics of Religion," 2011. http://lib.ugent.be/fulltxt/RUG01/001/786/448/RUG01-001786448_2012_0001_AC.pdf. Accessed 25 June 2015.

Blanford, Nicholas. "Iran and Region IV: Lebanon's Hezbollah." 28 January 2015. http://iranprimer.usip.org/blog/2015/jan/28/iran-region-iv-lebanons-hezbollah. Accessed 5 July 2015.

Cole, Juan. "Iran and Islam," *Special Report: United States Institute for Peace*. http://iranprimer.usip.org/resource/iran-and-islam. Accessed 25 June 2015.

Ehteshami, Anoushirvan. *After Khomeini: the Iranian Second Republic*. London & New York: Routledge, 1995.

Ezzati, Abul-Fazl. *The Revolutionary Islam and the Islamic Revolution*. Tehran: Ministry of Islamic Guidance, 1981.

Fuller, Graham E. "Islamist Politics in Iraq after Saddam Hussein," *Special Report: United Institute of Peace*. August 2003. URL: http://www.usip.org/publications/islamist-politics-in-iraq-after-saddam-hussein/. Accessed on 20 June 2015.

Grinstead, Nick and Iba Abdo. (2015) "Yemen: under fire, desperate for peace." 16 June 2015. https://www.opendemocracy.net/opensecurity/nick-grinstead-iba-abdo/yemen-under-fire-desperate-for-peace. Accessed 29 June 2015.

Johny, Stanly. "The hot Saudi-Iran cold war." 2015. http://www.thehindu.com/opinion/lead/the-hot-saudiiran-cold-war/article7315490.ece. Accessed 29 June 2015.

Martin, Vanessa. *Creating an Islamic State: Khomeini and the Making of New Iran*. New York: I.B. Tauris, 2003.

Mustafa, Tahir. "Islamic Iran's Resistance Economy and Culture." April 2014. http://www.crescent-online.net/2014/04/islamic-irans-resistance-economy-and-culture-tahir-mustafa-4375-articles.html. Accessed on 23 June 2015.

Pizzi, Michael. (2014) "In declaring a Caliphate, Islamic State draws a line in the Sand." 2014. http://america.aljazeera.com/articles/2014/6/30/islamic-state-caliphate.html. Accessed 25 June 2015.

Sariolghalam, Mahmood. "Transition in the Middle East: New Arab Realities and Iran," *Middle East Policy Council*, 2013.

Toossi, Sina. (2015) "Deciphering Iran's Strategic Vision." 2015. http://www.lobelog.com/deciphering-irans-strategic-vision. Accessed 24 June 2015.

Uyar, Mazlum. "The Concept of Sovereignty and position of the 'Ulama in both constitution of Iran," *EKEV AKEDMI DERGISI Yil*, 2007. http://ktp.isam.org.tr/pdfdrg/D01777%5C2007_31/2007_31_UYARM.pdf. Accessed 24 June 2015.

Westcott, Kathryn. "Who are Hezbollah?" 4 April 2002. http://news.bbc.co.uk/2/hi/middle_east/1908671.stm. Accessed 5 July 2015.

Zubaida, Sami. "Is Iran an Islamic State?" In *Political Islam: Essays from the Middle East Report*, Joel Beinin and Joe Stark (eds.). New York: I.B. Tauris, 1997.

5

Of Islam and Other Things

The Drivers and Rhetoric in Iranian Politics

Kingshuk Chatterjee

In its early stages the so-called Arab Spring made people and observers ask, whether Islam—or to be exact, Political Islam[1]—is finally redundant in Middle Eastern politics? Has the time finally come for Post-Islamism?[2] The experience, however, of the Ikhwan al-Muslimin and al-Nahda in power, and the drift of the civil wars in Libya and Syria, is supposedly giving cause for pause on a final verdict on the demise of Political Islam.

In the light of this twist in the debate on Political Islam and Post-Islamism, it is perhaps worth asking whether there was any major divide between the two. Most importantly, to understand the difference between Political Islam and Post-Islamism, it is useful to ask what actually makes an agenda Islamic? Does it necessarily have anything to do with Islam, the religion, or even the cultural space? Does anything—social values, economic practices, political institutions—have to acquire a particular form or institutional apparatus for it to qualify as Islamic?

This paper means to look into these questions by engaging with the considerations of what drives the formulation of agenda of the Islamic Republic of Iran, now as much as ever since the Islamic Revolution of 1979. The paper also means to look into the question of how such formulations that are 'packaged' by rhetorical usage as being related to considerations that make them Islamic. The paper is divided into four sections. The first part deals with the question what made the revolution of 1979 and the republic itself 'Islamic'. It then goes on to discuss how despite the identifiably 'Islamic' character of the discourse on economic order in the republic, the concerns are far less discernible to be so. The third section of the essay looks at the social sphere in the Islamic Republic and argues that the 'Islamic' values imposed by the republic are capable of a completely different (class-based) reading as well. In the last section of the essay, a brief foray is made into the Republics foreign policy to argue that the apparent convergence between the 'Islamic' and 'real-political' concerns is more contingent than is generally made out.

The Revolution of 1979 and the 'Islamic' Character of the Regime

Any inquiry into the character of Iranian politics post-1979 necessarily begs the question "what was Islamic about the Islamic Revolution?" While the most visible leaders belonged to the 'ulema hierocracy, it was not only the 'ulema that made the revolution. The democratic current in the 1979 revolution was just as strong as the Islamic current had been. It was only the radicalization of the milieu by the popular revolutionary committees and revolutionary courts which pushed the revolution firmly into the ambit of the 'ulema hierocracy. The invasion by Iraq in 1980 served to galvanize the country into resistance behind the banner of the 'ulema, and thus helped them consolidate their hold on the revolution. However, the 'ulemas much as the laity in Iran, have always fallen well short of any unanimity on what constitutes the Islamic character of the Islamic Revolution, and hence of the regime that followed as well.

The revolution of 1979 was shaped by forces of resistance to the Shah that drew their inspiration from two different (but not always unrelated) languages of politics that characterized the kingdom of Persia ever since the Mashruteh revolution of 1906: constitutionalism (*Mashrutiyat*) and Islamism [for want of a better word] (*Mashru'eh*). The period of instability which followed the ouster of the Shah, punctuated by major apprehensions of US intervention against the revolutionary forces (similar to the experience of 1953), served to radicalize the revolution by undermining the provisional government of Mehdi Bazargan, dominated by the (more moderate) votaries of constitutionalism, and strengthening the vigilante revolutionary committees (*Komiteh*) dominated by the votaries of Islamism.[3] The original draft of the proposed constitution for the Islamic Republic, which was demonstrably more democratic, was shot down at a referendum by the radicals, who then went on to firmly establish the domination of the 'ulema in the political system of the republic by means of the constitution that was passed in October 1979. By that time, concerned about the survival of the revolution Ayatollah Khomeini, having earlier endorsed the more democratic constitution, changed his mind and underwrote the radicalism of the new constitution.[4] The principle of *Vilayat-e Faqih*, elaborated upon earlier by Khomeini to justify intervention by learned Islamic jurists (*faqih*) in the matters of government, was enshrined in the constitution to accord him an immense array of powers unmatched by any elected functionary. Having earlier been accepted as the undisputed figurehead of the revolution, Khomeini's elevation to the position of the *Rahbar* (Supreme Leader) in his capacity of being an eminent jurist was pivotal to the identification of the revolution as Islamic by nature.[5] Nevertheless, the democratic current remained, which was evinced in the compromises between the elected (the President, the Majlis) and unelected centres (the Rahbar, the Council of Guardians, the Council of Experts, the Expediency Council) of power that ultimately characterised the constitution of the Islamic Republic of Iran. The cardinal principle underlying the constitution makes this clear—Sovereignty belongs to Allah, but no policy can be formulated unless it promotes the well-being of the people.[6]

A democratic compromise notwithstanding, the political establishment of the Islamic Republic was fashioned in large measure by the political exigencies unleashed by the war with Iraq. The invasion by Iraq threatened the stability of the fledgling revolutionary order considerably, resulting in a backlash from the revolutionaries that used the war as a smokescreen to virtually eliminate all sources of political dissent. As hundreds associated with the political opposition were jailed, executed, assassinated or driven to exile, clerical and lay defenders of the revolutionary order came to dominate all the major positions in the political establishment in course of the 1980s. The revolutionary logic that prompted such a systematic violation of the political rights of the people was packaged in Islamic terms of reference in a bid to attain legitimacy, thus suspension of civic rights of people suspected of treason was justified as the part of the larger *jihad-e defa'i* (defensive struggle, i.e. struggle in the defence of Islam).[7] Consequently, the discourse of politics in the Islamic Republic became completely Islamized in tandem with the Iraq war, virtually eliminating the scope of the non-sectarian language of politics associated with *Mashrutiyat* of the previous two generations. When the war came to an end, therefore, and 'normal' politics required making a comeback, the political discourse of the Islamic Republic stood far more 'Islamized' than it had been during the revolution itself. Politics in the Islamic Republic of Iran today, accordingly, has to be seen through the prism of this new language of politics.

It is worth mentioning, though, that even as the discourse has been thoroughly rid of any scope for a non-sectarian language of politics, the central concerns that tend to inform the secular language of politics has not disappeared; rather, they were subsumed within the language of political Islam after 1979 as much as they tended to be before it. The potency of political Islam in the run up to the revolution was principally on account of its critique of authoritarianism, of the inequitable economic order under the Pahlavi dynasty, and of the dislocations and problems ushered in by the Pahlavi agenda of modernisation.[8] Despite the Islamic terms of reference employed in the packaging of this critique, its impact was not so much on belief in (and practice of) Islam as on the lives of all Iranians, regardless of their faith. Similarly, once the Iraq war was over, the cardinal challenges before the Islamic Republic pertained not so much to the faith and practice of Islam as they did to the task of rebuilding the war-ravaged country.

Concerns in the aftermath of the Iraq war, in other words, pertained to questions of governance rather than faith. Indeed, much of the political contestations between the so-called Principalists (Osulgirans, i.e. the conservatives)[9] and the Reformists[10] have been portrayed as a struggle over the 'Islamic' character of the Islamic Republic. The reconstruction of the war-ravaged country undertaken in the mid-1980s as a *jihad*—the *jihad-e sazandegi* (the construction *jihad*); the opening up of Iran's social sphere and democratization through local government reforms under President Khatami was similarly depicted as realization of the promise of Islamic order. The conservative forces have, similarly, tried to stem the tide of reform (by means of the Council of Guardians disqualifying reformist candidates by questioning their 'reformist' credentials); the chief protagonists of the conservative political position have in the last decade even begun to refer to themselves as the Principalists (defenders of the principal [i.e. Islamic] features of the Islamic Republic).

It is, therefore, useful to understand that contrary to the popular perception about the Islamic Republic, the Iranians do not try to attain any definite universally accepted benchmark of 'Islamic order.' The wide diversity of secular political choices each tend to be conveyed in the political arena through the use of Islamic terms of reference largely for concerns of legitimacy, rather than on account of any particular 'Islamic' standard. Such choices are made in areas of concern as divergent as the economy, society, and even the foreign policy of the Islamic Republic.

The Elusive Quest for an Islamic Economic Order

In the three and a half decades since it came into being, the Islamic Republic of Iran has actively tried to establish an economic order, different from the pre-revolutionary one that would suit best the interests of its people. Towards this end, the regime has experimented in turn with both regulated economy (associated with the Prime Ministerial tenure of Mir Hussein-Mousavi, the war economy he put together, and the functioning of the bonyad-ha and the public sector), market economy (associated with private property and capitalist economic ideas advocated by Rafsanjani and his Jihad-e Sazandegi) and lately populism (associated with the tenure of Ahmadinejad), depending on the needs of the various political factions of the Islamic Republic of Iran at particular points of time. Support for all these positions were found in various readings of Islam. For instance left-wing Islamist ideologues dominated during the 1980s (highlighting the roles played by the underclass in the early days of Islam, championing the ideas of equity and equality propagated as a critique of the pre-revolutionary economic order by thinkers like Ali Shari'ati). By contrast the conservative plank was associated with the bazaars and championed private property (beginning with Morteza Motahhari in the 1970s, the Motalefeh in the 1990s and people like Larijani at present) and pushed for privatization. Even Ahmadinejad's populist agenda of redistribution was couched in terms of the chiliastic vision of Islam as an antidote to mercenary capitalism.

The Pahlavi state used to intervene extensively in the functioning of Iranian economy, pumping oil revenue into heavy and consumer goods industry alike, generating a prodigious degree of industrial activity and expanding economic opportunities in the country, particularly in the urban areas.[11] The benefits of such expansion in the scope of economy, however, were reaped mostly by a small segment of technocrats, bureaucrats, industrialists and cronies of the Shah, leaving a large segment of the educated and young population of the country disgruntled with the regime. Similarly, there was little trickle-down effect for the masses of urban poor that provided the supply of labour which was crucial to the economy. Parallel to this, the regime had systematically marginalised the bazaar (the market area which was traditionally the hub of commercial activities in the country) by regulating the asnaf (guilds) and imposing price-control at times of price rise; such interventionist practices had peaked in 1976-78.[12] The Islamic regime was expected somehow to address all of these concerns.

In response to these expectations, Islamic populism emerged as a major revolutionary agenda in the first post-revolutionary decade.[13] Representing primarily the educated youth and the urban poor, Islamic socialists comprised of a broad-ranging group of people with a redistributive agenda, determined to redress the problems of economic inequality that characterized Pahlavi Iran. They argued that equitable distribution of wealth in the society had to be the defining attribute of any Islamic order. In the initial stages, they encouraged the appropriation of the resources of the various *bonyad-ha* (foundations) and redistributing that wealth among the people;[14] they were also instrumental in the nationalization of the assets of the 51 largest industrialists in the early months of the revolution.[15] Subsequently, after the outbreak of the Iraq-Iran war, the need to reorient economy towards the war and the crisis occasioned by the flight of managerial professionals after the revolution necessitated nationalisation of major sectors of the economy, including all private banks, insurance companies, all heavy industries (including mining and metal industries as well as plane, ship and automobile manufacturing plants).[16] This strengthened the votaries of Islamic populism who favoured the idea of a heavily regulated economy.[17] Accordingly, the revolutionary order inherited the Pahlavi mantle of a strong state, and initially persisted with that same centripetalism even as it embarked on its agenda of redistribution.

The financial burden of the Iraq war proved so great for the Islamic Republic, however, that by the end of the 1980s it was considered imperative by many that the state withdrew from most industrial and economic enterprises outside the petroleum sector. The liberalization of the Iranian economy undertaken by Rafsanjani, and even by the left-inclined Khatami, steadily worked towards dismantling the large state.[18] The reformists emphasized on changing the rolc of the state from intervention and control to supervision, thereby allowing private capital and market to increase investment in infrastructure and industrial output. The mercantile element of the bazaar (with which the Iranian clergy enjoys close personal and social ties, and which thus constitutes the bedrock of the so-called Conservative camp), favoured this part of the reformist agenda of dismantling of the command economy. Hence Rafsanjani enjoyed full support of the Conservative dominated Majlis in the primary task of liberalisation, viz. deregulation of the economy.[19] However, the Conservative support for economic liberalisation ran out by early 1990s, when the sanction-ridden Iranian economy compelled the government to raise direct taxes and costs of public utilities.

However, while the denationalization of industrial and economic enterprises was carried out, they did not end up being completely privatized. In a manner quite similar to the economic adventures of the Pakistani and Egyptian military, the paramilitary Sepah (and from 2005 onwards the Basij) acquired a controlling stake in many of these enterprises. Thus, even as the government was able to shed the cost of running nationalized ventures, it had to expand the scope of economic privileges and concessions that the Sepah claimed as virtually its entitlements for 'public service'. Additionally, the huge industrial and financial conglomerates of the pre-revolutionary era that were taken over by sections of the revolutionary elite, the *Bonyad-ha* (Foundations) emerged as useful mechanisms for personal enrichment for the revolutionary elite without the handicap of governmental scrutiny. Both the economic stakes of the Sepah in particular and the revolutionary elite in general prevented optimum and efficient allocation of resources, which therefore hindered the reconstruction efforts in a big way.[20] By 1990s, as the pressure for divestment mounted on Foundations run by the Sepah and the Basij, they began to join the Conservatives in resisting the agenda of economic reform.

Economic liberalization brought in its wake considerable economic hardship, and was attacked by both the traditional conservative forces of the Motalefeh, and the Sepah-Basij axis as a betrayal of the promise of the Revolution towards the creation of 'Islamic' order. Once Khatami's term ended, the Basiji leader Mahmoud Ahmedinejad won the Presidency with his promise of a redistributive vision of the economy in a veritable chiliastic Islamic order. In the four years that followed, Ahmedinejad happened to preside over perhaps the largest bounty in terms of favourable global oil prices in the history of the Islamic Republic.[21] Since the need to cut corners that was felt by Khatami and Rafsanjani disappeared almost overnight, Ahmedinejad went on to undo many of the more unpopular economic reforms undertaken by his two predecessors, and indulged in a sustained exercise of populism on the one hand, and a redistributive agenda on the other from which the paramilitary Basij and the Sepah emerged as the principal beneficiaries. Behind the smokescreen of redistribution, though, the Ahmedinejad agenda seems to have been essentially to give the Sepah and particularly the Basijis access to a larger share of the country's resources. Quite apart from appointing his fellow Basijis to most positions in the myriad public offices at all levels, Ahmedinejad orchestrated the privatization policy in such a manner that they rank among the principal beneficiaries of the divestment of nationalized resources carried out since 2006.[22] Thus, privatization, which was meant to mobilize capital for industrial development and in particular for reinvestment in Iran's sanction-ridden oil sector, was instead carried out in the opposite direction where the state actually lost capital assets. The chiliastic vision of an Islamic economy benefits, clearly, its visionaries more than the people themselves.

The challenge before the incumbent President, Hassan Rouhani, is largely to salvage Iran from the misadventure of the Ahmedinejad era, and resume the task of restructuring in the economy of Iran. It is unlikely to be a smooth ride because the vested interests in the existing economic dispensation are too strong to be easily allowed to be dismantled. The task becomes even more daunting because of the greater propensity of the conservative lobby to use 'Islamic' justifications in their defence of their favoured economic dispensations. Thus any attempt at reform is likely to be defined as an assault on the Republic and Revolution itself.

Islam, Society and the Battle for the Skies

The greater propensity of the conservative lobby to resort to Islamic terms of reference with reference to matters that has little to do with faith flows out of a different aspect of their politics—that pertaining to Iranian society. Social conservatism couched as Islamic values (segregation of sexes, degrading the value of role played by women, the matter of *hejab*) are more like the social values of the traditional 'ulema and the mercantile elite trained within the rubric of traditional educational and social structures. By contrast the liberalism championed by people like Khatami, Rouhani and Karabaschi, etc., are hallmarks of the educated social elite that finds itself at home in the world. They typically tend to address the constituency that has enjoyed economic freedom, and are not necessarily dependent on the largesses of the state. However, when the "battle for the skies" was being waged between Khatami and Larijani in the 1990s, the discourse was heavily Islamic, using terms as *Ikhtilaf* (disagreement) and *fitna* (trouble); *amr bi'l ma'ruf wa nahy'an al-munkar* (enjoining good and forbidding evil).

The Islamic Republic, from its earliest days was plagued by the question of Islamic values and its manifestation in the public space. Since Pahlavi modernity championed a kind of sartorial uniformity (western outfits for men, outlawing of the traditional religious headgears and their replacement by the hat, discouraging the sporting of beards and encouraging clean-shaven appearances, outlawing of the veil for women, discouraging of the head-to-toe cover-all of the *chador*), a section of the revolutionaries solicited the imposition of a similar sartorial uniformity as a part of Islamization of the public space. Men were discouraged from wearing the tie (on account of it appearing like a crucifix), and the beard—or at the very least, the stubble—staged a comeback as well. Women were required to have their head covered at all times in accordance with the idea of *hijab* (modest dressing) regardless of whether one was a Muslim (or even an Iranian national); women were also discouraged from wearing western outfits as the *chador* staged an emphatic comeback in the Iranian public space. Just as the Pahlavi regime had forced women to come out into the public space, the Islamic regime attempted to push them back in.[23] Equality before law accorded to women by the Pahlavi regime was abrogated; the value of a woman's testimony was reduced to half that of the man; the practice of *muta'* (contract marriage) in vogue in Iran for centuries, invalidated by the Pahlavi regime, was revalidated. Desegregation of the sexes was enforced in public spaces, buildings and public transport; severe restrictions were imposed on movement of women. Vigilantes were encouraged to enforce public morality to conform to 'Islamic' values. Those who were found to be in violation of Islamic values would often be roughed up. Particularly vulnerable targets were those sections of the Iranian society who had adopted western mores, having succumbed to *gharbzadegi* (intoxicated with the West), and therefore prone to moral laxity.[24]

Appointed Minister for Culture and Islamic Guidance in 1982, Hujjatulislam Sayyid Khatami was a part of the establishment that had carried out the purges of intellectual dissidents and political opponents of the Islamic Republic. From 1984, even as he defended the autocratic policies of the regime, his misgivings grew about state repression, making him remark on the need to establish an Islamic state based on pluralist ideas that he saw as the essence of Islam. By 1987, even before the end of the Iran-Iraq war, Khatami began to call for a more open cultural regime, beginning the long-winded process of something like a *glasnost* in Iran.[25] As a member of President Rafsanjani's administration Khatami began to carry out his policy of emancipation of Iran's public space—cable and satellite television was permitted in Iran for the first time during Khatami's tenure, exposing Iranians to western cultural influences; censorship was relaxed on both print and electronic media; the number of newspapers and journals published increased from 102 in 1988 to 369 in 1992.[26] In 1990 he even established a 'press jury' to investigate issues involving the media.

The votaries of 'Islamic' morality opposed Khatami's programme for the liberalization of the cultural regime, but could not dislodge him because of the support he enjoyed from Khomeini. After Khomeini's death, Rafsanjani continued to back Khatami till the pressure became intense, and Khatami had to resign in 1992. In his last months as Minister for Culture and Islamic Guidance, Khatami came under sustained attack from his clerical opponents by refusing to censor foreign music video and films beamed through satellite television channels. Clerical Majlis deputies argued that such films and videos are 'agents of corruption and fornication'. Khatami tried in vain to explain that "if there is a dispute against a piece of film or music, we cannot declare films or music as inadmissible and thereby spoil the issue."[27] Warning that restrictive and exclusionary attitudes with different ideas to that of the regime would ultimately lead to a dictatorship, Khatami maintained that "freedom of thought and respect for intellectual honour are among the primary goals of the revolution."[28] Arguing later against Larijani's cautioning against *azad-andeshi* (free-thinking) and *ikhtilaf* (disagreement) as a potential source of *fitna* (trouble), Khatami emphasized that *ikhtilaf* results in *chand-arzaeshi* (pluralism), which has sanction in the Qur'an.[29]

Khatami's attempt at liberalization of the cultural policies of the Islamic Republic was opposed by two political positions. The conservatives in the Majlis and the Guardians—clerics as much as the lay members of the Mo'talefeh—considered such policies to be *taquti* ('Satanic', a term associated with secularization under the Shah), and condemned the laxity encouraged by the government. Significantly, the second source of opposition to the cultural policies came from the socially-conservative element among the populists of the 1980s, the Sepah, or more exactly the Basijis. During the 1980s, the Basij forces had worked in tandem with the regime to physically crush all domestic opposition. Frequently such activities took the form of enforcing Islamic virtues and punishing immoral or lax behaviour on part of the people, and were constitutionally underwritten by the injunction to engage in *amr beh al-ma'ruf wa nahy'an al-munkar* (lit. Enjoin what is known [to be Good] and forbidding the Evil). Determined to create a more open and free society, Rafsanjani was particularly wary of Basij tactics of physical assault and summary punishment. His support for the policies of

Khatami, thus, was directly in opposition to modus operandi of the Basij.[30]

Right after gaining control of the Majlis in 1992, the conservatives mounted an attack on the liberal cultural policies of the regime. Within three months, making use of the right of interpellation (Article 89 of the constitution), the conservative majority in the Majlis expressed its lack of confidence in the Minister for Culture and Islamic Guidance, Muhammad Khatami. In July 1992, accordingly, Khatami had to resign, and was replaced by the prominent Mo'talefeh member (and son-in-law of Morteza Motahhari, one of the most prominent disciples of Khomeini) 'Ali Larijani. Under Larijani, the MCIG went on to systematically dismantle Khatami's liberal cultural policies and involved conservative individuals and institutional strongholds with the making of socio-cultural policies. In December 1992 Larijani made public his ministry's intention to bankroll the mosques into becoming primary cultural headquarters.[31] In April 1993, mosque trusteeships were authorized to issue permits for printing and publishing houses and video clubs.[32] In September 1993, forty cultural centres were promised in various Tehran mosques to counter cultural blitz of the West.[33] In his avowed agenda of curtailing *azad-andeshi* (free-thinking) Larijani enjoyed full support of the conservatives in the Majlis and outside.

However, given that the ministry of interior was still beyond the pale of the conservatives, enforcement of such restrictive policies became somewhat difficult. Accordingly, the traditional conservative forces decided to use the social hardliners, the Basijis, as their physical arm. In November 1992, the Majlis passed a law for the "legal protection of the Basijis' authorizing them to assist the law enforcement forces in fighting crimes in the country."[34] The law, allowing the Basijis to become pro-active, emboldened them to manhandle individual offenders of 'Islamic sensibilities' in the name of custodianship of the Islamic character of the revolution.

Khatami's liberalization of the public space in Iran had thrown up a large array of possibilities that fitted in with Rafsanjani's general take on rebuilding Iran. One of these was the beginning of something like a municipal revolution in the country. It began essentially with the appointment of the middle-aged maktabi Gholam-Hussein Karbaschi as the Mayor of Tehran in the winter of 1989-90, after a successful stint as the Prefect of Isfahan. Karbaschi's tenure was characterized by a rapid development of the urban infrastructure of the capital, as also creation of open public parks. The highly energetic municipal administration of Tehran under Karbaschi set an example for other municipal administrations to follow. Most major residential localities in cities like Tabriz, Mashhad, Shiraz, etc., inevitably made similar open public spaces accessible to the people. Maintained principally by means of municipal taxes collected from citizens (*hamshahri*), these parks swiftly became a space that the citizens claimed as their own. While conservatives resented the principle of taxation that characterized this municipal revolution, inhabitants of the cities proved reasonably content with these 'pockets of freedom', exempted from being under the scrutiny of the state.[35]

The Iranian youth in particular found these 'pockets of freedom' exhilarating, after the enforced moral strictures during the war with Iraq. Exposed to images of the lifestyle of developed societies that was beamed into Iran through cable and satellite television during the relaxed years under Khatami, the youth in Iran availed of the various municipal parks as the arena of public sociability where the sexes could mingle at ease. In the social life of modern Iranians, 'heading out for the open' constitutes a fairly regular part. At the weekends as much as during holidays, Iranians tend to head for open public spaces, to let the hair down, as it were. The municipal parks became tremendously popular for these purposes from the 1990s. The parks were also popular among people who want to meet without the fear of being snooped upon. Couples engaged in courtship, young people engaging in flirtation, friends relaxing with board games, musicians playing instruments, families relaxing with children—all these became regular sights at the municipal parks.

In 1992, after the replacement of Khatami by Larijani, the parks began to come under fire from the conservatives as "promoting the western culture of unfetteredness."[36] In fact, one of the aims of the Majlis behind empowering the Basij in 1992 was to enforce restrictive Islamic morality in public spaces, such as the parks. By 1993, the alignment between the conservatives of Mo'talefeh with the social hardliner Basijis became particularly vicious in "turning back the cultural clock of Iran."[37] In this moral crusade of the conservatives and hardliners, Khamenei supported the conservative cause. In June

1993, Khamenei set up a new vigilante body, the *Setad-e Yahya-ye Amr beh Ma'aruf wa Nahy az Munkar* (Headquarter for the Revival of Enjoining the Good and Forbidding Evil, hereafter *Setad*) under the staunch conservative Ayatollah Jannati.[38] Composed primarily of recruits from the young Basijis, the *Setad* was sought to be used by the conservatives to undermine the cultural freedom that Khatami sought to promote. Thus the *Setad* became particularly active in the two arena where that ambience of cultural freedom had become most conspicuous—the municipal parks and the universities—and which provided the real catchments of leftist politics.

With its vigilante activities given constitutional authorization and endorsed by the conservative forces and the *Rahbar* himself, the Basijis in general and the *Setad* became active in endorsing a strict morality code in public place, especially in the municipal parks and the universities. The Basijis targeting of the universities being aimed specifically at breaking up leftist student unions under the cover of enforcement of Islamic morality (viz. segregation of the sexes in public place, proper dress code, etc.), the influential student organisation *Daftar-e Tahkim-e Vahdat* (Office of Strengthening of Unity) fought out a vicious turf war in the universities. In defence of Basiji vigilantism, the head of the *Setad*, Ayatollah Jannati pronounced at length upon the need for student associations to be under the supervision of the clergy to retain their Islamic character.[39] Khamenei himself expressed his disapproval of the weakening of the Islamic spirit in universities and emphasized the need to replace the 'ambivalent' approach of the intellectuals with the revolutionary spirit of the Basij.[40] Larijani used the platform of the Ministry of Culture and Islamic Guidance to spread the idea that proper culture in Iran was that of the Basij. In October 1993, Larijani announced that the ministry would coordinate its activities with the Basij.[41]

The deadliest salvo of the conservatives in this battle for the public space came in September 1993, when a report was released by a group of Majlis deputies detailing un-Islamic content of national TV and radio. The Majlis responded to this report by passing a bill to inspect the revolutionary credentials of its personnel, conformity of TV and radio programmes with the Shari'ah, and to ascertain if radio and TV were spreading western culture among the youth.[42] The committee found programmes to be neither revolutionary nor

Islamically oriented; films screened were found to be mostly foreign films that were un-Islamic; the personnel were found to be inadequately revolutionary in their orientation and that too many women were employed by these organizations. Worst of all, both the organizations were found guilty of improper use of funds.[43] The Majlis then moved a vote of no-confidence against its intended target Muhammad Hashemi, the head of Iranian TV and Radio. Soon after this, Hashemi resigned and was replaced at Khamenei's instructions by Larijani. Larijani's successor at the Ministry of Culture and Islamic Guidance was another rigidly puritan Mo'talefeh member, Mustafa Mir-Salim. The new minister immediately pronounced his unqualified support for Basiji vigilantism, and launched a campaign of cleansing the press. In September 1994, the ministry proclaimed that only houses with religious-nationalist qualifications would be given permission to publish. Left-leaning newspapers like *Havades, Gardun, Bahman, Payam-e Daneshju* and *Aineh-ye Andisheh* were closed in close succession. The ministry also withdrew support for renowned liberal film-makers like Mohsen Makhmalbaf, Majid Majidi, and others.[44]

Beyond the 'Islamic' rhetoric, though, a completely different reading of this battle for the public space (known as "battle for the skies") that took place in the 1990s. The educated middle class had been one of the biggest beneficiaries of the liberalization of the Iranian public space under the Pahlavis. Although a large segment of them eventually led the protests demanding democratic freedoms against the Shah, they were not inclined to throw the baby (their freedoms) out with the bathwater (the Pahlavi regime). The traditional mercantile elite of the *bazaar,* which had suffered directly from the modernizing agenda earlier, and were the principal patrons of the traditional socio-religious cultural order associated with Shi'i Islam, were determined to undo the whole gamut of what constituted this dislocation, and restore the traditional mores of public culture at the expense of the 'western' mores. The educated upwardly mobile lower-middle class, which had little but disgruntlement against the Shah on account of the dislocation caused by the Pahlavi agenda of modernization, were equally resentful towards the markers of a more westernized secularized cultural idiom. Accordingly, the radical revolutionaries began to solicit the creation of an Islamic order to address both the wealthy *bazaaris* as also the lower-middle class constituency. The middle class were on the defensive, which became more pronounced as a large section of the middle class left the country fearing persecution from the new regime, making life still more difficult for those who were left behind. With the war with Iraq being waged, the 'compradorial' middle class began to be looked at with considerable suspicion; by contrast the lower-middle and lower class elements of the Iranian society, volunteering for military service under the banner of the Sepah and its reservists the Basij, began to grow much more assertive. These were the mainstay of much of the 'Islamic' vigilantism in wartime Iran, and the backbone of the groups that sought 'Islamic' morality.

The role played by the educated middle class during the war remained in the background most of the time. However, when the war with Iraq was over and the need for reconstruction became pressing, the entrepreneurial and managerial role the middle class was needed to play in the rebuilding of the Iranian economy after it began to be pressed upon the regime by the more farsighted members like Khatami and Rafsanjani. It was clear that the socially repressive policies of the wartime were unsustainable after it; besides the educated middle class also needed to be given some stake in the regime. It was in this background that the emancipation of the public space began to be considered.

However, social conservatives associated with the *Motalefeh,* who represented a social coalition in which the bazaaris played a major role, were determined to stem this drift fearing that the return of the non-traditional socio-cultural mores would bring back the culture of modern consumerism. Unable to intervene directly with the reform-minded executive, though, the conservatives sought a new ally—the traditionalist hardliners of the predominantly lower-middle class Basij.

The Basij had begun to lose its relevance after the end of the Iraq war, and found it reasonably difficult to reinvent itself. Unlike the main core of the Sepah, which had gained access to industrial and other economic enterprises, the Basij did not quite benefit materially from the period of economic reconstruction that characterized the Rafsanjani era. Thus the predominantly lower-middle class elements of the Basij found in the November 1992 laws a vindication of their continued existence. The role the Basij played on behalf of the socially conservative judiciary in the 1990s, undermining Khatami and his associates in the "battle for the skies" made them a major force in its own right. When Karbaschi was removed from his position of Mayor of Tehran on clearly trumped up charges, the Mayoral office was made over to the Basiji leader, Mahmoud Ahmedinejad, thus paving the ground for his eventual election to the Presidency once Khatami's term came to an end in 2005. During the presidential tenure of Ahmedinejad, the scale and scope of Basiji vigilantism expanded to systematically penetrate not merely the public parks of the Khatami era, but also the universities, which were bastions of reformist support for long periods. Student demonstrations demanding greater freedom were severely cracked down upon by the Basijis with the police looking away; the faculties were purged on the flimsiest of grounds.[45]

It remains to be seen how far the Rouhani administration is going to engage this battle for the public space of Iran during his watch. What is perfectly clear, though, is that the social values being contended over in Iran are driven as much (if not more) by class considerations as by any understanding of what faith requires.

Where Islam is not the Solution, and Not Even a Part of the Question

It is a widely held position that Tehran's foreign policy manifests the deepest ideological commitment to Islam. Arguably driven by considerations of exporting the Islamic Revolution abroad, Tehran has been relentless in its animosity towards Israel and staunch in its support for Hamas in Palestine, Hizbollah in Lebanon, and for the embattled Assad regime in Syria. The problem is while many of these arguments appear weak from the standpoint of exporting Shi'i Islamic revolutionary traits, their real political considerations are considerably stronger. In the last decade, moreover, Tehran has been repeatedly accused of functioning as a force abetting instability in her immediate neighbourhood, especially in Iraq since 2005 and Bahrain since 2011. Even if one is to accept that Tehran is supposedly working towards regional hegemony, such a foreign policy direction would seem to be motivated more by strategic considerations than ideological ones. The matters of Hamas, Hizbollah, Iraq and even Bahrain may apparently indicate fascinating convergence between Islamic and strategic considerations, but such a reading is unlikely to stand closer scrutiny.

The deepest footfall (in the sense of duration of involvement) of the Islamic Republic in the regional politics of the Middle East is to be found in the Levantine region of Syria, Lebanon and Palestine. Tehran is at present one of the two principal mainstays of the embattled Syrian regime (Russia being the other) of Bashar al-Assad, locked into a civil war with a myriad group of his own countrymen, ranging from outfits associated with the Ikhwan al-Muslimin (Muslim Brotherhood), and even the al-Qaeda as also people who are simply disgruntled with the regime. It is now abundantly clear that so long as Tehran provides Damascus with crucial material and diplomatic support, it would require a massive and coordinated effort on the part of Assad's adversaries to overthrow him; and given the al-Qaeda connection of some of the adversaries such coordination is unlikely to emerge.

Additionally, Tehran has provided the militant Hezbollah movement from 1983 with a broad range of financial, military, logistic and political support.[46] While both Tehran and the Hezbollah find it convenient to deny Tehran's involvement, Iran is considered to have been the principal source of arms and ammunitions for the Hezbollah right from 1983, and to have operated training camps for the Hezbollah under the prominent Iranian revolutionary Mostafa Chamran.[47] After the end of the Lebanese civil war, Iran has continued to provide Hezbollah with logistical support to emerge as the principal force of opposition in Lebanon. Even Hezbollah's television and propaganda network, Al-Manar, was set up with support from Iran.[48]

Iran has also been involved in the Israeli-Palestine conflict from the latter part of the 1980s. Tehran has financed and possibly also trained the HAMAS (Harakat al-Muqawwamat al-Islamiyya or the Islamic Resistance Movement) from the late-1980s, and definitely from the mid-1990s. Estimates vary, but the general agreement has been that the quantum of Tehran's assistance to HAMAS has not been insignificant. US sources have estimated Iranian support to the HAMAS to have ranged between $30 million and $50 million during the 1990s; Canadian intelligence estimates the transfer for the same period to have been between $3 million and $18 million.[49] Despite the considerable difference in the two figures, the substance of Iranian assistance is yet to be disputed. US intelligence believes that Tehran's support for HAMAS operated on pay-for-performance principle, which peaked in 1995-96 with a plethora of suicide bombings. In 1995-96 alone, Tehran is supposed to have transferred between $25 million and $50 million.[50] The Intelligence and Terrorism Information Center at the Israel Intelligence Heritage and Commemoration Center suggests that Tehran's support for the HAMAS was pivotal in the latter's increased ability to launch its swathe of rocket attacks during 2006-07.[51]

While Iranian involvement with Hezbollah and HAMAS need not be disputed, the rationale behind such intervention needs be put in perspective. The usual explanation proffered was that the revolutionary regime was keen on exporting its revolutionary ideology, and that the Alawite Shi'i rulers of Syria and the Shi'ite organization of Hezbollah in Lebanon were natural constituencies for Tehran to address. This argument, to put it mildly, is silly. It does not explain Tehran's interest in HAMAS. Indeed it is not necessary that Tehran's support for all forces everywhere must be motivated by the same reason. That in fact was the reason pedlars of "export of ideology" thesis stood their ground, and explained away Tehran's support for HAMAS by contending that Khomeini had always taken his stand in favour of the Palestinian struggle, while the support for Hezbollah and 'Alawite rulers of Syria were motivated by ideological considerations. The last argument, i.e. support for Alawite rulers of Syria, is the most anomalous of the lot, because the Assad regime has been receiving the backing of an overwhelming majority of Syria's secularists and even the Christian population, fearful of the opposition which has a pronounced 'Islamic' character—a curious alignment, unless one looks for the answers in strategic considerations rather than ideological ones.

The war with Iraq had Tehran completely isolated in the neighbourhood with Saudi Arabia, Kuwait, UAE and the USA actively supporting Iraq at various stages of its war effort in various ways. Tehran's bid to break out of this diplomatic isolation took it to Damascus, where Syria's intervention in the Lebanese civil war had already made Damascus very unpopular with the West and its Arab neighbours. Tehran began supporting Syria, and then (once Israeli invasion of Lebanon made the Hezbollah mount a gallant resistance to the invaders) Hezbollah, principally in order to open a second front that could distract American interest and therefore concentrate less on Iraq.[52] Iran's interest in the HAMAS also was presumably driven by similar concerns of keeping the second front open after the Lebanese civil war was over—US preoccupation with the Arab-Israeli dispute would serve to reduce the heat on Iran. Additionally, in the light of the funding of Iraq during the Iran-Iraq war by Arab governments in the name of Arab solidarity, Tehran's espousal of the Palestinian cause was meant to send a powerful message to the Arab streets that on the crucial question of Palestine, Tehran remained more true to the Arab cause than all the Arab regimes.

How does this reading square with the relentless hostility that the Islamic Republic has been showing to Israel over the last three decades? A strategic explanation would suggest that Tehran is targeting the *Shaitan-e Kochak* (the Lesser Devil, i.e. Israel) to hurt the *Shaitan-e Bozorg* (the Great Satan, i.e. USA). Such an argument would explain why Iran supports Hezbollah and remains more Palestinian than the Palestinians. It would also explain why such support escalates whenever Tehran is under international (read, US) pressure on any issue (as in the 1980s, between 1994-96, during 2003, and 2006-08).

Such a reading sits easily as well with other cases where the ideological considerations have been considered to have played a still greater role in Tehran's foreign policy, viz. unrest among the Shi'i in Iran's Arab neibhbourhood and particularly Iraq after 2003. Right after the Islamic Revolution of 1979, the Shi'i communities in Iran's Arab neighbourhood, viz. in Bahrain, Iraq and Saudi Arabia, had become particularly enthused by Tehran's example. Apprehension of such repercussions were strong enough for Saddam to invoke it at the time of Iraqi invasion in 1980, and for Iran's Arab neighbours (Saudi Arabia, Bahrain and Kuwait) to extend support for Baghdad materially and/or diplomatically. Iran responded to such support by encouraging the export of its revolutionary model particularly among the Shi'i communities in the neighbourhood. What needs appreciation is that although Shi'i dissidence was growing in these Arab countries, Iran's prodding attained little success (particularly in Iraq, where they were a much-repressed minority). It also needs be noted that such flaunted 'exporting revolution' died a natural death by the mid-1980s itself.

Of late, especially from the days of Ahmedinejad, the idea has gained traction that Iran is gaining ascendancy in the region, capitalizing on the power-vacuum left behind by, first, the fall of Saddam, and then by the steady disengagement begun by USA from the region. Iraq's neighbours as much as the USA has persistently accused Iran of trying to destabilize Iraq ever since Saddam Hussein was toppled in 2003. They argue that Iran is trying to create a series of Shi'i centres of power in the Arab heartland by propping up various Shi'i forces in Iraq, Lebanon and, in 2011, in Bahrain.[53] King Abdullah II's comments about "the rise of a Shi'i crescent" out of the Iraq war have been periodically echoed by Saudi diplomats that US intervention in Iraq is effectively handing over the country to Iran.[54]

Despite persistent propaganda emerging from Manama and Riyadh, there is little evidence to suggest that Iran played any active role in creating an atmosphere of dissent in Bahrain in 2011. Tehran was mortified at the prospect that the Arab Spring might be followed by a Persian summer. Indeed, if the Shi'i came to power in Bahrain, Tehran would not have minded reaping its benefits. But that does not necessarily give Tehran any agency in the disturbances themselves.

The Americans tended to argue that once Saddam was toppled, Tehran became particularly active in trying to gain leverage in Baghdad. It began backing various factions (mostly Shi'i) at different points of time: viz. Ahmed Chelabi, the Supreme Council of Islamic Revolution in Iraq (SCIRI), the Badr militia of Muqtada al-Sadr and even Sunni insurgent groups. The strongest such indictment came from the US Ambassador to Iraq, Zalmay Khalilzad in February 2006, when he was charged with a "mixed policy towards Iraq," blending normal diplomatic relationship with making available the arms and ammunition that have kept the trouble brewing in Iraq.[55]

Conventional wisdom would suggest that since Tehran had fought the most destructive war in Iranian history with Iraq, it makes sense for Iran to keep her powerful neighbour considerably weakened. Indeed, Iran was uncomfortable having the USA in its backyard, and was keen that the Americans left Iraq quickly, lest they start using Iraq as their base for any potential invasion of Iran. This mood was reasonably pervasive from the early part of 2006 as US rhetoric against Tehran began to grow particularly bellicose. It did make strategic sense for Tehran for the Iraqi situation to go out of hand for USA, bogging

America down in Iraq to an extent that Washington DC would be neither willing nor able to launch an invasion of Iran in the near future.

There is little reason to doubt that Tehran would want at the very least a friendly regime in Baghdad. Having already fought the most destructive war in living memory with her western neighbour, Iran would be extremely uncomfortable with either an inimically disposed regime in Baghdad or even one that might allow the US a strategic depth against Tehran. Thus while Tehran tried to develop friendly relationship with the Nouri al-Maliki regime, it was equally keen on developing mileage with both forces in power and those in opposition that might give her some strategic depth in Baghdad, at least for the duration of US presence in the region. Indeed, Tehran seems to believe that its best chances of success would come with the Shi'i elements in Iraqi politics that have been hitherto repressed by the Sunni minority, but not by trying to establish a "theocratic" regime in Baghdad, which would be guaranteed to provoke Sunni Arab and Kurdish hostility. Iran is determined however to prevent the rise of a Saudi-backed Sunni insurgency in Iraq that would lend strategic depth to any anti-Tehran disposition. Hence, while Tehran disputed the allegations of its military and logistical support to Sunni and Shi'i insurgency in Iraq, and while no substantive evidence exists justifying either of these charges, the probability that Tehran supported Muqtada al-Sadr and the Badr militia loyal to the SCIRI till some years back was admittedly high.[56] Over time Tehran the shifted its support to prop up the Nouri al-Maliki regime, and even sent military advisors to help the Shi'i fightback in July-August 2014 in order to stem the seemingly relentless advance of the ISIS.[57] It then went on to throw its weight behind Haidar al-Abadi instead, when it became clear to all concerned that Maliki was more of a liability.[58]

Thus, to suspect Tehran as having any design to destabilize Iraq is to miss the plot completely. Unstable Iraq, with a central authority unable to control the regions, would invariably amount to greater autonomy for the Kurds in the north. This is against the interests of Tehran (as also Ankara), because the very introduction of autonomy for the Kurdish regions of Iraq had resulted in similar aspirations and demands in the adjacent Kurdish regions of the Islamic Republic. Further strengthening of the autonomous character of Kurdish autonomy would provide a fillip for the demand for independent

Kurdistan that is almost certain to destabilize Iran as much as Turkey. Hence, it might be safe to contend that, Iran would prefer a weak Iraq to strong Iraq, and a stable Iraq to an unstable one.[59]

Whether Iran's neighbourhood shares its religious or ideological inclinations has little resonance among policy-makers in Tehran, compared to the question whether they are good neighbours. In foreign policy, as in any other aspect of government policy, ideological considerations seem to offer little beyond rhetoric in the realm of policy formulation.

Conclusion

A careful study of the course and content of policy formulated in the Islamic Republic of Iran clearly reveals that there is little by way of intrinsically ideological considerations that inform these. Given the incremental Islamisation of the discourse of politics in the Islamic Republic, almost all major debates in Iran revolve around the issues of governance couched in terms of Islam—which is the copybook definition of what we understand as Political Islam. Having emerged as a discourse of opposition confronting the totalising discourse of the modern state, though, when protagonists of Political Islam themselves came to power in Iran, they found that the issues of governance cannot be addressed satisfactorily in terms of Islam.

There would seem to be a growing consensus in the Muslim world that "Islam is the solution" only while in opposition, seldom when in power. Islamic Republic of Iran is a good example of this, and in a way so is Turkey, as the experience of the Erdogan era seems to be reinforcing every day. The Ikhwan in Egypt in particular, and Islamists in the Middle East in general, came under attack from a large cross-section of the people having they failed on matters of governance after staging successful challenges to the previous regimes. They responded by pushing forth their 'Islamic' agenda, presumably hoping to be able to consolidate their hold over their core constituency. But the strategy could not be considered a satisfactory response to those issues of governance. Accordingly, the democratically elected government in Egypt was overthrown, and the military staged a return to power; Tunisia has fared marginally better, but dissent is growing.

Whether one sees Post-Islam as the transmutation of Political Islam or as a new wind altogether remains to be resolved. What is clear though is that while the rhetoric of politics may or may not be of Islamic vintage, the drivers of policy are essentially related to matters of governance that affect Muslims and non-Muslims, believers and non-believers alike.

References

1. Political Islam denotes an intellectual category in which Islam functions less as a religion, and more as a political ideology that lays down certain specific objectives to those in pursuit of it. It might range from a puritan dispensation of order, stressing upon the literal implementation of the shari'ah in a tribal monarchical framework (as in Saudi Arabia) to a parliamentary democracy. What makes such widely divergent political formulations Islamic is the pursuit of certain values or forms of social order identified as Islamic, and thought worthy of preservation as such.
2. Post-Islamism has been defined by Asef Bayat, who coined the term as "a conscious attempt to conceptualize and strategize the rationale and modalities of transcending Islamism in social, political, and intellectual domains. ... It represents the endeavour to fuse religiosity and rights, faith and freedom, Islam and liberty. It is an attempt to turn the underlying principles of Islamism on its head by emphasizing rights instead of duties, plurality in place of singular authoritarian voice, historicity rather than fixed scripture, and the future instead of the past." See Asef Bayat, *Making Islam Democratic: Social Movements and the Post-Islamist Turn*, Stanford, Ca: Stanford University Press, 2007, p. 11.
3. For two immensely readable treatments of the manner in which the revolution unfolded, *see* Shaul Bakhash, *The Reign of the Ayatollahs: Iran and the Islamic Revolution*, New York: Basic Books, 1984; Michael Axworthy, *Revolutionary Iran: A History of the Islamic Republic*, London: Allen Lane, 2013.
4. For a treatment of the course and significance of the formulation of the constitution of the Islamic Republic, See Asghar Schirazi, *the Constitution of Iran: Politics and State in the Islamic Republic*, London: I.B. Tauris, 1997.
5. It needs be pointed out that although Khomeini and his camp favoured institutionalizing the power of the 'ulema within the political system (and hence came to be labelled as the Islamic element in the body-politic), there was no precedent in the Islamic political tradition in Iran or elsewhere for the concept of the *Vilayat-e Faqih*, and was not easily accepted by contemporaries with greater erudition than Khomeini, such as Ayatollah Shariatmadari. The concept did not gain much currency anywhere in the Sunni world, and even in the Shi'i world its influence was conditioned

more by the promise of support from the revolutionary regime to those who sought it in other countries (viz. the Hezbollah in Lebanon) than by the doctrine on its own merits. Hence to argue the doctrine of the *Vilayat-e Faqih* as the principal Islamic component in the Islamic revolution is open to questioning from within the Islamic hermeneutical tradition. Even a revolutionary figure as prominent as Hossein Ali Montazeri (a close disciple and once-annointed successor of Khomeini) criticized the doctrine as being discordant with Islam.

6. Article 56 of the Iranian Constitution.
7. Saskia Gieling, *Religion and War in Revolutionary Iran,* London and New York: I.B. Tauris, 1990, p. 44.
8. *See* Kingshuk Chatterjee, *'Ali Shari'ati and the Shaping of Political Islam in Iran*, New York, Palgrave Macmillan, 2011).
9. The social coalition loosely referred to as 'conservatives' in this essay was represented by distinct but analogous groups from different periods after 1979, almost all of whom favour a regulated social and cultural space with little government control over the economy. In the 1980s, this denoted the right-wing members of the *Hizb-e Jomhuri-ye Islami* (Islamic Republic Party), with which the bazaar was closely associated. From the late 1980s, after the IRP was dissolved, the *Jame 'h-e Rouhaniyun-e Mobarez* (Society of Combatant Clergy) constituted the bedrock of this platform, and gradually began to work in tandem with the party of the lay politicians known as the *Jamiyat-e Motalefeh-ye Islami* (Allied Islamic Society, or *Motalefeh* for short, led by people like Mohsen Rafiqdust and the Larijani brothers), which dominated the conservative block during the Khatami years. By 2008, the JRM-Motalefeh axis began to label itself as *A'etelaf-e Firagir-e Osulgiran* or the *Osulgiran* (Principalists) for short.
10. Protagonists of reform also differ among each other on many matters, but are united on the cardinal assessment that the revolutionary order needs five restructuring if the Islamic Republic has to survive the changes that have crept in the post-war period. The reformist plank happens to comprise of two distinct shades of political opinion—the more moderate centre-right forces that dominated the 'struggle for reconstruction' (*Jihad-e Sazanadegi*) during the Presidency of Akbar Hashmi Rafsanjani, who eventually put together the political platform of *Hizb-e Kargozaran-e Sazandegi* (Party of the Executives of Reconstruction, hereafter Kargozaran), as also outfits like *A'etelaf-e Niruha-ye Melli Mazhabi* (Alliance of National Religious Forces) and *Hizb-e E'tedaal wa Towsiyeh* (Moderation and Development Party, with which the incumbent President Hassan Rouhani is associated); the other component of the reformist wing happens to be the numerous centre-left forces such as the *Majma'-ye Rowhaniyun-e Mobarez* (Association of the Combatant Clerics, with which former President Khatami used to be associated), *Jebhe-ye Mosharikat-e Islam-e Irani* (associated with his brother Reza Khatami), along with many others that together constituted the powerful *Dovvom-e Khordad*

Movement which carried Sayyid Muhammad Khatami to two landslide victories in the Presidential polls of 1997 and 2003.

11. For an exhaustive treatment of the Pahlavi economic agenda, see Homa Katouzian, *The Political Economy of Modern Iran: Despotism and Pseudo-Modernism 1926-79*, London and New York: Macmillan and New York University Press, 1981.
12. See Misagh Parsa, *the Social Origins of the Islamic Revolution*, New Brunswick and London: Rutgers University Press, 1989, pp. 90-125.
13. For a treatment of the phenomenon of Islamic populism, see Ervand Abrahamian, *Khomeinism: Essays on the Islamic Republic*, University of California Press, 1993.
14. *Bonyad*s are a variation of *awqaf* (sing. *waqf.*), i.e, autonomous charitable foundations in Muslim societies relying upon endowments by faithful, purported to provide material support to the less-privileged members of the Muslim community. Associated generally with religious shrines and orders, organisations such as the *Bonyad-e Astan-e Qods* or the *Bonyad-e Panzdah-ye Khordad* have prospered under the Islamic Republic. For instance, based at the shrine of Imam Reza in Mashhad, owning property all over Iran and receiving a steady stream of revenue from alms paid by pilgrims, the *Bonyad-e Astan-e Qods* is supposed to have an annual budget of around $2 billion. The Islamic Republic, however, has invested far greater assets to *bonyad*s that have no attachment with religious endowments. While there are some foundations that rely on private funds, most rely heavily on the government for either direct subsidies or special prerogatives, with considerable autonomy. Several of such quasi-public foundations, such as *Bonyad-e Mostazafin wa Janbaz* (Foundation for the Oppressed and the Self-Sacrificers, entrusted with protecting victims of the revolution and the war), the *Komiteh-ye Imdad-e Imam* (Imam's Relief Committee, providing medical, educational and social assistance to needy rural families), *Jihad-e Sazandegi* (Reconstruction Crusade, responsible for promotion of economic development in the countryside) were pivotal to sustained war effort and also economic activity all through the 1980s.
15. For a description of the major industrial families under the Shah and the process of nationalisation, see Anourshivan Ehteshami, *After Khomeini: the Iranian Second Republic*, London: Routledge, 1995, p. 83-8.
16. Suzanne Maloney, "Agents or Obstacles: Parastatal Foundations and Challenges for Iranian Development," in *The Economy of Iran: Dilemmas of an Islamic State,* Parvin Alizadeh (ed.), London and New York: I. B. Tauris, 2000, p. 154.
17. Prominent protagonists of this agenda included Ayatollahs Mohammad Beheshti and Hossein 'Ali Montazeri, Mir Hussein-Musavi (Prime Minister 1981-89), Behzad Nabavi, Hojjatulislam Muhammad Musavi-Khoeiniha, Mehdi Karrubi. In common parlance, this populist faction is referred to as the left-wing in post-revolutionary Iranian politics, which

dominated the Majlis during 1981-89. Following the populist school (*maktab*) in Islamic thinking represented by Khomeini himself, these Islamic populists called themselves *Maktabi*.

18. For nearly a decade, the government had controlled domestic prices and imposed a wage ceiling, and kept the foreign exchange rates artificially overvalued, subjected imports to government allocation, required a variety of permits for establishing new industrial enterprises, refused to allow foreign investments in Iran, and provided subsidies for nearly all basic foodstuffs. It was premised upon foreign exchange liberalization, decontrol of prices, elimination of subsidies and privatization of state-owned enterprises. For a very comprehensive treatment of Iran's economic liberalization under Rafsanjani, see Sohrab Behdad, "From Populism to Liberalism: the Iranian Predicament," in Alizadeh, *The Economy of Iran*, pp. 115-31.
19. Led in the initial stages by powerful ideologues of the Islamic state such as Ayatollah Morteza Motahhari, this minimalist position of the state was championed all through the 1980s by Ayatollah Muhammad Yazdi, Musavi-Ardabili, as also prominent political figures like 'Ali Khamenei (President 1981-89, Rahbar 1989 till date) and 'Ali Akhbar Nateq-Nouri (Speaker of the Majlis, 1989-97). From the 1990s, this group formed an axis called the Jamiyat-e Mo'talefeh-ye Islami (Allied Islamic Society, hereafter the Mo'talefeh)—dominated by lay Islamists like Mohsen Rafiqdust (later, head of the Bonyad-e Mustazafin) and brothers 'Ali and Javed Larijani, which became more prominent during and after the Rafsanjani era.
20. At the end of the war, these foot-soldiers of the Islamic Revolution were left in command over considerable share of nationalized economic resources, for which the Foundations began to claim autonomy from government control by the time liberalization was launched. It was always going to be a difficult task to get them to dissolve their stake in the economy. For a brief treatment of the role played by the Sepah and the Basij, see Frederic Wehrey, Jerrold D. Green, Brian Nichiporuk, Alireza Nader, Lydia Hansell, Rasool Nafisi, S. R. Bohandy, *The Rise of the Pasdaran: Assessing the Domestic Roles of the Islamic Revolutionary Guards Corps*, Arlington VA, RAND Corporation, 2009.
21. In 2005, when the prices began to rise sharply, Iran's oil export revenue stood at \$46.6 billion, double the high point of the Khatami presidency of \$23.7 billion in 2003. As oil prices jumped from \$55 per barrel to \$147, Iran's oil export stood at \$70 billion–more than two and a half times the average for the Khatami period. http://www.payvand.com/news/09/feb/1034.html. Accessed on 1 May 2009.
22. Under a new law regarding 'privatization' introduced by Ahmedinejad, nearly 2,000 nationalized entities valued at anything between \$100 and 140 billion were privatized. Almost 40 per cent of the shares so divested

were earmarked as "justice shares" for sale among low income households at heavily discounted prices. The value of such resources made over to 4.6 million people has been put at $2.7 billion. Eligibility for the "justice shares" was, primarily, participation in the Iraq war, which allowed both the Sepah and the Basij veterans to get these. Additionally, 40 per cent of these shares were released in the stock market, but having barely any takers who were willing to invest in enterprises in which they could not have controlling stake, even these shares were purchased by Foundations dominated by the Sepah and the Basij. *See* Nader Habibi, "The Economic Legacy of Mahmoud Ahmedinejad," *Middle East Brief*, Crown Centre for Middle East Studies, p. 3. http://www.brandeis.edu/crown/publications/meb/MEB74.pdf. Accessed on 31 January 2014.

23. Reza Shah made it mandatory for public servants to bring their wives and children to office gatherings. Any functionary found not complying with this injunction was subjected to disciplinary actions.
24. Even privacy of the home tended to be invaded, as parties in residences tended to be gate-crashed by *basijis*.
25. Mehdi Moslem, *Factional Politics in Post-Khomeini Iran*, New York: Syracuse University Press, 2002, p. 171.
26. *Salaam*, 24 November 1992.
27. "Culture, Islamic Guidance Minister on Policies," broadcast 3 May 1992, FBIS-NES-92-105, 1 June 1992.
28. *Salaam*, 17 March 1991.
29. Presidential address at *Hamaesh Jahani-ye Hikmat-e Motahari*, May 2004.
30. Kingshuk Chatterjee, *A Split in the Middle: The Making of the Political Centre in Iran*, IFPS/CPWAS Occasional Paper no. 2, New Delhi: KW Publishers, 2012, pp. 20-21.
31. *Ittela'at*, 31 December 1992.
32. *Kayhan*, 12 April 1993.
33. *Kayhan*, 30 September 1993.
34. Moslem, *Factional Politics*, p. 217.
35. Farhang Rajaee, in conversation with the author, April 2004.
36. *Salaam*, 24 June 1993.
37. *Salaam*, 3 July 1993.
38. Moslem, *Factional Politics*, p. 219.
39. *See*, for instance, *Ittela'at*, 29 October 1992.
40. *Ittela'at*, 5 November 1992.
41. *Ittela'at*, 5 October 1993.
42. Moslem, *Factional Politics*, p. 221
43. Moslem, *Factional Politics*.
44. Moslem, *Factional Politics*, pp. 221-23.
45. For instance, Fatemeh Sadeghi, a leading feminist activist and the daughter of the radical revolutionary Sadeq Khalkhali, was thrown out of her job at the Allameh Tabatabai University in Tehran for the offence of having a chewing gum during daytime in the month of Ramadan.

46. *See* Anthony H. Cordesman, "Iran's Support for the Hezbollah in Lebanon," http://csis.org/files/media/csis/pubs/060715_hezbollah.pdf. Accessed on 26 March 2011.
47. An Iranian academic on condition of anonymity, (whose father was instrumental in the negotiations that begun Iran's military and logistical involvement with Hezbollah) in conversation with the author in Beirut, 2005.
48. Ibrahim Mousawi, Director, Political Programmes, Al-Manar Television, in conversation with the author, in Beirut, May 2005.
49. Matthew Levitt, *HAMAS: Politics, Charity and Terrorism in the Service of Jihad*, New Haven and London: Yale University Press, 2006, p. 172.
50. Levitt, *HAMAS*, p. 172.
51. http://terrorism-info-org.il/malam_multimedia? English/eng_n/pdf/iran_e004.pdf. Accessed on 16 January 2011.
52. For a detailed argument along these lines, *see* Anoushiravan Ehteshami and Raymond Hinnebusch, *Syria and Iran: Middle Powers in a Penetrated Regional System*, London and New York: Routledge, 1997.
53. "Bahrain and Iran trade accusations at UN Rights Forum," *Reuters,* 6 March 2014, http://www.reuters.com/article/2014/03/06/us-bahrain-iran-unrest-idUSBREA250V920140306. Accessed 14 August 2014.
54. Anoushiravan Ehteshami, "Iran's Regional Policies Since the End of the Cold War," in *Contemporary Iran: Economy, Society, Politics*, Ali Gheissari (ed.), Oxford and New York: Oxford University Press, 2009, p. 345.
55. Nelson Hernandez, "US Ambassador Criticizes Iran's Role in Iraq," *The Washington Post*, 20 February 2006.
56. Ehteshami, "Iran's Regional Policies since the End of the Cold War," pp. 360-61.
57. "IRGC Commander: Iranian Regime helps Maliki using Methods Supporting Assad in Syria," *Iran News Update*, 30 June 2014. http://irannewsupdate.com/news/terrorism/1323-irgc-commander-iranian-regime-helps-maliki-using-methods-supporting-assad-in-syria.html. Accessed on 5 July 2014.
58. "Iran to continue support for Iraq against Terrorist groups," *Fars News Agency*, 14 August 2014, http://english.farsnews.com/newstext.aspx?nn=13930523000704. Accessed 14 August 2014.
59. For a succinct analysis of Iran's policy towards the new Iraq, *see* Mohsen M. Milani, "Iran's Persian Gulf Policy in the Post-Saddam Era," in *Contemporary Iran*, Gheissari (ed.), p. 359-63. *See also*, Kayhan Barzegar, "Iran's Foreign Policy Strategy after Saddam," *The Washington Quarterly*, 33, No. 1, January 2010: 173-89.

6

The Iranian Nuclear Issue

Contending Narratives, Emerging Dynamics and the Road Ahead

Sujata Ashwarya Cheema

Introduction

The controversy over the Iranian nuclear programme stems from proliferation concerns of the international community. The United States and its allies believe that Iran kept several aspects of its nuclear programme, particularly the uranium enrichment programme, 'concealed' for several years, indicative of an intention to produce fissile material for nuclear bomb. In addition, Iran also wants to control the entire fuel cycle, i.e. the process by which uranium ore is mined, processed, enriched, used, and reprocessed and disposed, which the western powers aver, demonstrates Iran's firm determination to obtain nuclear weapons. Reprocessing of irradiated uranium fuel also yields fissionable plutonium that can be extracted for producing nuclear weapons or can also be recycled back into mixed oxide fuel for thermal reactors. The view that Iran has been concealing its intention to develop a military nuclear programme has dictated international politics on the Iranian nuclear issue for more than a decade now. Iran contends that its nuclear programme is entirely peaceful and for civilian purposes, including production of electric power and medical isotopes.

At the core of the Iranian nuclear imbroglio is uranium enrichment, a technological process that can be used to produce fuel for nuclear reactors or fissionable material for nuclear weapons.

Nuclear reactors (research and power) use a form of uranium called uranium 235 or U235, a variant not found readily in nature. Naturally occurring uranium is dominated by another variant known as U238. The process of increasing the proportion of U235 in a natural mixture is called enrichment, which is commonly done in centrifuges. Nuclear reactors use uranium enriched up to 20 per cent but enrichment in the same centrifuges can be done up to 90 per cent, when the 'fuel' (Highly Enriched Uranium, HEU) becomes suitable to constitute the core of nuclear weapon. Under the universal Nuclear Non-Proliferation Treaty (NPT), only five countries have the right to enrich uranium for their military applications; the rest of the signatories *can* enrich uranium solely in a civilian nuclear programme. To implement this regime, the International Atomic Energy Agency (IAEA) closely monitors civilian nuclear complexes.

In order to restore international confidence in its nuclear programme, Iran agreed to suspend uranium enrichment for two years in 2003 and negotiate with the western powers to resolve all outstanding issues and controversies related to its nuclear programme. In 2005, Iran proposed an enhanced safeguards regime against the diversion of nuclear material for military purposes and full transparency with regard to verification procedures of the IAEA. A deal could not be reached because the US refused to accept that Iran had the right to enrich uranium on its own soil—and the European negotiators (Britain, France and Germany, EU3) complied.

Although Iran is in substantive compliance of the NPT, and the IAEA has detected no diversion of nuclear material for weapon-related activities, the United States and its allies have declared Iran's nuclear programme perfidious.[1] The powers assert that Iran has forfeited its right under the NPT to enrich uranium by running a 'clandestine' nuclear enrichment programme that came to light in 2002, in addition to 'evidences' of having conducted weaponization studies in the past. Therefore, Iran cannot be trusted with a nuclear process that brings it close to making nuclear weapons. This is the crux of the Iranian nuclear issue.

However, since 2007 at least, there is a remarkable consensus—almost paradoxical—on the basic question of the entire Iranian nuclear imbroglio: that Iran is not making a bomb. US intelligence first came to this conclusion in its November 2007 National Intelligence Estimate

(NIE) as: "We judge with high confidence that in fall 2003, Tehran halted its nuclear weapons programme. …We assess with moderate confidence Tehran has not restarted its nuclear weapons programme as of mid-2007."[2] James Clapper, director of US National Intelligence, on 18 April 2013, testified before the Senate Armed Services Committee that this remains the assessment of US intelligence till date: "Iran has the scientific, technical, and industrial capacity to eventually produce nuclear weapons. This makes the central issue its political will to do so."[3] In the same year US Defence Secretary Leon Panetta affirmed Clapper's assessment, saying, "What I've said [in the past], and I will say today, is that the intelligence we have is they have not made the decision to proceed with the development of a nuclear weapon. They're developing and enriching uranium. They continue to do that."[4] Even the Israeli Chief of Staff, General Benny Gantz, concurred with the American officials, saying, "I do not believe Iran will decide to develop nuclear weapons."[5]

However, the West's Iran policy is trapped in mistrust since 2003, when Mohamed ElBaradei, the erstwhile Director General of IAEA, reported that Iran had on many occasions failed to "facilitate the implementation of safeguards, through concealment,"[6] of several aspects of its nuclear programme. That mistrust has fuelled rhetoric demanding military attack against Iran's nuclear facilities and even regime change in the country from sections in the US Congress, Israel, and Saudi Arabia, and various political lobbies in these countries, who thrive on perpetuating hostility and belligerence towards Iran. They also have championed punitive sanctions against Iran's energy sector, the economic lifeline of the Islamic Republic. In the midst of pervasive reluctance to treat Iran as trustworthy, the western powers want to place physical limitations on the capacity and scope of Iran's nuclear activities, in combination with intrusive monitoring of its nuclear sites along the fuel cycle, so as to delay any possible 'breakout period', the time required to produce enough HEU for a nuclear weapon, should a country decide to build one.

A snapshot of that belief was evident in the Geneva Agreement of November 2013 signed between Iran and the P5+1 (the five permanent members of the Security Council plus Germany, the negotiating team since 2005). Also known as the Joint Plan of Action (JPA) or the interim agreement, it consisted of short-term freezing of key parts of the Iranian nuclear programme in exchange for sanctions relief, as both sides work towards a long-term agreement in a time-bound manner. Under the terms on the deal, Iran agreed to the following: stop enriching uranium beyond five per cent, and 'neutralize' its stockpile of uranium enriched beyond this point, i.e. the country would cast the stockpile of uranium enriched to 20 per cent for the production of medical isotopes in a form that precludes their potential for further enrichment; leave a large part of Natanz and Fordow uranium enrichment capability inoperable; give greater access to the IAEA inspectors at Natanz and Fordow nuclear enrichment sites, including access to uranium mines and centrifuge production facilities; and undertake not to produce, test, or transfer fuel to the heavy water reactor in Arak plant which was believed to have capability of producing plutonium.[7]

While Iran believes the interim agreement met one of its fundamental demands of indigenous uranium enrichment granted as a 'right' by the NPT, western powers contend that Iran and, indeed, any other signatory to the treaty have no such right. Iranian officials frequently argue that under Article IV (1) of the NPT, the signatories have the right to build technologies for nuclear power, including the right to control the fuel cycle.[8] It says, "Nothing in this Treaty shall be interpreted as affecting the inalienable right of all the Parties to the Treaty to develop research, production and use of nuclear energy for peaceful purposes without discrimination and in conformity with Articles I and II of this Treaty."[9] The western negotiators maintain that neither the treaty nor its 2000 review refer specifically to a right to enrich uranium. US denied any such right had been conceded in the interim deal; while UK Foreign Secretary William Hague, one of the negotiating members, said the text of the document says nothing outright on a 'right to enrich'.[10]

Iran's Nuclear Programme: An Overview

Iran's nuclear pursuit started as early as 1957, when the Shah of Iran signed a civilian nuclear cooperation agreement with the United States under the Atoms for Peace programme that provided for supply of civilian nuclear technology including technical assistance and fissile material to countries with less advanced research. Subsequently, the

Shah constituted the Atomic Energy Organization of Iran (AEOI). The first significant nuclear facility, the Tehran Nuclear Research Centre (TNRC), was established in 1967 and was equipped with a US-supplied, 5-megawatt nuclear research reactor. Iran became a signatory to the NPT in 1968, which expedited its nuclear cooperation with western countries. The Arab-Israeli War of 1973, and the subsequent huge increase in oil prices, provided Reza Shah with substantial resources to embark on a full-fledged nuclear programme.

With an atomic energy agency and NPT in place, Iran announced a grandiose plan of setting up 20 nuclear power reactors, a uranium enrichment facility, and a reprocessing plant for spent fuel. In the five years that followed, Iran concluded several contracts for the construction/establishment of nuclear plants, the supply of nuclear fuel and the training of personnel: with the United States in 1974 to buy eight reactors; Germany (1974) to build power reactors at Bushehr; and France (1977) to build two reactors at Darkhovin. In addition, the Nuclear Technology Centre at Isfahan was founded in the mid-1970s with French assistance in order to provide training to personnel for operating the Bushehr reactors. In 1976, Iran also purchased 10 per cent stake in Eurodif, a multinational uranium enrichment consortium based in France. In 1975, the Massachusetts Institute of Technology (MIT) signed a contract with the AEOI for providing training for the first cadre of Iranian nuclear engineers. Kraftwerk Union, a subsidiary of the Germany's Siemens, was awarded the contract to construct two 1,200-megawatt nuclear reactors in the port city of Bushehr.

In the immediate aftermath of the Islamic Revolution in January 1979, the Iranian nuclear programme came to a halt due to Ayatollah Khomeini's opposition to nuclear technology. Khomeini believed that nuclear weapons contradicted the Islamic tenets of peace and brotherhood and was, therefore, immoral. Further, the flight of several Iranian nuclear scientists after the fall of the Pahlavi regime and the withdrawal of support by western governments brought Iran's nuclear project to a standstill post-1979.[11] However, the eight-year devastating war with Iraq (1980-88) created new imperatives for Iran to revive its nuclear programme. Invasion by Iraq and the loss of a powerful ally, the United States, contributed to Iran's sense of political and military vulnerability.

Multiple bombings of the Bushehr reactor site, chemical attacks on its forces and missile strikes on its cities, and an overall drain on its resources shattered Iran's morale and produced intense feeling of insecurity. The international community failed to condemn Iraq and was notably indifferent towards Iran's vulnerabilities. This indifference and silence may have shaped the Iranian desire to acquire a deterrent nuclear capability and may also explain why the Khomeini government ultimately resumed its efforts to revive Iran's nuclear programme. In 1982, during the period of the war itself, the Iranian officials announced that they planned to build a reactor powered by indigenously made nuclear fuel. A new nuclear research centre was inaugurated at Isfahan in 1984.[12]

The Gulf War (1990-91) affirmed Iran's conviction that such a capability was a strategic necessity as "the threat of in-kind retaliation (or worse) deterred Iraq's use of chemical weapons in Desert Storm… the absence of such a retaliatory capability facilitated its decision to use chemical weapons against Iran."[13] However, in view of America's opposition to the Islamic regime, western governments refused to cooperate with Iran on nuclear matters. Unable to find a western partner, Iran turned to Russia and China for assistance. In 1990, Tehran signed nuclear cooperation agreements with Beijing and Moscow. Five years later, Russia agreed to a deal worth $800 million to complete the partially fabricated first reactor at Bushehr and build three additional reactors on the site.[14] China agreed to provide two reactors for the nuclear facility in Isfahan; it later cancelled the deal under US pressure.

In mid-2002, the National Council of Resistance of Iran (NCRI) or the Mujahidin-e Khalq (MEK)—an exiled Iranian opposition group bitterly opposed to the Islamic regime that was listed as terrorist organization by the US and Canada—unveiled the existence of two previously unknown and 'undeclared' nuclear facilities in Iran, a pilot uranium enrichment facility in Natanz and a heavy water production plant in Arak. The western countries and Israel immediately accused Iran of maintaining a clandestine nuclear weapons programme. Under increased international scrutiny and pressure, Iran signed the Additional Protocol to the NPT in 2003 that permitted aggressive IAEA inspections of its nuclear facilities. The IAEA inspectors, who conducted extensive inspections in January 2005, did not find much evidence of weaponization at Iran's nuclear sites. In February 2005, IAEA Director General ElBaradei pointed to the continued absence of 'smoking gun' to concretely assess Iran's programmatic goals without such evidence: "We at the IAEA lack concrete evidence. We've yet to see a smoking gun that would convict Tehran. I can make assumptions about intentions, but I cannot verify intentions, just facts."[15]

According to the 14 November 2013 IAEA report, in total Iran has about 10,000 IR-1 (first-generation) centrifuges operating at Natanz and Fordow enrichment plants. Iran has installed a total of 1,008 advanced centrifuges (IR-2m & IR-4) at Natanz. These centrifuges are not yet producing enriched uranium. Iran's stockpile of 20 per cent enriched uranium is at 196 kilograms, below the estimated 240-250 kilograms which, when further enriched to weapons grade, would be enough for one nuclear weapon. Tehran's decision to enrich uranium up to 20 per cent levels raised concerns about the production of weapon-grade material, because a stockpile of 20 per cent enriched uranium would cut by more than half the time needed to enrich to levels over 90 per cent—levels that are suitable for a bomb.[16] Tehran says it needs the material for production of medical isotopes and research.

Iran insists it needs to maintain an indigenous uranium enrichment capability to produce fuel for a network of nuclear power plants it plans to build, without having to rely on foreign suppliers, who have been unreliable. The Islamic Republic has had bitter experience with Eurodif, even though Tehran held an indirect share in the consortium. Iran cites this refusal as "proof of the unreliability of outside nuclear supplies and uses the Eurodif episode to argue its case for achieving energy independence by supplying all of the elements of the nuclear fuel cycle itself."[17] But some western officials draw attention to the fact that Iran does not have a short or medium term need for nuclear fuel, as it would take several years to build nuclear power plants of the scale envisaged by the country. Therefore, the underlying goal in enriching uranium is something else—the ability to yield fissile material for nuclear bombs at short notice, an allegation the Islamic Republic refutes. The Iranians consider the western hype about nuclear proliferation in their country and demand for limitation on uranium enrichment contrived, intended to deprive Iran the right of access to nuclear technology.

Iran's 'clandestine' Enrichment Programme?

The powers have levelled several charges against Iran's nuclear programme, one such being that Iran maintained a covert enrichment programme until the international community 'discovered' it in 2003. This section will examine that contention.

It is pertinent to recall here that the US and European countries had actively assisted the Shah of Iran in establishing a nuclear programme pre-1979, although Washington was always wary of Shah's penchant for nuclear weapons.[18] Iran and Israel in the late 1970s even discussed a plan to modify Israel's surface-to-surface Jericho missiles for use by Tehran—missiles that *could* be loaded with nuclear warheads.[19] The United States, however, not only refused to assist the Islamic Republic in the backdrop of the attack and seizure of the American Embassy in Tehran during 1979-80 but also actively thwarted the attempts by other countries from doing so. That 'informal' regime of non-cooperation with Iran adopted by the western countries on nuclear matters directly contravened Article IV (2) of the NPT, which enjoins "parties to the Treaty to facilitate, and have the right to participate in, the fullest possible exchange of equipment, materials and scientific and technological information for the peaceful uses of nuclear energy".[20] Up until now, there is no evidence, according to the IAEA reports, that nuclear assistance sought or acquired elsewhere was used for making weapons.

When Iran restarted the programme in the early 1980s, the IAEA was duly informed. In fact, the IAEA's assistance to Iran for uranium conversion under its Technical Assistance Programme was thwarted by the United States. Iran's plan to enrich uranium was openly discussed on national radio, as documented by *Iran Affairs*.[21] During a visit of the IAEA officials in November 1996, Iran informed the IAEA that it planned to build a uranium hexafluoride (UF6) conversion plant at the Nuclear Technology Centre in Isfahan. When China abandoned the UF6 project under pressure from the US, the Iranians informed the Agency that they would go ahead with the project nonetheless. Iran completed the project in 2000 using the blueprint and compensation provided by China and declared the facility to the IAEA. Therefore, Iran argues its nuclear programme, including uranium enrichment, was never 'secret' or 'clandestine' as portrayed by the western powers.

The US also thwarted the IAEA's attempt to assist Iran with restarting its nuclear programme in 1982. Marks Hibbs, currently a senior associate with the Nuclear Policy Programme at the Carnegie Endowment for International Peace, wrote the story about the United States' intervention thus:

Four years after the Islamic revolution, and two years after Iran's new leaders dusted off the nuclear programme of the deposed Reza Shah Pahlavi, IAEA officials were keen to assist Iran in reactivating a research programme to learn how to process U3O8 into UO2 pellets and then set up a pilot plant to produce UF6.[22] When in 1983 the recommendations of an IAEA mission to Iran were passed on to the IAEA's technical cooperation programme, the US Government then 'directly intervened' to discourage the IAEA from assisting Iran in production of UO2 and UF6. "We stopped that in its tracks," said a former US official.[23]

Therefore, both the IAEA and the US were aware of Iran's plan to develop fuel fabrication and uranium enrichment technology as far back as 1983. There was no attempt at concealment or deception. What more, the United States prevented the Agency from fulfilling its obligations under Article III.A.1 of the IAEA Statute, which specifies that one of the many functions of the IAEA is "to act as an intermediary for the purposes of securing the performance of services or the supplying of materials, equipment, or facilities by one member of the Agency for another."[24] That is, the IAEA is enjoined to act as an intermediary in the fulfilment of Article IV (2) of the NPT. David Morrison and Peter Oborne argue, "Had Iran been permitted to fulfil its desire for a nuclear programme by openly acquiring the necessary technology and material from abroad, with IAEA acting as intermediary, the world would have been much more aware of Iran's developing nuclear programme."[25]

The United States also intervened again to prevent Argentina's Invap from selling UO2 conversion technology to Iran in 1997. It is evident that the US was aware of Iran's intention to establish fuel enrichment capacities. The IAEA was also aware of several years of uranium mining in Iran, and the IAEA official Melissa Fleming confirmed that the Agency had inspected Iran's uranium mines in 1992, a decade before the Iran's enrichment programme was allegedly discovered.[26]

Were the nuclear facilities deliberately hidden? It is oft repeated by the security establishments and political elites in the United States, Europe, and Israel, reinforced by nearly a decade of shrill mainstream media coverage that the MEK 'revealed' Iran's secret nuclear facilities to the world, as Iran tried hard to hide them from the IAEA. But under Iran's safeguards agreement with the IAEA operational at that time (November 2002, when the alleged exposure of the plot occurred), required the Islamic Republic to notify the IAEA of any new nuclear facility and to provide information on the design no later than 180 days prior to the introduction of nuclear material into the facility. ElBaradei confirmed this in his June 2003 report to the IAEA Board of Governors in June 2003:

> The Subsidiary Arrangements General Part in force with Iran from 1976 to 26 February 2003 included what was, until 1992, standard text which called for provision to the Agency of design information on a new facility no later than 180 days before the introduction of nuclear material into the facility, and the provision of information on a new LOF [locations outside of facilities where nuclear material is customarily used] together with the report relating to the receipt of nuclear material at the LOF [location outside facilities].[27]

There was no requirement at all to declare the heavy water generation plant at Arak, since as the same report says "heavy water production facilities are not nuclear facilities under comprehensive NPT safeguards agreements, and are thus not required to be declared to the Agency."[28]

The argument that Iran is seeking to make uranium fuel without having a functioning nuclear power station to burn it, and therefore, the country is seeking enrichment technology for military rather than civilian purposes, is spurious, say Morrison and Oborne.[29] They aver that to seek enrichment capability before setting up power stations is a logical thing to do, because one needs to have enough fuel to run them not just for a few years, but also for their expected lifespan of 40 or 50 years. Since it was clear from the early 1980s that US and its allies were going to deny Iran access to assistance for its nuclear programme, Iran had no option but to develop an indigenous enrichment programme, if it was going to embark on a nuclear power programme and that's exactly what it did.[30]

Evidence of Weaponization Studies before 2002?

The narrative that Iran has had a nuclear weapon programme and is determined to obtain nuclear weapons is tethered to a dubious intelligence dossier imposed on the IAEA and on world opinion.[31] This dossier consists of files apparently compiled from a laptop, which the United States says was smuggled from Iran by a source and given to its intelligence in 2004. It apparently contains evidence that Iran conducted studies on weaponization. In the absence of corroboration from actual physical samples of alleged studies, the former head of the IAEA, ElBaradei, was understandably sceptical. In an interview with *The Hindu* on 1 October 2009, he declared, "The IAEA is not making any judgment at all whether Iran even had weaponization studies before because there is a major question of authenticity of the documents."[32]

Gareth Porter's investigation into the matter illustrates that the source was a former member of the MEK. The dossier was provided to the United States' intelligence agencies by Israel in an effort to pressure the US administration into considering military action against Iran,[33] a demonstration of political-strategic rivalry rather than a concern for state security, as it has been regularly portrayed by Israel in global forums.[34] Israel has held on to the narrative since the early 1990s that Iran's 'covert' nuclear weapons programme presents a threat to its existence. Several Israeli leaders for two decades have spoken of the imminent existential threat from Iran's purported pursuit of nuclear weapons. That is indeed ironical as Israel has about 80 nuclear warheads with the ability to produce 115 to 190 more[35] and possesses the means to deliver them across the region, including Iran.

A CRS report (2013) on US-Iran relations summarizes the Israeli position on Iran's nuclear programme thus:

> For several years now, Israeli leaders have described Iran and its reported pursuit of a nuclear weapons capability as an imminent threat to Israeli security. Israeli officials have claimed that their window of opportunity to act on their own to delay, halt, or reverse Iranian progress toward a nuclear weapons capability is closing. Consequently, they have sought increasingly punitive international measures against Iran's nuclear programme. Within this context, Israeli leaders have publicly hinted that absent a clear resolution of

> Iran's nuclear activity to their satisfaction, they may order the Israeli military to strike Iranian nuclear facilities.[36]

The IAEA report of September 2008 dealt with these so-called 'laptop files' in paragraphs 14-21. It reported that the Agency held a series of meetings with Iranian officials in April and May 2008 to seek additional clarifications relevant to the nature of Iran's nuclear programme, including the 'alleged studies' into nuclear weaponization. As a result, Iran provided several written replies, including a 117-page presentation, which confirmed the partial veracity of some of the allegations, but which also asserted that the allegations in the whole were based on 'forged' documents and 'fabricated' data. Iranian officials reiterated that although they had been shown electronic versions of the documentation, they had not received copies of the documentation to enable it to prove that they were fabricated and forged.

Basically, these paragraphs in the report say that the IAEA wants Iran to address the allegations of weaponisation in greater detail, even as the Agency regrets not able to provide Iran with copies of the documentation concerning the alleged studies. In the report, the Agency urges Iran to provide it with "substantive information to support its statements and provide access to relevant documentation and individuals" regarding the alleged studies as "a matter of transparency,"[37] which, as Cyrus Safdari argues, "means they are outside of what Iran is legally required to do."[38] The report went on to state that the IAEA itself has found no information "on the actual design or manufacture by Iran of nuclear material components of a nuclear weapon or of certain other key components, such as initiators, or on related nuclear physics studies. Nor has the Agency detected the actual use of nuclear material in connection with the alleged studies.[39]

In short, the IAEA in 2008 found no evidence of a nuclear weapons programme after four years of rigorous inspection and constant monitoring. Earlier in August 2007, in the "Modalities Agreement" between Iran and the IAEA, the former had agreed to resolve the "alleged studies" claims of weaponisation as a sign of good will, "upon receiving all related documents,"[40] which it did not receive from the "intelligence crowd" in order to "protect their sources and methods."[41] ElBaradei in his book wonders at the absurdity of hiding the document from Iran and then being goaded to take on Iran over violation of safeguards agreement: "How can I accuse a person, I asked, without revealing the accusations against him?"[42]

Back then ElBaradei stood accused by sections of the media of "censoring" a "secret IAEA summary" that incriminated Iran to its pursuit of nuclear weapons. The "intelligence summary" as the Associated Press called it "referred to an internal analysis, a rolling text compiled by the Agency's department of Safeguards that included all the various pieces of information that had come in from different intelligence organizations, most of which IAEA inspectors had been unable to verify or authenticate."[43] ElBaradei was naturally reticent to publish the summary, as the main problem was the inability of the IAEA officials to corroborate these various pieces of allegations. The analysis was largely based on paperwork; there were no physical evidence to examine, measure, or inspect.[44] The former chief of the IAEA put the predicament about the 'summary' succinctly in the context of the 'laptop allegations': "We were equipped to verify operations involving the use of nuclear material, where we could establish the facts through measurements and environmental sampling. We did not have the tool or expertise, however, to verify the authenticity of documents."[45]

ElBaradei went on record in 2009 asserting, "We have not seen diversion of nuclear material (from declared civilian uses), and we have not seen components of nuclear weapons. We do not have any information to that effect."[46] Yet the summary was annexed as 'credible' information in the November 2011 report of the IAEA, under its current head, Yukiya Amano, under the heading, "Possible Military Dimensions to Iran's Nuclear Programme."[47] It is pertinent to take note that the annex still spoke of a 'possibility'; in effect it remained unsubstantiated allegations. Under ElBaradei the IAEA had issued a press release in 2009 stating that "it has no concrete proof that there is or has been a nuclear weapon programme in Iran."[48]

The IAEA's change of course under Amano must be seen in the background of his ascension to the post of the IAEA chief. Flynt Leverett and Hillary Mann Leverett write, "Amano, unfortunately, [did] not bring the same kind of intellectual and political integrity to his job as his predecessor. The United States, Israel, and other western governments had to work hard to get the IAEA's Board of Governors to elect Amano in 2009, by the narrowest possible margin... Washington and its allies got what they wanted."[49] In a cable from the US mission in Vienna—published by WikiLeaks—titled "IAEA Leadership Team Transition and U.S. influence," described the change of guard in the IAEA as a "once-a-decade opportunity."

A later cable titled "IAEA: Amano Ready For Prime Time," the US charge d'affaires, Geoffrey Pyatt wrote, "Amano reminded [US] Ambassador on several occasions that he would need to make concessions" to the developing countries "but that he was solidly in the US court on every key strategic decision," including "the handling of Iran's alleged nuclear weapons programme."[50] Another analyst maintains, "The IAEA's willingness to accept unverified US intelligence is particularly strange given recent history. In 2002, British and American intelligence agencies alleged that Iraq had purchased uranium from Niger. Former US President, George W. Bush used this as a justification for the war in his 2003 'State of the Union' address. It was later found that these allegations were based on crude forgeries."[51] To have passed allegations as facts with its authoritative imprimatur, Amano-led IAEA not only accused Iran wrongly, but also raised concerns about its own credibility as a non-partisan body.[52]

The Israeli Narrative

Israel has maintained since the early 1990s that Tehran's 'covert nuclear weapons programme' presents an existential threat to the Jewish state. Israel believes that a negotiated settlement of the nuclear dispute alone cannot prevent Iran from acquiring nuclear weapon capability; it must be backed by a 'credible' military threat targeting Iran's nuclear facilities. A patent aspect of Israel's perception of Iran's nuclear programme is the fact that the political leaders of the Jewish state have been periodically claiming an imminent Iranian bomb since the 1990s.

As far back in October 1992, Israel's then-Foreign Minister Shimon Peres warned that Iran would be armed with a nuclear bomb by 1999.[53] Twenty years later, Netanyahu warned the United Nations on 27 September 2012 that Iran's progress toward a nuclear bomb would be irreversible by mid-2013.[54] That US State Department officials seriously doubt the accuracy and sincerity of Israeli predictions about when Iran will obtain a nuclear weapon is evident from an item in the Wikileaks cables. A senior American official, it was revealed, wrote to the State Department and the Pentagon, in response to an Israeli general's November 2009 prediction that it would take Iran one year to obtain a nuclear weapon and two and a half years to build an arsenal of three weapons: "It is unclear if the Israelis firmly believe this or are using worst-case estimates to raise greater urgency from the United States."[55]

Although the Bush administration (2001-2008) rebuffed Israel's request for bunker buster bombs (that could be used for targeting Iran's nuclear sites) in 2005,[56] the 'war against Iran' rhetoric gained traction during that period, driven by the alliance of Israel, American Israel Public Affairs Committee (AIPAC), the neoconservatives, and a few Christian Zionists. It was the same alliance that had pushed President Bush to authorize America's war in Iraq to disastrous consequences. The alliance or the Israel lobby, influential in Washington's beltway, has been trying to provoke a war against Iran ever since. As Sahimi writes, "Their efforts have been multi-pronged, ranging from spreading exaggerations, half truths, and even outright lies about Iran's nuclear programme, to planting anti-Iran articles in the mainstream media, and pressuring the Congress to pass tough resolutions for sanctions against Iran."[57]

Since US President Barack Obama declared his new engagement policy with Iran 2009, Israel has feared erosion of its strategic value in America's strategic perception and, therefore, intensified its 'war on Iran' rhetoric. Israel's Prime Minister Benjamin Netanyahu has sought to ratchet up pressure by proffering predictions on when Iran could cross a critical threshold in its capacity to build a weapon, which have been misleading every single time. Much to the chagrin of Netanyahu and his right-wing coalition partners, Obama has followed a course of slow diplomacy, waiting out a possible deal with Iran. However, by issuing periodic threats of military strikes against Iran, Israel has played a key role in driving the harsh European and economic sanctions against Iran's oil and financial sectors.

Israel's perception of Iranian nuclear programme is underscored by security concerns and question of survival of the state in a hostile regional environment. Israel's lack of strategic-territorial depth aggravates this sense of vulnerability. The country has a small population concentrated in a few prominent cities. An overwhelming military attack by conventional or non-conventional weapons could put the survival of the state in danger. Israel, additionally, relies on a reservist-based military, which magnifies civilian and military losses on its small population. These potential drawbacks in the country's security environment shaped the strategic thinking of Israel's first leaders. They came to believe that a nuclear weapons capability would counteract the advantages of Israel's adversaries and bridge the geostrategic gap in their state's national security.

Along with assigning centrality to nuclear weapons in the security strategy of the state, Israeli leaders also elaborated a military doctrine whose critical parameters are: First, Israel's conventional military power should be qualitatively superior to that of its adversaries (individually or collectively). In other words, a credible deterrent posture is imperative to state's security and survival. Second, Israel should be able to carry out pre-emptive strikes against such adversaries to ward off any perceived threat to its survival. Third, Israel's adversaries must be prevented from acquiring a nuclear option.[58] The latter two parameters of this military doctrine were displayed in Israel's pre-emptive air strike against Iraq's breeder reactor in Osiraq in the early 1980s and air strike against Syrian nuclear facility in 2007.

Former Israeli defence minister Shaul Mofaz declared in 2003, "a nuclear Iran was intolerable" because it would "erode Israel's strategic edge."[59] Alan Roth, Associate Director of National Security Studies at the Johns Hopkins University's Krieger School of Arts and Sciences, explains,

> Israel fears that Iran's nuclear ambitions could undermine its qualitative superiority of arms and its consistent ability to inflict disproportionate casualties on adversaries—the cornerstones of Israel's defence strategy. Although some idealists dream of reconciliation in the Middle East based on a genuine and mutual recognition of all parties' legitimate rights, most Israelis believe the key to enduring peace in the Middle East is convincing Israel's adversaries that ejecting Israel through force is an impossible task not worth pursuing.
>
> Essential to inducing that sense of despair is Israel's ability to continuously trounce its enemies on the battlefield and suffer far fewer losses than it inflicts. The Iranian nuclear programme threatens Israel's ability to do this in two ways. First, an Iranian nuclear

> capability would likely force Israel to restrain itself due to fears that Iran's nuclear weapons could provide an implied security guarantee to other anti-Zionist forces—the sort of guarantee that would prevent Israel from causing the massive losses it has in the past, while giving anti-Israel forces the confidence to keep up the fight.[60]

The option of an Israeli military strike on Iranian nuclear facilities has been gaining traction with the inauguration of Netanyahu's premiership in 2009, the goal of such an act being to prevent Iran from reaching the technological threshold of fabricating a bomb. However, the threat of military action, many analysts believe (and so does Iran), is part of the psychological war intended to rattle the Iranian regime and sow divisions within its leadership.[61]

Nonetheless, there is an agreement at least on three aspects of Tehran's nuclear programme in Washington, Brussels and Tel Aviv: Iran does not have a nuclear weapon (bomb), has not decided to build one (an order to produce a weapon has not been handed down from the top level of the leadership), and is not making significant progress towards having a deliverable nuclear warhead.[62] This was also the crux of the 2007 National Intelligence Estimate of the US spy agencies. Some key Washington allies, however, never wholly accepted the report. The Europeans believed while the centrally directed weapons programme may have stopped in 2003, Iran could be covertly pursuing the programme in bits and parts, some of them in military or scientific installations, some in obscure academic institutions.[63] Israel also pointed out that Iran did have a programme until 2003 and the global community could never be sure that it will not be resumed in the future.

Under pressure from both European allies and Israel, American intelligence agencies took a second look at the 2007 estimate. Eventually, at the very end of 2010, an updated version was circulated within the government. Although no public extract of this document was released, the 2010 Estimate is understood to have largely endorsed the principal assessments of the 2007 report.[64] While the European allies of the United States largely accepted the revised assessment, Israel has remained circumspect. The intelligence findings of the US spy agencies have honed Washington's belief that Iran does not have a running nuclear programme since 2003 and that after the exposure of the Fordow enrichment site in 2009, it has no secret nuclear installations either. The US officials are also certain that 'eyes in the sky', i.e. intelligence satellites and sensors (both European and American) would detect any move by the Iranians to assemble a nuclear device. After all, the Fordow underground enrichment site was disclosed by the US intelligence service. This perception of Iran's nuclear issue underscores Obama's initiative to engage in negotiations with the Iranians.

Alarmed by the prospects of American-Iranian rapprochement, Israel has renewed its threat to take unilateral military action against Iran's nuclear programme. "Israel's strategy is to use the Iranian nuclear issue to drag the US into a devastating war with Iran if possible," says Mousavian.[65] Israel and the US have already taken on Iran's nuclear programme through cyber attacks. Iran's enrichment effort was set back by almost eighteen months by the Stuxnet computer virus—developed and deployed by both the US and Israel—which found its way into Iran's Natanz uranium enrichment facility, destroying hundreds of centrifuges in early 2010. Obama is said to have authorized the Stuxnet cyber attack to have latitude on diplomacy and sanctions, and prevent Israel from carrying out a conventional military attack on Iran, prompting a conflict that could spread throughout the region.[66]

The Arab Narrative: Saudi Arabia and the Other Gulf Countries

The Arab countries of the Persian Gulf are convinced that Iran is pursuing a nuclear weapons programme, or, at least, that is their official position. William Broad and David Sanger of *The New York Times* reported in 2007 that the neighbouring Gulf countries were extremely hostile to Iran's nuclear programme, which they believed had a military dimension: "Many diplomats and analysts say that the Sunni Arab governments are so anxious about Iran's nuclear progress that they would even, grudgingly, support a United States military strike against Iran."[67]

In July 2010, the Ambassador of the United Arab Emirates (UAE) to the United States, Yousef al-Otaiba, publicly endorsed the use of the military option for countering Iran's nuclear programme, if sanctions fail to stop the country's quest for nuclear weapons. "We cannot live with a nuclear Iran. I am willing to absorb what takes place at the expense of the security of the UAE," al-Otaiba is reported to have said in response to a question after a public interview session with the *Atlantic* magazine at the Aspen Ideas Festival in Colorado. Asked if he wanted the US to stop the Iranian nuclear programme by force, al-Otaiba remarked, "Absolutely…I think we are at risk of an Iranian nuclear programme far more than you are at risk."[68] "Otaiba's remarks may or may not be a gaffe but they certainly reflect official thinking in Abu Dhabi," says Christopher Davidson, a Gulf expert at Durham University. "They want to see more American boots on the ground, and they don't want to live in the shadow of a nuclear Iran."[69] The UAE's ambassador underlined the wider nervousness in the Gulf about Iran's nuclear programme.

Expectedly, the support for a military elimination of Iran's nuclear programme was echoed at the highest level of decision-making in the Persian Gulf countries, such as Saudi Arabia and Bahrain, and was evident in no uncertain terms by the diplomatic cable released by the Wikileaks in 2010. In one cable King Abdullah of Saudi Arabia repeatedly asks America to attack Iran to stop its nuclear programme so as to "cut off the head of the snake."[70] In another cable King Hamad bin Isa al-Khalifa of Bahrain argued forcefully for the termination of the Iranian nuclear programme, even by military means. "That programme must be stopped…. The danger of letting it go on is greater than the danger of stopping it." The leaked cable also revealed that in November 2009, US ambassador to Bahrain reported that King al-Khalifa had "argued forcefully for taking action to terminate [Iran's] nuclear programme, by whatever means necessary."[71]

The Saudi officials are the most worried of the entire lot. They are extremely circumspect about the growing political influence of Iran in the region—Iraq, Bahrain, Yemen and Syria—and what that would mean for their own regime's survival. Iran's nuclear programme is viewed within Saudi Arabia as physical proof of the growing Shia threat in the region, which heightens fears of "unbridled Iranian support for an active 'Shia Crescent' from the Levant through the Eastern Province of Saudi Arabia to Bahrain."[72] Thus, the Iranian nuclear issue is a particularly important point of tension between Saudi Arabia and Iran. King Abdullah of Saudi Arabia warned Dennis Ross, visiting US special envoy to the Middle East, in 2009 that if

Iran crossed the threshold, "we will get nuclear weapons."[73] A similar sentiment was echoed by Prince Turki al-Faisal, a senior Saudi diplomat and former head of Saudi Arabia's General Intelligence Directorate, in a meeting with NATO officials at Royal Air Force Molesworth, UK, declared, "If Iran develops a nuclear weapon, that will be unacceptable to us and we will have to follow suit."[74]

Saudi Arabia's fear is not so much that Iran would use nuclear weapons for an actual physical attack but that such weapons would embolden Tehran to "pursue its own, more hegemonic foreign policy in the region,"[75] so as to change the balance of power in the Middle East to the disadvantage of Riyadh. Abdulaziz Sager, head of the Geneva-based Gulf Research Centre, argues that nuclear weapons would turn Iran into

> A hegemonic power over the [Persian Gulf] states of the region, through its control of Iraq, its holding fast to the continued occupation of the UAE's [United Arab Emirates] islands, and its intervention in the domestic affairs of countries in the region through the agitated Shiite groups in these countries, which could push the GCC [Gulf Cooperation Council], namely Saudi Arabia, to seek, in turn, the acquisition of a nuclear weapon to confront Iran.[76]

Lewis Dunn aptly summarized the concerns of Gulf countries including Saudi Arabia in a paper for the US Naval Postgraduate School (2009), "Among virtually all of Iran's neighbours, there is considerable concern that once in possession of nuclear weapons, the Iranian leadership could intensify its interference in those neighbours' domestic politics, step up support for extremist groups, and use the shadow of nuclear weapons to shape regional relations in a manner more favourable to it."[77]

Saudi Arabia views the "developments in Iran very negatively," says David Albright, the president of the Institute for Science and International Security and a former weapons inspector. "The Saudis are thinking through how do you create a deterrent through capability?" he adds.[78] A RAND analysis sums up Saudi fear thus, "The advent of nuclear-armed Iran would likely be perceived as an existential threat to Riyadh, possibly pushing Saudi Arabia to acquire its own countervailing deterrent." Fear of a 'Saudi bomb' has resurrected in the wake of Riyadh's differences with Washington over

Iran and Syria. The US security umbrella has to date provided the Saudis with unprecedented level of protection, which they believe may be weakening over several strategic differences over events in the region. A major deterioration in US-Saudi relations leading to withdrawal of Washington's security guarantees could compel Riyadh to take the nuclear weapons option more seriously. In such a scenario, Saudi policymakers believe, a nuclear-weapons-capable Iran would be a grave strategic threat to the kingdom as well as the region. It would undermine Saudi regional influence, and threaten the domestic stability of the Gulf countries through incitement of their Shia population.

In November 2006, the IAEA named six Arab countries—Algeria, Egypt, Morocco, Saudi Arabia, Tunisia, and the UAE—as having shown interest in development of civilian nuclear technology. In the backdrop of the controversy over Iran's nuclear programme, many independent experts believe that the surge in interest vis-à-vis nuclear energy in the Middle East represents a reaction by the countries to Iran's nuclear programme.[79] Others suggest the drive for civil nuclear power in the region should be understood as a security initiative. It has created the perception that having nuclear energy facilities, especially the fuel cycle facilities, gives the country a sense of power and strength. In the light of concerns that the US security guarantees for its Middle Eastern allies might not remain forever, there is a sudden rush for developing nuclear programmes in the region. "It's a long term hedging option," says Hibbs, "particularly in light of concerns that the US security guarantees will become weaker."[80] Saudi officials' persistent complain that the US top priority in the region under President Obama is to resolve the long-standing nuclear dispute with Iran, explains the fear of the Persian Gulf countries of diminishing commitment of the United States parallel with the rise of Iran, which has been the main beneficiary of the America's Iraq war.[81]

The Past as Prologue and the Emerging Dynamics

A deal on the Iranian nuclear issue of the kind agreed to in the JPA could have been reached almost ten years ago. In exchange for limited uranium enrichment right, Iran was prepared to concede limitations and safeguard measures, over and above those required under the

NPT way back in 2005. Javad Zarif, then Iran's ambassador to the UN, submitted a comprehensive proposal to the EU3 to resolve the nuclear issue. It included a number of unprecedented measures that would have virtually eliminated the possibility of Iran producing highly enriched uranium or plutonium, the fissile material for nuclear bomb. Specifically, it contained: a) immediate conversion of all enriched uranium to fuel rods; and b) no reprocessing of spent fuel, thereby preventing the production of plutonium. The proposal also provided for enhanced monitoring and legislative and regulatory measures to limit the scope of the nuclear programme, including, continued implementation and ratification of the Additional Protocol and continuous on-site presence of IAEA inspectors at the uranium conversion and enrichment facilities. The Iranians also proposed ceiling of enrichment at Light Enriched Uranium (LEU) level (three per cent enrichment suitable for reactors) and limitation on the extent of the programme, i.e. the volume of uranium production in the future by limiting the number of Iranian centrifuges at 3,000.[82]

The European negotiators ignored this offer, because the Bush administration was against having enrichment centrifuges running on Iranian soil. At that time Iran had just 164 centrifuges compared to 19,000 it has now.[83] This occurred at a time when Iran's cooperation with the IAEA remained robust and both parties were making wholesome progress toward resolving outstanding issues. As ElBaradei writes, "At the March 2005 Board meeting, Iran's nuclear programme was not on the agenda for the first time in almost two years."[84] Talking about Iran's right to enrichment, the present US Secretary of State, John Kerry, while serving as chairman of the Senate Foreign Relations Committee four years ago, held in June 2009, "They [Iranians] have a right to peaceful nuclear power and to enrichment in that purpose." He added that the Bush administration's no enrichment argument was "bombastic diplomacy" and "hardened the lines."[85] That's exactly what happened in subsequent years.

A new phase in the Iranian nuclear crisis began, with the EU3's refusal to respond to Iran's proposal. A European counter-proposal offered "few of the benefits... [and] simply made vague statements about giving access to the foreign nuclear technology markets," in return for "a ban on nuclear fuel activities,"[86] i.e. uranium conversion and enrichment. It was rejected by the new hard line government in Iran, which authorized cessation of two-year self-imposed moratorium on uranium enrichment, paving way for censure of Iran for 'non-compliance' and imposition of economic sanctions by the Security Council.

Did Sanctions Force Iran's Hand?

Many argue that sanctions effectively squeezed Iran to a conciliatory stand at the negotiating table, resulting in the interim agreement. For instance, Tom Donilon, former national security adviser to the Obama administration, traced a clear link between President Obama's decision to implement sanctions against Iran and the deal brokered with the Islamic Republic in November 2013: "You wouldn't have had a negotiation under way right now," Donilon said on ABC (American Broadcasting Corporation), adding that sanctions campaign spearheaded by the president of the United States "forced the choice" of election of Hassan Rouhani and softening of Iranian position on negotiations.[87] This belief/myth is the reason why lawmakers in the Congress want to impose more sanctions on Iran. "Current sanctions brought Iran to the negotiating table and a credible threat of future sanctions will require Iran to cooperate and act in good faith at the negotiating table," said Foreign Relations Committee Chairman Robert Menendez, while introducing a bipartisan legislation in the US Senate on 19 December 2013, that would authorize new economic sanctions on Iran, if it breaches the interim agreement to limit its nuclear programme or failed to strike a final accord on it.[88]

Quite the reverse, several reports suggest that sanctions are feeble instruments to ensure compliance by a 'recalcitrant' regime or government. Sometimes they even propel the regimes' detractors to rally in support for sake of national pride.[89] An International Crisis Group paper assesses the efficacy of sanctions on their own terms as following:

> Without doubt, they are crippling Iran's economy. But are they succeeding? By at least one important criterion (the intensity of Western concern over nuclear progress), plainly they are not...There, the one thing considered more perilous than suffering from sanctions is surrendering to them; persuaded the West is intent on toppling the regime, the leadership views economic steps as just one in a panoply of measures designed to destabilise it...rather than adjusting its nuclear

> policy to remove the sanctions, the regime [will] continue[s] to adjust its economic policy in order to adapt to them.[90]

Hence, sanctions do not appear to have slowed down Iran's nuclear technology development, but has punished the common people by depriving them of many basic provisions. If sanctions forced Iran's hand, it is worth recalling that in 2003 the Islamic Republic offered a grand bargain proposal to the Bush administration addressing all major areas of conflict between the two countries. Among many other things pertaining to the region, the Iranians offered to open up their nuclear programme for transparency, in return for recognition and resumption of diplomatic relations.[91] Again, the 2005 offer discussed above, was another Iranian attempt to settle every contentious issue related to its nuclear programme, which the US rejected off-hand because Iran was a 'rogue state' and ranked first on the so-called 'axis of evil'. In September 2005 speech at the United Nations, even the much-reviled Iranian figure in the beltway, President Mahmoud Ahmadinejad, offered:

> As a further confidence building measure and in order to provide the greatest degree of transparency, the Islamic Republic of Iran is prepared to engage in serious partnership with private and public sectors of other countries in the implementation of uranium enrichment programme in Iran. This represents the most far-reaching step, outside all requirements of the NPT, being proposed by Iran as a further confidence building measure.[92]

The Iranian leaders reached out to the P5+1, with the obvious blessings of the Supreme Leader, Ayatollah Khamenei, the final voice on Iran's nuclear policy, even before US and EU sanctions started devastating the economy of the Islamic Republic. It was the United States and its allies that maintained an inflexible approach, leading to repeated breakdown of negotiations.

Did Threat to Use Force Compel Iran?

Up until the November 2013 nuclear agreement, the conventional wisdom was that the only way to elicit cooperation from Iran is to threaten it into submission, either by use of punitive sanction and/or by use of actual force, aimed at regime change. Both the neocons (in think-tanks, intelligence, and military establishments as well as leaders) and the bipartisan hawks in the Congress have spoken of more credible threats in addition to sanctions, meaning, to use military force in dealing with Iran. It is worth recalling that Obama's policy of engagement with Iran came in the background of the December 2007 National Intelligence Estimate on Iran. The NIE report undercut much of the foundation of neocons' and hawks' aggressive foreign policy on Iran. It did not portray Iran as a rogue, ideological state zealously trying to develop nuclear weapons, as they fiercely argued, but rather a rational political actor whose "decisions are guided by a cost-benefit approach rather than a rush to a weapon irrespective of political, economic and military costs."[93]

The inconsistencies of the Bush administration in dealing with Iran weighed heavily on the successor, which constituted combining the appeal of engagement, i.e. prospect of talks with the pressure of economic sanctions, dubbed the "dual-track" policy, a brainchild of former Secretary of State Condoleezza Rice and her deputy Nicholas Burns. "The problem with dual track policy with Iran was that it relied on a single track: economic pressure," writes Vali Nasr, a former State Department advisor from 2009 to 2011 and now the dean of John Hopkins' School of Advanced International Studies, which gave Bush "a punitive course of action short of war that could placate other stakeholders in the dispute, such as Saudi Arabia, the Emirates and Israel." While "Obama [too] assumed that the Iran problem could be managed without resort to military action," engagement became "a cover for a coercive campaign of sabotage, economic pressure, and cyber warfare,"[94] in the midst of rising domestic talk of war.

Under severe pressure from the neocons-bipartisan hawk's coalition, Obama led a worldwide effort to give teeth to economic sanctions started by his predecessor. The Obama administration "succumbed to exaggerated Israeli and Arab fears of Iran and exaggerated promises of Arab support for American action against Iran," in the same way that Bush had.[95] In a March 2012 interview with Jeffrey Goldberg of the *Atlantic*, the president affirmed specifically that all options were on the table and that the final option remained the "military component."[96] When US Vice President Joe Biden told AIPAC's annual conference in March 2013 that President Obama was not "bluffing about using force to thwart Iran's nuclear ambitions if all else fails,"[97] he was merely reiterating the president's military threat to Iran over the prior two years.

With the election of moderate Rouhani as the President of Iran, voices from several quarters within the United States urged Obama to take the first step in bringing the new Iranian government to the negotiating table. They argued, "Expressions of belligerence by the US have seriously undermined moderate voices inside the Iranian government calling for compromise, and strengthened more radical, hard line factions who believe that no compromise with the U.S. is possible, or even desirable."[98] Writing in *Foreign Policy*, Nasr pointed out, "For the past eight years, US policy has relied on pressure—threats of war and international economic sanctions—rather than incentives to change Iran's calculus. Continuing with that approach will be counterproductive. It will not provide Rouhani with the cover for a fresh approach to nuclear talks, and it could undermine the reformists generally by showing they cannot do better than conservatives on the nuclear issue."[99]

Conceivably, Washington realized that it was able to rally the international community against Iran largely due to the bombastic style of President Mahmoud Ahmadinejad (the predecessor of President Rouhani),[100] who made it easy to paint Iranian leaders irrational and threat to international community. The fact that the Iranian people voted for a reformist president, who publicly distanced himself from his predecessor and sought his election on the platform of rapprochement with the West, made it problematic for the United States to threaten 'pre-emptive war' or foist more stifling sanctions on the Islamic republic. As Laura Secor writes, "Rouhani is a pragmatist who came to power, in part, on the strength of disaffection, both popular and élite, with the confrontational foreign policy of his predecessor."[101] With moderation emanating from Iran and backed by Supreme Leader Ayatollah Khamenei, it also became difficult to sell the 'war on Iran' discourse to the American people. Thus, Obama warmed up to better relations with Iran, taking a retreat from threats of impending military punishment or further economic isolation. Even as "there exists a tendency and a power structure inside the Beltway that keeps readiness and permanent preparedness for war despite the Vietnam disaster,"[102] this is not an "active goal" for the Obama administration any longer.[103]

Implementing 'Dialogue Without Preconditions'

Stephen Walt points out that threats of punishment (sanctions, war) rarely work on states (or even individuals) unless the threatened punishment is really terrible, because giving into threats elicits more demands from the threatening party. For instance, Khamenei's rejection of Biden's offer of direct talks in February 2013 is instructive. Biden is reported to have said during a security conference in Munich, "There is still time, there is still space for diplomacy *backed by pressure* to succeed. The ball is in the government of Iran's court."[104] To this, Khamenei had replied, "The ball, in fact, is in your court. Does it make sense to offer negotiations while issuing threats and putting pressure? You are holding a gun against Iran saying you want to talk. The Iranian nation will not be frightened by the threats." It is not surprising that Khamenei went on to say, "Negotiating with America will not solve any problems," to an audience of air force personnel who had gathered as part of anniversary celebrations of the 1979 Islamic revolution.[105]

Walt draws attention to 'backscratching' as opposed to 'blackmail'—a concept proposed by MIT political scientist Kenneth Oye[106] — is more likely to elicit cooperation in inter-state relations:

In international politics, giving in to one state's threats might convey weakness and invite demands by others. By contrast, states (and people) routinely engage in acts of 'backscratching', where each adjusts its behaviour to give the other something that it wants in exchange for getting something that *it* wants. Backscratching—which is the essence of trade agreements, commercial transactions, and many other types of cooperation—establishes a valuable precedent: it shows that if you'll do something for me, then I'll do something for you.[107]

It was neither the squeeze of sanctions nor the threat of the use of force that lead to the JPA. When the United States and its allies also decided to make concessions on their longstanding 'red line'—the view that Iran needed to suspend enrichment as a precondition for talks—and agreed to ease sanctions that an agreement was achieved. In other words, when the P5+1 evolved a compromise formula and gave up threats in favour of inducements, that the Iranian interlocutors sat across the table with a mind to resolve the imbroglio. As Trita Parsi writes:

> Diplomatic opening came about [when] both sides compromised. Tehran stopped advancing sensitive parts of its programme and agreed to greater transparency. And Washington finally accepted enrichment on Iranian soil in the November 2013 interim agreement. Tehran had long insisted that if its enrichment was accepted, it would agree to transparency as well as restrictions.[108]

The Developing Scenario

The text of the Geneva Interim Agreement (24 November 2013) admits that Iran should "fully enjoy its right to nuclear energy for peaceful purposes" but within "a mutually defined enrichment programme with mutually agreed parameters consistent with practical needs." The critics of the interim deal see in the retention of some enrichment capacity as paving the way for a nuclear Iran, ignoring the high price that the Islamic Republic paid to retain what is enjoined to it in the universal non-proliferation regime. In other words, Marc Finaud says, "for the first time, a sovereign state party to the NPT has accepted to place its nuclear activities under the control not only of the IAEA like any other NPT non-nuclear weapon state, but also the five NPT nuclear-weapon states plus Germany.[109] Or, as Gary Samore, former non-proliferation advisor to the Obama White House, says, "On balance… the interim agreement is probably more acceptable to the P5+1 than it is to Iran because we are essentially freezing their nuclear programme without giving up very much in sanctions leverage." In *quid pro quo*, some trade sanctions have been eased and some frozen funds (actually Iran's own money in foreign bank accounts) released. There is also an assurance not to impose new sanctions during the six months interim period.[110] Despite the fears of the critics, "the overall sanctions regime remains intact, mainly because the US and EU governments have warned companies and other governments not to take actions that would draw sanctions."[111]

This 'right' to enrich uranium as part of the fuel cycle, imbricated in the principles agreed at Geneva, is most likely to be retained in the final agreement. However, the permissible future size and scope of Iran's nuclear fuel enrichment continues to be an intractable issue. The powers' primary aim is to get Iran to sharply reduce its uranium enrichment capability that would lengthen the breakout period. An *Al-Monitor* report states that the Iranian negotiators would be willing to consider short-term constraint on the size of its enrichment programme. The starting point would be to keep the 9,000 IR-1 centrifuges—the number of centrifuges currently operational under the six month interim deal—for a few years before gradually expanding to an industrial scale of 50,000 or more IR-1 centrifuge machines. At the end of this yet-to-be-agreed period (Iran is disposed for five), in which it would agree to restrictions and extensive inspections, monitoring and safeguards, Iran wants to have its status as a member of the NPT normalized, so that, theoretically, there would be no restrictions on the size of its enrichment programme.[112]

Instead, the P5+1 would find a deal under which Iran operated 3,000 IR-1 centrifuges while maintaining a small stockpile of 3.5 per cent enriched uranium, which extends the breakout period to a year or more and remains in place for a decade or more "politically defensible" on the domestic front.[113] Moreover, Iran wants its nuclear enrichment limits to be considered in 'separative work units' or SWU—a complex unit, indicating energy input, enrichment and depletion levels—rather than any specific number of particular kind of centrifuges, so it can gradually replace IR-1s with more advanced machines when they come on line and maintain the same overall enrichment capacity.[114] In terms of sanctions relief, the P5+1 proposal brings on a decade or more time frame for their phased removal, while Iran wants this aspect of the future deal to be immediate and comprehensive, for the nuclear concessions it would make as soon as the deal get underway.[115]

Another aspect related to uranium enrichment is the question of centrifuge research and development. Iran says it has the 'right' to install advanced centrifuges to enrich uranium. The powers want strict restriction on Iran developing new generation centrifuges, as that would shorten the time of a nuclear breakout scenario. Iran intends to replace its first generation IR-1 centrifuges now operating its enrichment plants at Fordow and Natanz with IR-2m centrifuges. In 2003, it installed around a 1,000 IR-2m centrifuges at Natanz, but has not made them operational. A final agreement on the scope and future development of Iran's nuclear programme hinges on the definition of Iran's "practical needs" with respect to uranium enrichment. The P5+1 and Iran have considerably different interpretations of just how much uranium Iran needs to enrich to fuel its proposed nuclear power plants.[116]

Undeniably, the risk of proliferation—diversion of nuclear material for military purposes—cannot be ruled out wholly in nuclear energy programmes. The 1946 Report on the International Control of Atomic Energy (also called the Acheson-Lilienthal report) stated that "the industry required and the technology developed for the realization of atomic weapons are the same industry and the same technology which play so essential a part in man's almost universal striving to improve his standard of living and his control of nature."[117] Physicist Amory Lovins and attorney Hunter Lovins call attention to the dual nature of nuclear technology in their book *Energy/War: Breaking the Nuclear Link*, "Every known route to bombs involves either nuclear power or materials and technology which are available, which exist in commerce, as a direct and essential consequence of nuclear power." Further, "All nuclear fission technologies both use and produce fissionable materials that are or can be concentrated. Unavoidably latent in those technologies, therefore, is a potential for nuclear violence and coercion which may be exploited by governments, factions," they write. In effect, civilian nuclear power technology, they emphasize, provides the way to make nuclear weapons, furnishing the materiel and personnel.[118]

Because nuclear technology has dual use potential, that there are perennial concerns of diversion of nuclear material for making weapons. Iranian officials have repeatedly asserted that the Islamic republic's nuclear programme is civilian and they have the 'right' to nuclear enrichment for peaceful purposes. Iran has been abiding by its safeguards agreement and the IAEA since 2008 has repeatedly confirmed the non-diversion of nuclear material in its reports. The point here is whether Iran can be trusted at its words. A pointer in this direction is an IAEA report of 20 February 2014, in which Director General Amano reported to his board (and indirectly to the P5+1) that Iran was fully implementing its share of the JPA. Iran's compliance with the interim agreement was reaffirmed in subsequent IAEA reports in March and April. The way to go, Ali Vaez outlines in his Crisis Group report is:

> A compromise that satisfies both sides' irreducible, bottom-line requirements: for Iran a meaningful enrichment programme, continued scientific advancement and tangible sanctions relief; and for the P5+1, a firewall between Iran's civilian and potential military

> nuclear capabilities, airtight monitoring mechanisms and sufficient time and Iranian cooperation to establish trust in the exclusively peaceful nature of the country's nuclear programme. Such a solution would enable them to sell the deal at home and serve as a springboard for developing a different kind of relationship.[119]

That said, Iran has already accepted an "unprecedented transparency and intrusive monitoring" according to the US official fact-sheet about the agreement, which includes daily access by "IAEA inspectors to enrichment plants and continuous video monitoring; access to centrifuges production, assembly, and storage facilities; access to uranium mines and mills; and provision of other key data and information among others."[120] If Iran's nuclear concessions were to be reciprocated by significant and swift easing of economic sanctions, a long-term settlement could be in offing.

The Road Ahead

"A civil nuclear energy programme has an implied military deterrent value because it keeps opponents guessing about whether the state also has a hidden nuclear weapons capability,"[121] says Ian Jackson. This is one of the crucial implicit reasons why Iran wants to control the entire fuel cycle and why Israel, Saudi Arabia and other regional countries are so wary of the Islamic republic's nuclear programme. Iran, like Japan, would like to remain at the nuclear threshold and enjoy legitimacy conferred by transparency, while conscious that nuclear weapons are within reach.[122] In contingent situations, Japan would have a short timetable to weaponization because of advanced civil nuclear facilities. As Juan Cole says, Iran is not pursuing a bomb, just nuclear latency—the ability to produce nuclear weapon fast, rather than have a standing arsenal.[123]

Iran's aspiration for latent nuclear capability is intolerable to Israel and Arab countries of the Persian Gulf. Alan Roth, Associate Director of National Security Studies at the Johns Hopkins University's Krieger School of Arts and Sciences, explains the Israeli case:

> Israel fears that Iran's nuclear ambitions could undermine its qualitative superiority of arms and its consistent ability to inflict disproportionate casualties on adversaries—the cornerstones of Israel's defence strategy... The Iranian nuclear programme threatens

> Israel's ability to do this in two ways. First, an Iranian nuclear capability would likely force Israel to restrain itself due to fears that Iran's nuclear weapons could provide an implied security guarantee to other anti-Zionist forces—the sort of guarantee that would prevent Israel from causing the massive losses it has in the past, while giving anti-Israel forces the confidence to keep up the fight.[124]

Similarly, Saudi Arabia is sceptical of the efforts by P5+1 (led by Washington) to negotiate a deal with Iran, expressing the fear that Iran could be left with a breakout capacity to make the fuel for a nuclear weapon at a time of their choosing. While the Saudis recognize there is no easy military response to Iran's nuclear programme and no military strike can eliminate the country's advancement in nuclear knowledge, they are irked with the decision of the Obama administration to ease sanctions, instead of tightening them further and causing a plausible collapse of the Islamic regime which has pursued the nuclear programme so assiduously. The Gulf countries have rallied behind the Saudis in opposing any deal on the Iranian nuclear issue. The Persian Gulf States are afraid of an American-Iranian rapprochement, as that would change the strategic balance of the region in favour of the Islamic Republic. They would rather see the United States and Iran remain at loggerheads and prefer a permanent US commitment to secure the region by maintaining the status quo.

What both Israel and the Gulf countries ignore is the fact that with comprehensive sets of checks and constraints on Iran's nuclear programme in place, the region would become a more secure place to live. They also miss the crucial element of any deal that although Iran has crossed the nuclear threshold—recognised by many experts—it has agreed to place limitation on its nuclear programme indeed not to cross that threshold. In the same vein, George Perkovich asserts, contrary to the arguments of the naysayers of the deal, "the United States is not in any position to prevent Iran from [enriching uranium]. Iran is one of 14 countries that already enrich uranium… neither more sanctions nor military strikes will push Iran out of the enrichment club."[125]

Moreover, Ian Jackson writes:

> …the proliferation of military nuclear weapons does not automatically follow the acquisition of nuclear energy technology. Many countries possess advanced nuclear skills but have not

> deployed nuclear weapons systems. Any country with significant nuclear technology should probably be regarded as a latent nuclear weapon power. Yet only one-third of the 30 countries that possess civil nuclear energy programmes have weaponized them… it seems proliferation is a choice, not a certain outcome of a state nuclear energy programme.[126]

Jacques E.C. Hymans, associate professor of international relations at the University of Southern California, says there are few grounds to ring an alarm bell if the talks fail to deliver the final deal by a stipulated time. He says there will not be a quick Iranian nuclear weapons breakout, followed by a proliferation race in the region or even in other regions, primarily for three reasons: a) states may not be hell-bent upon getting the bomb, even though their actions may look like it as the case of Argentina demonstrates so unambiguously; b) it is simply not easy to develop nuclear weapons on one's own because of technological and management constraints in the developing county, the typical nuclear weapons aspirants in recent years, and Iran is no exception to this; and c) there is a huge "nuclear breakout capacity" and an actual possession of nuclear weapons arsenal, as it is very hard for most states to jump suddenly from a notional breakout capacity to an actual breakout for political (detection, sanctions, ostracism, war) as well as technical (actual testing, design failure) reasons.[127]

According to Hymans, Iran's nuclear programme is actually rudimentary, despite the promises and hype. It has a "very long record of failing to live up to expectations" and "has long remained stuck in first gear despite an estimated $100 billion investment by the regime."[128] Ominous predictions of an imminent Iranian nuclear threat made for decades have not materialized[129] and the country has faced several technical hurdles to build a robust programme. Even the enrichment plants, the much discussed and supposedly developed component of Iran's nuclear programme, houses mostly the first generation IR-1 centrifuges.

Iran's current nuclear trajectory posits uranium enrichment as the *sine qua non* of nuclear energy programme, guided by false nationalism and producing "embarrassingly little peaceful nuclear benefit," aver Siegfried S. Hecker and Abbas Milani, faculty members at Stanford University.[130] They add that the Iranian nuclear programme can see a turnaround from the current difficulties, if it shifts gear from the focus on fuel enrichment to the development of "economically profitable parts of the nuclear fuel cycle—reactor component fabrication, fuel fabrication, and reactor construction—while eschewing the proliferation-sensitive steps of uranium enrichment and spent-fuel reprocessing." This would allay concerns about Iran's nuclear programme, and also propel the country on the path of "civilian nuclear development similar to the one South Korea has successfully pursued." They recommend that the P5+1 should "incorporate Iran into the international nuclear energy community" by assisting in the construction of a viable civilian programme in the middle of the nuclear fuel cycle.[131]

Conclusion

The resolution of the Iranian nuclear issue is prelude to more real problems that confront the powers, namely, how would Iran fashion its relations internationally, and whether the deal would herald Iran's political and economic reintegration into the international community. Normalization of Iran brings us to the question of Iran's security needs in the region, which feeds Iran's desire for a latent nuclear deterrent. It is proposed that regional security architecture—mediated by the United States—that takes into account the legitimate security interests of Iran, along with, those of Persian Gulf states and Israel, the two constituencies greatly effected by Tehran nuclear 'rise', would go a long way in relieving the strategic competition that feeds into negative perception of one another. West Asia would generally be safer if the US-Iran relations were normalised and the scope and purpose of Iran's nuclear programme were endorsed in a multilateral agreement. Iran, with its population, size, natural resources and historical achievements, has far more potential to become a hegemonic power than any other state in West Asia, and will loom large, if it does manage to escape the constraints perpetuated by sanctions and isolation in the years ahead. The US as a predominant great power in the region, then, has its task cut out. It would make great realist sense, if the United States were to play the role of an offshore balancer, ensuring that no single state is able to threaten others in the region and emerge a dominant actor.

A balance-of-power strategy in the region would, in fact, address Iran's aspiration to be recognized as a regional power with a rightful role. The resolution of Iranian nuclear impasse could also serve as the beginning of Iran's cooperation with major powers in the crises in Syria and Iraq. Some suggest that Iran could also play the role of a balance to rising Sunni extremism in the region, but that could be a dangerous proposition with the potential to further tear the region asunder along sectarian lines. In the end, Iran may not embrace the new reality in the post-deal scenario in a way that benefits the West, but it would definitely herald a relationship that is free of acrimony and ready for cooperative engagements.

References

1. Mohamed ElBaradei, the former Director General of the IAEA, confirmed that nuclear material was not diverted to prohibited activities in his 10 November 2003 report (paragraph 52) and 15 November 2004 report (paragraph 112) to the Board of Governors, during the two years that Iran's nuclear programme came under intense scrutiny. Ten years later, the Agency continued to verify the non-diversion of declared material in safeguarded and location outside facilities (LOF) vide its Report dated 21 February 2013 (paragraph 7). *See* these reports at www.iaea.org.
2. "We judge with high confidence that in fall 2003, Tehran halted its nuclear weapons programme; we also assess with moderate-to-high confidence that Tehran at a minimum is keeping open the option to develop nuclear weapons. We judge with high confidence that the halt, and Tehran's announcement of its decision to suspend its declared uranium enrichment programme and sign an Additional Protocol to its Nuclear Non-Proliferation Treaty Safeguards Agreement, was directed primarily in response to increasing international scrutiny and pressure resulting from exposure of Iran's previously undeclared nuclear work." "Iran: Nuclear Intentions and Capabilities," *National Intelligence Estimate* (NIE) from the Office of the Director of National Intelligence, November 2007, www.odni.gov.
3. James R. Clapper, "Statement for the Record, Worldwide Threat Assessment of the US Intelligence Community, Senate Committee on Armed Services, Director of National Intelligence," *Office of the Director of National Intelligence* (http://odni.gov/), 18 April 2013, https://www.hsdl.org/?view&did=746570.
4. Leon Panetta in "Meet the Press" with Chuck Todd, *NBC News*, 3 February 2013, http://www.nbcnews.com/id/50666148/ns/meet_the_press-transcripts/#.U5K5mDlYyfT.

5. Amos Harel, "IDF chief to Haaretz: I do not believe Iran will decide to develop nuclear weapons," *Ha'aretz*, 25 April 2012, http://www.haaretz.com/news/diplomacy-defense/idf-chief-to-haaretz-i-do-not-believe-iran-will-decide-to-develop-nuclear-weapons-1.426389.
6. "Report to the Governor General to the Board of Governors," *International Atomic Energy Agency* (IAEA), 10 November 2003.
7. Idir Ouahes and Ben Smith, "The Deal with Iran," *International Affairs and Defence Section* (House of Commons Library), December 2013.
8. "The various activities associated with the production of electricity from nuclear reactions are referred to collectively as the nuclear fuel cycle. It begins with the mining of uranium and ends with the disposal of nuclear waste. To prepare uranium for use in a nuclear reactor, it undergoes the steps of mining and milling, conversion, enrichment and fuel fabrication. These steps make up the 'front end' of the nuclear fuel cycle. After uranium has spent about three years in a reactor to produce electricity, the used fuel may undergo a further series of steps including temporary storage, reprocessing, and recycling before wastes are disposed. Collectively these steps are known as the 'back end' of the fuel cycle." World Nuclear Association, "The Nuclear Fuel Cycle," http://www.world-nuclear.org/info/Nuclear-Fuel-Cycle/Introduction/Nuclear-Fuel-Cycle-Overview/, December 2012. *See also* Maryam Sinaee, "Khatami defends Iran's 'nuclear right'," *The National*, 10 March 2009, http://www.thenational.ae/news/world/middle-east/khatami-defends-irans-nuclear-right; "Iran Demands Affirmation of 'Nuclear Rights'," *Global Security Newswire* (NTI), 5 June 2012, http://www.nti.org/gsn/article/iran-demands-affirmation-nuclear-rights/; Shahram Chubin, "The Politics of Iran's Nuclear Programme," *The Iran Primer*, United States Institute of Peace (USIP), http://iranprimer.usip.org/resource/politics-irans-nuclear-programme; "West unwilling to recognize Iran's nuclear rights: Analyst," *Press TV*, 3 May 2013, http://www.presstv.com/detail/2013/05/03/301638/west-ignores-iran-nuclear-energy-right/; Max Fisher, "9 questions about Iran's nuclear programme you were too embarrassed to ask," *The Washington Post*, 24 November 2013, http://www.washingtonpost.com/blogs/worldviews/wp/2013/11/25/9-questions-about-irans-nuclear-programme-you-were-too-embarrassed-to-ask/.
9. The United Nations, "The Treaty on the Non-Proliferation of Nuclear Weapons," http://www.un.org/en/conf/npt/2005/npttreaty.html.
10. "Iran deal does not mention 'right to enrich', Britain says," *Yalibnan*, 24 November 2013, http://yalibnan.com/2013/11/24/iran-deal-does-not-mention-right-to-enrich-britain-says/; "Britain says Iran deal does not mention 'right to enrich'," *Channel News Asia*, 25 November 2013, http://www.channelnewsasia.com/news/specialreports/mh370/news/britain-says-iran-deal/898566.html.
11. In February 1979, when the Islamic Revolution toppled the Shah, the Bushehr-1 (reactor 1) was 90 per cent complete while Bushehr-2 was 50

per cent complete. If the 1979 Revolution had not happened, the Kraftwerk Union would have continued its work in all likelihood with the cooperation of the United States' Bechtel Power, which was the former's joint-venture partner in many power plant projects around the world. The revolutionary government of Prime Minister Mehdi Bazargan then decided that Iran did not need nuclear energy and, therefore, the work at Bushehr was halted in February 1979. The German firm had left Iran earlier. *See* "Country Profile: Iran," *Nuclear Threat Initiative*, July 2013, http://www.nti.org/country-profiles/iran/nuclear/; Mohammad Sahimi, "Iran's Nuclear Programme," *Payvand Iran News*, 10 February 2003, http://www.payvand.com/news/03/oct/1015.html.

12. *See* "A History of Iran's Nuclear Programme," *Iran Watch*, Wisconsin Project on Nuclear Arms Control, Washington, D.C., http://www.iranwatch.org/our-publications/weapon-programme-background-report/history-irans-nuclear-programme, 1 March 2012; Sahimi, "Iran's Nuclear Programme," *Payvand Iran News*; "Iran: Nuclear Overview," *Nuclear Threat Initiative*, July 2013; Ze'ev Schiff, *Weapons of Mass Destruction and the Middle East: The View from Israel*, Houston: James A. Baker III Institute for Public Policy, Rice University, March 2003, p. 7.
13. Shahram Chubin, Director of Studies at the Geneva Centre for Security Policy, quoted in Gabriel G. Tabarani, *How Iran Plans to Fight America and Dominate the Middle East*, Bloomington, Indiana: Author House, 2008, p. 165.
14. Andrew Koch and Jeanette Wolf, *Iran's Nuclear Facilities: A Profile*, Monterey Institute of International Studies: Centre for Non-proliferation Studies, 1998, p. 2.
15. ElBaradei quoted in Anthony H. Cordesman and Khalid R. Al-Rodhan, "Iran's Weapons of Mass Destruction: The Real and Potential Threat," *Significant Issues Series* 28, no. 3, 2006: 154, Washington, D.C.: Centre for Strategic and International Studies; Dieter Bednarz and Erich Follath, "Interview with Mohamed ElBaradei: 'We Are Moving Rapidly towards an Abyss'," *Spiegel Online International*, no. 36, 2007.
16. "Pilot Fuel Enrichment Plant (PFEP)," *Nuclear Threat Initiative*, http://www.nti.org/facilities/172/, 10 October 2013; Kelsey Davenport, "The November IAEA Report on Iran's Nuclear Programme: No Significant Advances," *Arms control Now*, 14 November 2013, http://armscontrolnow.org/2013/11/14/the-november-iaea-report-on-irans-nuclear-programme-no-significant-advances/; Report by the IAEA Director General to the Board of Governors, 14 November 2013, www.iaea.org.
17. Oliver Meier, "Iran and Foreign Enrichment: A Troubled Model," *Arms Control Association*, January/February 2006, https://www.armscontrol.org/act/2006_01-02/JANFEB-IranEnrich; also see, "Iran: Nuclear History," *Nuclearenergy.ir*, http://nuclearenergy.ir/history/

18. Abbas Milani, "The Shah's Atomic Dreams," *Foreign Policy*, 29 December 2010, http://www.foreignpolicy.com/articles/2010/12/29/the_shahs_atomic_dreams.
19. Devin T. Hagerty, "The implications of a nuclear-armed Iran," in *Nuclear Proliferation in South Asia: Crisis Behaviour and the Bomb*, Sumit Ganguly and Paul S. Kapur (eds.), Abingdon: Routledge, 2009, pp. 216-17; "Iran: Missile," *Nuclear Threat Initiative*, Washington, D.C., July 2014, http://www.nti.org/country-profiles/iran/delivery-systems/.
20. The United Nations, "The Treaty on the Non-Proliferation of Nuclear Weapons."
21. Cyrus Safdari, "Iran's not-so-hidden enrichment programme," *Iran Affairs*, 13 December 2007, http://www.iranaffairs.com/iran_affairs/2007/12/irans-not-so-hi.html.
22. It is the feedstock for a centrifuge enrichment plant.
23. Mark Hibbs, "U.S. in 1983 stopped IAEA from helping Iran make UF6, *Nuclear Fuel* 28, No. 16, 4 August 2003: 12, quoted in Safdari, "Iran's not-so-hidden enrichment programme."
24. "The Statute of the IAEA," *International Atomic Energy Agency*, http://www.iaea.org/About/statute.html#A1.2.
25. David Morrison and Peter Oborne "Does the BBC not trust US intelligence on Iran?" *Open Democracy*, 8 August 2013, http://www.opendemocracy.net/ourkingdom/david-morrison-peter-oborne/does-bbc-not-trust-us-intelligence-on-iran.
26. Safdari, "Iran's not-so-hidden enrichment programme."
27. With the acceptance by Iran on 26 February 2003 of the modifications to the Subsidiary Arrangements proposed by the Agency, the Subsidiary Arrangements General Part now requires Iran to inform the Agency of new nuclear facilities and modifications to existing facilities through the provision of preliminary design information as soon as the decision to construct, to authorise construction or to modify has been taken, and to provide the Agency with further design information as it is developed. Information is to be provided early in the project definition, preliminary design, construction, and commissioning phases (Paragraph 15). "Report by the Director General to the Board of Governors," *IAEA*, 6 June 2003, http://www.iaea.org/Publications/Documents/Board/2003/gov2003-40.pdf.
28. "Report by the Director General to the Board of Governors," footnote 3.
29. Morrison and Oborne, "Does the BBC not trust US intelligence on Iran?"
30. Morrison and Oborne, "Does the BBC not trust US intelligence on Iran?"
31. Gareth Porter, "Demonising nuclear Iran," *Aljazeera*, 17 May 2014, http://www.aljazeera.com/indepth/opinion/2014/05/demonising-nuclear-iran-2014517195752572663.html.
32. Siddharth Varadarajan, "The ElBaradei interview: Language of force is not helpful on Iran issue," *The Hindu*, 3 October 2009.

33. Gareth Porter, "The Mysterious Laptop Documents: 'Evidence' of Iran Nuclear Weapons Programme May Be Fraudulent," *Global Research*, 18 November 2010, http://www.globalresearch.ca/the-mysterious-laptop-documents-evidence-of-iran-nuclear-weapons-programme-may-be-fraudulent/21994.
34. Trita Parsi, *Treacherous Alliance: The Secret Dealings of Israel, Iran, and the US*, New Haven and London: Yale University Press, 2007.
35. Hans M. Kristensen and Robert S. Norris, "Global nuclear weapons inventories, 1945-2013," *Bulletin of the Atomic Scientists* 69, no. 5, September/October 2013: 80.
36. Jim Zanotti, "Israel: Background and U.S. Relations," *Congressional Research Service*, 12 June 2013, p. 1.
37. Report of the Director-General to the Board of Governors (Paragraph 21), *IAEA*, www.iaea.org, 15 September 2008.
38. Cyrus Safdari, "Analysis of Sept 2008 IAEA report on Iran's nuclear programme," *Iran Affairs*, 15 September 2008, http://www.iranaffairs.com/iran_affairs/2008/09/analysis-of-latest-iaea-report-on-iran.html.
39. *IAEA Report*, 15 September 2008.
40. "Understandings of the Islamic Republic of Iran and the IAEA on the Modalities of Resolution of the Outstanding Issues," *IAEA Information Circular*, INFCIRC/711, 27 August 2007, www.iaea.org.
41. Mohamed ElBaradei, *The Age of Deception: Nuclear Diplomacy in Treacherous Times*, London: Bloomsbury publishing, 2011, p. 291.
42. ElBaradei, *The Age of Deception*.
43. ElBaradei, *The Age of Deception*, p. 290.
44. ElBaradei, *The Age of Deception*, pp. 290-1.
45. ElBaradei, *The Age of Deception*, p. 290.
46. Mark Heinrich, "IAEA denies report it is sure Iran seeking atom bomb," *Reuters*, 17 September 2009http://www.reuters.com/article/2009/09/17/us-nuclear-iaea-iran-sb-idUSTRE58G60W20090917?sp=true.
47. "Report of the Director General to the Board of Governors, *IAEA*, 8 November 2011, www.iaea.org; Peter Crail, Daryl G. Kimball, Greg Thielmann, "The IAEA's Iran Report: Assessment and Implications," *Arms Control Association*, 8 November 2011, https://www.armscontrol.org/issuebriefs/The-IAEAs-Iran-Report_Assessment-and-Implications.
48. "Recent Media Report on Iran," *IAEA Press Release*, 17 September 2009, http://www.iaea.org/newscenter/mediaadvisory/2009/ma200919.html; Bob Drogin, Kim Murphy, "Most U.S. tips fingering Iran false—envoys / No intelligence given U.N. since '02 led to big discoveries," *Los Angeles Times*, 25 February 2007, http://www.sfgate.com/politics/article/Most-U-S-tips-fingering-Iran-false-envoys-2646358.php.
49. Flynt Leverett and Hillary Mann Leverett, "Pulling the IAEA Into the 'Attack Iran' Debate Will Backfire," *The Race for Iran*, 8 November 2011,

http://www.raceforiran.com/pulling-the-iaea-into-the-“attack-iran”-debate-will-backfire.

50. “US embassy cables: New UN chief is ‘director general of all states, but in agreement with us’,” *The Guardian*, 2 December 2010, http://www.theguardian.com/world/us-embassy-cables-documents/230076.
51. Suvrat Raju, “The disingenuous debate on Iran,” *The Hindu*, 27 May 2012, http://www.thehindu.com/opinion/op-ed/the-disingenuous-debate-on-iran/article3446670.ece.
52. Julian Borger, “Nuclear watchdog chief accused of pro-western bias over Iran,” *The Guardian*, 22 March 2012, http://www.theguardian.com/world/2012/mar/22/nuclear-watchdog-iran-iaea; “Ex-IAEA officials accuse agency chief of anti-Iran bias,” *Press TV*, 23 March 2012, http://www.presstv.in/detail/232880.html.
53. Shimon Peres in an interview with France 3 Television; Parsi, *Treacherous Alliance*, p. 163.
54. There are many other examples of such assertions. In 1995, Benjamin Netanyahu wrote, “the best estimates at this time place Iran between three and five years away from possessing the prerequisites required for the independent production of nuclear weapons.” Israeli Defence Minister Binyamin Ben-Eliezer claimed in July 2001 that Iran would be ready with a bomb by 2005. Again in February 2009, Netanyahu told an American Congressional delegation that Iran is only one or two years away from having nuclear weapons. In July 2013, he again warned that Iran was only weeks away from crossing the ‘red line’ on developing a nuclear weapon. *See* Jonathan Tepperman, “Israel vs. Iran, Again,” *The New York Times*, 26 July 2013, http://www.nytimes.com/2013/07/27/opinion/global/israel-vs-iran-again.html?_r=0; Seyed Hossein Mousavian, “Netanyahu’s Threats Undermine Possible Nuclear Deal With Iran,” *Al-Monitor*, 21 July 2013, http://www.al-monitor.com/pulse/originals/2013/07/iran-israel-netanyahu-rouhani-nuclear-weapon.html#; Jacques E.C. Hymans, “Iran Is Still Botching the Bomb: It is Time for Israel and the United States To Stop Overreacting,” *Foreign Affairs*, 18 February 2013, http://www.foreignaffairs.com/articles/139013/jacques-e-c-hymans/iran-is-still-botching-the-bomb; Nima Shirazi, “Benjamin Netanyahu Cries ‘Wolf’ ... Again,” *Foreign Policy Journal*, 18 July 2013, http://www.foreignpolicyjournal.com/2013/07/18/benjamin-netanyahu-cries-wolf-again/; Ronen Bergman, “Will Israel Attack Iran?” *The New York Times*, 25 January 2012, http://www.nytimes.com/2012/01/29/magazine/will-israel-attack-iran.html?pagewanted=all; Tony Karon, “What Do Israel’s Leaders Really Think about Iran?” *Time World*, 10 May 2011, http://world.time.com/2011/05/10/what-do-israels-leaders-really-think-about-iran/.
55. WikiLeaks cable item, “Wikileaks cables: Don’t trust Israel on Iran,” *Salon*, 2 December 2010, http://www.salon.com/2010/12/02/wikileaks_israel_on_iran/, quoted in Justin Elliot, “Israel on Iran: So wrong for so long,”

Salon, 6 December 2010, http://www.salon.com/2010/12/05/israeli_predictions_iranian_nukes/.

56. Israeli request for bunker-buster bomb was declined not because it could be used against Iran but because, at the time, the Pentagon had frozen almost all US-Israeli joint defence projects out of concern that Israel was transferring advanced military technology to China. However, in 2007, Bush informed Ehud Olmert, then Prime Minister of Israel, that he would order the bunker busters for delivery in 2009 or 2010. The Israelis wanted them in 2007. President Obama is reported to have finally released the weapons in 2009. *See* Eli Lake, "Inside Obama's Israel Bomb Sale," *Newsweek*, 25 September 2011, http://www.newsweek.com/obama-arms-israel-67479.
57. Muhammad Sahimi, "The Israel Lobby, the Neocons, and the Iranian-American Community," *Antiwar.com*, 21 November 2009, http://original.antiwar.com/sahimi/2009/11/20/the-israel-lobby-the-neocons-and-the-iranian-american-community%C2%A0/.
58. *See* Louis Rene Beres *et al.*, "Israel's Strategic Future: The Final Report of Project Daniel," *NATIV Online*, April 2004, Ariel Centre for Policy Research, Israel, http://www.acpr.org.il/ENGLISH-NATIV/03-issue/daniel-3.htm.
59. Nicole Gaouette, "Israel: Iran is Now Danger No. 1," *Christian Science Monitor*, 28 November 2003, http://www.csmonitor.com/2003/1128/p06s01-wome.html.
60. Ariel Ilan Roth, "The Root of All Fears: Why Is Israel So Afraid of Iranian Nukes?" *Foreign Affairs*, 24 November 2009, www.foreignaffairs.com.
61. Farideh Farhi, "What to do about U.S. Sanctions and Israeli Threats: Iran's Muted Nuclear Debate," *Middle East Brief*, no. 61, April 2012, Crown Centre for Middle East Studies, Brandeis University, www.brandeis.edu/crown/.ý
62. *See* Tabassum Zakaria and Mark Hosenball, "Special Report: Intel shows Iran nuclear threat not imminent," *Reuters*, 23 March 2012, www.reuters.com.
63. Jack Boureston and Charles D. Ferguson, "Schooling Iran's Atom Squad," *Bulletin of the Atomic Scientists* 60, no. 3, May-June 2004: 32-35.
64. "The Iran Nuclear NIE of 2007: Revise, Reject, or Reiterate?" *Issue Brief Arms Control Association*1, No. 18, 12 August 2010, www.armscontrol.org.
65. Seyed Hossein Mousavian, "The Iran Nuclear Dilemma: The Peaceful Use of Nuclear Energy and NPT's Main Objectives," *Iran Review*, 6 November 2012, http://www.iranreview.org/content/Documents/The-Iran-Nuclear-Dilemma-The-Peaceful-Use-of-Nuclear-Energy-and-NPT-s-Main-Objectives.htm.
66. *See* David E. Sanger, *Confront and Conceal: Obama's Secret Wars and Surprising Use of American Power*, New York: Broadway Paperbacks, 2012, pp. 188-225.

67. William J. Broad and David E. Sanger, “With Eye on Iran, Rivals Also Want Nuclear Power,” *The New York Times*, 15 April 2007, http://www.nytimes.com/2007/04/15/world/middleeast/15sunnis.html?pagewanted=print&_r=0.
68. Eli Lake, “U.A.E. diplomat mulls hit on Iran’s nukes,” *The Washington Times*, 6 July 2010, http://www.washingtontimes.com/news/2010/jul/6/uae-ambassador-endorses-bombing-irans-nuclear-prog/?page=all.
69. Christopher Davidson, quoted in Ian Black, “UAE ambassador backs strike on Iran‘s nuclear sites,” *The Guardian*, 7 July 2010, http://www.theguardian.com/world/2010/jul/07/uae-envoy-iran-nuclear-sites.
70. “Saudi King Abdullah and Senior Princes on Saudi Policy toward Iraq (Cable 08RIYADH649),” http://www.wikileaks.ch/cable/2008/04/08RIYADH649.html.
71. *See* Yaakov Katz, Yoaz Hendel, *Israel Vs. Iran: The Shadow War*, Dulles, Virginia: Potomac Books, 2102, p. 5; Barry Rubin, “Wikileaks Confirm Our Analysis of U.S. Policy and Middle East Politics,” *GLORIA Center*, 29 November 2010, http://www.gloria-center.org/2010/11/wikileaks-confirms-gloria-analysis/; Michael Busch, “WikiLeaks II: Saudi Arabia on Iran—“Cut off the head of the snake,” *Foreign Policy in Focus*, 29 November 2010, http://fpif.org/wikileaks_ii_saudi_arabia_on_iran_-_cut_off_the_head_of_the_snake/.
72. Robert Mason, “Establishing equilibrium in the Gulf: in search of a pragmatic agenda for stability and security,” *Open Democracy*, 7 May 2014, http://www.opendemocracy.net/arab-awakening/robert-mason/establishing-equilibrium-in-gulf-in-search-of-pragmatic-agenda-for-stabi.
73. “Israel, Saudi Arabia Unite against Iran,” *Al-Manar*, 17 November 2013, http://www.almanar.com.lb/english/adetails.php?fromval=1&cid=31&frid=31&eid=121251,
74. Jason Burke, “Riyadh will build nuclear weapons if Iran gets them, Saudi prince warns,” *The Guardian*, 29 June 2011, http://www.theguardian.com/world/2011/jun/29/saudi-build-nuclear-weapons-iran.
75. Bradley Bowman, “Chain Reaction: Avoiding a Nuclear Arms Race in the Middle East,” *Report to the Committee on Foreign Relations*, US Senate, February 2008, p. 11.
76. Abdulaziz Sager quoted in Naser al-Tamimi, “Will Riyadh Get the Bomb? ?Saudi Arabia‘s Atomic Ambitions,” *Middle East Quarterly*, Spring 2013, http://www.meforum.org/3509/saudi-arabia-nuclear-bomb.
77. Lewis A. Dunn, “Strategic Reassurance if Iran ‘Goes Nuclear’: A Framework and Some Propositions,” *Strategic Insights* 8, no. 5, December 2009, http://calhoun.nps.edu/public/bitstream/handle/10945/11160/dunnDec09.pdf?sequence=1.
78. “Saudi Arabia May Go Nuclear Because of Obama’s Iran Deal,” *The Daily Beast*, February 14, 2014, http://www.thedailybeast.com/articles/2014/02/14/saudi-arabia-may-go-nuclear-because-of-obama-s-iran-deal.html.

79. Richard Weitz, "Gulf Cooperation Council Moves Forward with Nuclear Energy Plans," *WMD Insights*, http://www.nti.org/country-profiles/saudi-arabia/nuclear/.
80. Mark Hibbs, "Saudi Arabia's Nuclear Options," *Carnegie Endowment for International Peace*, April 2007, http://carnegieendowment.org/2010/07/20/saudi-arabia-s-nuclear-ambitions/58v, July 10, 2010.
81. *See* Parmit Pal Chaudhuri, "US' changing role in West Asia," *Hindustan Times*, 13 July 2014, p. 21.
82. Anthony H. Cordesman, Bryan Gold, and Chloe Coughlin-Schulte, *Iran: Sanctions, Energy, Arms Control, and Regime Change*, Washington, D.C.: Center for Strategic & International Studies, 2014, pp. 125-26; *see also* Gary Samore (ed.), *Iran's Strategic Weapons Programmes: A Net Assessment*, New York: Routledge, 2005.
83. David Ignatius, "Will history repeat in Iran nuclear negotiations?" *Washington Post*, 17 November 2013, http://www.washingtonpost.com/blogs/post-partisan/wp/2013/11/17/will-history-repeat-in-iran-nuclear-negotiations/?tid%3DhpModule_ea22e378-b26e-11e2-bbf2-a6f9e9d79e19.
84. ElBaradei, *The Age of Deception*, p. 143.
85. Nima Shirazi, "Iran's nuclear rights vs. the West's 'bombastic diplomacy'," *Mondoweiss*, November 11, 2013, http://mondoweiss.net/2013/11/nuclear-bombastic-diplomacy.html; Seyed Hossein Mousavian and Shahir Shahid Saless, "Iran nuclear deal may be start of new era in Persian Gulf," *AlMonitor*, December 1, 2013, http://www.al-monitor.com/pulse/originals/2013/12/iran-nuclear-deal-right-to-enrich-new-era-in-persian-gulf.html#. However, in November 2013, Kerry denied that the interim agreement recognized Iran's right to enrich: "There is no inherent right to enrich," Kerry said on ABC's "This Week." *See* Aaron Blake, "Kerry on Iran: 'We do not recognize a right to enrich'," *Washington Post*, November 24, 2013, http://www.washingtonpost.com/blogs/post-politics/wp/2013/11/24/kerry-on-iran-we-do-not-recognize-a-right-to-enrich/.
86. ElBaradei, *The Age of Deception*, p. 144.
87. Jason Seher, "Ex-national security adviser: 'Direct line' between Iran sanctions and Rouhani's election," *CNN Politics*, 1 December 2013, http://politicalticker.blogs.cnn.com/2013/12/01/ex-national-security-adviser-direct-line-between-iran-sanctions-and-rouhanis-election/.
88. Colin H. Kahl, "The Danger of New Iran Sanctions," *The National Interest*, 31 December 2013, http://nationalinterest.org/commentary/the-danger-new-iran-sanctions-9651.
89. *See* Robert A. Pape, "Why Economic Sanctions Do Not Work? *International Security* 22, no. 2, Autumn 1997: 90-136.
90. "Spider Web: The Making and Unmaking of Iran Sanctions," *Crisis Group*, 25 February 2013, http://www.crisisgroup.org/en/regions/middle-east-north-africa/iraq-iran-gulf/iran/138-spider-web-the-making-and-unmaking-of-iran-sanctions.aspx.

91. Daniel Dombey, "Bolton rejects 'grand bargain' with Iran," *Financial Times*, 9 June 2006, http://www.ft.com/intl/cms/s/0/3016bd02-f7e9-11da-9481-0000779e2340.html#axzz38DhgQy2s; Meir Javedanfar, "The grand bargain with Tehran," *The Guardian*, 3 March 2009, http://www.theguardian.com/commentisfree/2009/mar/03/iran-nuclear-weapons; Suzanne Maloney, "U.S. Policy Toward Iran: Missed Opportunities and Paths Forward," *The Fletcher Forum of World Affairs* 32, no. 2, Summer 2008: 25-44.
92. "Full text of President Ahmadinejad's speech at General Assembly," *Global Security.org*, 17 September 2005, http://www.globalsecurity.org/wmd/library/news/iran/2005/iran-050918-irna02.htm.
93. NIE, "Iran: Nuclear Intentions and Capabilities," November 2007.
94. Vali Nasr, *The Dispensable Nation: American Foreign Policy in Retreat*, New York: Doubleday, 2013, pp. 97, 110, 111, and 114.
95. Nasr, *The Dispensable Nation*, p. 97.
96. Jeffrey Goldberg, "Obama to Iran and Israel: 'As President of the United States, I Don't Bluff'," *The Atlantic*, 2 March 2012, http://www.theatlantic.com/international/archive/2012/03/obama-to-iran-and-israel-as-president-of-the-united-states-i-dont-bluff/253875/.
97. Matt Spetalnick and Paul Eckert, "Biden, Netanyahu set tone on Iran for Obama visit to Israel," *Reuters*, 4 March 2013, http://www.reuters.com/article/2013/03/04/us-israel-iran-netanyahu-idUSBRE92312720130304.
98. "The "Axis of Evil" speech by President George W. Bush in 2002, stymied "the possibility of rapprochement that had recently arisen from US-Iran cooperation in Afghanistan establishing the Karzai government, undermining Iranian moderates and empowering their hawkish opponents." "US should tread lightly on Iran," *Politico*, Editorial, http://www.politico.com/story/2013/06/united-states-should-tread-lightly-on-iran-93545_Page2.html#ixzz36oLfM8yQ.
99. Vali Nasr, "Regime Change Obama can Believe In," *Foreign Policy*, 16 June 2013, http://www.foreignpolicy.com/articles/2013/06/16/regime_change_iran_nuclear_weapons_deal.
100. In denying the Holocaust, calling for Israel to be wiped off the map, and deliberately escalating tensions with the West, Ahmadinejad portrayed the Iranian ruling elites irrational, unreasonable and incapable of diplomacy.
101. Laura Secor, "Talking or Walking," *The New Yorker*, 25 November 2013, http://www.newyorker.com/talk/comment/2013/11/25/131125taco_talk_secor.
102. Gareth Porter, quoted in Ludwig Watzal, "Manufactured Crisis. The Untold Story of the Iran Nuclear Scare," *Global Research*, 21 March 2014, http://www.globalresearch.ca/manufactured-crisis-the-untold-story-of-the-iran-nuclear-scare/5374677?print=1.
103. "Iran: The United States Should Take the Threat of Military Force 'Off the Table' (Interview with Stephen M. Walt)," *Global Research*, 23

February 2014, http://www.globalresearch.ca/iran-the-united-states-should-take-the-threat-of-military-force-off-the-table/5370208.

104. Jonathan Tirone, "U.S. Ready for 'Serious' Direct Nuclear Iran Negotiations," *Bloomberg*, 2 February 2013, http://www.bloomberg.com/news/2013-02-02/u-s-ready-for-serious-direct-nuclear-iran-negotiations.html.
105. "Khamenei Comments: US-Iran Talks Won't Solve Any Problems," *The Iran Primer*, United States Institute of Peace, 26 February 2013, http://iranprimer.usip.org/blog/2013/feb/26/khamenei-comments-us-iran-talks-won't-solve-any-problems.
106. Kenneth Oye, "The Domain of Choice," in *Eagle Entangled: U.S. Foreign Policy in a Complex World,* Kenneth Oye, Donald Rotchchild, and Robert J. Lieber (eds.), New York: Longman, 1979, pp. 3-33; *See also* Robert A. Keohane and Joseph S. Nye, "Power and Interdependence Revisited," *International Organization* 41, no. 4, Autumn, 1987: 725-53.
107. Stephen Walt, "On Iran, try backscratching, not blackmail," *Foreign Policy*, 22 February 2013, http://www.foreignpolicy.com/posts/2013/02/22/on_iran_try_backscratching_not_blackmail.
108. Trita Parsi, "No, Sanctions Didn't Force Iran to Make a Deal," *Foreign Policy*, 14 May 2014, http://www.foreignpolicy.com/articles/2014/05/14/sanctions_did_not_force_iran_to_make_a_deal_nuclear_enrichment.
109. Marc Finaud, "The Geneva Accord on Iran's Nuclear Programme: Historic Chance or Historic Mistake?" Web Editorial, *Geneva Centre for Security Policy*, 29 November 2013, http://www.gcsp.ch/Emerging-Security-Challenges/Programme-News/Web-Editorial-The-Geneva-Accord-on-Iran-s-Nuclear-Programme-Historic-Chance-or-Historic-Mistake#footnote%202.
110. Joby Warrick, "Nuclear pact's fine print: A temporary halt in advances," *Washington Post*, 24 November 2013, http://www.washingtonpost.com/world/national-security/nuclear-pacts-fine-print-a-temporary-halt-in-advances/2013/11/23/0f71640a-54be-11e3-9e2c-e1d01116fd98_story_1.html.
111. "Gary Samore's speech on the distance still to go in Iran nuclear talks," *Iran Matters*, Harvard's Belfer Center, 19 May 2014, http://iranmatters.belfercenter.org/blog/gary-samore-speech-distance-still-go-iran-nuclear-talks.
112. Laura Rozen, "Enrichment capacity seen as key hurdle to Iran deal," *The Back Channel* (*Al-Monitor*), http://backchannel.al-monitor.com/index.php/2014/05/8311/identifying-key-hurdles-to-iran-deal-both-sides-want/, May 21, 2014; "Bayanat dar deedar-e masaulane-nizam," *Khamenei.ir* (Persian), http://farsi.khamenei.ir/speech-content?id=26908, 16.4.1393 (July 7, 2014).
113. "Gary Samore's speech," 19 May 2014.
114. "Gary Samore's speech," 19 May 2014.

115. Arash Karami, "Iran official cites 'intense disagreements' between Iran, P5+1," *Al Monitor*, 21 May 2014, http://www.al-monitor.com/pulse/originals/2014/05/iran-official-discloses-intense-disagreements-iran-p51.html#.
116. Hossein?Mousavian, "A dose of realism is needed to resolve Iran's nuclear crisis," *Financial Times*, 14 July 2014, http://www.ft.com/intl/cms/s/0/a59f2232-0b48-11e4-9e55-00144feabdc0.html#axzz37TIVCWWy.
117. "The Acheson-Lilienthal Report on the International Control of Atomic Energy, March 16, 1946," http://fissilematerials.org/library/ach46.pdf, p. 9.
118. *See* "Nuclear Power and Nuclear Weapons," *Nuclear Energy Information Service*, Illinois' Nuclear Power Watchdog, 31 August 2004, http://www.neis.org/literature/Brochures/weapcon.htm; Karl Grossman, "Nuclear Power/Nuclear Weapons—and a Precarious Future," *Huff Post*, 11 March 2013, http://www.huffingtonpost.com/karl-grossman/nuclear-powernuclear-weap_b_2851985.html; "Outline History of Nuclear Energy," *World Nuclear Association*, March 2014, http://www.world-nuclear.org/info/Current-and-Future-Generation/Outline-History-of-NUclear-Energy/.
119. Ali Vaez, "Iran and the P5+1: Solving the Nuclear Rubik's Cube," *Crisis Group*, 9 May 2014, http://www.crisisgroup.org/en/regions/middle-east-north-africa/iraq-iran-gulf/iran/152-iran-and-the-p5-plus-1-solving-the-nuclear-rubik-s-cube.aspx?utm_source=iran-report&amp%3Butm_medium=1&amp%3Butm_campaign=mremail.
120. "Fact Sheet: First Step Understandings Regarding the Islamic Republic of Iran's Nuclear Programme," *The White House*, 23 November 2013, http://www.whitehouse.gov/the-press-office/2013/11/23/fact-sheet-first-step-understandings-regarding-islamic-republic-iran-s-n. It is worth remembering that Brazil, Argentina and Japan have even more developed nuclear technology programmes and the first two have not signed the Additional Protocol.
121. Ian Jackson, "Nuclear energy and proliferation risks: myths and realities of the Persian Gulf," *International Affairs* 85, no. 6, 2009: 1159.
122. Dan Drollette Jr., "The historic debate about Iran's nuclear programme," *Bulletin of the Atomic Scientists*, 20 May 2014, http://thebulletin.org/historic-debate-about-iran's-nuclear-programme7176; "Iran's nuclear programme will follow Japanese model: Larijani," *Payvand Iran News*, 25 February 2010, http://www.payvand.com/news/10/feb/1260.html; James Rupert, "To Disarm Iran's Threat, Offer It a Nuclear Future Like Japan's," *Atlantic Council*, 15 February 2014, http://www.atlanticcouncil.org/blogs/new-atlanticist/to-disarm-iran-s-threat-offer-it-a-nuclear-future like-japan-s; Robert A. Manning and James Clad, "Iran: Rethinking the Endgame," *The National Interest*, 3 February 2014; Ray Takeyh, "Introduction: What Do We Know?" in *Iran: The Nuclear*

Challenge, Robert D. Blackwill (ed.), Washington, D.C.: Council on Foreign Relations Press, 2012.

123. Juan Cole, "Does Iran really want the bomb?" *Salon*, 7 October 2009, http://www.salon.com/2009/10/07/iran_nuclear/.
124. Ariel Ilan Roth, "The Root of All Fears: Why Is Israel So Afraid of Iranian Nukes?" *Foreign Affairs*, 24 November 2009, www.foreignaffairs.com.
125. George Perkovich, "No Endgame in Sight," *Foreign Affairs*, 15 January 2014, http://www.foreignaffairs.com/articles/140650/george-perkovich/no-endgame-in-sight.
126. Ian Jackson, "Nuclear energy and proliferation risks," p. 1157.
127. Jacques E. C. Hymans, "Don't panic if the Iran nuclear negotiations fail," *Bulletin of the Atomic Scientists*, 2 February 2012, http://thebulletin.org/don't-panic-if-iran-nuclear-negotiations-fail; *see also* Jacques E.C. Hymans, Matthew S. Gratias, "Iran and the Nuclear Threshold," *The Nonproliferation Review* 20, No. 1, 2013: 13-38.
128. Hymans, "Don't panic," *Bulletin of the Atomic Scientists*, 2 February 2012.
129. Scott Peterson, "Imminent Iran nuclear threat? A timeline of warnings since 1979," *Christian Science Monitor*, 8 November 2011, http://www.csmonitor.com/World/Middle-East/2011/1108/Imminent-Iran-nuclear-threat-A-timeline-of-warnings-since-1979/US-joins-the-warnings-1992-97.
130. Siegfried S. Hecker and Abbas Milani, "A nuclear energy programme that benefits the Iranian people," *Bulletin of the Atomic Scientists*, 21 January 2014, http://thebulletin.org/nuclear-energy-programme-benefits-iranian-people.
131. Hecker and Milani, "A nuclear energy programme."

7

The Rise of Contentious Politics in Turkey after the Arab Spring

Alper Y. Dede

Introduction

The sudden mass uprisings and the consequent changes of bureaucratic-authoritarian regimes across the Middle East, known as the Arab Spring, shocked the whole world as many analysts studying the region had not expected the sudden collapse of such status-quo oriented, bureaucratic-authoritarian regimes through mass protests. Besides daunting socio-economic and political factors, the Arab Spring would most likely have been impossible without two significant factors: "i) the availability of modern means of communication, and ii) the well-educated young masses' high levels of frustration as a result of stagnancy and inefficiency of the regimes whose only purpose was to maintain the status quo."[1] However, the masses poured on the streets when certain opportunities became available for them.

Historically, the literature on the region regarding prospects of political and social change revolved around the central concept of long-term gradual change. Authoritarian regimes of the region, it was thought, would change as a result of piecemeal liberalization through domestic and/or international pressures. The Arab Spring proved those historical analyses wrong in a fundamental way because such analyses crucially failed to recognize the possibility of sudden mass uprisings as a means of political change across the region. Arab people put their lives in danger by demonstrating on the streets for more freedoms under highly risky situations that could have potentially threatened their lives. This alone proved that there was substantial demand for democracy in the Arab world. The Arab Spring produced different outcomes in different countries. In other words, the course of the Arab Spring did not turn out satisfactorily for all countries that had experienced such large scale mass protests for ousting authoritarian regimes. So far, for instance, Tunisia was able to ensure a successful transition from authoritarianism to democracy and the writing of a liberal constitution. In Egypt, the authoritarian status-quo oriented Mubarak regime had been replaced by the Islamists (the *Ikhwan*); however, the Egyptian military took over one year after Muhammed Moursi, the *Ikhwan*'s presidential candidate, won the country's first democratic elections. In Syria, the Assad regime is still in power and the country is on the course of becoming a failed state with endless fighting between the insurgency and the Assad regime, hundreds of thousands of casualties, and the resulting destruction of the country's infrastructure and cities. Iraq did not experience protests during the Arab Spring; however, the initial stability that was in place after the election of the Maliki government is now being threatened by the ISIL (Islamic State of Iraq and the Levant).

The Arab Spring definitely had a spillover effect and similar protests erupted across the Middle East including Turkey. Thus, at the peak of the Arab Spring, Turkey also was not immune to contentious politics as large scale protests erupted in Turkey in summer of 2013 as people from different walks of life protested the government's plan to demolish the Gezi Park next to the Taksim Square right at the heart of Istanbul and redevelop the area by rebuilding a historical landmark, a mosque and several shopping malls around it.

This paper will analyse *three points* regarding the protests by using concepts taken from the social movement literature: i) how the Arab Spring affected contentious politics in Turkey; ii) what kind of social and political reasons contributed to the rapid spread of the protests across the country, and iii) how the government responded to the protests and why the protests died out quickly.

On 27 May 2013, bulldozers entered the Gezi Park at midnight to uproot the trees in the park and prepare the ground for construction which was part of an urban development project, earlier planned in

2011, with the name "Project for the Pedestrianization of Taksim." In the morning of 28 May, a handful of environmentalists came to the park and set their tents at the park to prevent its demolition. At first, no one could have predicted that such a small environmentalist protest would turn into large scale mass protests in the next several weeks in almost all major cities shaking the whole country. The response from the local police towards the first small group of protestors was very harsh and it exacerbated the whole situation. The protestors were brutally attacked and their tents, which were camped out at the park, were burned down. Some protestors were severely injured. The initial expectation by the local authorities was that the protestors would quit and the protest would come to an end promptly. However, the pictures of the brutal attack by the local police, burned tents, injured protestors and messages about what had happened at the Gezi Park spread all over the social media and suddenly the Gezi Park became the most hotly debated issue on the social media in Turkey. Contrary to the expectations of the local authorities, the protestors did not quit, and the number of protestors exponentially grew as people started to organize solidarity with the protestors on the social media. Indeed, on the evening of 28 May, more people moved into the park with more tents, and suddenly the park turned into a festival ground despite the presence of heavy construction machinery and large number of riot police in and around the park. During the protests, the Turkish Prime Minister R. Tayyip Erdoğan was on a diplomatic trip to North Africa. When the protests erupted, he cut his trip short and returned to Turkey promptly. When he came back, and reporters asked his opinion of the ongoing protests his first reaction was to label the protestors as a handful of *çapulcular* (looters).

The Gezi protests initially started due to an environmentalist concern. But the harsh reaction and the uncompromising attitude of the government about the issue further exacerbated and inflamed the whole situation and a small environmentalist protest escalated into large scale protests across the country. However, there is more to the issue than the environmentalist concerns and debates on urban planning and public spaces. Thus, one needs to analyse and understand the socio-political roots of contention in Turkey to understand why a humble environmentalist protest in the Gezi Park spread immediately and caused a huge political controversy.

The Socio-Political Roots of the Gezi Park Contention

First, the Taksim Square is more than a square because it is a cultural and political icon. In other words, for many people, Taksim is just more than a square; it has a high symbolic and sentimental value in their collective memory. Primarily, the Taksim area represents the modern and secular *façade* of Turkey with its roots in the late Ottoman period as a modern neighbourhood with its multicultural residents. The area is also an attractive location for international tourism hosting regular events of art and culture. It also has a vibrant night life with many cafes and bars which allow people to socialize. Thus, it has a central place in the collective memory of many people. Taksim's significance is not just limited to its attractiveness as an economic, touristic, and social place. More importantly, Taksim has a political significance as it has been historically the most well-known iconic place of political protests including the 1 May rallies. Despite the intermittent prohibition of 1 May rallies at Taksim since 1 May 1977, when 34 people were killed during the rally, Taksim has remained as the *sine qua non* of 1 May rallies in Turkey. Thus, the announcement of the "Project for the Pedestrianization of Taksim" which came with the government's ban on organizing any kind of rallies at Taksim contributed significantly to the intensification of the Gezi protests. The protests were not simply based on environmental concerns or the ongoing political debates in Turkey in summer of 2013. People protested because they perceived the government's new urban plan as an attempt to destroy an iconic place which has a highly sentimental and symbolic value in their collective memories. Additionally, the government's plan to construct a mosque at the square put the secular characteristic of Taksim on debate as the protestors perceived in the government's plan an attempt to dilute the secular characteristics of the Taksim neighbourhood. [2]

Second, and more importantly, it was not just environmental concerns that brought the crowds together. People who had any sort of grievance with the ruling AKP (*Adalet ve Kalkýnma Partisi*-Justice and Development Party) joined the protests. Although the majority of the protestors were young citizens, it was quite possible to see people from different walks of life with varying degrees of ideological commitment on different sides of the political spectrum. In that regard, as Göle argues, the Gezi movement was a pluralistic movement which brought different people together "against the polarizing rhetoric and politics of the government."[3] Especially after the images of the local police forces' brutal treatment of the protestors had spread all over the social media, masses joined the protestors at the Taksim Square and similar protests erupted in almost all cities across the country. Indeed, each attempt at dispersing the crowds attracted more protestors.

Third, the driving force behind the demonstrations, which turned into an extensive social outburst, is not necessarily sole ideology, but about lifestyles.[4] The ruling AKP has over the years become more intrusive into the lifestyles of people who do not share the same ideology with the conservative ruling party. Prime Minister Erdoğan's rhetoric has become overly authoritarian and conservative through the last several years of his tenure in office.[5] For instance, he declared that one of the most important goals of his government would be educating a religious generation and he asked his party members to support a new legislation to introduce more elective courses on religion in basic education. Indeed, the legislation was passed despite criticism from the secular opposition. On a different occasion, the Prime Minister urged his party's members to support a legislation that would introduce tighter restrictions on alcohol sales. Similarly, this legislation was also passed despite criticism from the secular opposition.

Secular Turks believe that the AKP has become overly intrusive into their secular lifestyles. The secularists' fear is indeed real. There is actually a genuine fear among secular Turks that AKP could use legislation to corner secularists and limit their freedoms through its majority in the Turkish parliament.[6] In fact, conservatism and religious symbols have become more visible in the Turkish public space since the late 1980s. As urbanization in Turkey had been accelerating since the late 1960s and early 1970s, well before the establishment of the ruling AKP, increasing number of rural conservatives started to move to bigger cities and they became more visible in urban public spaces. As a result, one of the hottest political debates in the 1990s in Turkey was the headscarf ban which prevented conservative females from wearing their headscarves to universities and public institutions. Indeed, this type of conservative visibility was not perceived as intrusive by the majority of Turkish secularists. However, the AKP's imposition of certain conservative political agenda by relying on its majority in the Turkish parliament actually alienated the Turkish secularists.[7] Thus, it was not just environmentalism or disagreements on urban planning that angered the masses on the streets. One of the underlying causes of the protests was about the battle on secularist and conservative lifestyles as the ruling AKP over the years had been pushing its conservative agenda in the parliament on a variety of different occasions which had alienated the secularists in Turkey.

Fourth, part of the reaction against the AKP stemmed from the feelings of resentment among Turkish liberals who initially supported the AKP. The AKP had followed a more pluralist, democratic and liberal legal and political agenda in its early years in power and introduced openings on a variety of issues that caused political controversy in Turkey. However, liberal Turks parted their way with the AKP as the party became less tolerant and less liberal in legal and political issues. As Göle (2013: 11) puts it, for the past few years, Turkey has experienced "personalization of power" where Erdoğan refrained from consulting citizens while making major decisions about almost every issue in Turkey.[8] He also "monopolized discourse" which resulted in undermining the powers of others who are directly responsible for or related to political issues such as the major of Istanbul, and major of Beyoğlu where the Taksim neighbourhood is located. Thus, the Gezi protests reflect the anger against this type of personalization of power and his omnipresence in the public space.

A comprehensive study conducted during the protests on the protestors reveals significant facts about the protestors and why they protested. Based on the data from KONDA's survey[9] conducted on 6-8 June 2013 on 4,411 Gezi protestors, 50.8 per cent of the protestors were female while 49.2 per cent of them were male. According to the data, 30.8 per cent of the protestors were between the ages of 21-25 and 20.3 per cent of them were between the ages of 26-30, which means that roughly about half of the protestors were between the ages of 21-30. This quite overlaps with the Gezi protestors' demands regarding the ruling AKP's infringement upon their lifestyles because it is usually the young generation which complains about the AKP's pushing of its conservative agenda. The educational profile of the protestors supports the arguments about the socio-economic roots of contention at the Gezi Park. According to the data presented in the KONDA report, roughly about half of the protestors were university graduates who are more sensitive about political issues whereas only about one tenth of Turkish population is a university graduate. The educational profile of the Gezi protestors is well above the Turkish average. Additionally, students are overrepresented among the protests as 36.6 per cent of the protestors were students whereas only 7.8 per cent of the whole Turkish population was students.

The protestors' responses about why they protested is even more revealing: 58.1 per cent of the protestors stated that they protested because freedoms in Turkey had been infringed upon. 37.2 per cent of them stated that they were against the policies of the ruling AKP, and 30.3 per cent of them were protesting against the inflammatory and controversial statements of the prime minister (consider the fact that the respondents were able to provide multiple reasons regarding why they protested). Additionally, the three most important demands of the protestors from the government were more freedoms (34.1 per cent), eliminating infringements of rights (18.4 per cent) and eliminating dictatorship (9.7 per cent).

Understanding the Gezi Protests: The Centre-Periphery Clash Theory or Social Movements Theory?

When the Gezi protests began in late May and early June 2013, the Prime Minister Erdoğan was on a diplomatic trip in North Africa. Upon his return to the country, the Prime Minister called the protestors *çapulcular* (looters). In the following weeks, he did not hesitate to label the protestors as marginal, thugs, scum or even drunkards.[10] Upon the direct orders from the Prime Minister, the city officials' response against the protestors was very harsh. For instance, according to the data collected by The Turkish Medical Association (TMA), in June and July of 2013, 8163 people went to the hospitals in 13 cities with various injuries, 63 of them with severe injuries. Additionally, five people died, and 11 people lost an eye as a result of hitting of pepper gas canisters thrown by the police at the protestors at a short distance.[11] In a month, the police sprayed 3000 tons of water and fired 150,000 pepper gas canisters at the people which is the annual amount of tear gas canisters ordered for the Turkish police by the Turkish Ministry of Interior from Brazil.[12]

For those who are familiar with the studies of Turkish politics, centre-periphery theory describes how political change and/or conflict take place in Turkish politics.[13] According to the theory, a status-quo oriented centre, dominated with westernized and educated elites, rules with little disregard for the political demands of the parochial periphery that represents large uneducated rural masses. As the theory goes, this tension between the secular authoritarian-bureaucratic centre and the relatively more religious periphery has existed for years since the Ottoman times. The new Turkish republic, established by M. Kemal Atatürk and his friends, actually did nothing to eliminate this clash. The westernizing-modernizing elites of the new Turkish republic tried to impose their values, which are the values of the centre, on the periphery despite the periphery's resistance.[14] Thus, the new republic's elites actually reinforced the existing centre-periphery clash. The theory also posits that tensions that arise from the clash between the authoritarian-bureaucratic centre and the periphery with demands for more political participation had shaped future decades of Turkish politics. Although, from time to time, the periphery exerted considerable amount of pressure on the centre mostly through democratic demands, the centre remained dominant as it remained a pivotal actor as praetorian protectors of the main pillars of the Turkish republic outlined by M. Kemal Atatürk's secular ideology.[15]

The centre in Turkey has always had a transformative impact on those who aspire to become part of the centre as a result of upward social mobilization. In other words, the centre imposes its own values and worldview on those who join the ruling elite from the periphery with its deep traditions and tendencies that originate from the authoritarian-bureaucratic, status-quo oriented, statist ideology. Although, the AKP had at first appeared to challenge the centre with claims to represent the periphery, some observers argue that the AKP itself had become the centre, alienating those who are in the periphery. For many years the Turkish politics had been dominated by the military that represents the core values of the Kemalist ideology created by M. Kemal Atatürk, the founder of modern Turkey. However, the AKP has eliminated the military threat by putting some of generals of the military into trial for allegations of plotting against the civilian government known as the *Ergenekon* case. Thus, the ascendancy of the military on Turkish politics significantly declined after the trials. After eliminating the military, and after enjoying three consecutive electoral majorities in the Turkish parliament, the AKP became more authoritarian.[16] In other words, once part of the periphery, the AKP later became the centre by imposing its own worldview and understanding on the centre while ignoring democratic demands coming from the periphery. Therefore, considering the centre-periphery clash theory, one might assume that the Gezi protests represent the resentment of the new periphery that is composed of those who are now left out and alienated under the AKP rule like liberals, secularists, nationalists, and small groups of conservatives with democratic concerns who do not necessarily share the AKP's version of conservatism. As discussed above, this argument holds that the AKP itself has become the centre and it has started to alienate those who have become the new periphery. This could be true to a larger extent; however, the Gezi protests can't be easily understood with the old centre-periphery clash theory that had been widely used by those who study Turkish politics.

We need better explanatory tools to understand the reasons and dynamics of the Gezi protests, and the social movement literature provides us such explanatory tools. Such explanatory tools could be taken from the social movements' literature because the Gezi movement is a social movement. Snow, Soule and Kreisi define social movements as:

> One of the principal social forms through which collectivities give voice to their grievances and concerns about the rights, welfare, and well-being of themselves and others by engaging in various types of collective action, such as protesting in the streets, that dramatize those grievances and concerns and demand that something be done about them.[17]

Thus, social movements are a form of collective action that arise outside of institutional political channels as challengers to or defenders of existing authority organized around and/or mobilized around certain types of collective action. Social movements and social movement organizations use resources to identify and influence political issues and decisions. To influence those who make decisions, social movements must benefit from certain political opportunities as those opportunities become available to them. Thus, political opportunity structures refer to changes in the political environment that influence the chances of success of social movements. Tarrow defines dimensions of political opportunities as: i) the opening of access to political participation, ii) the evidence of political realignment within the polity, iii) the appearance of influential allies, iv) emerging splits within the ruling elite, and v) a decline in the state's capacity or will to repress dissent.[18] The following sections are going to examine the Gezi protests as a social movement by two key concepts taken from the social movements' literature: political opportunity structures and frames.

Ete labels Turkey's oppositional parties as "dysfunctional" and maintains that the Gezi protests should not be perceived solely as manifestations of political dissent against the ruling AKP, but also as a reaction to the failure of the opposition parties to respond to their constituencies' demands.[19] This leads us to conclude that lack of powerful opposition in itself had become an opportunity for the Gezi protestors to voice their demands against the ruling party. In other words, in the absence of real and meaningful political opposition, people took it upon themselves to oppose to defend their rights and lifestyles. Additionally, sharing of brutal images of protestors getting attacked by the police prompted many more protestors to go to Taksim and support the ongoing protests thus opening access to political participation. Thus, the social media provided opportunities for the protestors to get organized, communicate and to spread their messages. Considering the number of young people who had joined the protests, the power of the social media in motivating the protestors should not be overlooked. Despite the diverse background of the protestors, the Gezi movement was able to form a collective spirit holding those diverse people together against the attitude of the ruling AKP which they perceive as an infringement into their lifestyles.

Frames are essentially about how social movements, social movement organizations and their leaders create and use meaning, i.e. about how events and ideas are framed by them. Frames are conceptual containers, and every social interaction is understood through a frame of reference. Benford and Snow argue that frames inspire and legitimate political activities of social movements. Frames must resonate with their audiences.[20]

Another factor that helped the Gezi protestors build a collective spirit, mobilize the masses, and spread their messages was how the protestors framed their grievances. The Gezi protestors were successfully able to frame their grievances in cleverly prepared social media messages as well as reframing the official frames generated by the Prime Minister and the AKP officials. One such frame was the protestors' reframing and embracement of the word *çapulcu* (looter), originally used by the Prime Minister to denigrate the protestors. Protestors frequently shouted on the streets or texted "we are all looters." Among others, the most widely used frames during the Gezi protests were frames specifically about authoritarianism, injustice, and the ruling AKP's intrusion into their secular lifestyles. Indeed, it was the protestors' fear of losing the freedom to enjoy their lifestyles that brought populations with opposing political views.[21] Indeed, the frames created by the protestors were supported by more general frames about equality, democracy, rights and freedoms. Although the mainstream media in Turkey hesitated to cover the events at first, a few days after the protests started, people were able to get live coverage of the protests in Istanbul and in other major cities. Millions of messages and photos were also shared on the social media about the events.

Regardless of the mainstream media's attitude about the Gezi protests, activists on the streets had already been organizing demonstrations, sit-ins and marches over the social media and they shared millions of messages and used innovative methods to mobilize masses. For instance, 13.5 million tweets were posted with the tags of "*direngeziparki, occupygezi, direnankara, direntaksim* and *direngezi*" (*diren* means resist in Turkish). In the repertoire of those who supported Gezi protests, the slogan 'Everywhere is Taksim, resistance everywhere' (*Her yer Taksim, her yer direniş*) was one of the most popular slogans shouted almost everywhere including football matches, university graduation ceremonies, and various demonstrations.[22]

Due to the mainstream media's lack of coverage of the events, the Gezi protestors used social media to get to know what was happening and to communicate. The mainstream media's failure of covering the protests is about the ruling AKP's authoritarianism. Many journalists, indeed, before and after the Gezi protests lost their jobs due to restrictions on freedom of expression and the political pressures of the ruling AKP on the mainstream media in Turkey.[23] However, auto-censorship in Turkey became widespread during and after the Gezi protests as the government used a wide array of tools to subdue the mainstream media. For instance, the AKP government sent an army of financial inspectors to audit financial records of the Doğan Media Group which has various TV channels and newspapers in Turkey. After the audit, enormous fines were assessed for the group and it was forced to sell off several media properties, including *Milliyet*, one of the leading dailies.[24] On different occasions, Turkish Prime Minister directly targeted dozens of journalists and columnists who are critical of the AKP. For instance, recently, at an election rally in Malatya, a city in southeastern Turkey, Erdoğan referred to Amberin Zaman, a successful young female journalist, as a "shameless militant" and added "You shameless woman! Know your place!"[25]

The Decline of the Gezi Protests

Understanding how resource mobilization processes work might help us understand why the Gezi protests ended soon after. One key resource mobilization process is creating organizations and building organizational capacity once a social movement starts. Although the Gezi movement was relatively successful in mobilizing activism through organizing over the social media by arranging various types of protests, sit-ins, occupations and marches, the movement indeed failed to build an organizational capacity with a solid leadership that would help the movement to coordinate their activities further, to communicate with the members of the movement, political elites and the public, and to mobilize material and non-material resources.

The second reason why the Gezi movement failed to build an organizational capacity was that it was a large coalition composed of dedicated but small atomistic groups. We must admit that there was something that we might call a "Gezi spirit" during the protests. However, that spirit was not strong enough to move masses for further political activism over extended time periods. Additionally, those small atomistic groups later dominated the protests which in a way marginalized the rhetoric of Gezi movement keeping the "mainstream Gezi protestors" somewhat alienated from the whole process. When the small atomistic groups dominated the protests on the streets, they resorted to violence which deterred the mainstream Gezi protestors who are less committed than the marginalized protestors. In other words, the Gezi movement lost its appeal among those who might have otherwise supported the movement due to marginalization and violence in the absence of a strong leadership of the movement.

The third reason why the Gezi movement failed to build a larger base of support was about the changes in the demands of the protestors. At first, the demands of the protestors were reasonable such as ending police violence and stopping the construction project at the park. When small atomistic groups dominated the protests, the demands of the movement have become too vague and unreasonable. For instance, a platform established by one of such small atomistic groups gave a list of demands to the government which included issues that were not directly related to the protests, such as their criticisms about construction of the third bridge on the Bosphorus and a new airport in Istanbul. For many mainstream Gezi protestors, as discussed above, the protests were about the threat on their secular lifestyles posed by the ruling AKP. Thus, unlike the members of those small atomized groups that dominated the Gezi discourse, issues like construction of the third bridge or the new airport did not occupy an important place in the political agendas of the mainstream Gezi protestors. Thus, in a way, the small atomized and marginalized groups hijacked the Gezi protests, and more importantly, they made the mistake of trying to act like a political party, which is part of formal politics, while ignoring the fact that as a social movement, they were part of informal politics.

Conclusion

A humble environmentalist protest at the Gezi Park of Istanbul in June of 2013, spreading immediately to all major cities of Turkey, had left a significant mark on Turkish politics. A year after the protests, it might be too early to claim that Turkish politics would be divided in two parts as before the Gezi and after the Gezi. However, since the turbulent 1970s, for the first time in its political history, Turkey had experienced large scale protests of this magnitude. There is very little doubt that the driving force behind the demonstrations, which turned into an extensive social outburst, was people's fears about losing the freedoms and enjoying their lifestyles. Indeed, it was this fear that united people from different sides of the political spectrum. Additionally, the power of social media was evident during the events and people relied on the social media to get their news about the protests instead of the traditional mainstream media. The Gezi protests were not a reaction to religion, but a reaction against authoritarianism which has been on the rise in Turkey under the AKP rule. As of 10 August 2014, Turkish Prime Minister Erdoğan was voted as the first publicly elected president of Turkey which has a parliamentarian system. It appears that the two most heavily debated issues of the upcoming days are going to be: i) who is going to replace Erdoğan as the prime minister, and ii) whether Erdoğan is going to be able to introduce the presidential system that he had always wanted.

After the Arab Spring, Turkey has faced contentious politics decades after the turbulent times of the 1970s when urban guerillas of opposing extreme right and left had clashed on the streets. However, unlike the extreme right and left urban guerillas of the 1970s, this time regular Turks, with concerns about protecting their lifestyles, were mobilized through peaceful collective action. Despite sporadic violence and harsh crackdown of the security forces, Gezi protests in most cities were mostly peaceful and those who joined the protests had positive and life transforming political experiences. Politics of Turkey had always been controversial; however, the Gezi park protests had changed how political controversies are resolved in Turkey: it was not sheer violence but contentious politics with feelings of solidarity and a new level of political consciousness through mostly peaceful means.

Notes

1. Alper Y. Dede, "The Arab Uprisings: Debating the 'Turkish Model'," *Insight Turkey* 13, no. 2, 2011: 23-32.
2. Ahu Karasulu, "If a Leaf Falls, They Blame the Tree: Scattered Notes on Gezi Resistances, Contention, and Space," *International Review of Sociology: Revue Internationale de Sociologie* 24, No. 1, 2014:164-175.
3. Nilufer Göle, "Gezi—Anatomy of a Public Square Movement," *Insight Turkey* 15, No. 3, 2013: 10
4. Hatem Ete, "The Political Reverberations of the Gezi Protests," *Insight Turkey* 15, no. 3, 2013: 15-25.

5. Tayfun Atay, "The Clash of Nations in Turkey: Reflections on the Gezi Park Incident," *Insight Turkey* 15, no. 3, 2013: 39-44.
6. Atay, "The Clash of Nations in Turkey: Reflections on the Gezi Park Incident," 2013:39-44.
7. Nikos Moudouros, "Rethinking Islamic Hegemony in Turkey through Gezi Park," *Journal of Balkan and Near Eastern Studies* 16, No. 2, 2014: 181-95.
8. Göle, 2013: 11
9. KONDA Gezi Raporu (KONDA Gezi Report), http://www.konda.com.tr/tr/raporlar/KONDA_GeziRaporu2014.pdf Released on 5 June 2014. Accessed on 1 August 2014.
10. Göle 2013: 11
11. The Turkish Medical Association, "Göstericilerin Sağlýk Durumlarý (The Health Status Of The Demonstrators)" Released on 1 August 2013. http://www.ttb.org.tr/index.php/Haberler/veri-3944.html Accessed on 14 July 2014.
12. Amnesty International, "Turkey: Fresh Protests Spark Fears over Pending Tear Gas Shipments," 2013. http://www.amnesty.org/en/news/turkey-fresh-protest-death-underscores-urgent-need-halt-tear-gas-shipments-2013-09-10 12 September 2013, Accessed on 21 July 2014.
13. Mardin, Şerif "Centre-Periphery Conflict: A Key to Turkish Politics?" *Daedalus* 102, no. 1, 1973: 169-190.
14. Levent Köker, "Local Politics and Democracy in Turkey: An Appraisal," *Annals of the American Academy of Political and Social Science*. 540, 1995: 51-62.
15. Metin Heper and E. Fuat Keyman, "Double-Faced State: Political Patronage and the Consolidation of Democracy in Turkey," *Middle Eastern Studies*34, no. 4, 1998: 259-77.
16. Ahmet T. Kuru and Alfred Stepan, *Democracy, Islam, and Secularism in Turkey*, New York: Columbia University Press, 2012.
17. David Snow, Sarah A. Soule and Hanspeter Kriesi, "Mapping the Terrain," in *Blackwell Companion to Social Movements*, New York: Wiley-Blackwell, 2008, p. 3.
18. Sidney Tarrow, *Power in Movement. Social Movements, Collective Action and Politics*, New York: University of Cambridge Press, 1994, pp. 86-88.
19. Ete, "The Political Reverberations of the Gezi Protests," 2013:18.
20. Robert D. Benford and David A. Snow, "Framing Processes and Social Movements: An Overview and Assessment Micromobilization, and Movement Participation," *American Review of Sociology* 26, 2000: 611-39.
21. Ete, "The Political Reverberations of the Gezi Protests."
22. Efe Can Gürcan and Efe Peker, "Turkey's Gezi Park Demonstrations of 2013: A Marxian Analysis of the Political Moment," *Socialism and Democracy* 28, No. 1, 2014: 70-89.

23. Bilge Ye°il, "Press Censorship in Turkey: Networks of State Power, Commercial Pressures, and Self-Censorship," *Communication, Culture & Critique* 7, no. 2, 2014:154-73.
24. S. Corke, A. Finkel, D. J. Kramer, C. A. Robbins and N. Schenkkan, "Democracy in Crisis: Corruption, Media, and Power in Turkey," Freedom House Report, 2014.
25. *Todays Zaman*, "Know Your Place You Shameless Woman, Erdoğan Tells Journalist," 2014. http://www.todayszaman.com/newsDetail.action?newsId=354923 Accessed on 9 August 2014.

References

Amnesty International. "Turkey: Fresh Protests Spark Fears over Pending Tear Gas Shipments." 2013. http://www.amnesty.org/en/news/turkey-fresh-protest-death-underscores-urgent-need-halt-tear-gas-shipments-2013-09-10 12 September 2013, Accessed on 21 July 2014.

Atay, Tayfun. "The Clash of Nations in Turkey: Reflections on the Gezi Park Incident." *Insight Turkey* 15, No. 3, 2013: 39-44

Benford, Robert D. and David A. Snow. "Framing Processes and Social Movements: An Overview and Assessment Micromobilization, and Movement Participation." *American Review of Sociology* 26, 2000: 611-39.

Corke, S., A. Finkel, D.J. Kramer, C.A. Robbins and N. Schenkkan. "Democracy in Crisis: Corruption, Media, and Power in Turkey." Freedom House Report, 2014.

Dede, Alper Y. "The Arab Uprisings: Debating the 'Turkish Model'." *Insight Turkey* 13, No. 2, 2011: 23-32.

Ete, Hatem. "The Political Reverberations of the Gezi Protests." *Insight Turkey* 15, No. 3, 2013: 15-25.

Göle, Nilufer. "Gezi—Anatomy of a Public Square Movement," *Insight Turkey* 15, No. 3, 2013: 7-14.

Gürcan, Efe Can and Efe Peker. "Turkey's Gezi Park Demonstrations of 2013: A Marxian Analysis of the Political Moment." *Socialism and Democracy* 28, No. 1, 2014: 70-89.

Heper, Metin and E. Fuat Keyman. "Double-Faced State: Political Patronage and the Consolidation of Democracy in Turkey." *Middle Eastern Studies* 34, No. 4, 1998: 259-77.

Karasulu, Ahu. "If a Leaf Falls, They Blame the Tree: Scattered Notes On Gezi Resistances, Contention, and Space." *International Review of Sociology: Revue Internationale de Sociologie* 24, No. 1, 2014: 164-75.

KONDA Gezi Raporu (KONDA Gezi Report). 2014. http://www.konda.com.tr/tr/raporlar/KONDA_GeziRaporu2014.pdf. Released on 5 June 2014. Accessed on 1 August 2014.

Köker, Levent. "Local Politics and Democracy in Turkey: An Appraisal." *Annals of the American Academy of Political and Social Science* 540, 1995: 51-62.

Kuru, Ahmet T. and Alfred Stepan. *Democracy, Islam, and Secularism in Turkey*. New York: Columbia University Press, 2012.

Mardin, Şerif. "Centre-Periphery Conflict: A Key to Turkish Politics?" *Daedalus* 102, No. 1, 1973: 169-90.

Moudouros, Nikos. "Rethinking Islamic Hegemony in Turkey through Gezi Park." *Journal of Balkan and Near Eastern Studies* 16, No. 2, 2014: 181-95.

Snow, David, Sarah A. Soule and Hanspeter Kriesi. "Mapping the Terrain" in *Blackwell Companion to Social Movements*. New York: Wiley-Blackwell, 2008, pp. 3-16.

Tarrow, Sidney. *Power in Movement. Social Movements, Collective Action and Politics*. New York: University of Cambridge Press, 1994.

The Turkish Medical Association (TMA). "Göstericilerin Sağlýk Durumlarý (The Health Status Of The Demonstrators)." 2013. Released on 1 August 2013. http://www.ttb.org.tr/index.php/Haberler/veri-3944.html. Accessed on 14 July 2014.

Todays Zaman. "Know Your Place You Shameless Woman, Erdoğan Tells Journalist." 2014. http://www.todayszaman.com/newsDetail.action?newsId=354923. Accessed on 9 August 2014.

Yeşil, Bilge. "Press Censorship in Turkey: Networks of State Power, Commercial Pressures, and Self-Censorship." *Communication, Culture & Critique* 7, No. 2, 2014: 154-73.

8

The Changing Dynamics of Turkey's Relations with Israel

The Arab Spring and its Aftermath

Mujib Alam

Introduction

Turkey's relations with Israel plummeted in the mid-2000s after a series of critical events that took place at the bilateral levels between these two countries. The downturn in the relations appeared stunning and dramatic, keeping in view their close relations that had developed in the 1990s[1] and continued even during the early years of the AK Party (*Adalet ve Kalkınma* or Justice and Development) which has been at the helm of affairs in Turkey since November 2002. Several factors, either direct or indirect—at regional, domestic and individual levels—can be enumerated for the development of the strained relationship between Turkey and Israel. One of the direct causal factors was the 31 May 2010 Mavi Marmara incident, in which the Turkish ship, the *Mavi Marmara*, of the Gaza Freedom Flotilla came under attack by the Israeli Defence Forces (IDF) resulting in the death of nine Turkish citizens on board the flotilla. There is no denying the fact that the Palestinian issue was also one of the major determinants of this strained relationship. Though the Mavi Marmara incident led to sharp decline in Turkey-Israel relationship at political/diplomatic or military levels, the economic relations has not only been continuing without much sliding but has constantly been growing during all these years.

The 'Arab Spring' phenomenon that started since mid-December 2010 has caused tremendous ramifications in one form or the other in the length and breadth of the West Asian and North African region. Besides bringing huge transformations at domestic affairs of some countries, the Arab Spring has affected and wrought, positively or negatively, bilateral and multilateral relations between/among the countries of the region. Turkey's relations with Israel are also to be seen against this background. The developments due to the Arab Spring in the region and especially in neighbouring Syria has produced a different regional context and has inflicted new challenges upon both Turkey and Israel.[2] The rigidity between Turkey's and Israel's stances with regard to the Mavi Marmara incident seemed to be decreasing due to emerging security scenario in Syria and the region. Another emerging dimension is related to the Eastern Mediterranean energy resources. There is potential for cooperation in the context of gas discoveries off the Israeli coasts in which Turkey and Israel may cooperate for its consumption and export. Turkey can be a transit route for exports of these energy resources. In spite of the aforesaid challenges, if the process of normalization that are taking place after Israeli apology (2013) and talk for compensation to the victims of Mavi Marmara incident does in fact ensue, there could be a positive impact in a number of areas. New areas of cooperation could become a game changer benefiting both Turkey and Israel.

This paper argues that because of the changing security scenario that has emerged with the Arab Spring phenomenon and other factors especially economic ones, Turkey's relations with Israel has not been frozen completely and in the future it will improve though not to the level that existed in the 1990s. Before analysing the state of Turkish-Israeli relationship during the past four years in the context of the Arab Spring, it is imperative to muse over the past relationship of the two countries.

Turkey-Israel Relations, 1948-2008: An Overview

The history of relationship between Turkey and Israel has remained inconsistent during the past 65 years. However, for analytical purposes scholars have divided these two countries' relationship broadly into four phases.[3] For our purpose we can combine the first three phases as well as some of the initial years of the AKP period to give a historical background and analyse the present phase which basically began since the mid-2000s.

Turkey was opposed to the creation of the State of Israel.[4] However, after the establishment of Israel in 1948, Turkey extended its recognition on 28 March 1949 and established diplomatic relations. It became the first predominantly Muslim country to recognize the Jewish state and within the framework of the western backed-military alliance system in West Asia, Turkey developed close relations with Israel.[5] Besides this, the close relationship of both Turkey and Israel with the US was important factor in the closeness between the former two countries. During the period between 1949 and 1955 Turkey-Israel relations were generally normal which got deteriorated, nevertheless, after the signing of the Baghdad Pact (1955).[6] However, by 1958 Turkey became a part of Israel's "Periphery Alliance" which also included Iran and Ethiopia. It was basically an anti-Arab coalition and an informal alliance of Middle Eastern 'others'.[7] Under the auspices of the alliance of periphery, Turkey and Israel established discreet security and intelligence cooperation in the late 1950s.

During the 1960s and 1970s Turkish-Israeli relationship generally fluctuated during which period Turkey tried to balance its relations with Israel and Arab states and often tilted towards latter countries which had problems with Israel due to the Palestine issue. Because of the effect of the Cyprus issue in Turkey's foreign policy arena and also because of the country's domestic economic problems during these decades, Turkey established better relations with several Arab states and got membership in the OIC (Organization of Islamic Countries). Consequently, the Palestinian issue became one of the important factors in Turkish foreign policy which in turn resulted in fluctuating relationship between both the countries during the 1960s and 70s.[8] In 1980 after the Israeli parliament, Knesset, passed Jerusalem Act to claim the entire city under Israel's administration, Turkey downgraded its diplomatic relations with Tel Aviv from the level of *Chargé d'affaires* to the status of only a Legation and throughout the decade the relationship between the two countries was very cold. The Palestinian issue remained one of the prime factors for this state of affairs.

Since the beginning of 1990s several far-reaching developments at regional and international levels led to changes in general Turkish foreign policy approach and also in its relations with Israel. One important aspect was the emergence of new threats and challenges to Turkey's security from its southern neighbours.[9] Hence the Turkish-Israeli relations that developed in the 1990s were basically strategic and military in nature besides having economic dimensions. The other significant development was related to the West Asian peace process. Turkey, officially citing "positive developments in Israel-Palestinian relations following the Madrid Conference," upgraded its diplomatic representation to the ambassadorial level on 19 December 1991, just six weeks after the Madrid peace talks.[10] It is to be noted that Turkey upgraded relations with both Israel and the Palestinian entity to the ambassadorial level simultaneously. Hence, the starting of the peace process provided Turkey an opportunity to establish close relations with Israel.

The operational environment mainly related to security that brought Turkey and Israel closer during the 1990s were shaped by both regional (strategic) as well as domestic level factors. In order to balance threats from its southern neighbours particularly Syria due to the latter's support to the Kurdistan Workers' Party (PKK), Turkey needed strategic alliance with Israel. Turkey's threat perception was also high due to the signing of military agreement in 1995 between Syria and Turkey's the then adversary Greece. On the domestic level, the 1990s witnessed the expansion of the role of military in Turkish politics, which evolved out of the challenges posed by the Kurdish issue. Besides, the military which was dominant player in foreign policy making was the driving force behind the Turkish-Israeli alliance.[11]

Hence, a combination of factors steered Turkey and Israel in the 1990s to develop close relations in military, economic and technical fields. The close relations of the 1990s were built up on the basis of the following wide-ranging agreements and treaties: (i) Framework agreement (1993), comprising tourism, economic cooperation and educational exchanges; (ii) Environmental cooperation agreement (1994); (iii) Free trade agreement (1996); (iv) Military training and cooperation agreement (1996), which outlined a set of joint training and intelligence-sharing activities; (v) Double-taxation prevention treaty (1997); and (vi) bilateral investment treaty (1998), as well as cooperation in the fields of telecommunications, postal services and drug trafficking. However, the core of the Turkish-Israeli relationship during the 1990s was basically in military and strategic fields.

With the beginning of the twenty-first century the Turkish-Israeli relationship, which was robust during the preceding decade, started deteriorating due to Turkey's changing security environment as well as because of the breakdown in the Palestinian-Israeli peace process.[12] During the period of three-party coalition government (1999-2002) Turkey's relations with Israel began to sour.[13] It is to emphasize here that it all started even before the AKP came to power in November 2002, though the downturn in their relations accelerated during the AKP rule. Turkey's relations towards its southern neighbours in general, and Syria in particular, began to turn from conflict to a cautious rapprochement. With the capture of Kurdistan Workers'Party (PKK) leader Abdullah Ocalan in 1999 and the signing of the Adana Accords with Syria, Turkey's security-based foreign policy towards West Asia started to change.[14] Turkey began to downplay hard security issues in its foreign policy, and especially during the AKP period soft-power began to be emphasized. During the AKP rule most of the factors that were determinants for close alliance with Israel in the 1990s had evaporated or became less important. Thus one can clearly observe their impact on Turkish-Israeli relationship, particularly at military and diplomatic levels. Consequently, the raison d'être of Turkey's overdependence on Israel's support for military and strategic fields started to fade away since the beginning of the 2000s.[15]

The Palestinian-Israeli conflict has remained as one of the vital determinants in Turkish foreign policy circles irrespective of the government at Ankara. Often the Palestinian issue engages the Turkish public almost as a national cause irrespective of their political divide.[16] With the collapse of the West Asian peace process (Oslo I & II) and the eruption of *Intifada II*, deterioration in Turkish-Israeli political relations became visible. In 2002 the then Turkish PM of DSP-MHP-ANAP coalition government Bulent Ecevit accused Israel of committing "genocide" in Jenin.[17] In May 2004, pointing to an Israeli operation in a Gaza refugee camp where about 60 Palestinians were killed, including several children and civilians, PM Erdogan accused Israel of perpetrating 'state terrorism'.[18] When Israel and the West were completely at odds with Hamas after its sweeping victory in the

2006 Palestinian parliamentary elections, Turkey accorded much-needed political legitimacy to the isolated faction and invited its leader-in-exile Khaled Masha'al to Ankara despite Israel's stern resentment.

As mentioned before, the downturn in vibrant relations that Turkey and Israel had enjoyed in the 1990s had started even before the coming to power of the AKP in 2002. However, even during the initial years of the AKP rule, the relationship were maintained at certain level and continued till the downslide started post-2008. In early 2005 prime ministers of Turkey and Israel – Recep Tayyip Erdoğan and Ariel Sharon – signed an agreement to establish a "hotline" for the exchange of intelligence on terrorism-related matters. Erdoğan paid official visit to Israel in the later part of the same year.[19] Israeli President Shimon Peres visited Turkey in 2007 and during his visit he addressed the Turkish Grand National Assembly (TGNA). This was the first time an Israeli head of the state had addressed the parliament of a Muslim-majority country.[20] Cooperation in economic, commercial and military spheres between Turkey and Israel continued apace during the AKP government's first term (2002-07).[21] In 2007 both the countries concluded negotiations over a grand project, named the Med Stream project, to connect their countries across the Mediterranean Sea through five subsea pipelines transporting oil, natural gas, water, electricity and fibre optic cables.[22] In 2008 both the countries agreed to construct an oil pipeline from southern Turkish port of Ceyhan to Israeli port of Ashkelon. Turkey was so optimistic that during his visit to India in 2008, Turkish foreign minister Ali Babacan proposed for an energy corridor for transporting Central Asian hydrocarbon to India via Turkey and Israel.[23] Normalcy in bilateral relations between Turkey and Israel continued till the end of 2008 when Israel's Prime Minister Ehud Olmert paid an official visit to Ankara.

Post-2008 Political and Diplomatic Relations

Turkey's relations with Israel underwent a sharp downturn in diplomatic and military arenas post-2008. A series of events led to the emergence of this situation. The first major source of strain in relationship started due to the Israeli military operations in Gaza Strip (Operation Cast Lead) that started in December 2008 just a few weeks after Ehud Olmert's Ankara visit. Turkish Government vehemently criticized the Israeli actions in Hamas-led Gaza Strip which led to the killing of several thousands of Palestinians, majority of whom were civilians. Ankara also considered this an instance of disregard for its mediation role and challenge for its regional influence. A month later in January 2009 Turkish PM Erdoğan lambasted Israel in the presence of its President Shimon Peres at the World Economic Forum (WEF) in Davos. Erdoğan walked out of the discussion forum after expressing his angst against Israel in his much-talked about "one minute" speech which left President Peres embarrassed and berated.[24] Another thorny incident (2010) was the 'lower chair' issue in which Israel's Deputy Foreign Minister Danny Ayalon made Turkish ambassador Ahmet Oğuz Çelikkol sit on a lower chair in a meeting in order to humiliate the latter.

The most critical point in Turkish-Israeli bilateral relations was the Mavi Marmara incident of 31 May 2010. The Gaza-bound Turkish ship, the *Mavi (Blue) Marmara*, one of the six ships of the Gaza Freedom (Aid) Flotilla carrying humanitarian relief goods, was attacked by the IDF in international water while approaching Gaza. At least eight Turkish citizens and one Turkish-American national were killed in the raid. In reaction to the event, Turkey recalled its ambassador from Israel in June. Ankara demanded for an international enquiry for the incident, and apology from Israel, and insisted on the lifting of Israeli blockade of the Gaza Strip. However, Israel tried to rationalize the IDF action and rebuffed the Turkish demand for an apology. Subsequent to the incident several investigations were carried out by different forums, including the one by the UN which was constituted in August 2010.[25] The panel of inquiry constituted by the UN Secretary General and headed by Sir Geoffrey Palmer, found IDF's action excessive and unreasonable, but at the same time questioned the motivations of the backer of the *Mavi Marmara* trip, the Turkish NGO named IHH (Humanitarian Relief Foundation). It also affirmed Israel's naval blockade of Gaza Strip as legal. Turkey was critical of the Palmer Report which was leaked to the press in September 2011 before its formal release. In reaction to the Report, Turkey expelled Israel's ambassador to Ankara (Gabby Levy) and froze military relations. Consequently, the Turkish-Israeli diplomatic relations entered into a phase of deep crisis.

Economic Relations since 2000

Despite the low level of political and military relations after mid-2000s, which has largely been moulded by Turkey's new foreign policy approach towards the region and the Palestinian issue (based on Ahmet Davutoğlu's 'Strategic Depth Doctrine'),[26] economic relations between Turkey and Israel have continued to remain vibrant and even thriving. Economic relations between the two countries started to grow since the 1990s along with the relationship in political and strategic arenas.[27] Except the tourism sector Israeli-Turkish economic ties have prospered during the AKP period. Bilateral trade between the two countries has quadrupled since 2000 and in 2013 it totalled over $5 billion. Notwithstanding the downturn in political realms, both sides have tried to keep economic relations separate from the political one. All the treaties relevant for trade and investment which were signed in the 1990s have remained effective even after the ongoing political and diplomatic crisis.[28] In the aftermath of the Mavi Marmara incident, Turkish PM Erdoğan pronounced that Turkey would cut off all relations with Tel Aviv. However, the Turkish Government later on desisted from downgrading the commercial relations with Israel.[29] Likewise, from Israeli side also initiatives were taken in order not to hurt commercial interests of both the countries.[30]

Table 8.1: Turkey-Israel Trade Relations, 2000-2013

	Turkey's export to Israel / Israel's Import from Turkey	*Turkey's Import from Israel /Israel's export to Turkey*	*Total Trade (in million $)*
2000	650	506	1156
2001	805	529	1334
2002	861	544	1405
2003	1083	459	1542
2004	1315	714	2029
2005	1467	805	2272
2006	1529	782	2311
2007	1658	1082	2740
2008	1935	1448	3383
2009	1522	1075	2597
2010	2080	1360	3440
2011	2391	2057	4448
2012	2329	1710	4039
2013	2651	2418	5069

As shown in the Table 8.1, Turkish-Israeli bilateral trade increased steadily over the years, from $1.1 billion in 2000 to $5.06 billion in 2013, despite the collapse in diplomatic and military relations. The trade which stood at $3.4 billion in 2008 before the downslide started, rose to $4.4 billion in 2011 and further increased to $5.06 billion as per the latest figure available. Bilateral trade which increased at the rate of 14.6 per cent per year on average from 2002-2008, it has increased by 30.7 per cent from 2010 to 2012. A closer look at each other's exports show that the trend in bilateral trade is not only positive but also reciprocal. If we take into account the major export categories of each country, one can observe that they grew by almost 50 per cent between 2007 and 2011.[31]

However, bilateral economic relations in military sphere have undergone sharp decline due to the Mavi Marmara fallout. In September 2011, Turkey announced the suspension of defence ties with Israel and afterwards froze more than a dozen defence projects. Major deals that were cancelled included a $5 billion deal for hundreds of Merkava Mark III main battle tanks and a proposed $800 million sale of two Israeli patrol aircraft and an early-warning radar plane.[32]

The Arab Spring Effect on Turkey-Israel Relationship

The Arab Spring phenomenon that started towards the end of 2010 and its aftermath has had great impact on the Turkish-Israeli relations, besides inflicting wide-ranging ramifications on the countries of the region as well as the region as a whole. While, unlike Israel, Turkey found itself in an advantageous position during the initial years of the Arab Spring, it encountered security threats due to the protracted crisis in Syria. The civil war in Syria has huge implications on Turkey's regional role[33] which in turn has also impacted Turkish-Israeli relations and both countries are pushed to find some common ground for cooperation. On account of Turkey's changing strategic orientation, it has lifted its veto against Israeli participation in non-military activities within the NATO framework. It is to note that all military ties between Turkey and Israel had been suspended after the Mavi Marmara incident. Besides this, the discovery of hydrocarbon in the Mediterranean basin mainly off the Israeli and Cyprus shores has added to the changing dynamics of the region and which in turn has implications on the Turkish-Israeli relations. The new discovery of huge energy resources especially in Leviathan gas field off the Israeli coast has opened up possibilities for cooperation between Israel and Turkey with regard to export and consumption of these energy resources. Turkish option is cheap and viable one in comparison to other options that would be available to Israel to export its surplus gas.

During the past four years, i.e. since the beginning of the Arab Spring, several positive developments have taken place in the Turkish-Israeli relationship because of changing dynamics, attributable to the effect of Arab Spring phenomenon. In March 2013 Israeli PM Benjamin Netanyahu apologized for the death of Turkish citizens during the Mavi Marmara incident by calling his Turkish counterpart Erdoğan over telephone.[34] This was an important development for mending soured Turkish-Israeli relationship as the 'Israeli apology' was one of the main Turkish demands ever since the Mavi Marmara episode. After the apology, several rounds of talks have taken place for the mitigation of other Turkish demands. Talks for compensation began in April 2013. In a statement in early February 2014, the then Turkish Foreign Minister Ahmet Davutoğlu revealed that the Turkish-Israeli relationship was closer to normalization.[35] Turkey is demanding $30 million in compensation. Recently Israel has offered to pay $20 million, with an extra $3 million if necessary to secure an agreement. Though the Israeli apology is being interpreted from various angles,[36] it can be considered as an indication of coming of Turkey and Israel closer to each other. However, both Turkey and Israel have to go a long way to mend their differences. The final agreement related to the Mavi Marmara incident eventually has to be approved by the respective countries' parliament. Both Turkey and Israel have to take their domestic compulsions into consideration. Furthermore, the trial in absentia of four senior IDF commanders—former Chief of Staff Gabi Ashkenazi, Navy Vice Admiral Flizer Marom, head of Air Force intelligence Avishai Levi and military intelligence chief Amos Yadlin—in an Istanbul court which found them guilty in a recent judgement,[37] will come on the way of reducing tension in bilateral relationship. Another main Turkish demand, i.e. the ending of Gaza blockade was also under consideration, though of late the matter has become complicated due to the fresh Israeli offensive in Gaza which began in July 2014.

The Arab Spring effect is also seen in the economic spheres as well. Due to the Syrian civil war and Turkey's ensuing problems with Syria, which has deprived Turkey of its main export route to the rest of West Asia, Israel has helped Turkey in the transportation of goods to and from Jordan. [38] According to a new report by the Israel Export and International Cooperation Institute, between January-September 2013, chemical exports to Turkey noted a significant 66 per cent rise in 2013, amounting to $1.8 billion, making it Israel's third-largest market.[39] Another sphere where restoration of relations is visible is the two countries ties in civil aviation. Air traffic between Israel and Turkey has soared by over 150 per cent since the 2010 Gaza flotilla episode. However, there are still some disparities between the two nations. While the total number of Turkish Airline flights out of Ben Gurion Airport each week is 112, Israel has no airline flights on the route.[40] The Israeli national carrier El Al flights had stopped flying to Turkish airports and they have remained suspended since 2007 after Turkey refused to comply with Israeli security demands at Turkish airports. Recently, in December 2013, the two countries reached at an agreement that would facilitate in the resumption of the Israeli national carrier El Al flights to Turkey.

Notwithstanding the tension in political relations, both Turkey and Israel have been often exhibiting good gestures at the time of each other's crisis. In December 2010, only a few months after the Mavi Marmara incident and beginning of the diplomatic crisis, Turkey provided assistance in combating Mount Carmel forest fires near Haifa town in Israel. Reciprocating this, in October 2011 during the earthquake in Turkey's Van province, Israeli assistance was offered to Turkey. Soon after a mine tragedy in Turkey in May 2014 (near the town of Soma), the Israeli embassy in Ankara cancelled an Israeli Independence Day ceremony out of respect for Turkey's tragedy.[41] The Israeli Government even offered to provide any technical or medical support for the rescue operations if required by Turkey.

As part of public diplomacy, in January 2012 Turkey's state-run television channel TRT aired episodes of an eight-hour famous documentary on Holocaust.[42] This was for the first time that a Muslim-majority country transmitted such type of documentary on public television. The AKP government's decision to send a high-level representative from the Ministry of Foreign Affairs to participate in the Holocaust commemorations in Istanbul in January 2014 is one of the positive steps taken by the Turkish side aiming at repairing relations with Israel. Naci Koru, the Deputy Foreign Minister, represented the Turkish Government at the event.[43] The Holocaust Remembrance Day is organized by Istanbul's Jewish community along with the Istanbul-based Kadir Has University on 27 January each year since 2011. Another example is that despite the crisis in diplomatic relations, in October 2011 Turkey mediated for a deal between Israel and Hamas for the release of Israel's corporal Gilad Shalit from Hamas in exchange of some prisoners belonging to Hamas from Israel.

Assessment and Conclusion

Most of the literature on the present state of Turkish-Israeli "conflict" or "disengagement" indicates either of two lines of arguments: (i) ideological reasons; and (ii) balance of power perspective. However, for a realistic assessment, we have taken into consideration a combination of factors at domestic, regional and international levels that were relevant during the pre-AKP period as well as those which are pertinent for the present scenario. The discussion above clearly shows that the contemporary Turkish-Israeli relationship especially during the AKP rule has been moulded by various factors, though the Palestinian issue, shaped by the AKP's ideological leanings, has been very visible and dominant for the downturn in their relationship. Though the AKP does not champion political Islam, it partly emphasizes Turkey's Muslim identity at domestic level and associates with Muslim causes particularly in the region (Palestinian issue).

In the context of changing security environment of Turkey due to the Syrian crisis and overall transitioning of the West Asian and North African region, strong bilateral relations can perhaps be reinstated through a revitalization of the peace process and the materialization of a more integrated economy of the region.[44] Because of the strong public opinion within Turkey as well as in the Arab world in favour of resolution of the Palestinian issue, the revival of peace process is one of the important factors for better Turkish-Israeli relations in future. Due to the changing dynamics in Turkey's neighbourhood, the Turkish-Israeli political and diplomatic relationship has been improving and it is likely that it will further improve if the situation in the region remains volatile. Moreover, Turkey's own national interest necessitates it to mend its relations with Israel. At present it does not have a resident ambassador in three important West Asian capitals: Cairo, Damascus and Tel Aviv.[45] If Turkey wants to play a greater regional role it cannot afford to remain in isolation diplomatically.

It is argued by several scholars that while Israel wishes to repair relations, the AKP's and especially its main leadership's interest in doing so is limited. Erdoğan's rhetoric against Israel is cited by many in this regard. For example, he alleged that there is an "interest rate lobby," targeting Israel and that the Jews are behind the recent upheavals in Turkey (Gezi Park controversy and corruption allegations against the AKP government). These types of allegations and counter-allegations are primarily motivated by domestic consumptions of the respective country and will not necessarily impede the improvement in the relationship between Turkey and Israel.

References

1. For detailed analysis of this period, *see* Amikam Nachmani, "The Remarkable Turkish-Israel Ties," *Middle East Quarterly* 5, No. 2, Spring 1998; D. Waxman, "Turkey and Israel: A New Balance of Power in the Middle East," *The Washington Quarterly*, Winter 1999; Dietrich Jung and Wolfgango Piccolli, "The Turkish-Israeli Alignment: Paranoia or Pragmatism?" *Security Dialogue* 31, No. 1, 2000; Ofra Bengio and Gencer Ozcan, "Changing Relations: Turkish-Israeli-Arab Triangle," *Perceptions* 5, No. 1, March-May 2000.
2. Moran Stern and Dennis Ross, "The Role of Syria in Israeli-Turkish Relations," *Georgetown Journal of International Affairs*, Summer/Fall 2013: 120.
3. Writing in the beginning of the present century, Alptekin Dursunoğlu, in his book *Stratejik Ittifak: Turkiye-Israil Iliskilerinin Oykusu* [*The Strategic Alliance: History of Turkey-Israel Relationship*], Istanbul: Anka publications, 2000, mentioned about three phases: first period spread through the 1950s, 60s and 70s which had begun after the initiation of formal diplomatic relations in 1949; second, the 1980s; third, the 1990s. Besides these three phases, many scholars consider the AKP period (post-2002) as distinct phase in Turkish-Israeli relationship.
4. As a member of an UN-created 3-member commission (Reconciliation Commission) to look into the issue of Palestine before Israel's

establishment, Turkey opposed the creation of Israel. When the UNSCOP proposed its plan for the solution in Palestine, Turkey favoured a federal solution (a minority plan) rather than a majority 'partition plan' (UNGA Resolution 181, 1947) which paved the way for the creation of Israel.

5. *See* Nedim Yalansiz, "Turkey-Middle East Relations in the Cold War Era and the Great Powers," *History Studies: International Journal of History* 4, issue 2, July 2012: 393-402.
6. Joshua Walker, "Turkey and Israel's Relationship in the Middle East," *Mediterranean Quarterly* 17, No. 4, Fall 2006: 67-69.
7. Towards the end of the 1960s, this alliance gradually disappeared due to the factors such as the 1967 Six-Day Arab-Israeli War, removal of the Shah of Iran (1979) and the Emperor of Ethiopia.
8. Walker, "Turkey and Israel's Relationship in the Middle East," p. 73.
9. Serget Minasian, "The Turkish-Israeli Military and Political Cooperation and Regional Security Issues," *Iran and the Caucasus* 7, nos.1-2, 2003: 310-11.
10. Beshir Abdel Fattah, "Where are the Turkish-Israeli relations headed?" *Arab Affairs Journal*, no. 140, Winter 2009: 1.
11. Gencer Özcan, "The Changing Role of Turkey's Military in Foreign Policy Making," *UNISCI Discussion Papers*, no. 23, May 2010: 23-45.
12. Karen Kaya, "Changing Trends in Israel-Turkey Security and Military Relations: Their Perspectives," *FMSO-JRIC Analyst*, Foreign Military Studies Office (FMSO), Department of Defence, Government of USA, January 2011, pp. 1-17, http://fmso.leavenworth.army.mil/documents/Changing-Trends-in-Israel-Turkey-Security-Relations.pdf , accessed 8 September 2014.
13. Tarik Oğuzlu, "The Changing Dynamics of Turkey-Israel Relations: A Structural Realist Account," *Mediterranean Politics* 15, No. 2, 2010: 274.
14. Ozlem Tur, "Turkey and Israel in the 2000s–From Cooperation to Conflict," *Israel Studies* 17, no. 3, 2012: 50.
15. Gabriela Özel Volfová, "Changes in Turkish-Israeli Relations: Implications for the Regional Security Environment," *CEIJSS*, no. 1, 2014: 85-86.
16. Before joining Israel's Peripheral Doctrine, Turkey under the Menderes government had downgraded the diplomatic post to Israel to that of *Chargé d'affaires* level in the wake of the Suez crisis (1956); it further downgraded diplomatic relations with Israel after the Jerusalem Act (1980). Ankara recognized the PLO in 1976 and allowed it to establish an office in Turkey in 1979. Gokhan Bacik, "Turkish-Israeli Relations after Davos: A View from Turkey," *Insight Turkey* 11, No. 2, 2009: 35-38.
17. The coalition government (1999-2002) of three political parties, namely Democratic Left Party, Nationalist Movement Party and Motherland Party. Jonny Dymond, "Turkey accuses Israel of genocide," in *BBC News*, 4 April 2002, http://news.bbc.co.uk/2/hi/europe/191109.stm
18. *Hurriyet*, 20 May 2004.

19. During his tour, the Turkish PM paid emotionally important visit to Israel's Holocaust memorial, Yad Vashem, in Jerusalem.
20. Mathew S. Coben and Charles D. Freilich, "Breakdown and Possible Restart: Turkish-Israeli Relations under the AKP," *Israel Journal of Foreign Affairs* 8, no. 1, 2014: 41.
21. Banu Eligür, "Crisis in Turkish–Israeli Relations (December 2008–June 2011): From Partnership to Enmity," *Middle Eastern Studies* 48, no. 3, 2012: 433; Carol Migdalovitz, "AKP's domestically-driven Foreign policy," *Turkish Policy Quarterly* 9, No. 4, Winter 2010-11:.37-45.
22. Daniela Huber and Nathalie Tocci, "Behind the Scenes of the Turkish-Israeli Breakthrough," *IAI Working Papers*, nos. 13-15, April 2013, p. 5.
23. http://timesofindia.indiatimes.com/India/Turkey_offers_alternative_to_Iran_pipeline/articleshow/2770237.cms
24. Aljazeera.com, http://www.aljazeera.com/indepth/opinion/2013/07/201371112018720461.html
25. Huber and Tocci, "Behind the Scenes of the Turkish-Israeli Breakthrough," p. 6.
26. Umut Uzer, "Turkish-Israeli Relations: Their Rise and Fall," *Middle East Policy* 20, no. 1, Spring 2013: 108. For a detailed analysis *see* Can Kasapoglu, "The Turkish-Israeli Relations under the Davutoğlu Doctrine in Turkish Foreign Policy," *Ege Stratejik Arastirma Dergisi* (*Agean Strategic Research Journal*) 3, no. 2, 2012: 1-20.
27. The bases of economic relations were: The 1993 framework agreement, which included economic cooperation; the free trade agreement (1996); the double-taxation prevention treaty (1997); and the bilateral investment treaty (1998).
28. Soner Cagaptay and Tyler Evens, "The Unexpected Vitality of Turkish–Israeli Trade," Washington Institute for Near East Policy, *Research Notes 16*, June 2012, p. 1.
29. *Today's Zaman*, http://www.todayszaman.com/news-255903-pm-turkey-to-impose-more-sanctions-on-israel-boost-presence-in-east-med.html.
30. When an Israeli investment firm declared its intention to divest from Turkey, the head of the Tel Aviv and Central Israel Chamber of Commerce (TACICC) urged firms to refrain from taking any action that might upset Turkish-Israeli economic relationship.
31. Israel's two main categories of exports to Turkey (chemical products and plastic), and Turkey's largest export category to Israel (base metal) as well as other important categories such as vehicles, aircraft, vessels and transport equipment grew more than 50 per cent. Cagaptay and Evens, "The Unexpected Vitality of Turkish–Israeli Trade," p. 2.
32. United Press International, "Israel Scraps Military Deal with Turkey," U PI.com, 3 January 2012: 22. http://www.upi.com/Business_News/Security-Industry/2012/01/03/Israel-scraps-military-deal-with-Turkey/UPI-94711325614535/

33. *See*, Ziya Onis, "Turkey and the Arab Revolutions Boundaries of Regional Power Influence in a Turbulent Middle East," *Mediterranean Politics* 19, No. 2, 2014: 203-19.
34. During his visit to Israel US President Barak Obama persuaded Netanyahu to apologize. The conversation between the PMs took place after almost three years. Barak Ravid, "Netanyahu Phones Erdoğan to Apologize for Deaths of Turkish Citizens on Gaza Flotilla," *Haaretz*, 22 March 2013.
35. Tulin Daloğlu, "Davutoğlu says Turkish-Israeli relationship nears normalisation," www.turkeytribune.com, 11 February 2014.
36. Emre Osman Olkun, "The Reflections of Israeli Apology to Turkey after Mavi Marmara Crisis on Turkish Press: Examples from Daily Newspapers-Cumhuriyet, Hürriyet, Sözcü, Yeni Şafak and Zaman," *Academic Journal of Interdisciplinary Studies* 2, No. 9, October 2009: 757-63.
37. The Istanbul 7th Court of Serious Crimes ordered the arrest of four Israeli commanders on 26 May 2014, who are all being tried in abscntia for their involvement in the raid on the Mavi Marmara in 2010 and also decided to request an Interpol Red Notice for the arrest of who were allegedly involved. *Hurriyet Daily News,* http://www.hurriyetdailynews.com/turkish-court-orders-arrest-of-four-israeli-generals-over-mavi-marmara-.aspx?pageID=238&nid=66979.
38. John Daly, "Trade can be an Ice-Breaker in Turkish-Israeli Relations," *Turkey Analyst* 6, no. 23, 18 December 2013, http://www.turkeyanalyst.org/publications/turkey-analyst-articles/item/78-trade-can-be-an-ice-breaker-in-turkish-israeli-relations.html
39. Daly, "Trade can be an Ice-Breaker in Turkish-Israeli Relations."
40. Al Arabiya Institute for Studies, http://estudies.alarabiya.net/content/'turkey's-ban-israeli-flights-could-bring-down-el-al'
41. *Asharq al-awsat*, http://www.aawsat.net/2014/06/article55332966
42. Documentary of Claude Lanzmann
43. "Turkey marks Holocaust Remembrance Day," *Today's Zaman,* January 27, 2014. http://www.todayszaman.com/news-337779-turkey-marks-holocaust-remembrance-day.html; Dy. Foreign Minister's speech can be found at http://www.projetaladin.org/en/international-holocaust-remembrance-day-in-istanbul.html
44. Kilic Bugra Kanat, "Turkish-Israeli Reset: Business As Usual?" *Middle East Policy* 20, No. 2, Summer 2013: 119; Can Kasapoğlu, "The Turkish–Israeli Relations in 2013: Modest Expectations," *Ortadogu Analiz* 5, No. 49, January 2013: 10-20.
45. Yasar Yakis, "Turkey after the Arab Spring: Policy Dilemmas," *Middle East Policy* 21, No. 1, Spring 2014: 105.

9

Hizbullah's Axis and Turkey

Joseph Alagha

Background

As the so-called 'Arab Spring' or the Arab Uprisings turned into Sunni-Shi'a conflict (discord) and a domino effect of failing states, the Lebanese Hizbullah deepened its regional involvement in Syria, Iraq, and Yemen, thus joining the Iranian axis (with Russia and China) against the Turkish, Gulf Cooperation Council (GCC), and the US, UK, French axis. Think tanks concerned with security studies estimate that there are about 15000 foreign fighters in Syria who originate from 75 countries. Turkish citizens fighting in Syria seem to be immune from prosecution when they return home, since they continue their normal lives without police and intelligence harassment, while those who hail from European countries are held accountable, can go to jail, and have their passports confiscated. This seems to be the case in Western European countries such as France, Belgium, the Netherlands, Germany, Britain, etc., and also in Australia, Canada, and the US.[1]

Hizbullah's Secretary, General Sayyid Hasan Nasrallah, has repeatedly accused Turkey of complicity in the Syrian civil war by being on the side of the rebels and the militant Sunni Islamists. In particular, Nasrallah bashed Turkey for harbouring and buttressing the "Victory Front" (*Jabhat al-Nusra*) and "Islamic State in Iraq and the Levant" (ISIL). For instance, on 15 January and 27 March 2015, he accused Turkey of being the orchestrator of ISIL and *Nusra*, and that it is opening its boarders to them and supporting them logistically and militarily, as well as turning a blind eye and a deaf ear to the foreign fighters' infiltration to Syria across the porous border with Turkey. Nasrallah claimed that ISIL is the brainchild of Turkey, with the US's, France's, and UK's blessings and help. He claimed that Turkey is the major buyer of ISIL's oil, which is against the UN's resolutions.[2] After one year of claiming its Caliphate by military conquest on 9 June 2014, ISIL gained more land. It now controls 50 per cent of Syria and 40 per cent of Iraq, in spite of the continuous airstrikes by the coalition forces. Thus, unfortunately, the 15 October 2014 US-led 'Operation Inherent Resolve'[3] did not curtail ISIL and its expansionist policy. Has the International Community failed in controlling transnational *jihadi* networks?

Introduction: The Coexistence of Militancy and Moderation

Hizbullah, better known as the Islamic Resistance in Lebanon, is infamous for its 'terrorist' global reach and militant face. In the 1980s and early 1990s, Hizbullah abducted Westerners in Lebanon and fought the Israel army till it withdrew its forces in 2000. In the wake of the Arab Uprisings, Hizbullah is fighting alongside the Alawi (Shi'ite) Syrian regime and is lending logistical support to the Iraqi and Yemeni Shi'ite armed militias.[4] Hizbullah's propaganda machine is portraying it as a protector and defender of Eastern Christians and minorities in Lebanon, Syria, Iraq, and Yemen. In light of its Pan-Arabism and Pan-Islamism, what are Hizbullah's domestic and regional ambitions? Do they waver between militancy and moderation?

Hizbullah altered its Islamist ideology and militant character of the 1980s ? when it anathematized the political system and regarded the Lebanese state as an apostate ? to a gradual integration process in the political system since the end of the civil war in 1990 and the party's acceptance of the Ta'if Agreement, which became Lebanon's new constitution. In its post-Islamist trajectory domestic *infitah* (opening-up) project, Hizbullah has reformulated some of its central ideas and strategies. In response to the Lebanese national context, the country's multi-religious realities, and the new post-civil-war-possibilities of successfully operating within a democratic system, prompted Hizbullah to integrate into the Lebanese political system.

Its political ideology changed in so far as its leaders meanwhile concede that the establishment of an Islamic state would need the full legitimacy and sovereignty from the Lebanese people. Hizbullah's former top-down strategy of forcibly imposing an Islamic state against the will of significant parts of the Lebanese society has changed toward an integrative, bottom-up strategy of *infitah*.

Hizbullah's Domestic Ambitions: Control the Political System

The Lebanese resistance movement Hizbullah (Party of God) is notorious for its militant face. Since its inception, Hizbullah has been keen to control the Lebanese political system, initially through a top-down revolutionary process aimed at obtaining power by military force. Regionally and internationally, Hizbullah's reputation as an Islamic resistance movement has been marred by the West's accusation of 'terrorist' operations of global reach; the majority of which were claimed by the Islamic Jihad.[5] Some of the hard power attacks which made Hizbullah gain global attention were the US embassy suicide attacks on 18 April 1983[6] and 20 September 1984; the 23 October 1983 twin-suicide attacks that led to the death of 241 US marines[7] and 58 French paratroopers in Beirut; the Buenos Aires bombing of the Israeli embassy on 17 March 1992:[8] and the holding of Western hostages. The Israeli government and the US Administration claim that Hizbullah's Islamic Resistance constitutes a semi-clandestine organization and that Islamic Jihad is its clandestine wing.[9] In an endeavour to ward off the charges of terrorism, Hizbullah's ideologues, leaders, cadres and intellectuals voice a consensus that has systematically and constantly denied any connection or link to Islamic Jihad or acts it has claimed as its own. This radicalism proved futile in the 1980s.

Hizbullah witnessed remarkable transformations in the past three decades or so. From its founding as an Islamic movement of social and political protest during 1978-1985 it evolved into a full-fledged social movement between 1985 and 1991 and then to a parliamentary political party since 1992 to the present. Since its inception, Hizbullah has adopted Ayatollah Khomeini's theory of *wilayat al-faqih* (guardianship of the jurisprudent) as its ideology in the Lebanese social and political conditions. Khomeini's *wilayat al-faqih* was imported to Lebanon, serving as a blue print of a progressive Islamic state to be emulated by Hizbullah in its constituencies. Illustrating the vital importance given to becoming a member of '*Ummat* Hizbullah,' a Hizbullah cadre told me, on condition of anonymity, that a person, who tried to join the party but failed the process of screening (*ta'tir*) that Hizbullah's prospective members undergo three times, came with an assault rifle and killed his recruiting officer. Another member told me that as practice of indoctrination and as an initiation ceremony, new Hizbullah recruits had to repeatedly state: "If the jurisprudent told you to kill yourself, then you have to do it."[10] This not only illustrates indoctrination, but also the total obedience to the *faqih* (jurisprudent).

In the early 1980s, Khomeini instructed Ali Khamina'i, who was at the time deputy Minister of Defense, to take full responsibility of the Lebanese Hizbullah. Since then, Khamina'i became Hizbullah's 'godfather.' That is why, since its inception, Hizbullah, based on a religious and ideological stance, fully abides by the ideas and opinions of Khomeini as communicated by Khamina'i. During that period, the religious-ideological bond between the Islamic Republic of Iran and Lebanon could be examined from the following declarations by Hizbullah and Iranian officials. Shaykh Hasan Trad: "Iran and Lebanon are one people in one country;" Sayyid Ibrahim Amin Al-Sayyid: "We do not say that we are part of Iran, we are Iran in Lebanon and Lebanon in Iran;" Ali Akbar Muhtashami: "We are going to support Lebanon politically and militarily like we buttress one of our own Iranian districts;" Shaykh Hasan Srur: "We declare to the whole world that the Islamic Republic of Iran is our mother, religion, *Ka'ba*, and our veins."[11]

In the 1980s, Hizbullah advocated the establishment of an Islamic state in Lebanon and maintained the *ahl al-dhimma*[12] category with respect to non-Muslims. In spite of Hizbullah's exhortation of the Christians to convert to Islam, it did not seek to impose this conversion by force. Rather, the party applied its theory of tolerance to those Christians living in its constituencies, as well as to other Christians, as long as they were not 'treacherous or aggressive.' In conformity with the Prophetic tradition and the Qur'an, Hizbullah stressed that there should be "no compulsion in religion" (Qur'an 2:256) and an "equitable world" (Qur'an 3:64) or common grounds that should guide relationships between Muslims and Christians. As such, Hizbullah stressed that the common grounds between *ahl al-dhimma* and Muslims are the social values of mutual tolerance, respect, brotherhood, and solidarity. On this basis, Hizbullah recognized the human freedom, i.e. social and religious freedom of Christians, but *not* the political autonomy as was the case in the 1926 French Mandate Constitution and 1943 Independence Constitution. Thus, in the 1980s, contrary to the Prophetic tradition that granted non-Muslims partnership in political structures, Hizbullah's tolerance or 'inclusiveness' excluded Christians from political life, which could be regarded as a discriminatory practice. Hizbullah's then policy seemed to imply that tolerance is the responsibility of the 'majority' and integration is the responsibility of the 'minority.'

Since 1985, there developed a number of changes in Hizbullah's ideological-identification with Iran's ruling elite. Hizbullah argued that during the early phase of its formation, it needed a unifying religious-political ideology, rather than an elaborate political programme. Thus, it based itself on *wilayat al-faqih* and regarded Khomeini as the jurisconsult of *all* the Muslims.[13] In the beginning, Hizbullah was, ideologically, completely dependent on Khomeini. Later on this dependency witnessed some leeway in the sense that Hizbullah did not blindly follow the Iranian regime; rather it had some specificity (*khususiyya*), since in his capacity as the Supreme Leader (*Rahbar*) he was endowed with the sole right to determine the legitimacy (legitimate authority) to Hizbullah. Khomeini highlighted certain precepts within which Hizbullah could move freely; however, he left their implementation to the party's discretion. Thus, although Hizbullah was ideologically dependent on the Iranian regime, it had some room to manoeuvre in its decisions pertaining to some cases in Lebanese domestic affairs. Even though the fragmentation of religious authority, i.e. the multiplicity of *marja's* among the Shi'ites, continued after Khomeini's death, in Hizbullah's case the issue of religious authority (*marja'iyya*) has been determined on the doctrinal-ideological basis of following the official authority of emulation (*marja' al-taqlid*), who is recognized by the Islamic Republic of Iran. Thus, Hizbullah's religious authority was, still is the Iranian *faqih*. This made the transition after Khomeini's death in June 1989 smoother. Khomeini was succeeded by Imam Ali

Khamina'i, who is the Iranian Spiritual leader, and by default, he is also Hizbullah's religious authority (*marja*). Since then, Hizbullah has experienced a considerable ideological shift.

Since the early 1990s, Hizbullah regarded founding an Islamic state as a 'legal abstraction' and dropped its demands for its implementation in Lebanon. This paved the way for the party to employ the concept of *muwatana* (citizenship) instead of *ahl al-dhimma*. Hizbullah's intellectuals based this current practice on a novel interpretation of the Prophetic tradition, as sanctioned by Shi'ite jurisprudence. Thus, since the 1990s and into the 21st century, Hizbullah has made great strides forward in acknowledging the human, civil, economic, social, cultural, and most importantly the political rights of the so-called ex-*dhimmis*, recognizing their right to full citizenship, citizens of equal status and rights. This is not a rhetorical shift, rather it is a major policy alteration being implemented and aimed at making the 'other' secure in a shared Lebanese polity that might one day be dominated by the Shi'ite majority. Within this new policy of alliances, diplomacy, negotiations, and bargaining, Hizbullah was able to spread its wings and flanks to a tangible part of the Christian constituents of the country.

In the 1990's, Hizbullah reformulated some of its central ideas and strategies. Its former top-down strategy of forcibly imposing an Islamic state against the will of significant parts of the Lebanese society has changed toward an integrative, bottom-up strategy, not only in politics but also in the public sphere. From a *realpolitik* perspective, Hizbullah reconstructed its identity, altered its political strategy, and recognized the 1990 Ta'if Agreement, Lebanon's new constitution. Since then, Hizbullah played within the narrow confines of the political system, by following a bottom-up integration process, which culminated in 2011 to ruling Lebanon through democratic means after the party obtained majority in the parliament, named the prime mister, and formed its government. All this took place, while the new winds of Arab Uprisings were shaping a new Middle East and North Africa (MENA) region.

Benefiting from the Syrian influence that controlled Lebanon militarily (1976-2005), Hizbullah played its cards well and was able to extract an important concession from the Lebanese government by being classified as a resistance movement and not a militia. This meant that Hizbullah was the notable exception to the Ta'if Agreement stipulation of disbanding all militias. As such, the party was able to keep its arms and continue resisting the Israeli occupation, while the militias of all the Lebanese political parties—which had participated in the sixteen-year civil war—had to disband and surrender their weapons to the Lebanese Army. This exception made Hizbullah the strongest military player in Lebanon, even more powerful than the Lebanese Army and security forces. Hizbullah continues to hold a considerable arsenal—mainly of missile stockpiles—even after the nearly complete Israeli withdrawal from Lebanon in May 2000 and the Syrian withdrawal in 2005.

From the early 1990s onwards, Hizbullah readjusted its identity by endeavouring to control the political system through a bottom-up process of gradual participation and integration into the democratic system, starting with the parliament, the municipal councils, and the cabinet or council of ministers, the main executive body of the country. Thus, Hizbullah shifted to acceptance of, and engagement in, the democratic process under a sectarian-confessional political and administrative system that it previously regarded as an apostate. More dramatically, Hizbullah modified its demand, from the abolition of political sectarianism, to the adoption of the Maronite (Christian) political discourse, which stresses abolishing political sectarianism in people's mentality, before officially abolishing it in written laws. The party also called for upholding the principle of consensual democracy. However, based on its demographic strength, Hizbullah called for reducing the voting age from 21 to 18 and changing the electoral system to proportional representation, which the party believed would give the 18 ethno-confessional communities more equitable representation, but in reality it would give the Muslims a numerical 75 per cent advantage over the Christian voters who are estimated to number not more than 25 per cent, by the most generous estimates.[14] Thus, Hizbullah's identity has undergone a considerable transformation from the propagation of its first Manifesto, the "Open Letter" of February 1985, passing through its nine clandestine conclaves, to the dissemination of its second Manifesto a quarter of a century later, in November 2009.

Moderation? Hizbullah's 2009 Manifesto

> Lebanon is our country and the country of our fathers and forefathers; it is also the country of our children and grandchildren and all future generations. We want it sovereign, free, independent, strong and unified... we reject partition and federalism.[15]

Bearing in mind that there are multiple paths of modernity available to the emerging Muslim public sphere leading to the creation of a new civil society, where Islamic values can be created and injected into new senses of a public space that is "discursive, performative, and participative,"[16] Nasrallah clarified that Hizbullah benefits from its jurisprudential vision which believes in the doctrine of *wilayat al-faqih* that gives it the legitimacy of having a political programme in a multicultural, multi-religious country characterized by pluralist groupings and forces, without encroaching upon its doctrinal-ideological, Islamic-religious convictions.[17] In May 2008, after the Hizbullah-led opposition gained veto power in the Lebanese cabinet, Nasrallah reiterated:

> I am honoured to be a member of the party of *wilayat al-faqih*. The just, knowledgeable, wise, courageous, righteous, honest, and faithful *faqih*... *Wilayat al-faqih* tells us [Hizbullah] that Lebanon is a multi-confessional, multi-religious (*mutanawwi', muta'adid*) country that you have to preserve and uphold.[18]

With this unshakable commitment to *wilayat al-faqih*, Hizbullah reformulated what it meant by an Islamic state by making a categorical distinction between *al-fikr al-siyasi* (political ideology) that it maintained and *al-barnamaj al-siyasi* (political programme) that it promoted. From an ideological perspective Hizbullah is committed to an Islamic state, and it will not be dropped as a legal abstraction. However, Hizbullah's political programme has to take into account the political status quo and the overall functioning of the Lebanese political system. Hizbullah characterizes the Lebanese political situation as a complicated mould of sectarian-confessional specificities that prohibit the establishment of an Islamic state, not only from a practical perspective, but also from a doctrinal one. Hizbullah's political ideology stipulates that an Islamic state should be established on solid foundations having full legitimacy and sovereignty from the people. Since the general will of the Lebanese people is against the establishment of an Islamic state, then it is not plausible to establish one.[19] On 30 November 2009, after revealing Hizbullah's new political platform/manifesto, which mentioned neither the Islamic state nor referred to *wilayat al-faqih*, Nasrallah affirmed in answer to a question that there is no contradiction/opposition between belief in *wilayat al-faqih*, on the one hand, and the erection of a strong institutionalized Lebanese state, on the other. On the contrary, *wilayat al-faqih* sanctioned and allowed Hizbullah's integration into the political system. Not only that, in line with the Vatican's position and the papal guidance, Nasrallah added that Hizbullah believes that Lebanon is a blessing and has accomplished great historical achievements. He reiterated Imam Musa al-Sadr's stance that "Lebanon is the definitive nation to all its citizens (*Lubnan watan niha'i li-jami' abna'ihi*)," which is in conformity with the Lebanese constitution.[20]

Thus, Hizbullah shifted its position through its acceptance of and engagement in the democratic process under a sectarian-confessional political and administrative system. More dramatically, Hizbullah's political programme modified its demand from the abolition of political sectarianism, to the adoption of the political Maronite discourse, which stresses the abolition of political sectarianism in mentality, before eradicating it in the texts.[21] In line with the Ta'if Agreement, its earlier election programmes, and Nabih Berri's recent call,[22] Hizbullah's 2009 Manifesto, called for the establishment of the 'National Body for the Abolition of Political Sectarianism' since sectarianism is perceived as a threat to consensual democracy and national coexistence.[23] Although Nasrallah deemed the sectarian system a tribal system, he clarified:

> Let us be realistic. The abolition of political sectarianism is one of the most difficult issues and cannot be accomplished overnight… nobody can dictate how to abolish it in a sentence or two. Rather, if after years of debate, ranging from five to thirty years, we find out that political sectarianism cannot be abolished, then let us be bold enough to say that what we agreed upon in the Ta'if Agreement cannot be realized. But till then, the Lebanese need to found the 'National Body for the Abolishment of Political Sectarianism' in order to initiate the debate in a constructive manner.[24]

The 2009 manifesto delineates an almost complete 'Lebanonization' of Hizbullah, at least in discourse, since it no longer included transnational links such as *wilayat al-faqih* and Islamic state in its primary frame of authority. Furthermore, it gave primacy to the national political arena for achieving national goals that would be beneficial to almost all the Lebanese. This manifesto represents Hizbullah's ideological shifts by assimilating more into the political system to accomplish its goals through political initiatives and continued cooperation with other parties. Moreover, this manifesto might signify Hizbullah's trajectory towards a post-Islamist trend in practice, thus transcending Islamism, its exclusivist platform, evolving into the pluralistic political reality of Lebanon even though certain Islamist rhetoric might still be voiced, and even though Hizbullah's political interests and regional ambitions keep it an ally of the Islamist regime in Iran and the civil-war ridden Ba'thist regime in Syria; the former from an ideological stance, the latter from a strategic alliance.

The party has gone a long way in its attempt to display its new post-Islamist face, all the way to the beginnings of the Arab Uprisings,[25] when setbacks started to accumulate. The US, Israel, Canada, Australia, the Netherlands, and other Western countries classify Hizbullah as a "terrorist organization." The UK differentiates between Hizbullah's "political wing" and its "military wing," dubbing the latter a terrorist organization. On July 26, 2013, the EU followed the UK's classification. After more than three decades of its founding, Hizbullah succeeded in merging its domestic agenda with its regional ambitions, thus boosting its geopolitical role in the shaping of a new Middle East in the wake of the calamities and misfortunes brought about by the Arab Uprisings.

Hizbullah's Regional Axis: Syria, Iraq, and Yemen

Does Hizbullah's buttressing of the Syrian regime and the Iraqi and Yemini Shi'ite militias damage its propaganda image as protector of minorities? Noteworthy, Hizbullah gave arms and supplied logistical training to Lebanese, Syrian, and Iraqi Christians who are facing danger from the "Islamic State in Iraq and the Levant" (ISIL) and similar radical Islamist mindsets such as the "Victory Front" (*Jabhat al-Nusra*) in Lebanon and Syria.

Hizbullah supported the Arab street with the notable exception of Syria, where it adamantly stood by the Syrian regime, its indispensable strategic ally. Hizbullah issued euphoric political declarations exalting the Tunisian and Egyptian people, in particular, and the Arab masses, in general, for their drive for "freedom and dignity." Hizbullah's Secretary General Sayyid Hasan Nasrallah added, "This is the true path when people believe in their resolve... this is the new Middle East created by its own people." He concluded, "Your Spring has begun; no one can lead you to another winter. Your belief, vigilance, and resilience will overcome all difficulties and make you triumphant."[26]

Hizbullah lent its coreligionist Bahraini populace unwavering vocal support in the face of the ruling elite. This stance led some political analysts to criticize such 'double standards.' Being on the defensive, Nasrallah tried to defend, justify, and legitimize Hizbullah's policies. In terms of geopolitics, Hizbullah has repeatedly stated that it would not interfere in any military attack targeting Syria and Iran, unless there is an existential danger facing the two regimes, whereby Hizbullah's joining the fight would tilt the balance in favour of the aggressed upon parties. Therefore, Nasrallah repeatedly stated that Hizbullah will only resort to fighting in Syria in case of extreme necessity.

In the wake of the Arab Uprisings, Hizbullah is fighting alongside the Syrian regime and lending logistical support to the Iraqi and Yemeni Shi'ite armed militias. Hizbullah seems to shift within the parameters of pan-Islamism and pan-Arabism, while maintaining its Lebanese national identity at the centre. Notwithstanding, Hizbullah moves between militancy and integration, the former exemplifies its hawkish policy during the Arab Uprisings, while the latter illustrates its dovish domestic face of being an integral part of the Lebanese state, from which it derives its legitimacy. This shift fuelled Sunni-Shi'a divide or discord (*fitna*), threatening a serious spillover of the Syrian civil war into Lebanon after ISIL and *Jabhat al-Nusra* battled Hizbullah and the Lebanese Army on Lebanese soil.

Hizbullah's Involvement in the Syrian Crisis and the Lebanese Spill-Over

On 25 May 2013, Nasrallah deemed it an existential necessity and blatantly announced that Hizbullah has entered the Syrian fight on the side of the regime. Invoking the 'Divine Victory' legacy of 2006 July War with Israel, Nasrallah emphatically promised his constituency another victory, which materialized on 12 June 2013, when the party 'liberated' *Qusayr* from the Syrian opposition fighters.[27]

Employing anti-takfiri (anathema) discourse, Hizbullah interfered in the sovereignty and territorial integrity of Syria in order to protect its back and fend off the militant Sunni fundamentalist threat originating from there. Of course, Hizbullah's military involvement was welcomed by its strategic ally, the Syrian regime, which it (Syrian regime) considers a boost in its fight against 'armed gangs' such as the Free Syrian Army (FSA), and 'international terrorism' or 'jihadis affiliated with al-Qa'ida,' as the Syrian regime labels the military opposition. Hizbullah accused the FSA—as being traitors, collaborators with the 'enemy,' as the defunct South Lebanon Army (SLA) did during the Israeli Defence Forces' (IDF) occupation of southern Lebanon. As such, Hizbullah accused the FSA of furthering the Israeli-US agenda in the Middle East, or of creating the 'New Middle East of Condoleeza Rice,' the ex-Secretary of State.

Domestically, Hizbullah traded accusations with the Western-backed *March 14* coalition, which compared Hizbullah's military intervention in Syria with the IDF's occupation of Lebanon in order to protect Israel from the attacks of the Lebanese and Palestinian resistance. According to *March 14*, Hizbullah behaved like the IDF by invading and occupying land and encroaching on the 'sovereignty and territorial integrity' of Syria, a UN member country, in order to protect its back. Furthermore, *March 14* argued that Hizbullah's involvement in the Syrian civil war is diminishing its availability across the Lebanese-Israeli border and is distracting its vigilance in dealing with any Israeli imminent threat.

Due to its strategic interest and its fear of losing its backyard, its 'vital space' (élan vital), as well as an easy weapon's supply route, Hizbullah involved itself in the Syrian quagmire. It sent fighters, in spite of the heavy blood price it has to pay and the fear of depleting its human and material resources, especially after losing fighters on a daily basis. Sayyid Nasrallah conceded Hizbullah's limited capabilities and argued that his party cannot change the outcome of the Syrian war, but can offer logistical and material help to the Syrian Army and train it for guerrilla warfare: "We went to Syria to defend

Lebanon… we did it by a personal decision, rather than heeding an Iranian order." Nasrallah accused Saudi Arabia[28] of waging proxy wars in Iran, Iraq, Lebanon, and more importantly in Syria by its material and military support of radical Islamist groups fighting the regime.[29]

In addition to many radical Lebanese Sunni Islamists volunteering to fight against the Syrian regime, jihadi Salafis such as the Shaykh Ahmad al-Asir of Sidon and Shaykh Salem al-Râfi'i of Tripoli sent fighters en masse. The Sunni-Shi'a strife (*fitna*) in Lebanon appeared to be unavoidable. On June 23, 2013, violent military clashes in Sidon erupted between Hizbullah and Shaykh Ahmad al-Asir supporters. After many dead and wounded fell, the Lebanese Army intervened and ended the fight, but at a high price. Al-Asir's headquarters were destroyed and many of his supporters were arrested. Al-Asir fled and his whereabouts are unknown to date. The author's prediction of Sunni-Shi'a *fitna* became a painful reality when, on November 19, 2013, two supporters of al-Asir conducted a twin-suicide operation against the Iranian Embassy, located at *Dahiya*—the heart of Hizbullah's den and stronghold of the southern suburb of Beirut, killing 23 people. Previously, the *Dahiya* was targeted by rockets and two massive explosions: the first on July 7, 2013 led to a few deaths, while that of August 15, 2013, killed 31 people, after which Hizbullah agreed to the deployment of the Lebanese Army and security forces. On January 16, 2014, a suicide bomber detonated a car in *Hirmel*, Hizbullah's stronghold in the *Biqa,'* killing two and wounding more than 46. For the next two days, the Syrian Islamists continued to target *Hirmel* with sporadic rockets. On January 21, 2014, another suicide bomber detonated a car in *Dahiya* killing three and wounding 35 people.

On September 28, 2013, violent confrontations erupted between militant Sunnis and Hizbullah fighters in the *Balbaak*, in the outskirts of the Eastern *Biqa'* valley. As was the case in *Dahiya*, this eventually led to the deployment of the Lebanese Army and security forces in the city, thus returning sovereignty to the state after the apparent failure of private security measures for a second time. On August 23, 2013, two car bombs targeted two Sunni mosques in Tripoli, north Lebanon—the second largest Sunni city after Beirut. Regular skirmishes and seven mini-wars in Tripoli erupted between the Sunnis, who support *March 14*, and the ‘Alawis, who support the Syrian regime. In short, unfortunately, what *Hizbullah's DNA* admonished against two years ago—namely that the Syrian uprising will spill over to Lebanon with drastic and detrimental consequences, the most salient of which is the feared *fitna*—became a painful reality.

In August 2014, the most serious spillover of the Syrian civil war occurred when takfiri jihadis from the “Islamic State in Iraq and the Levant” (ISIL) and “Victory Front” (*Jabhat al-Nusra*) raided and occupied the border town of ‘Irsal. The Lebanese Army intervened. After a few days, the takfiris were defeated and they headed back to Syria, but they were able to kidnap 30 Lebanese soldiers and security forces personnel. The takfir's executed four Lebanese military, threatening more executions if the Lebanese government does not comply with their demands and release a number of hardcore Sunni militants responsible for earlier deadly confrontations with the Lebanese Army.

On 6 October 2014, the “Victory Front” stormed a Hizbullah post near the border village of *Brital* killing 11 Hizbullah fighters. The party reinforced its positions and took back its lost post after a fierce battle that led to the death of 16 “Victory Front” fighters. On 2 December 2014, the takfiris ambushed seven Lebanese Army soldiers—near the arid boarder area of *Ras Ba'albak*—killing six and wounding one. Therefore, the tendency of targeting the Lebanese Army and Security Forces is on the rise.

On 16 January 2015, the Lebanese Army defused a car carrying 120kg of explosives near ‘Irsal. Most probably it was heading to Hizbullah's stronghold of *Dahiya*. On 10 January 2015, two Lebanese suicide bombers from “Victory Front” targeted the ‘Alawi area of *Jabal Muhsin* in Tripoli killing seven and wounding more than 30. Hizbullah engaged in dialogue with the *Future* Movement of the March 14 Trend—the most moderate and the largest Sunni political party in Lebanon—in an attempt to defuse the *takfiri* threat and grant itself more legitimacy after Sunni-Shi'a discord (*fitna*) threatened to cause civil unrest in Lebanon. In a firebrand speech on 27 March 2015—mainly aimed at voicing his criticism against the Saudi-led military operation in Yemen and lending his support to the Yemeni Houthis—Nasrallah reiterated that his party is engaging the *Future* with dialogue from the stance of national interest, stressing that the different modus operandi of the two parties on regional issues should not tarnish domestic politics. Although both parties have a conflict of interest since Sa'd Hariri the leader of Future supports the Saudis, Hariri reiterated that his party stresses the need to continue dialogue in order to protect Lebanon because dialogue is of national interest, thus above all considerations. Hence, both Nasrallah and Hariri agreed that dialogue is of paramount national interest. Nasrallah stressed that Hizbullah is not an Iranian proxy and does not take orders from Iran, stressing the party's independence of Iran in domestic and regional decision making.

> I do concede that we have a relationship of friendship and love with Iran. I believe that Imam 'Ali Khamina'i *al-waliyy al-faqih* is the jurisprudent of all the Muslims. In spite of that, I firmly state that Iran did not tell us, or order us, to do anything in domestic and regional affairs. We are an independent decision body: we study, we evaluate, and then we decide. Nevertheless, sometimes we are guided by Iranian experiences and views, so we might ask for their wise counsel on certain issues. However, the decision and the course of action we take are ultimately ours; as we do not heed Iranian orders of 'do' or 'do not do.'[30]

The Battle of *Qalamun* and the Euphoria of Victory: Blitzkrieg?

On 16 February 2015, Nasrallah announced that the snow has melted and that his party is preparing for the *Qalamun* battle. After three months, on 16 May, in a one-hour televised fiery speech, Nasrallah boasted another "Divine Victory," in which Hizbullah's military machine was able to reclaim, in less than two weeks, 330 square kilometres (93 in Lebanon and 237 in Syria) of strategic-rugged terrain across the Lebanese-Syrian north-eastern boarder that was previously held by ISIL and the Nusra Front. According to him, the battle cost the party 13 dead and tens of wounded, which is an indication of Hizbullah's military prowess that was able to engage the "enemy" across a 30 kilometre front, with 10 kilometre depth (3 months of preparations and only 2 weeks of actual fighting). Nasrallah's propaganda threatened to carry the battle to the *'Irsal* heights if the Lebanese Army does not take drastic measures to reign in the Syrian rebels who are constantly infiltrating Lebanese land, wrecking havoc in it, and terrorising the local population through kidnapping, theft, and extortion. Nasrallah euphorically allayed the fears of the Christian villages—surrounding the historic city of *Ba'albak*—affirming that the *takfiri* (anathema) threat is over, thereby promoting his party as a protector of minorities and defender of their civil and religious liberties: 'we [Hizbullah] are capable of defeating the takfiri threat, no matter who is backing it up and the enormous logistical and military support it is receiving from Turkey and its allies', which is a reference to the GCC, the US, the UK, and French axis, as opposed to Iranian axis of Iraq, Syria, and Lebanon. Comparing the *takfiri* threat to the *Nakba* (the "great misfortune" or historic loss of Palestine in 1948), Nasrallah asserted in a pun that the *Nakba* of the *takfiri* threat is much graver and dangerous than the *Nakba* of 1948'. Nasrallah threatened that the battle is open and that there are no red lines.[31]

Nasrallah: "We'll Wipe Out the Takfiris and End the Existential Threat"

On 10 June 2015, after Hizbullah and the Syrian Army took control of all the hill tops across the Eastern Lebanese-Syrian border – with the notable exception of 'Irsal where the Syrian militants still hold 25 Lebanese Army and Security personnel as hostages—Nasrallah boasted that his party will terminate the "existential takfiri threat." Addressing via video conference the 'Second Congress on the Innovation of Imam Khomeini's Thought', he affirmed: "We are determined to terminate this despicable terrorist-takfiri threat no matter how high the costs are. And we will win."[32]

Conclusion

The Lebanese Shi'ite political party Hizbullah labels itself as an Islamic *jihadi* movement, whose primary concern is the preservation of its identity in light of the Arab Uprisings, which resulted in dramatic developments and turmoil that are rupturing the Middle East and North Africa (MENA). While al-Qa'ida's offshoot *The Islamic State in Iraq and the Levant* (ISIL) wrecks havoc in the MENA, especially in failing states such as Iraq, Libya, and Syria, Hizbullah did not remain idle. The 'Shi'ite' resistance movement Hizbullah joined the

Syrian regime, and to a lesser extent, the Iraqi regime in their fight against 'Sunni' transnational anathema (*takfiri*) *jihad*. Hizbullah dubs as *takfiri* the Sunni militants who are nibbling the Syrian and Iraqi sovereignty and territorial integrity, in a regional and international war where superpowers and regional powers are contesting spheres of influence. Russia, China, Iran, and Hizbullah support the Syrian regime; while the US, France, Britain, Qatar, and Saudi Arabia support the moderate rebels, who have been trying to topple the Syrian regime for the past four years. After ISIL declared its war against the US and Western Europe and beheaded US and British citizens, on 15 October 2014 'Operation Inherent Resolve' was born: a US-led coalition of 40 countries, including 10 Arab countries, most notably Saudi Arabia, Qatar, UAE, Bahrain, and Jordan. Noteworthy, the coalition airstrikes did not lead to the demise of ISIL. On the contrary, after one year of declaring its Caliphate, ISIL still controls around 50 per cent of Syria and 40 per cent of Iraq. Regionally, in the wake of the Arab Uprisings, Hizbullah's militant face is portrayed via its fighting alongside the Syrian 'Alawi (Shi'ite) regime and its lending logistical support to the Iraqi and Yemeni Shi'ite armed militias, while at the same time promoting its moderate face as the protector of minorities, especially the Christians living in Syria and Iraq. Domestically, Hizbullah's *infitah* ('opening-up') policy since the 1990s led the party to become a major player in the Lebanese public sphere.

Notes

1. Such as: http://carnegie-mec.org/?lang=en; http://www.crisisgroup.org/; http://www.clingendael.nl/
2. It seems Nasrallah was referring to the United Nations Security Council (UNSC) Resolution 2718 of 24 September 2014: http://www.un.org/press/en/2014/sc11580.doc.htm. *See* http://www.almayadeen.net/ar/news/lebanon-nTCX90g_DkKC0aQhATmO3A/;http://www.moqawama.org/essaydetails.php?eid=32120&cid=325#.VLpSD6F0_bg (accessed 16 Jan. 2015); and *al-Safir* 13032 (28 March 2015): 1, 3, 11; *al-Akhbar* 2553 (28 March 2015): 1-2.
3. http://www.newsweek.com/americas-next-war-will-be-called-operation-inherent-resolve-277735 (Accessed 15 Oct. 2015).

4. It is estimated that since the beginning of the Arab Uprisings, Hizbullah has lost more than 1500 fighters, around 3000 wounded and many handicapped in its war of attrition against the Sunni militants in Syria, Iraq, and Yemen.
5. The now defunct 'Islamic Jihad' was at the time the spearhead of radical Shi'ite military factions mobilized on the ideology of fighting Israel, the US, and the West. This Shi'ite 'Islamic Jihad' should not be conflated with the Sunni Islamic Jihad, a Palestinian organization founded by Fathi al-Shaqaqi and Abd al-Aziz 'Awda in Syria during the 1970s.
6. According to US political analysts, this incident served as a blueprint for the Marine's bombing six months later. On this basis, it ought to have served as an omen to the CIA to try to prevent the Marine's bombing. (Brent Sadler, CNN, 11 GMT News, 23 October 2003). The death toll of the US Embassy in West Beirut was 63 people, out of whom 17 were Americans, including the entire Middle East contingent of the CIA. Ann Byers, *Lebanon's Hezbollah: Inside the World's Most Infamous Terrorist Organizations* (London: Rosen Publishing Group, 2003), 26-35.
7. The same sources claim that the 12,000 ton explosion was the largest non-nuclear device that resulted, in one instance, in the largest number of US casualties since WWII. Till now, the US holds Iran and Hizbullah responsible for the incident. Byers, Lebanon's Hezbollah, 28-33.
8. In retaliation to Israel's assassination of Sayyid Abbas al-Musawi, Hizbullah's second Secretary General, on 16 February 1992.
9. Shaul Shay, The Axis of Evil: Iran, Hizbullah, and the Palestinian Terror (London: Transaction Publishers, 2005), 89-100; Byers, Lebanon's Hezbollah, 36-49; Ely Karmon, Fight on all Fronts: Hizbullah, the War on Terror, and the War on Iraq. Policy Focus, no. 46. (Washington, DC: The Washington Institute for Near East Policy, December 2003), 1-29.
10. Mahdi N. And 'Abdallah S., interviews by the author conducted in Beirut, October 21 and 25, 2004, respectively.
11. *Al-'Ahd* 8 (21 Dhul-Qadah 1404/August 17, 1984): 6.
12. Where minorities, such as Christians and Jews, were treated as residents holding limited rights and required to pay a poll tax in lieu of alms giving (*zakat*).
13. Sayyid Hasan Nasrallah, (National Broadcasting Network, July 21, 2002).
14. Joseph Alagha, Hizbullah's Identity Construction (Amsterdam: Amsterdam University Press, 2011), 150-1, 224.
15. Hizbullah's 30 November 2009 Manifesto, Chapter II: "Lebanon," Section 1: "The Homeland," 30.
16. Dale Eickelman and Jon Anderson, (Eds) *New Media in the Muslim World: The Emerging Public Sphere* (Bloomington, IN: Indiana University Press, 2003), 2.
17. Nasrallah as cited by Hasan 'Izzeddine, "How is Hizbullah looked upon and how does it introduce itself?" *Al-Safir* (12 November 2001).

18. *Al-Intiqad* 1267 (30 May 2008).
19. Nasrallah, *AL-JAZEERA* TV, 24 September 1998; Na'im Qasim, Hizbullah: Al-Manhaj, Al-Tajriba, Al-Mustaqbal /Hizbullah: The curriculum, the experience, the future, 7th rev. and updated ed. (Beirut: Dar Al-Mahajja Al-Bayda', 2010), 51-52; and MP Ali Fayyad, as cited in Fadeel M. Abun-Nasr, Hizbullah: Haqa'iq wa Ab'ad /Hizbullah: Facts and Dimensions (Beirut: World Book Publishing, 2003), 127.
20. Nasrallah's press conference was broadcast live on *Al-Manar* TV, 30 November 2009, at 1:30 GMT.
21. Nasrallah's 2001 call for the abolition of political sectarianism in mentality, before abolishing it in the texts (10 July 2001 Speech; *al-Safir* 11 July 2001) bears a striking resemblance to the Maronite bishops' declaration that cautioned that deleting political sectarianism from legal texts before wiping it out from Lebanese people's mentality ? through an efficient education of coexistence and mutual respect ? is hazardous (*Daily Star* 5 February 2004). *See* Joseph Alagha, The Shifts in Hizbullah's Ideology (Amsterdam: Amsterdam University Press), 160.
22. A few days before revealing Hizbullah's Manifesto.
23. Hizbullah's 30 November 2009 Manifesto, Chapter II: "Lebanon," Section 3: "The State and the Political System," 38-39.
24. Idem, Nasrallah's press conference (30 November 2009).
25. Joseph Alagha, Hizbullah's Documents: From the 1985 Open Letter to the 2009 Manifesto (Amsterdam: Amsterdam University Press, 2011).
26. Alagha, Hizbullah's Identity Construction, 188.
27. http://www.moqawama.org/essaydetails.php?eid=27814&cid=141#.UaXNXaFKSSo
28. The Saudi King repeatedly and vehemently bashed ISIL and its medieval mindset, arguing that their practices have nothing to do with Islam, which preaches tolerance and acceptance of the other.
29. *See* his interview with OTV on December 3, 2013, and his speech of December 20, 2013, commemorating the assassination of Hassan al-Laqis, a leading cadre of the Islamic Resistance, Hizbullah's military wing.
30. http://www.moqawama.org/essaydetails.php?eid=32301&cid=199#.VRakxaF0_bg; *See also al-Safir* 13032 (28 March 2015): 3; *al-Akhbar* 2553 (28 March 2015): 2; http://www.alahednews.com.lb/108932/149/.
31. http://www.alahednews.com.lb/110866/7#.VVhZT6F0_bg; *al-Safir* 13071 (18 May 2015): 3, 12; *al-Akhbar* 2592 (18 May 2015): 1-4. http:/ /www.moqawama.org/essaydetails.php?eid=32379&cid=199#.VVhavKF0_bg *al-Akhbar* 2593 (19 May 2015): 2-3, 5.
32. http://www.moqawama.org/essaydetails.php?eid=32441&cid=199#.VYKlXaF0_bg; http://www.alahednews.com.lb/111833/149/ (Both accessed 11 June 2015).

References

Such as: http://carnegie-mec.org/?lang=en; http://www.crisisgroup.org/; http://www.clingendael.nl/

It seems Nasrallah was referring to the United Nations Security Council (UNSC) Resolution 2718 of 24 September 2014: http://www.un.org/press/en/2014/sc11580.doc.htm. *See* http://www.almayadeen.net/ar/news/lebanon-nTCX90g_DkKC0aQhATmO3A/;http://www.moqawama.org/essaydetails.php?eid=32120&cid=325#.VLpSD6F0_bg (accessed 16 Jan. 2015); and *al-Safir* 13032 (28 March 2015): 1, 3, 11; *al-Akhbar* 2553 (28 March 2015): 1-2.

http://www.newsweek.com/americas-next-war-will-be-called-operation-inherent-resolve-277735 (Accessed 15 Oct. 2015).

It is estimated that since the beginning of the Arab Uprisings, Hizbullah has lost more than 1500 fighters, around 3000 wounded and many handicapped in its war of attrition against the Sunni militants in Syria, Iraq, and Yemen.

The now defunct 'Islamic Jihad' was at the time the spearhead of radical Shi'ite military factions mobilized on the ideology of fighting Israel, the US, and the West. This Shi'ite 'Islamic Jihad' should not be conflated with the Sunni Islamic Jihad, a Palestinian organization founded by Fathi al-Shaqaqi and Abd al-Aziz 'Awda in Syria during the 1970s.

According to US political analysts, this incident served as a blueprint for the Marine's bombing six months later. On this basis, it ought to have served as an omen to the CIA to try to prevent the Marine's bombing. (Brent Sadler, CNN, 11 GMT News, 23 October 2003). The death toll of the US Embassy in West Beirut was 63 people, out of whom 17 were Americans, including the entire Middle East contingent of the CIA. Ann Byers, *Lebanon's Hezbollah: Inside the World's Most Infamous Terrorist Organizations* (London: Rosen Publishing Group, 2003), 26-35.

The same sources claim that the 12,000 ton explosion was the largest non-nuclear device that resulted, in one instance, in the largest number of US casualties since WWII. Till now, the US holds Iran and Hizbullah responsible for the incident. Byers, Lebanon's Hezbollah, 28-33.

In retaliation to Israel's assassination of Sayyid Abbas al-Musawi, Hizbullah's second Secretary General, on 16 February 1992.

Shaul Shay, *The Axis of Evil: Iran, Hizbullah, and the Palestinian Terror* (London: Transaction Publishers, 2005), 89-100; Byers, Lebanon's Hezbollah, 36-49; Ely Karmon, Fight on all Fronts: Hizbullah, the War on Terror, and the War on Iraq. *Policy Focus*, No. 46. (Washington, DC: The Washington Institute for Near East Policy, December 2003), 1-29.

Mahdi N. and 'Abdallah S., interviews by the author conducted in Beirut, October 21 and 25, 2004, respectively.

Al-'Ahd 8 (21 Dhul-Qadah 1404/August 17, 1984): 6.

Where minorities, such as Christians and Jews, were treated as residents holding limited rights and required to pay a poll tax in lieu of alms giving (*zakat*).

Sayyid Hasan Nasrallah, (National Broadcasting Network, July 21, 2002).

Joseph Alagha, *Hizbullah's Identity Construction (Amsterdam*: Amsterdam University Press, 2011), 150-1, 224.

Hizbullah's 30 November 2009 Manifesto, Chapter II: "Lebanon", Section 1: "The Homeland", 30.

Dale Eickelman and Jon Anderson, (Eds) *New Media in the Muslim World: The Emerging Public Sphere* (Bloomington, IN: Indiana University Press, 2003), 2.

Nasrallah as cited by Hasan 'Izzeddine, "How is Hizbullah looked upon and how does it introduce itself?" *Al-Safir* (12 November 2001).

Al-Intiqad 1267 (30 May 2008).

Nasrallah, *AL-JAZEERA* TV, 24 September 1998; Na'im Qasim, Hizbullah: Al-Manhaj, Al-Tajriba, Al-Mustaqbal /Hizbullah: The curriculum, the experience, the future, 7th rev. and updated ed. (Beirut: Dar Al-Mahajja Al-Bayda',

2010), 51-52; and MP Ali Fayyad, as cited in Fadeel M. Abun-Nasr, *Hizbullah: Haqa'iq wa Ab'ad /Hizbullah: Facts and Dimensions* (Beirut: World Book Publishing, 2003), 127.

Nasrallah's press conference was broadcast live on *Al-Manar* TV, 30 November 2009, at 1:30 GMT.

Nasrallah's 2001 call for the abolition of political sectarianism in mentality, before abolishing it in the texts (10 July 2001 Speech; *al-Safir* 11 July 2001) bears a striking resemblance to the Maronite bishops' declaration that cautioned that deleting political sectarianism from legal texts before wiping it out from Lebanese people's mentality ? through an efficient education of coexistence and mutual respect ? is hazardous (*Daily Star* 5 February 2004). See Joseph Alagha, The Shifts in Hizbullah's Ideology (Amsterdam: Amsterdam University Press), 160.

A few days before revealing Hizbullah's Manifesto.

Hizbullah's 30 November 2009 Manifesto, Chapter II: "Lebanon", Section 3: "The State and the Political System", 38-39.

Idem, Nasrallah's press conference (30 November 2009).

Joseph Alagha, *Hizbullah's Documents: From the 1985 Open Letter to the 2009 Manifesto* (Amsterdam: Amsterdam University Press, 2011).

Alagha, Hizbullah's Identity Construction, 188.

http://www.moqawama.org/essaydetails.php?eid=27814&cid=141#.UaXNX aFKSSo

The Saudi King repeatedly and vehemently bashed ISIL and its medieval mindset, arguing that their practices have nothing to do with Islam, which preaches tolerance and acceptance of the other.

See his interview with OTV on December 3, 2013, and his speech of December 20, 2013, commemorating the assassination of Hassan al-Laqis, a leading cadre of the Islamic Resistance, Hizbullah's military wing.

http://www.moqawama.org/essaydetails.php?eid=32301&cid=199#.VRakxaF0_bg; See also *al-Safir* 13032 (28 March 2015): 3; *al-Akhbar* 2553 (28 March 2015): 2; http://www.alahednews.com.lb/108932/149/.

http://www.alahednews.com.lb/110866/7#.VVhZT6F0_bg; *al-Safir* 13071 (18 May 2015): 3, 12; *al-Akhbar* 2592 (18 May 2015): 1-4. http://www.moqawama.org/essaydetails.php?eid=32379&cid=199#.VVhavKF0_bg

al-Akhbar 2593 (19 May 2015): 2-3, 5.

http://www.moqawama.org/essaydetails.php?eid=32441&cid=199#.VYKlXaF0_bg; http://www.alahednews.com.lb/111833/149/ (Both accessed 11 June 2015).

10

The Divergent Trajectories of Arab Dignity Revolts

Egypt and Tunisia

Mustapha Kamel Al-Sayyid

Introduction

Arab Dignity revolutions which started in Tunisia in December 2010 and in Egypt few weeks later, promised a fundamental change of the political systems in the Arab countries from authoritarian rule to democratic governments elected in fair and free elections. Such hopes were dashed in all the countries where the spark of the revolution ignited masses of the people to revolt against their rulers. The authoritarian regimes gave way to protracted civil war in Libya and Syria, military intervention by neighbouring Arab countries to consolidate a minority led regime in Bahrain and a shaky government that was easily overthrown by the rebel Houthis in Yemen.

The only case of Arab Dignity revolutions where success in attaining at least the political goals of the revolution was registered was Tunisia. Tunisian political parties and civil society organizations managed, despite many difficulties to draft a constitution that provides unambiguously civil and political rights, was approved by both its secular and religious political parties, and elected a pluralist parliament and a civilian president. The case of Tunisia stands in stark contrast to that of Egypt, the second Arab country to remove an authoritarian leader, which finds itself engulfed in a protracted conflict between the Military supported government and supporters and sympathisers with the country's Islamist movement.

The contrast between these two cases stimulated a wide ranging debate among political scientists and observers of the political scene in the Arab world, all of them wondering about causes of these divergent paths of Arab revolutions. They all ask: why did the Tunisians succeed where all other Arab revolutions, and foremost that of Egypt, failed.[1]

Some found the explanation in their belief that the two countries, Tunisia and Egypt, represent two political cultures, one more hospitable to democratic institutions while the other has been perceived as marked by centuries-old authoritarian traditions. Others pointed to a fundamental difference between the leading Islamist movement in each country, namely Ennahda Party in Tunisia and the Muslim Brethren in Egypt. This chapter would use the rational actor's model as a way of comprehending the different trajectories of the two countries. It will start by pointing out the commonalities between the two countries, contrasts the opposed outcomes of the two revolutions and ends by offering what could be an explanation of these divergent paths.

What the Two Countries have in Common?

Given the opposed outcomes of the revolution in the two countries, it is amazing how many features they have in common. A keen observer of the political scene in the two of them could count no less than eight features they share in common.

To start with, their revolutions were the shortest in Arab countries and relatively the most peaceful. In Tunisia, Jasmine Revolution started on 17 December and was crowned with the departure of Ben Ali that brought him down finally to on 14 January 2011, twenty-eight days after the start of the revolution. The Egyptian Revolution was ten days shorter, lasting only eighteen days from January 25 till 11 February 2011. The two revolutions had their victims: 338 people died in Tunisia and 846 died in Egypt. However compared to what happened in Libya and Syria, these were almost peaceful revolutions, compared to tens of thousands killed during the civil wars that marked the revolution in Libya and Syria.

Undoubtedly, both the short duration and the peaceful character of both revolutions were due largely to the role played by their armed forces. Police forces in the two countries could not contain the angry masses. Both Ben Ali and Mubarak had therefore to rely on the armed forces to remain in power. Commanders of the armed forces in the two countries decided not to stand in the face of angry masses and told the authoritarian leader that he no longer was guaranteed of their protection. The Supreme Council of the Armed Forces in Egypt led by Marshall Hussein Tantawi, the then Defence Minister and Commander in Chief, wanted Mubarak to get gradually the message that armed forces were no longer on his side. Mubarak, or his closest entourage including his son, did not want to understand that message. In the face of hundreds of thousands of people threatening to storm his presidential palace and the army expressly unwilling to resist their imminent onslaught, Mubarak had to leave to Sharm El Sheikh. In Tunisia, General Rashid Ammar, general commander of the Tunisian army persuaded Ben Ali to board a plane that was would presumably take him to France on 14 January 2011. With French authorities refusing to grant him permission to land in Paris, he opted instead to go to Saudi Arabia.[2]

The use of social media was a third important feature of the revolution in the two countries, which led observers to call these, and other revolutions in the Arab world, "Face Book revolutions." The Face Book page "Kollona Khaled Sa'eid-We are all Khaled Sa'eid" was instrumental in mobilizing hundreds of thousands of young people to take part in the angry protests months before the January revolution in Egypt. A similar development had been observed in Tunisia as well. Despite efforts by the two governments to suspend Internet services during the days of the revolution, such attempts failed and militants found ways to communicate through social media and other ways. The use of social media marked Arab revolutions for the first time in history.[3]

The pre-revolutionary po6 litical systems had also much in common. They ran short on legitimacy. The two countries were ruled by republican regimes, which betrayed republican ideals. Mubarak acquiesced to the presidential ambitions of his son Gamal. But it was rumoured in Tunisia that the successor to Ben Ali would be a member of his wife's family, as he himself had no son. The corruption that was pervasive in the two countries further eroded their legitimacy. The adoption of neo-liberal economic policies although successful from the point of view of international financial institutions gave rise to wide gaps in the distribution of wealth and income and left large numbers of young people unemployed. The self-immolation of Mohammed Bouazouzi, a frustrated young educated man was shared by many young people in the two countries and fuelled their resentment of the corrupt regime and its economic policies.

Compared to other Arab countries where Dignity revolts took place, the two societies in Tunisia and Egypt were relatively homogeneous. The vast majority of Tunisians were Muslims with a relative absence of large minorities. In Egypt, although Christian Copts account for between 8-12 per cent of total population, they share with the majority Muslim population the same language and culture and are not racially different from their fellow Muslims. This relative homogeneity stands in contrast to the ethnically divided societies in Syria, Yemen and Bahrain or even Libya divided along regional, tribal and even ethnic lines.

Moreover, the composition of political parties in the two countries was marked by the presence of an Islamist dominant party, namely Ennahda in Tunisia and the Muslim Brothers in Egypt. The presence of such dominant party largely shaped the agenda of political debate in the two countries at least for a while after the revolution, with the question of the adoption of Shari'a as a basic source of legislation becoming a focal point of this debate. The opposition between Islamists and their allies on the one hand and secular forces on the other seemed at times to be a threat to national unity.

Finally, each country exerted a demonstration effect on the other. Success of the Tunisians in removing Ben Ali encouraged young people in Egypt to do the same. Young people opposed to the Islamists in Egypt called themselves "Tamarrod–Rebellion" and anti-Islamist parties formed a Salvation Front, as did their Tunisian counterparts in the summer of 2013.

Revolutionary Political Change?

Despite these common features in the context of the two revolutions, the last four years have seen a divergence in their political trajectories with progress towards achieving at least some of the political goals of the revolution in Tunisia and bloody conflicts pointing to uncertain outcome in Egypt. Four years after the start of the two revolutions, Tunisia is now endowed with the infrastructure and institutions of a democratic government while Egypt is struggling to set up similar institutions with practices that do not conform to any definition of democratic governance.

In order to compare "revolutionary" achievements in the two countries, the concept of political change could be a useful framework. As defined by the late Samuel Huntington, political change is a change in the power or the content of any of the components of the political system. Huntington identified five of these components, namely culture, structure, groups, leadership and policies.[4] While it will take a while to find out what change in political culture took place in the two countries, it is easier perhaps to come to some conclusion about the change in the other four components. The two countries still share some continuity between the leaders who were part of the authoritarian regime and who remain in positions of power including in fact their heads of state. They also share a certain continuity of economic policies stressing the importance of a market economy and openness to foreign investments. It does not seem so far that the kind of ruling bloc made up of senior officials of the government and private business groups will not emerge in the medium term as the effective holders of political power in the two countries.[5]

However it is on the qu estion of building new structures that differences emerge between Egypt and Tunisia. This process has been relatively slow in the case of Tunisia, marked by sharp disagreements among principal political forces, but progress has been steadily coming to Tunisia finally with a working constitution that is approved by all these forces. It was quite the opposite in the case of Egypt with several deadlines not respected, and with two constitutional documents, none of which enjoys consensus of all political forces. At the time of writing in February 2015, Tunisia has already an elected assembly, an elected civilian president and a government that got the approval of the elected Assembly of the Representatives of the People and consists of principal figures of the parties that won the majority in this assembly. Egypt, on the other hand, had two elected presidents, one of whom was removed one year after his election, and the second was the Commander in Chief of the army who had removed the elected civilian president. During the interval, Counsellor Adly Mansour who was president of the Constitutional Court was appointed as interim president between the removal of Morsi and the election of former Field Marshal Abdel Fattah El Sisi, and served as acting president between 4 July 2013 and 8 June 2014.

The new constitution of Tunisia was adopted in 2014 by an elected constituent assembly in which the Islamist Ennahda Party had the plurality but not an absolute majority. Its representatives tried to endow it with an Islamic character but the vehement opposition by secular parties got them finally to accept a compromise that eventually produced a document providing unambigiuosly for full respect of civil and political rights. The preamble of the constitution referred to the Tunisian people's "commitment to the teachings of Islam and to their spirit of openness and tolerance" but the same second paragraph immediately added commitment to human values and to universal human rights. In the same conciliatory manner article one of the constitution which defined the identity of the state included Islam as the religion of the state, but Article 2 insisted that Tunisia is a "civil state" based on citizenship, the will of the people and rule of law. Article 3 clarified the matter adding that people is sovereign and exercises its authority through their elected representatives and by referendum.[6]

The first two articles of the Tunisian Constitution are rigid. The constitution insisted that they must not be amended. This was the compromise reached by the opposing camps in the constituent assembly. Supporters of Ennahda had pushed for including a reference to Islamic Shari'a as a principal source of legislation, while secular members resisted this attempt and were determined not to accept such idea insisting instead on a reference to universal human rights. The compromise provided this formulation of Article 1 stipulating that Islam is a religion of state, Article 2, identifying Tunisia as a civil state governed in Article 3 by popular sovereignty.

Another important feature of the new Tunisian Constitution is that it did not offer a particular status to the army and security forces. It stressed in article 17 that the task of the army is to support civilian authorities. It left organizational matters of armed forces to the law.[7]

The importance of this compromise could be seen when the texts of the two constitutions are compared. The Egyptian Constitution was promulgated after the January Revolution. The first document was approved in a referendum in December 2012. The preamble of this constitution expressed pride in the Egyptian people who opened the way to monotheism and knowledge of the creator and embraced prophets. Article 2 stated that principles of Islamic Shari'a are the principal source of legislation. Article 3 recognized the cannon principles of Christians and Jews. Article 4 assigned to Al-Azhar a consultative authority over all matters related to religion. Finally article 219 provided a vague and controversial definition of principles of Islamic Shari'a mentioned in Article 2. Article 43 called on the state to guarantee religious practice to people of divine religions, understood in Egypt to be only Christianity and Judaism.[8] Article 1 described the state system as democratic, but the term "civil state" was not mentioned in this document.

This constitution was drafted by a second constituent assembly dominated by Muslim Brothers. The first constituent assembly of which the author was member had met briefly for a week but failed to hold further sessions as members from secular parties withdrew arguing that Islamists dominated it. It was declared by the Supreme Administrative Court of the Council of State not in conformity with the provisional constitutional text of March 2011. The People's Assembly, which had a massive majority of Islamists, formed the second constituent assembly, which produced a constitutional text that was strongly criticized by secular parties and several civil society organizations. A major demand of these groups was to draft a new constitution, a demand which was vaguely accepted by President Morsi who promised to put it on the agenda of a future people's assembly to succeed the first one elected after the revolution.[9]

Following the removal of Morsi from office on 3 July 2013, the interim president Counsellor Adly Mansour formed the so-called Committee of the Fifty to draft a new constitution, which was put to the people in a referendum on 16 January 2014. The new constitution, an amended version of the 2012 document, purged the former of those controversial provisions through which the Islamists, Muslim Brothers and Salafis strove to shape the Egyptian political system along what they considered Islamic lines. Article 219 was dropped. Al-Azhar was mentioned as an important Islamic institution but stripped of the consultative power that was entrusted to it in the 2012 constitution (Article 7). And all references to the exercise of rights to be in conformity with Islamic Shari'a were dropped. But it also adopted a restrictive definition of religious practice calling on the state to guarantee religious practices of adherents to heavenly religions (Article 64).

However both the constitutions, drafted by Muslim Brothers and their supporters as well as the new one produced after their eviction from power, shared one feature absent in the Tunisian Constitution, namely strengthening the autonomy of the armed forces. Thus article 195 of the Muslim Brothers' constitution required the Minister of Defence to be chosen from among active army officers and Article 197 made the National Defence Council responsible for the budget of the armed forces. Article 198 of the same constitution allowed military tribunals to try civilians if they commit acts harmful to the armed forces.[10]

This autonomous position of the armed forces was further strengthened in the amended constitution of 2014. Article 234 required the approval by Supreme Council of the Armed Forces of the appointment of the minister of defence. This Article should be enforced under the two successive terms of the president of the republic following approval of the constitution in a popular referendum. Article 203 added that the budget of the armed forces would be submitted as one figure by the National Defence Council to the government to be included in the budget that would be considered by the Assembly of the Deputies. Article 204 maintained the jurisdiction of military tribunals to try civilians but strove to define the type of situations, which could bring civilians before these tribunals.[11]

The Tunisians thus succeeded in getting a constitution that reflects the aspiration for freedom that was a hallmark of their revolutions. Despite explicit statement of civil and political rights in the amended constitution of 2014 in Egypt, it still limited freedom of religion to adherents of the three heavenly religions of the Middle East, thus depriving Baha'is for example from the right to practice publicly rituals of their religion. Shi'a Muslims have difficulty even celebrating their religious festivities, as their beliefs are seen by Al-Azhar to be alien to Islam. More importantly, the 2014 constitution expanded the autonomy of the armed forces to make it approach a "state within the state."[12]

With the Tunisians adhe ring to the road map they drew for their institution building following their revolution, they find their country in early January 2015 possessing an elected pluralist legislature, a government formed of the parties that got the majority seats in this legislature, a powerful opposition and a civilian president elected in a second round of a highly competitive election. The Egyptians, having failed to adhere to several road maps, find themselves four years after their revolution with no parliament. The Judicial Electoral Commission in charge of elections took many months before it finally decided to fix the date of the first round of elections on March 21-22, and the second round a month later. The newly elected Assembly of Deputies would have probably no more than two months maximum to convene as the parliamentary session has to end late June, leaving the executive authority with no checks on its exercise of power for over two years during which it has adopted several controversial laws. While being proud of the new constitution, the new president failed to observe several of its provisions.[13] A non-elected interim president led this executive authority from July 2013 till June 2014. The elected president was the former minister of defence who won easily 97 per cent of the popular vote. He faced only one other candidate who lacked the resources to wage a successful and effective campaign.[14] He was moreover disadvantaged by the popular elusion that the powerful commander in chief of the armed forces was the "man of the moment" as described by the prestigious Mohammed Hasanein Heykal, considered the wise man of Egypt. More importantly, while acts of terrorism have taken their toll in Tunisia, a large number of the Egyptian people do not accept the new constitution and all its institutions, considering what happened in July 2013 to be a military coup d'état. Many of those Egyptians do not keep their anger to themselves, but they do engage in riots in different parts of the country. Some of them have taken to armed struggle targeting military and police forces, the transport and energy infrastructure of the country deliberately stirring fear for personal security among citizens of the country, punishing them for their "support of the coup."

Is it a Matter of Different Cultures?

The two countries have to face enormous difficulties meeting the basic needs to employment, poverty alleviation, improvement of public services and many other challenges that had pushed millions of people in the two countries to revolt against the highly corrupt repressive regimes led by Ben Ali and Mubarak. There is no doubt however that Tunisians were more successful so far in managing their differences peacefully and moving to build the foundations of a more liberal political order. But why did Egyptians fail to do the same?

There are two broad answers to this question. One that is not easy to test and is more of an essentialist character: Tunisians are very different from Egyptians. Therefore even when the two peoples find themselves confronting the same situation, they will deal with this situation in dissimilar ways, and the outcomes would not be the same. The other answer would suggest that the conditions under which Tunisian political actors operated were different from those of the Egyptians, and therefore the outcome had to be different in each case.

The first answer flows from a proposition made by the late Moroccan philosopher Dr. Mohammed Abed El Gabri, who had argued that people of the Maghreb, of Mauritania, Morocco, Algeria, Tunisia and probably Libya are different from the people of Masher, of Egyptians, Syrians, Lebanese, Jordanians, Palestinians and those of the Gulf. They share mostly the same language and religion, but they have different histories and geography. The Maghrebins had distinct cultural traditions marked more by the enlightenment of Andalusia and are closer to Europe with its diversity of languages and social conditions. They do not share this hostility to the West, which is a feature of Mashreqi people where Arab nationalist feelings are strongest. They are more willing to learn from the West and to admire western democratic institutions, which they experienced as migrants and students.[15]

A look at the political trajectory of countries of the Arab Maghreb could point to some shaky foundations of this argument. The majority of Maghrebi people live in Algeria. The recent history of Algeria was not marked by love of western institutions, or by willingness to compromise. The Algerians suffered almost ten years of a bloody civil war between their army and supporters of the Islamic Salvation Front, which probably cost lives of close to one hundred thousand people. In fact it was the Algerian army backed by a considerable number of westernized intellectuals who did not like the outcome of fair and free elections in 1991. This election would have led to a government of Islamists. Tunisia also is one of the countries who send thousands of young people to fight in Syria with organizations such as Jabhat el Nusra and ISIS who manifest resentment of western democratic institutions. The Libyans are also Maghrebi people but their warring militias find it even difficult to accept UN call for a meeting in Geneva to settle their differences.

A similar argument is that while it is true that both Ennahda and Muslim Brothers are Islamist movements and are influenced by the same ideas of Hassan El Banna, the founder of Muslim Brotherhood in Egypt, they evolved in different ways. Leaders of Ennahda are of a different mindset compared to leaders of MB in Egypt. They find it easier to accept notions of gender equality and are more inclined to seeking consensual decisions. Leaders of Muslim Brothers in Egypt were often described as Qutbis, in reference to their adherence to a radical trend of Islamist thought attributed to the late Sayyid Qutb. Some of them were even arrested and went to trial with him in 1965-1966 for alleged conspiracy to assassinate Nasser and declare an Islamist state in Egypt.

The debates on the constitutional provisions related to the place of Shari'a in the two countries give support to this line of argument. Ennahda representatives in the constituent assembly got eventually to cede grounds to the secular opposition and accepted dropping of reference to Shari'a as a source of legislation. Muslim Brothers and Salafis were adamantly opposed to any watering down of reference to this notion in the constitution of Egypt. In fact immediately after the fall of Mubarak, they battled in the campaign over the post-revolution constitutional document, charging those who wanted a new constitution that they aimed at deleting reference to Islamic Shari'a in the Mubarak era constitution, and therefore were in favour of amending that constitution, rather than opting for a new one. They went as far as strengthening reference to Shari'a by adding the controversial article 219. Was this unwillingness to compromise on the part of Egypt's Islamist a product of a different mind set?[16]

No matter how important these cultural or psychological differences between the two countries and their political leaders are, there is no doubt that the conditions under which they operated were not the same and were more conducive for negotiations in Tunisia than in Egypt. These conditions related to the role of the armed forces in the two countries, electoral imperatives and the role of third parties.

Role of Armed Forces

The armed forces in the two countries played a crucial role in ousting authoritarian rulers. But the Tunisian armed forces were content to leave the political scene to politicians once they were sure that there was no prospect of return of the deposed leader and his family. The Supreme Council of the Armed Forces in Egypt was determined to run the country alone following departure of Mubarak. It had its own agenda, which it imposed on all other political actors. Inexperienced in politics, it made the wrong moves which it regretted later. It refused any call to share power with civilians in a presidential council. It is true that getting civilian political forces, the youth, Muslim Brothers and liberal parties to agree on who should represent them in this council would have been an ardours task, but it did not even consider giving it a try. It initially took the side of Muslim Brothers hoping to rule the country with them. It persuaded them to accept this arrangement by appointing a committee to draft amendments to the constitution led by an Islamist figure and included a member of the Muslim Brotherhood among its five members. It favoured them by preferring to amend the Mubarak era constitution rather than endeavouring to get the country to adopt a new constitution. It violently repressed youth protests on several occasions and did not even consider holding accountable those who committed these violations of human rights. It lost the trust of secular political forces who refused later to cooperate with it. The same arrogant attitude continued to mark relations with civilian political forces in the second phase of army rule following the events of 30 June-3 July 2013 which led to the ousting of Muslim Brothers from the government. A flagrant example is rejection by President Abdel Fattah El Sisi to reconsider amending either the electoral law of the new Assembly of Deputies or the law of demonstrations, both severely criticized by most political parties in the country. Following their successful removal of Ben Ali, Tunisian armed forces, on the other hand, opted to get out of the political scene and to leave political forces in the country to decide its future.[17]

Electoral Realities

It is almost a mathematical rule of electoral politics that parties who get the plurality of seats in a legislative body need to seek partners in order to ensure the required majority for them to govern, to pass legislation or simply get their way through the legislature. That was the case of Ennahda party in Tunisia. It did not get more than 37 per cent of the vote and the seats in the first elections for a constituent assembly. Three fifths of Tunisian voters preferred to support secular parties. Ennahda wanted to govern and to take an active part in drafting the constitution of post-revolutionary Tunisia. It had to seek allies and could only find these allies among secular parties. It had to concede some ground for them to keep them as government and political partners.[18] The events in Egypt in the spring of 2013 also convinced el Ghannoushi to persist in seeking reconciliation with secular parties in Tunisia, some of whom were already contemplating going the Egyptian way.[19]

That was not the case of Muslim Brothers. They won every electoral consultation they contested since March 2011. It is true they did not get massive majorities but they could count on the support they could get from ideological fellows such as Salafis and former Islamist militants of the Islamic groups Jama'a Islamiyyah and Jihad Organization. Together they won 78 per cent of the vote on constitutional referendum in March 2011, 73 per cent of the vote in legislative elections in late 2011 and early 2012, 51.7 per cent in the second round of presidential elections in June 2012 and 64 per cent of the vote in the constitutional referendum in November 2012.[20] Believing they could easily 39 win at least an absolute majority in any election, counting on the support of fellow Islamists and discounting army intervention against their rule, Muslim Brothers, the dominant party in Egypt after the January revolution, disregarded all other parties and did not manifest any willingness to come to an agreement with these other parties except on their own terms.

Role of Third Parties

In the two countries, relations between Islamists and secular parties were often very tense and situations of sharp confrontation were not rare. At some of these points it seemed that the parties to the many disputes that marked the post revolutionary trajectory had reached the point of no return. Other actors stepped in. Those other actors failed hopelessly in Egypt but were quite effective in Tunisia.

The most important mediation effort in Egypt was undertaken by foreign actors who included the US ambassador but more importantly Catherine Ashton, the EU Foreign Affairs Commissioner. She continued to try to mediate between leaders of MB and the secular parties and later the Egyptian interim government following the ousting of Morsi in July 2013. Positions of the two parties were diametrically opposed. MB wanted return of the elected government and even punishment of whom they considered coup leaders. The secular parties wanted first removal of the unpopular and incompetent prime minister appointed by Morsi and revoking his controversial constitutional declaration, which had put him above the law. Later the interim government wanted Morsi to recognize that he was no longer president. The mediation failed.[21]

Civil society organizations in Egypt were not involved in these mediation efforts. They were too polarized to be credible mediators. Fortunately in Tunisia, they were party to the political process and were independent from all political parties. They also had the political weight to make them effective mediators. These were the Tunisian Federation of Labour with its historical role in the struggle for independence, the Tunisian League for Human Rights, one of the oldest in the Arab World, The Bar Association and the Business Federation. When matters came to a deadlock whether in the constituent assembly or in the government, they would step in, offer the compromise arrangement and use their clout get the opposed political factions to move closer to a meeting point.[22]

In Guise of a Conclusion

What could be said to conclude this account of the good fortunes of the Tunisian people and the bad fortune of the Egyptians. I recall this phrase of Karl Marx. "People make their own history, but they make it under conditions not of their own choosing."

References

1. Laura K. Landolt and Paul Kubicek, "Opportunities and constraints: comparing Tunisi^ and Egypt to the cultured revolutions," *Democratization*21, no. 6, October 2014: 984-1006; Niklas Plaetzer,

"Civil Society as Domestication: Egyptian and Tunisian Uprisings Beyond Liberal Transitology," *International Affairs* 68, No. 1,Fall/winter 2014: 255-65; Maria Syed, "Egypt and Tunisia: Testing Grounds for Goldstone's Assertion on the Revolutionary Process," *Security Strategies Journal*, October 2013: 1-33; Mohammad Fadel, "Modernist Islamic Political Thought and the Egyptian and Tunisian Revolutions of 2011," *Middle East Law & Governance* 3 Issue 1 / 2, February 2011: 94-104.

2. Michael Makara, "Coup Proofing, Military Defection and the Arab Spring," *Democracy and Security*, 2013, http://dx.doi.org/10.1080/17419166.2013.802983. Accessed on 9 February 2015; Taghreed Alqudsi-Ghabra, "Creative Use of Social Media in the Revolutions of Tunisia, Egypt & Libya," *International Journal of Interdisciplinary Social* Sciences 6, No. 6, 2012:147-158; Kevin Koehler, "Antimilitary elites and regime trajectories in the Arab Spring. Egypt, Syria, Tunisia and Yemen in comparative perspective," European University Institute, Florence, 2013.
3. Alqudsi-Ghabra, "Creative Use of Social Media in the Revolutions of Tunisia, Egypt & Libya."
4. Samuel Huntington, "The Change to Change: Modernization, Development and Politics," *Comparative Politics* 3, No. 3, April 1971: 316-17.
5. A good number of businessmen won elections to the People's Assembly in Tunisia and are prominent candidates in the forthcoming Assembly of Deputies in Egypt.
6. *See* text of the Constitution of Tunisia. For an English translation *see* www.constituionproject.org. Accessed on 5 February 2015.
7. Constitution of Tunisia.
8. *See* an English translation of the Constitution of the Arab Republic of Egypt, signed into law by President Mohammed Morsi on 26 December 2012. Preamble and articles 1-4, 219, www.Icln.org/research/library/files/Egypt/cons-2012-en.pdf. Accessed on 6 February 2015.
9. The first assembly had been elected in terms of an electoral law some of whose provisions were declared unconstitutional. That assembly had therefore to suspend its meetings.
10. Read in Constitutions of the Arab Republic of Egypt.
11. For the 2014 constitution, *see* Constitution of the Arab republic of Egypt in www.sis.gov.eg. Accessed on 6 February 2015.
12. Read analysis of the 2014 constitution by Nathan Brown. *see*: http://carnegieendowment.org/2013/12/04/egypt-s-draft-constitution-rewards-military-and-judiciary
13. *Al-Masry Al-Youm*, an Egyptian newspaper counted no less than 10 articles not observed by the president including the article calling on a new president to declare his wealth upon assuming office. *Al-Masry AL-Youm*, 21 January 2015.
14. For results of presidential elections in June 2014, see http: www.elections.eg.

15. Rafiq Abdel Salaam, "Bayna al-mashreq wa al-maghreb" (Comparing Mashreq and Maghreb), *Al-Sharq Al-Awsat*, 4 September 2010.
16. This is the point of view of Professor Alfred Stepan. Alfred Stepan, "Tunisia's Transition and the Twin Tolerations," *Journal of Democracy*23, No. 2, April 2012: 89-103.
17. *See also* Daniel Silverman, "The Arab Military in the Arab Spring: Agent of Continuity or Change/ a Comparative Analysis of Tunisia, Egypt, Libya and Syria," www.politicalscience.osu.edu/intranet/cprw/silverman%20cprw%202012.pdf.
18. On Tunisian election results see site of the national election commission, www.isie.tu/ar/.
19. Similar to what happened in Egypt, secular parties in Tunisia formed so-called Salvation Front, and young people established Tunisian Tamarrod-Rebellion movement.
20. On election results in Egypt, visit the site of the High Electoral Commission, www.elections.eg.
21. "European Union to continue Egypt mediation," www.reuters.com/./us-egypt-protests-ashton-conference-idUSBRE96TO,on February 11,2015, "US envoy leaves Egypt after mediation efforts fail.www.haaretz.com/news/middle-east/1 540259.
22. Hamada Redissi, "What role for Tunisia's National Dialogue under the Interim Unity Government," Arab Reform Initiative, *Policy Alternatives*, 7 February 2014.

11

The Tunisian Spring and the Egyptian Winter

Paul Rivlin

Introduction

At the beginning of 2011 the leaders of Tunisia and Egypt were ousted from power, each after decades in office. This occurred as a result of massive public protests calling for democracy. The fact that this happened in two Arab states, within one month, suggested that there must be significant factors in common between the two countries, which indeed there were. Now, three years later, the differences between them have emerged. After many difficulties and uncertainties, Tunisia has experienced an Arab Spring while Egypt has experienced what can only be called an Arab winter. This chapter examines the similarities and differences between the two countries and some of the implications for the rest of the Arab world.

The Events of December 2010-February 2011

On 17 December 2010, Mohamed Bouazizi's self-immolation in the Tunisian town of Sidi Bouzid gave rise to a wave of sympathy that was quickly politicized by the mass recognition of his desperation: the long-term failure of Arab states to deliver on promises of citizenship, political freedom and economic development. His subsequent death triggered a powerful movement of political mobilization challenging the governing elites of the Arab world. Within a month this movement had forced the president, Zine El

Abidine Bin Ali, to flee to Saudi Arabia after twenty-four years in office.

Ten days after Ben Ali's departure, mass demonstrations began in Egypt and especially in Cairo. Faced with a popular movement of Cairo's youth, the army chose not to fire on the crowd and on 11 February 2011, President Hosni Mubarak, who had ruled Egypt for thirty years, was forced to resign.

The events of late 2010 and early 2011 suggest that, apart from being Arab, the two countries had much in common. They both had largely homogenous populations and unambiguous borders together with a strong national identity. Both had been ruled by secular dictators for decades and had experienced Arab Socialism. Both regimes had fought against Islamic movements and were aligned with the West. Despite economic liberalization, both countries were dominated by the state, although they experienced relatively fast economic growth in the years leading up to the Arab Spring. They suffered extensive corruption that centred on the ruler, his family and followers. In Egypt and Tunisia as well as in other Arab (and non-Arab) countries, the living standards of the middle class were affected by the withdrawal or decline of state support. All these factors contributed to the wave of discontent that spread in the Arab world at the end of 2010, leading, among other things, to the fall of Ben Ali and Mubarak. The political developments that followed in Egypt and Tunisia seemed similar with Islamic forces taking a dominant role. Free elections were held and Islamic governments were elected but there the similarities and the paths that the two countries followed ended.

The Economies

The most obvious differences between the two countries were economic and demographic. In 2012, Egypt's population was ten times larger than Tunisia's and its national income over five times as large. As a result, national income per capita was over 30 per cent higher in Tunisia than in Egypt. Population growth was significantly higher in Egypt at 1.7 per cent adding about 1.4 million to the population annually. In Tunisia population growth, at one per cent, added about 100,000 annually. Poverty was a bigger problem in Egypt both absolutely and relatively. While 25 per cent of the population lived in poverty, at least 15 per cent more lived close to the poverty line and as a result, 40 per cent of the population—32 million people—had an income of $2/day or less. In Tunisia, 15.5 per cent of the population, i.e. 1.7 million, lived below the poverty line. (*See* Table 1)

While export growth has been rapid (averaging 15 per cent in Egypt, seven per cent in Tunisia over the last decade) and economic growth was healthy in the years to 2011, the structural transformation that typically accompanies rapid economic growth has been very limited.[1] Exports have been dominated 2 by traditional, and the structure of industry has remained largely unchanged over the past decade. There was little technological progress or knowledge spill-over from more sophisticated industries.

The shares of industry in GDP and employment have changed relatively little over the past fifty years. The share of agriculture in output and employment has fallen and productivity in agriculture has grown more slowly than that in other sectors. The decline in agriculture's share in GDP and employment was largely absorbed by the service sector. However, employment in high-productivity service activities, such as banking, insurance and finance, has grown very slowly, while employment in low-wage, low-productivity informal sectors has grown rapidly. In Egypt the public sector remains dominant, despite privatization.

Tunisia has developed from being semi-closed and inward-oriented economy into an outward-oriented and export-fuelled market one, based on manufacturing production and, in contrast to Egypt, run by private entrepreneurs. The share of industry in output increased during the 1970s and 1980s but has remained stable since then. The share of services also rose, while that of agriculture declined. Between 1980 and 2010, the share of manufactures products in total exports increased from 35 per cent to 75 per cent. Furthermore, 6.1 per cent of total exports were high-technology products in 2010.[2] Although Tunisia has gone fu4 rther in terms of economic reforms than most Arab countries, it has not been able to break through a glass ceiling and achieve the higher growth rates and lower unemployment rates prevailing in fast-developing countries outside the Middle East.[3]

Although the private sector has played a much larger role in Tunisia than in Egypt, the way in which it developed explains part of its weakness. During the modern colonial period from 1881, the

French bought agricultural products from Tunisia and sold industrial products there. Virtually no French investment was made in Tunisian industry. In 1904, this pattern was formalized with the creation of a customs union between France and Tunisia that ensured free access for French industrial products in Tunisian markets. The situation changed in the late 1930s and during the World War II, when the absence of French goods encouraged industrial production in Tunisia. France started to promote industrial development in 1942 in order to maintain the economy, but French personnel dominated the industries set up, thus preventing the creation of a locally based private sector. This continued until independence in 1956.

Tunisia's independence was followed by a debate on how the economy should be run. There were two main schools of thought: one favoured the private sector and the other favoured the public sector. In the early years, the private sector was encouraged with loans, tax and other benefits. However, its response was weak and in 1962, in an attempt to encourage economic growth, a state-led policy was implemented. While the state invested in public sector industries, it never wholly discredited the private sector as happened in other Arab countries during their socialist phase. The aim of the policy was to concentrate economic decision making in the government rather than implement socialism. During the period 1962-71, the public sector accounted for 72 per cent of gross fixed investment.[4] All this took place within the context of import substitution: tariffs and other restrictions on imports meant that local markets were reserved for domestic production, something that was to continue until the 1980s.

Failures in agricultural production and a fiscal crisis resulted in a change of direction in the early 1970s. Emphasis was placed on the private sector: extensive help and encouragement were provided. In the words of the minister of national economy, the state would create a generation of private sector industrialists who would take over economic leadership in the future.[5] The results were dramatic: in the 1970s, industrial growth grew rapidly.

These patterns of development show that the private industrial sector was neither parasitic nor dominant. The early 1980s brought economic crisis when oil revenues fell as a result of lower Tunisian production and lower world prices. Agricultural production fell due to drought and as a result of the combination of these factors, both the state budget and the balance of payments deteriorated. In 1986, the government announced comprehensive reforms designed to stabilize and restructure the economy. These were based on agreements with the IMF and the World Bank and included a liberalization of foreign trade. This reduced the extent of import substitution, gradually exposing parts of industry to foreign competition. With the signing of an Association Agreement with the European Union in 1995, Tunisia committed itself to much more extensive reductions on taxes on imports from its major market.

Compared to fast growing developing economies, Tunisia has suffered from a lack of private investment. Despite satisfactory macroeconomic conditions and structural reforms, growth has relied more on public investment, and private investment remains limited, at around 14 per cent of GDP in the early 2000s. This was even a lower rate than in the 1980s and early 1990s. One reason for the low private investment ratio is the limited openness of services markets and network industries, particularly in information technology and transport. This kept the cost of key services high, hindered competitiveness, and deprived Tunisia from significant opportunities for private investment. Another reason was the uncertainty of the business environment, reflecting the risks in Tunisia's international economic environment. But these factors only partly explain the large private investment gap in Tunisia. The World Bank provides a further explanation. Interference by the government was often arbitrary, limited competition and favoured those who had personal connections to officials. The regulatory framework lacked transparency and predictability as did that for government contracts. All this limited competition, efficiency, investment and production.[6]

The weakness of the private sector, notwithstanding the fact that it is more developed than in many other Arab countries, has meant that total investment, as a share of GDP, was lower after the economic reforms of 1986 than before. In 1988, it fell to its lowest level as a share of GDP since 1960.[7] From 1988 until 1993, there was an increase in investment from 22 per cent of GDP to 31 per cent. Although these were higher levels than in many Arab states, they were lower than those experienced in Tunisia in the 1960s and 1970s. The share of private sector investment in GDP rose in the 1970s from 11-12 per cent to 15-16 per cent. In the 1990s it fell, reaching 12-13 per cent in 1995-99.[8]

The private sector faces government-imposed limitations. First, privatization of the telecommunications, transport and other sectors has been limited. In other developing countries, including Arab ones, these sectors have attracted substantial private capital and foreign investment. Partly because these sectors remain publicly owned or dominated, competition is limited and so costs and prices are high. This is closely related to weaknesses in the regulatory environment. Government officials retain a high degree of discretion in regulating economic activity. The arbitrary powers used by government officials reflected the state of play in government-private sector relations. Although the government has long recognized its limitations as an entrepreneur and financier, it has not been willing to share power with the private sector. One of the ways that it maintains its control is to act arbitrarily, and avoid excessive transparency and clarity.[9]

Ben Ali maintained a large bureaucracy and public sector so that he could dispense patronage and retain control. As the domestic market was small, economies of scale in production were limited and so the development of manufacturing industry for the local market was limited. Tariffs on imports offered opportunities for rents, but they were threatened by international trade agreements. As a result of its relatively high living standards, Tunisia did not receive much foreign aid, so the government encouraged the development of exports, including manufacturing and tourism.

Tunisia failed to integrate the export sector into the oligarchy close to the ruling elite. As the regime lacked legitimacy, it prevented either economic or political competition. The regime favoured trusted, individual capitalists, rather than the capitalist class as a whole.[10] The uneven resuscitation of capitalism was too incomplete and discontinuous to create a new class of independent capitalists and so the accumulation of capital did not translate into political power.[11] The new capitalist class was reliant on the state for licenses and even access to capital.

During the period of economic liberalization, since 1986, Tunisia's ruling party abandoned its traditional attempt to represent a broad segment of society and became a vehicle representing the interests of the rural bourgeoisie and urban manufacturers, many of whom were previously rural notables. As a result, the regime represented the rural bourgeoisie and the urban bourgeoisie was merely an offshoot. At the same time, an increasingly globalized economy and stagnant state-led growth strategies within Tunisia led to constraints on the state, as international forces pressed for increased market reforms. Currently the Islamist movement serves as the strongest organized resistance to the ruling party.[12]

Social conflict was depoliticized or privatized and this disciplined and divided the business community and the trade unions. The business community was split between the state orientated, anti-liberalization group and the market-orientated, pro-liberalization group. The latter was a tiny minority of private entrepreneurs, although it did control the Tunisian Union of Industrialists, Merchants and Artisans (UTICA) and export industries.[13]

Table 11.1: Egypt and Tunisia: Basic Indicators, 2012

	Egypt	*Tunisia*
Population (millions)	80.7	10.8
GDP ($ millions)	262	46
GDP per capita ($)	3,247	4,259
Population growth (average annual rate, 2009-2013)	1.7	1.0
Poverty (percentage of the population living below the national poverty line)	25	15.3

Source: World Bank, http://data.worldbank.org/country

The Armed Forces

One of the biggest differences in the development of Egypt and Tunisia has been the role of the armed forces. Egypt's standing army numbers 450,000, with reserves of 254,000 and 405,000 in the paramilitary. Tunisia has an army of 35,500 and 9,000 in the paramilitary.[14] These figures do not, however, reveal the difference between the roles of the military in the political development of the two countries.

The Egyptian army has controlled Egypt since the coup of 1952, with the exception of Islamic President Mohamed Morsi's one year in office. Under its rule, the private sector was largely replaced by public ownership and modern enterprise with "monstrous bureaucracy."[15] The question of whether to restore democracy was determined in 1954 when General Mohammed Naguib, the nominal leader of the coup who wanted to restore democracy and return the army to the barracks, was replaced by Gamal Abdul Nasser.[16] Since then the army has ceded much power to the president and thus remained out of the limelight. Its military failures in 1956 and 1967 wars against Israel and in the prolonged war in Yemen (1962-67) were partly compensated for by its initial success in the 1973 war. The entry of the army into the civilian economy accelerated after the 1973 war with the need to demobilize large numbers of soldiers while retaining their loyalty.

The militarized state that developed in the aftermath of the 1973 war passed through three different phases. In 1979, following the peace agreement with Israel, the military, which then numbered about 900,000, had to be downsized. The need to find alternative employment for large numbers of officers resulted in many of them being absorbed by the military industries. It also resulted in the military entering civilian production. Some 250,000 officers were retired during Mubarak's 30-year presidency and to retain their loyalty and to offer future prospects for those still in service, the army's economic empire was developed. Maintaining this huge force is one of the key ways in which the government keeps unemployment down.

In 1978, the Egyptian Ministry of Defence created an economic unit called the "National Service Products Organization" (NSPO), which contributed to public infrastructure projects and produced cheap civilian goods.[17] In the 1990s when Egypt adop30 ted an economic liberalization plan in accordance with the IMF and World Bank's requirements, the military expanded production of civil goods and services. The military established new companies; built new factories and cultivated vast farms that were neither taxed nor audited. They were given special autonomous status in competition with the expanding private sector and the privatized public sector.

During the last ten years of President Hosni Mubarak's rule, retired senior army officers took high administrative positions in the bureaucracy and the public sector and further expanded their military businesses. Mubarak gave the officers administrative and economic influence in order partly to encourage them to accept the planned succession of his son, Gamal, who had no military background. Under Mubarak three major military bodies were engaged in non-military manufacturing and services: the National Service Products

Organization (NSPO), the Ministry of Military Production (MOMP), and the Arab Organization for Industrialization (AOI). NSPO specializes in civilian manufacturing, farming and services. MOMP owned eight manufacturing plants. 40 per cent of their production is geared to civilian markets. AOI owns eleven factories and companies. 70 per cent of their production goes to civilian markets. The three bodies produce a wide variety of household goods including foodstuffs. The army owns a large number of gas stations, hotels, entertainment halls, supermarkets, parking lots, transportation and shipping companies. Piped gas is supplied by the military as are foodstuffs, cement, and gasoline. Another source of the military's wealth is its landholding, which is increasingly being converted into gated communities and resorts. The military has other advantages in that it does not pay taxes nor does it have to deal with a bureaucracy that strangles the private sector.

Furthermore a class of military administrators and managers developed within the central government bureaucracy, the public sector, and the military enterprises. They received pensions from military sources in addition to salaries from the government. As a result much of the public sector was highly militarized, with retired senior officers managing natural gas and oil companies, parts of the commercial transportation system including the Suez Canal and Red Sea ports.[18]

The army's main interest is to maintain its position as the ultimate arbiter in the political process and to protect its assets. These are huge: it is estimated to control up to 40 per cent of the economy. The military economy includes the numerous factories and production facilities that are controlled by the Ministry of Defence and Ministry of Military Production. These also include companies affiliated with the Arab Organization for Industrialization and National Services Production Organization. In theory, these are state-owned entities but their accounts are not subject to financial oversight by the government's Central Auditing Organization.

The revolutionary regime, led by Gamal Abdel Nasser and his successors, especially Hosni Mubarak, were in constant conflict with the Muslim Brotherhood (*see* below). This conflict, which was accompanied by much bloodshed, over many years, led to the polarization of Egyptian politics. Hence in June 2012, most Egyptians voted for Islamic parties that did not subscribe to democratic values. Mohamed Morsi gained 51.7 per cent of the votes with a turnout of 51.6 per cent in what was considered Egypt's first democratic elections. By July 2013, most Egyptians seemed to have backed the coup against the elected Islamic president. In May 2014, the former commander-in-chief of the armed forces and Minister of Defence and Military Production, Abdel-Fattah El-Sisi was elected president, gaining 96.1 per cent of the vote, but with a turnout of only 47.5 per cent.[19]

In contrast to Egypt, the army in Tunisia did not bring about the country's independence, nor did it throw out the *ancien régime*. For most of its history it has concentrated on protecting the country's borders and public institutions and only in a few instances has the Tunisian army intervened to restore public order. During the uprising against Ben Ali's regime it distanced itself both from the demonstrators and the security services. This contributed to its popularity and to the belief among Tunisians that the army was the best defence against the repressive police force. The army's status as a preventive and neutral establishment rather is embedded in Tunisia's social history, which radically differs from Egypt's.

While the Tunisian army acted as a buttress to the ruling regime, the government was tightening its grip on the military in order to maintain its neutrality. The army therefore emerged as a republican body respectful of state institutions rather than just a servant of the regime. The voluntary retirement in 2013 of General Rachid Ammar illustrates this point. Ammar, who was head of the army under Ben Ali, became a national hero during the revolution for refusing to fire on protesters. In February 2011 after Ben Ali's fall, demonstrators demanded that Ammar take over the government. Unlike the support for Sisi in Egypt, support for army rule was based on its neutrality rather than just its opposition to Islamic fundamentalism.[20]

In Tunisia the army and the regime were not synonymous as they were in Egypt. Ben Ali relied on the security forces to maintain control, while encouraging the development of professional norms. To achieve this end he dispatched a large number of Tunisian officers to the US for training and invited numerous US military training missions to the country. A standard objective of such US military training was development of professional norms for officers, a component of which is civil-military relations in democracies. By contrast, the primary external source of training and supply for security forces, which numbered between 120,000 and 180,000, was France.

As spending on internal security escalated, allocations to the military fell from two per cent of GDP in the 1990s to less than 1.4 per cent in the 2000s. The annual budget for military procurement in 2010 was $70 million, the lowest in the Arab world. In 2011, the National Guard, the backbone of the security forces, was allocated 50 per cent than the Tunisian army, navy and air force combined.[21]

The Labour Movement

As well as a very polarized political system, Egypt has suffered for many years from a very weak civil society. One of the most important arenas in which this was felt was industrial relations.

The Egyptian Trade Union Federation (ETUF) was the product of the post-independence regime in Egypt and was created in 1957 by Nasser as a tool to control workers' discontent.[22] Since its creation the ETUF 40 has been the sole legal trade union organization in Egypt, a status formalized in 1976. Despite the dramatic changes in economic and social policy since the 1950s, was always an arm of the state. In the 2000s, ETUF claimed a membership of 3.8 million out of a wage labour force of about 27 million. Almost all its members work in the government or public sectors of the economy, as ETUF's structure is predicated on the dominance of the public sector created in Nasser's era.

Under Nasser, rank-and-file workers were given economic benefits, including job security, in exchange for their political quiescence. Within the frame-work of a state-dominated economy, unions played no collective bargaining role but were rather used as instruments for political control. The ETUF was given monopoly over workers' representation, and the formation of more than one union per profession or industry was prohibited by law. The ETUF's leadership enjoyed access to substantial institutional resources. Critics in the independent labour community charge that this led to rampant corruption within the organization, especially at higher leadership levels. Nasser's successors continued to use the ETUF as a tool to maintain control over workers while retrenching the economic benefits previously bestowed upon workers.

Nearly two years before Mubarak's removal from power, a group of real estate tax collectors formed Egypt's first independent union since 1957. Within two years, three groups—pensioners, teachers, and health technicians—had followed suit.[23] In the early 2000s independe42 nt union activity emerged among public sector workers. There were many strikes in the textile industry and the Mubarak regime responded with both violence and pay rises.

The Egyptian Federation of Independent Trade Unions (EFITU) was founded during the revolution of January 2014. Independent unions of Real Estate Tax Authority workers, healthcare technicians, and teachers initiated the new federation, joined by representatives of textile, pharmaceutical, chemical, iron and steel, and automotive workers from industrial zones in Cairo, Helwan, Mahalla al-Kubra, Tenth of Ramadan City, and Sadat City. This independent trade union federation was the first new institution to emerge from the popular uprising, and it linked the workers to what had become a revolutionary movement.

The origins of trade unionism in Tunisia go back to the early twentieth century and has had have had both local and international features since its inception. Farhat Hached developed a strong organization: he learned union activism and organizing within the French CGT for 15 years before splitting from it to start the Tunisian General Labour Union, known by its French acronym UGTT in 1946. His union quickly gained support, clout and international ties, which it used to pressure the French for more social and political rights for Tunisia and to consolidate the union's position as a key component of the national liberation movement. Because of that birth in the midst of the struggle against French colonialism, the union had political involvement from the start, a line it has maintained ever since.

The UGTT was formed a decade before Tunisia gained its independence. Its role in the struggle for independence made it difficult for the regime of Habib Bourguiba to bring it under its complete control, as the union's bases maintained a commitment to the independence from Tunisia's rulers. Gradually, the UGTT experienced internal that resulted in relations with the regime varying between periods of tight political cooperation and periods of relative autonomy.

Between 1978 and 1985, the UGTT openly opposed the regime's economic policies and organized strikes. In January 1978, the UGTT organized a general strike, resulting in severe repression and the imprisonment of the organization's secretary general. On other occasions, however, especially during the 1960s and 1990s, the UGTT vowed to respect the regime's economic policies and restrain workers' activism. In addition, the UGTT's leadership demonstrated its loyalty to Ben Ali by supporting his presidential campaigns in 1995 and 1999. Nevertheless, even during periods where the top leadership was loyal to Ben Ali, the UGTT's local branches managed to retain a certain level of independence. Still, local UGTT branches did not support the 2008 revolt in the Gafsa mining basin. The revolt, which lasted over a period of six months, involved a wide range of activists who protested unemployment and the economic marginalization of the region. It was harshly repressed by security forces.

The UGTT has enjoyed a historical continuity and presence across the country which is paralleled only by the ruling party under Bourguiba and Ben Ali. It has 150 offices across the country, an office in every governorate and district, and over 680,000 members, it constituted a credible alternative to the governing party's power and a locus of resistance to it. To be a unionist became a euphemism for being an opponent or an activist against the ruling party and in December 2010, the UGTT, particularly the teachers' unions, became the headquarters of the revolt against Ben Ali.[24]

The Islamic Movement

In Egypt and Tunisia, Islamists won elections. This made many inside and outside the region wonder if the Arab Spring had simply replaced secular dictatorships with religious ones. In fact the differences between the two countries in this respect were greater than the similarities. In Egypt, the Islamist president was removed from power after one year in office while in Tunisia the Islamists agreed on significant compromises with secular forces that enabled a democratic constitution to be adopted.

The Brotherhood began in the 1920s, whereas Ennahda began in the 1980s and after a long hibernation, it became more active in 2011. A key difference lies in the character of the Islamist groupings that won the first free elections in each country: Ennahda in Tunisia, and the Muslim Brotherhood in Egypt. While Ennahda moved cautiously and aimed for consensus, the Brotherhood drafted a constitution that many revolutionaries rejected. While the Brotherhood largely managed to resist the crackdowns in the early 1980s and 1990s, that on Ennahda in the early 1990s led either to their arrest or to their being forced to flee the country.

Both the groups took advantage of the revolutions in their countries as they progressed (there were parallels to the Iranian revolution of 1979). They rapidly organized themselves once Ben Ali and Mubarak were ousted, and sent out messages signalling their moderateness and openness. Both groups enjoy good relationships with Qatar and Turkey, but poor relationships with Saudi Arabia and the United Arab Emirates. Their rivals include secular groups, former regime affiliates, the army in Egypt and a strong police apparatus, as well as the powerful general labour union (UGTT) in Tunisia. They were also opposed by Salafist, extreme Muslim groups.

In Egypt, the Brotherhood movement needed to show distance from its newly created political wing, the Freedom and Justice Party (FJP) headed by Mohamed Morsi. As a political party, the situation was different for Ennahda, which elected Rachid Ghannouchi as its president.[25] In the 1989 elections, the party was banned from participating. However, some members ran as independents, and received between 10 per cent and 17 per cent of the vote nationally according to official figures. In 1991, Ben Ali turned against Ennahda, jailing 25,000 activists. Ennahda militants attacked the ruling party headquarters, killing one person and splashing acid in the faces of several others.

Ennahda was legalized after the revolution in March 2011. Following the revolutions, both Ennahda and the Brotherhood pledged not to run for the presidency. Then the Brotherhood reneged on its word and presented Morsi as its candidate.

In October 2011, in the Tunisian Constituent Assembly election, the first free election in the country's history was held. The turnout was only 51.1 per cent and Ennahda won 37 per cent of the popular vote and 89 of the 217 assembly seats (41%). From 2011 until 2013, Tunisia experienced political paralysis and violence including the assassination of two secular opposition leaders. Against this background the economy continued to deteriorate: tourism dried up, economic growth was minimal and unemployment increased.

Looking for a compromise that would break the political log-jam, Ennahda abandoned its call for the inclusion of Shari'a in the constitution after the secular opposition threatened to quit the Assembly. In Egypt, the Brotherhood ignored all objections and included it. When the opposition later walked out of the Egyptian constituent assembly, that body became exclusively Islamist. The Brotherhood, working alone, had a constitution rapidly written and ratified. On the contrary, in Tunisia, the work of the assembly slowed down each time the opposition withdrew. Tunisia, moreover, has never witnessed anything like Morsi's 2012 temporary presidential decree that granted him almost absolute powers.

National dialogue never worked in Egypt; the opposition kept on insisting on a governmental reshuffle while Morsi refused to make concessions. And whenever there was a ministerial reshuffle, more Brotherhood affiliates were added. It was a deadlock. In Tunisia, on the other hand, the UGTT initiated a dialogue in 2012, which was later boycotted by Ennahda and President Moncef Marzouki's party, the Congress for the Republic. Another round was then hosted by the Presidency, without the UGTT. A third round took place in May 2013, led by the UGTT, with almost everyone in attendance. The dialogue has had its stops and starts, but it is still ongoing. When anti-Ennahda demonstrations took place in February this year over the assassination of secular opposition leader Chokri Belaid, Jebali, the prime minister and Ennahda member, resigned, and a semi-technocratic government replaced the coalition. When a second crisis erupted, the party announced its readiness to leave power. As anti-Morsi protests spread in Egypt, the Brotherhood sent their men to face them and many died in these clashes. In Tunisia, Ennahda's members also resorted to violence, and so did their Leagues for Protection of the Revolution (a mixture of thugs, Islamists and unorganized, working-class demonstrators). Their brutality was limited, however, and there were few casualties. The Tunisian government was harsher than its Egyptian counterpart in acting against terrorism. In January 2014, Ennahda stepped down in order to make way for the final drafting of a constitution by a neutral interim government, followed by planned elections based on the new constitution.

The removal of Egyptian President Mohammed Morsi in July 2013 and the following massive repression against the Muslim Brotherhood in Egypt acted as a wake-up call for key actors in Tunisia. This is particularly true for the Islamist Ennahda party, the dominant party in the former government coalition. After Morsi's removal, representatives of Ennahda publicly expressed their concern about a similar development in their own country and drew their lessons. They engaged seriously in the national dialogue process, and showed a surprising willingness to compromise as the constitution was drafted.

Furthermore the rise of Jihadist groups in Libya, in the Sahel, and in Syria affected Tunisia's politics. Initially, the Ennahda government turned a blind eye to potentially militant Tunisian Salafis. Also, no obstacles were put in the way of young Tunisians departing for Syria to join the battle there. Yet, Ennahda again—even if hesitantly—drew conclusions from Tunisian militants' linking up with international jihadis and attacking Tunisian security forces. Over time, the Islamist party dissociated itself explicitly from the militant Salafi camp.

The increasing anarchy in Libya, where weapons circulated freely and Jihadists could move freely, increased the readiness for dialogue in Tunisia. With the progressive falling apart of Libya, Tunisia's political elite as well as important social forces became acutely aware that only by standing together would the country avoid the chaos affecting some of its neighbours. The Tunisian opposition also drew conclusions from developments in Egypt. At first it felt encouraged to call for the toppling of the Islamist led-government, but the violent confrontations in Egypt convinced key opposition figures, begin a dialogue with the Ennahda.[26]

Conclusion

The Egyptian army took over the state in 1952 and destroyed what little democracy there was. It proceeded in the late 1950s and early 1960s to destroy the private sector. In taking these steps it reduced the scope of pluralism in the country to a minimum and created a socio-economic reliance on the state that has continued ever since, despite economic liberalization and even privatization.

The main force opposing the army has been the Muslim Brotherhood and these two forces have literally battled it out, with the army winning but opposition continuing. Political groups in the centre have had little room for manoeuvre and their role has been small because the regimes of Nasser, Sadat, Mubarak and Sisi have all opposed pluralism.

Tunisia has had a very different history. Forces demanding change, such as the trade unions, were powerful before independence. When it came, the army did not exist and so it could not claim to be the liberator from colonial or feudal forces as it did in Egypt. The main priorities of Habib Bourguiba's regime were the improvement of the country's educational system, enhancing gender equality, developing the economy and maintaining a neutral foreign policy. Military spending was minimal and overseas military involvements were seen as irrelevant; a complete contrast to Nasser's policies. This made Bourguiba an exception among Arab leaders and that was a legacy that served Tunisia well.

Islamic and secular forces also stepped back from the brink and were willing to compromise. They felt that that they would do better if they did not insist on their maximalist demands. The examples of what had happened in Egypt and Libya influenced their thinking.

Countries live with legacies that are hard to change: that in Egypt is much more onerous than that in Tunisia.

References

1. Paul Rivlin, *Arab Economies in the Twenty-First Century*, New York: Cambridge University Press, 2011, chapters 5 and 12.
2. African Development Bank, *Comparative study on export policies in Egypt, Morocco, Tunisia and South Korea*. http://www.afdb.org/fileadmin/uploads/afdb/Documents/Project-and-Operations/Comparative%20Study%20on%20Export%20Policies% 20in%20Egypt%20Morocco%20Tunisia% 20and%20South%20Korea.pdf undated.
3. IMF, Article IV, *Consultation and Staff Report Tunisia*, 2006, p. 18.
4. Eva Bellin, "Tunisian Industrialists and the State," in *Tunisia: The Political Economy of Reform*, I. William Zartman (ed.), Boulder and London: Lynne Reinner, 1991, p. 9; IMF, Article IV, pp. 18, 49
5. Bellin, "Tunisian Industrialists," p. 50.
6. World Bank, *Country Assistance Strategy for the Republic of Tunisia, 2004*, pp. 7-8.
7. UN, *World Economic and Social Survey 1996*, New York: United Nations, 1996, p. 163.
8. Paloma Anos Casero and Aristomene Varoudakis, *Growth, Private*

Investment, and the Cost of Doing Business in Tunis: A Comparative Perspective, Washington, DC.: World Bank, January 2004, p. 19.

9. Clement M. Henry and Robert Springborg, *Globalization and the Politics of Development in the Middle East*, Cambridge: Cambridge University Press, 2001, p. 136.
10. Henry and Springborg, *Globalization and the Politics of Development*, p. 156.
11. Stephen J. King, "Economic reform and Tunisia's Hegemonic Party: The End of the Administrative Elite. Beyond Colonialism and Nationalism in North Africa," *Arab Studies Quarterly*, Spring, 1998: 1.
12. Steffen Erdle, *Tunisia: Economic Transformation and Political Restoration, in Arab Elites Negotiating the Politics of Change*, Boulder: Lynne Rienner, 2004, pp. 227-28.
13. World Bank, "World Bank approves US$36 Million to Boost Tunisia's Exports," Press Release no. 2004/465/MNA, Washington DC: World Bank, 2004.
14. Institute for National Security Studies. *Military Balance Files*. http://inss.web2.moonsite.co.il/uploadimages/SystemFiles/Egypt.pdf.
15. Bent Hansen, *The Political Economy of Poverty, Equity and Growth: Egypt and Turkey*, New York: Oxford University Press, for the World Bank, 1991, p. XIV
16. Hansen, *The Political Economy of Poverty*, p. 111.
18. Zeinab Abul-Magd, *The Egyptian Military in Politics and the Economy: Recent History and Current Transition Status*, CHR Michelson Institute, 2013. http://www.cmi.no/publications/file/4935-the-egyptian-military-in-politics-and-the-economy.pdf.
19. ahram.org.eg/NewsContent/1/64/102841/Egypt/Politics-/BREAKING-PEC-officially-announces-AbdelFattah- ElSi.aspx.
20. Mohamed Kerrou, *Tunisia's Historic Step Toward Democracy*, Carnegie Endowment for International Peace. 22 April 2014. http://carnegie-mec.org/2014/04/22/tunisia-s-historic-step-toward-democracy/h8sv?reloadFlag=1
21. Querine Hanlon, *Security Sector Reform in Tunisia A Year after the Jasmine Revolution*, United States Institute of Peace, March 2012. http://www.usip.org/sites/default/files/S.
22. Joel Beinin, "Rise of Egypt's Workers," *Carnegie Papers*, June 2012. http://carnegieendowment.org/files/egypt_labour.pdf
23. http://www.theguardian.com/world/2011/aug/05/mubarak-trade-federation-dissolved-egypt.
24. Youssef Cherif, "The Muslim Brotherhood versus Ennahda," *The Majalla*, 26 December 2013. http://www.majalla.com/eng/2013/12/article 55247739; Mohamed-Salah Omri, "Trade unions and the construction of a specifically Tunisian protest configuration." *openDemocracy*, 24 September 2013. https://www.opendemocracy.net/mohamed-salah-omri/

trade-unions-and-construction-of- specifically- tunisian-protest-configuration.

25. Ghannouchi had founded the "al-ittijah al-islami" or Islamic Tendency Movement in 1981. The Movement described itself as based in *non-violent Islam*, and called for a "reconstruction of economic life on a more equitable basis, the end of single-party politics and the acceptance of political pluralism and democracy." He and many of his followers were arrested, sentenced to eleven years in prison and were tortured. He was released in 1984, but returned to prison in 1987 with a life sentence, then was again released in 1988. He moved to Europe as a political exile, where he lived for twenty years.

26· Isabelle Werenfels, *Tunisia's democratization: Learning from the disasters of others*, SWP German Institute for International and Security Affairs. http://www.swp-berlin.org/en/publications/point-of-view/tunisias-democratization-learning-from-the-disasters-of-others.html. 30.01.2014.

12

Contentious Politics, Economic Crisis and Regime Change in Egypt

Nadine Sika

According to recent research in comparative politics, the stability of autocracies can be explained through three major variables: "legitimation, repression and co-optation."[1] Regime survival during Mubarak's tenure in office, especially through the 2000s decade, was based on repression and co-optation, much more than legitimation. The introduction of forceful structural adjustment programmes in the 1990s and the instigation of neoliberal economic policies in the 2000s have gravely affected the regime's legitimacy. Street contention by different protest groups increased since the early 2000s, which ultimately led to the end of the Mubarak regime in February 2011. Since Mubarak's ousting from power until today, Egypt has been subjected to four different rulers, ranging from the Supreme Council of the Armed Forces, to Mohamed Morsi, to Adli Mansour to Abdel Fattah el-Sisi. Meanwhile there have been different waves of contention with high and low levels of public mobilization, which culminated in the ousting of Mohamed Morsi from office. With the emergence of the Sisi regime in 2014 the question remains as to whether social contention will decrease or will remain the rule rather than the exception. This essay argues that the economic factors, which led to mass mobilization and protests prior to the January 2011 uprising and during Egypt's transitional period, are still prevalent and are even more pressing with the emergence of the Sisi regime. However, unlike the Mubarak and Morsi regimes, this regime has more legitimacy in addition to its ability to co-opt and repress its opposition. Social contention by different segments of society, especially workers, Islamists and human rights activists will remain high; however, regime survival is more likely to endure.

The Political Economy of Mubarak and Beyond

Egypt ventured on macroeconomic reform measures since the 1990s, which have been in line with the International Monetary Fund and the World Bank's structural readjustment programmes. In accordance with the IMF and World Bank's reform policies, fiscal discipline, priorities of public expenditures, tax reforms, financial liberalization, floating of exchange rates, trade liberalizations, foreign direct investments, privatization, deregulation and property rights, are the most important ingredients for development.[2] In line with these measures, Egypt's government spending was reduced to limit the widespread budget deficit, which included encouraging and facilitating private sector growth. This was through liberalizing the economy and through privatizing state-owned enterprises.[3] For instance, government subsidies to the transport sector were reduced, and public investments were held constant at 11 per cent of the GDP.[4] Tariffs have also decreased 7 from an average of 42.4 per cent in 1991 to 26.6 per cent in 1998 to 19.9 per cent in 2005.[5] Egyptian exports which could have helped in balancing the budget, have not developed; on the contrary these have not undergone any structural readjustments processes, with industrial exports stagnating at 37 per cent from 1990 until 2007.[6]

Stagnation in industrial exports, however, did not mean stagnation in the industrial process; on the contrary, industries have been catering to the local market instead of competing internationally.[7] This stagnation in exports, along with a slowdown in the privatization process, led the Mubarak regime, headed by his son Gamal Mubarak to enforce more structural readjustment programmes. In 2004 Ahmed Nazif was appointed prime minister, and created a cabinet that was composed of businessmen and neoliberal technocrats. Nazif increased the privatization process, and moved away from state-led economy and state-guaranteed privileges in the social and economic realms. Food and transportation prices increased exponentially, which led to high inflation.[8]

Investment Law 8 enacted by the Egyptian Government in 2005 relieved investors from rigid state regulations, and offered tax exemptions, as well as duty and custom free zones. One enacted law (91 of the year 2005) cut income and personal taxes by 50 per cent, and imposed a 20 per cent flat rate for taxes for individuals with personal income averaging $7,000 per year.[9] Thus, corporate taxes were brought in line with personal income taxes. On the other hand, the higher rate of taxes, namely 40 per cent, remained on all publicly owned enterprises. "Drastically reducing corporate taxes for the private sector, while maintaining the rate for public sector enterprises was a measure sure to force privatization because state owned enterprises would go bankrupt in no time due to unfair competition (higher prices born of higher tax rates) from the private sector companies."[10] The process of privatization was problematic, with no transparency. The government did not disclose information regarding the privatization process, and most of the public enterprises were sold at exceptionally low rates. Banks have not been impartial in providing investment loans to all businesses; they have only provided loans to the business elite that were associated with the ruling political party.[11] The partnership between the Egyptian Government and the business elite was evidenced with the increased corruption and nepotism. It was impossible for business to flourish without having contacts with the ruling party or with the executive office. The judiciary, civil services and the rule of law were weakened while the relative importance of personal contacts to the ruling elite increased. The most successful entrepreneurs were members of the National Democratic Party (NDP), the then ruling party, like Ahmed Ezz for instance who was initially a steel tycoon but was soon to become the secretary of organizational affairs for the NDP.

GDP growth was at its highest levels between 2006 and 2008 with an average of seven per cent; however, this growth was highly volatile, with the share of services being higher than 50 per cent. This was at the expense of agriculture, manufacturing, and industrial production.[12] These measures have had their impact on budget constraints and on social inequality. For instance, the percentage of population living under the national poverty line increased from 16 per cent in 2000 to 25.2 per cent in 2011.[13]

Legitimacy, Coercion and Co-optation under Mubarak

The Mubarak regime maintained some legitimacy levels amongst various segments in the Egyptian society, through maintaining a minimum wage for some public workers. The regime also maintained subsidies on food, oil and energy, to reduce the standard of living for the citizens. Even though the regime had ventured on the structural adjustment programmes, the percentage of public wages and subsidies in major areas of the economy remained high to maintain the regime stability, which had been dependent on these subsidies since the Nasser era.[14] Though these policies were important in maintaining some social support for the regime, many citizens were disenchanted, especially the middle class. Mubarak's legitimacy was weaning in the early 2000 decade. However, with the forceful implementation of Nazif's neoliberal project that was tied to corruption and nepotism, the Mubarak regime reached its lowest legitimacy by the end of the decade, which ultimately led to mass protests and the 25 January uprising. In various survey studies, citizens have manifested their frustration against corruption, and nepotism under the Mubarak regime.[15] Meanwhile, though forceful neoliberal reforms had been enacted, to eliminate public discontent Mubarak ensured the maintenance of food and gas subsidies.

Literacy rates have also increased in the past two decades, from 44.4 per cent in 1990 to 66.4 per cent in 2010, increasing citizens' awareness of the world around them.[16] Though the standard of Egypt's education systems is low, the prevalence of an educated citizenry, able to read, write, which has access to the Internet and with the ability to acquire knowledge from different sources, was an important eye opener to the increasing corruption, and rising inequality levels between the upper and lower echelons of society.

The Mubarak regime was mainly dependent on coercion and co-optation of its opposition to maintain its hold on power. Hence, the size and the capacity of the state security apparatus increased tremendously in response to domestic and international terrorism. The resources allocated to the Ministry of Interior increased in the 2000s. For instance the number of central security forces was almost 450,000 personnel by the end of the 2000, which do not pose any budgetary constraints on the Ministry, since these serve their military service in the security forces instead of the military.[17] During the

1990s, the security apparatus was adept at using force against Islamist insurgents or terrorists, against which massive arrests and human rights abuses were committed. With the increasing neoliberalization process under Nazif's leadership, state-led coercion and repression increased and was not only directed at the political opposition but has rather transcended to different segments of society.[18]

Contention in Egypt peaked during the 2000s with the outbreak of the second *intifada* in September 2000, which brought about the grouping together of activists from different political backgrounds, like leftists and Muslim Brotherhood. They established The Egyptian People's Committee for Solidarity with the Palestinian *Intifada*, which was able to mobilize for demonstrations in Tahrir Square in September 2001 in solidarity with the Palestinian cause. This gathering was an important milestone in contentious politics. However, the security apparatus arrested the committee's members. Public demonstrations against Israel were widespread from 2001 until 2002 not only in Cairo but in different areas of Egypt. By 2003 public mobilization against the American invasion of Iraq was widespread. Tahrir Square became the main scene of demonstrations, but security apparatus used extensive force against protestors.[19] While these protests were ma34 inly focused on regional politics, these were soon to change to become instances of contention against the Mubarak regime itself. An important milestone was the establishment of the Kifaya movement in 2004. This movement crossed all red lines through its slogan, which said "No to [Mubarak's] extension, no to [Gamal's] inheritance." Kifya opened the door for the establishment of more protest movements, like the youth for change movement and the 6 April movement, whose members, like the Kifaya movement members were constantly threatened and detained by the security apparatus.

The regime was more lenient with other movements, especially labour movements. The labour movement was successful in furthering its targeted demands precisely because it presented itself as largely disinterested in politics.[20] They had no leader; they called for specific socio-economic rights, at the same time they avoided challenging the existing authoritarian nature of the regime. By avoiding overt antagonism with the regime, they were able to negotiate and obtain many of their demands.[21] The Egyptian Government often tolerated these types of protests and was able to bargain with the demonstrators.

An important example of this tolerance is the demonstration of more than 27,000 workers in al-Mahala al-Kobra in 2006 to receive a two-month salary bonus, which had been promised by the prime minister. The government initially ignored the demonstrations, but this led to sit-ins and an expansion of the workers' demands to include wage increases and the establishment of a minimum wage. At this stage, the regime did not stop the demonstrators, but chose to negotiate with the workers. After extensive negotiations between the prime minister and the workers, the government gave in to the workers' demands and the factory's board of directors was dissolved and a new one was installed.[22]

Co-optation was another important strategy of the Mubarak regime. Political parties were tolerated in general, and were venues for the opposition figures to voice their opinion against the regime. The NDP remained the dominant power around which the governing elite held its rallies, its political appointments, and its power structure. Before the ousting of Mubarak, there were 26 political parties, albeit with marginal power and great restrictions on their freedoms. These parties were mired with corruption and internal struggles, but the political system under which they operated was the chief impairment to their effectiveness in the Egyptian political scene. The NDP retained exclusive political and economic power, legislative elections were held from 1981 to 2010, but they were never free and fair.

According to Jason Brownlee, political parties represent an important legitimating process for authoritarian regimes, and are the backbone of political stability in most authoritarian countries. Accordingly parties function as the support for the authoritarian leader, while at the same time, they side line opposition forces in different areas. Within the realm of the ruling political party, dominant forces and elites in society cooperate to keep their power and status quo. The ruling parties are able to regulate the differences in power struggles and competitions between different elites. Accordingly, successful loyal elites are able to become parts of the cabinet, the military or the police. These parties assure elite contestants that they always have an opportunity in the future to advance their political and power ambitions.[23] The ruling elite within the ruling party has mostly leadership and influence over different segments of society. The ruling party becomes the regulator of disputes, which arise between different elite forces in the nation. It is able to find solutions to problems, which could otherwise not be managed beyond the party ranks. "Thus, beyond managing competition *for* power, parties restrain the conflicts of actors *in* power."[24] Thus the ruling party is able to re-enforce and maintain a leadership cadre within its own ranks, in which the elites believe that their own survival depends on this power structure, which is able to renew itself. Henceforth, their short and long term benefits become tied to the ruling power, making it of utmost importance to marginalize any other opposition force. The ruling party ensures elite survival and socio-economic return to their loyalty, to maintain its power structure over politics and society.

The economic and political liberalization measures enacted in the 1990s largely opened up the public space for relatively free press, free to criticize the regime's political and economic policies, to accuse ministers of corruption and electoral fraud, but criticism of Mubarak remained banned until the 25 January 2011 uprising. The measures also allowed for a fairly pluralist political party system and for civil society organizations to flourish, but they constricted the possibility of any real opposition to take place. In 2005, the Muslim Brotherhood won 88 the 444 National Assembly seats, which posed a threat to the ruling National Democratic Party. By 2010, the regime was moving away from its co-optation strategy, especially with the Brotherhood, to exclusionary and coercive strategies. The 2010 parliamentary elections are clear manifestations of the regime's exclusionary policy. In November the first round of parliamentary elections were held, in which the NDP won 86.4 per cent of the 508 People's Assembly. The opposition held only 16 seats, compared to its 23 per cent representation in the 2005 parliamentary elections. The Brotherhood won only one seat, compared to the 88 seats they had won in 2005. The rest of the seats were won by independents, which in general are known to be NDP defectors.[25] These elections were widely perceived as fraudulent and a showcase for NDP corruption, excluding all political opposition from their only chance of political engagement in politics. When a month later protest movements called for the "end of the regime" in Tahrir Square, the traditional political opposition that was co-opted, like the political parties and the Muslim Brotherhood were reluctant at first; however, after a week of demonstrations, they too called for "the end of the regime."

The Political Economy After 2011

In the 2012/13 fiscal year, the budget deficit rose to almost 12 per cent of the GDP, while social expenditure increased and government revenues decreased. External rents from oil, natural gas, the Suez Canal and grants from aid agencies either declined or stagnated since 2011, while government expenditure remained high, almost 30 per cent of the GDP, due to the high expenditure on certain regime interests, like public wages, universal subsidies and oil subsidies. Oil subsidies were almost 20 per cent of the total government expenditure in 2008.[26] On the other hand, according to the World Bank estimates, Egypt's GDP growth fell from 7.15 per cent in 2008 to 2.21 per cent in 2012, while the unemployment rate increased from 8.7 per cent in 2008 to 12.7 per cent in 2012, marking the highest unemployment rate since 1991. Youth unemployment soared at 38.8 per cent in 2012 compared to 25.8 per cent in 2008. There is no policy of industrialization, or of revisiting previous economic policies to achieve sustainable development and an equitable distribution of income. The main negotiations it has undertaken with the IMF in January 2012 was concerning the further development of a market economy, tourism and foreign direct investments. There have been no negotiations concerning industrialization or problems associated with the informal market in Egypt.[27]

While in power, Mohamed Morsi, the Islamist president in the interim, did not embark on economic reform measures, though there were budgetary constraints. He feared widespread mass opposition against any austerity measures. During his tenure in office, Egypt enacted some tax reform measures, with an increase of five per cent tax on the upper classes. The main sources of Egypt's national income remained largely dependent on worker's remittances and the Suez Canal revenues. The economy was also dependent on services rather than industrialization and exports. Due to the escalation of violence and demonstrations on the streets during Morsi's tenure in office, the number of tourists declined, which had a dire impact on the economy.

While in power, Morsi's discourse was that of inclusion and co-optation at first. However two months into his presidency, his policies became largely exclusionary of all political opposition. These policies resulted in increased demonstrations against his rule. First in November 2012, then to mass demonstrations in June 2012, which ended with his ousting. In November, Morsi tried to increase his hold on power through exempting his decisions from judicial review and through making himself the sole guardian of the 25 January revolution. This move ensured that the Egyptian court could not dissolve the controversial Constituent Assembly, which mostly consisted of Islamists, the majority of whom either belongs to the Brotherhood or were sympathetic to its cause. One of Morsi's main promises during his election campaign was to make the Constituent Assembly more balanced between Islamist and secular members. Morsi failed to follow through on this promise and the Freedom and Justice Party (FJP) retained the majority in the Assembly. This assembly drafted an overwhelmingly Islamist constitution, that engendered substantial opposition, and led to the resignation of its minority secular and Coptic members.

Two days after the 22 November decree, the Constituent Assembly hastily rushed through and approved a final draft constitution. The Shura Council quickly gave its approval. The President, who declared that a popular referendum on the Constitution would take place a few weeks later on the 15th of December, then ratified the document. Morsi also mandated Talaat Abdallah, who was widely believed to belong to the Brotherhood to become Attorney General. In addition, the Freedom and Justice Party (FJP), the Muslim Brotherhood's political wing, has acted as Egypt's dominant political party since the fall of the Mubarak regime. In addition to controlling the presidency, the Brotherhood holds the majority of seats in the upper house of Parliament (Majlis al-Shura), which was the only functioning legislature in Egypt at the time.[28]

In the days that followed, protest movements, opposition parties, and the Judges Club, an association representing Egypt's judges, took to the streets. Widespread demonstrations ensued. Challenges to Morsi and the Brotherhood increased quickly, with two incidents generating substantial political pressure on the ruling elite. The first was the decree's condemnation by the Judges Club. The judges argued that the decree was a clear threat and assault on the judiciary's independence. Soon thereafter, the Club announced its refusal to supervise the 15 December constitutional referendum. The second important development was the establishment of the National Salvation Front, a coalition of opposition parties, social movements, and influential political figures such as former presidential candidates, Amr Mousa and Mohamed al-Baradei, who had also served as chief of the IAEA. As the Front's coordinator, the movement chose al-Baradei, who has widely been perceived as a democratic icon against authoritarianism in Egypt. The coalition has had a significant impact, bringing together rival groups and political parties. For the first time since the 25 January uprising, a wide coalition of organizations has united to counter balance the Islamists' hold on power. The tactics of the National Salvation Front have involved mobilizing demonstrations against the regime. It has also formed wider coalitions with human rights organizations in an attempt to oversee the referendum. This coalition was able to uncover evidence of varied strategies developed by the regime to rig the referendum results. Though the regime used widespread divide and rule tactics, the coalition held on until the ouster of Morsi in July 2012.

Many of Egypt's youth movements were not members of the Front, such as the April 6 and Ultras movements; however, they have also mobilized against the increasing Islamization and autocracy in Egypt. In response to the increased discontent with his rule, Morsi resorted to his own followers, thugs and Brotherhood sympathizers to stop the demonstrations, rather than depending on state institutions like the police force.[29] Economic problems amalgamated with political inefficiency and exclusionary polices, have led to more controversy and more social tumult, which ultimately led the army to return back to the forefront of Egyptian politics. On 2 July 2013, the army, headed by then general Abdel Fattah el Sisi decided to oust Morsi from power, leading to more social tumult and unrest, between those in favour of Morsi and those against him.

Post July 2012 Egypt: Back to Square One?

The ousting of Morsi from power brought about a military backed interim government headed by Adly Mansour, the chief judge of the Supreme Constitutional Court. The economy under Mansour remained constrained, with the same problems precipitating unemployment, budgetary constraints, lack of tourism revenues and the like. Insecurity was also mounting, especially with the Muslim Brotherhood adherents demonstrating months long against the ousting of Morsi. The Rab'a affair, in which the military and the police have killed almost 3000 of the Brotherhood supporters aggravated demonstrations and insecurity. There have been no drastic economic policies during this interim period, however, state-led violence increased. According to Amnesty International, "a surge in arbitrary arrests, detentions and harrowing incidents of torture and deaths in police custody recorded by Amnesty International provide a strong evidence of the sharp deterioration in human rights in Egypt, in the year since President Mohamed Morsi was ousted…thousands of people have been detained, with figures varying. According to official estimates published by the Associated Press in March, at least 16,000 people have been detained over the past year as part of a sweeping crackdown against Mohamed Morsi's supporters and other groups and activists that have expressed dissent.[30] In addition, many laws have been issued during Mansour's interim presidency. Amongst these is the Presidential Decree 107/2013 that regulates the right of assembly and protest. This law has been enacted specifically to restrict mass protests from taking place. It grants the police force enormous powers to disperse protestors through different means like rubber pellets and teargas. In addition, the police can also arrest any person involved in protest activities, whose sentence could range from two to seven years imprisonment. Many young activists have been imprisoned as a result of this law.[31]

These measures, along with the mobilization of independent media in favour of the interim government and the increased rhetoric against the Muslim Brotherhood, have been able to curb public discontent against the military backed interim president and his government.

Before the Rab'a affair, most of the secular opposition was in favour of the military backed government; nevertheless, with the escalation of violence, prominent figures like al-Baradei defected, while others, like Amr Moussa, the former Secretary General of the League of Arab States, were co-opted into the military-backed regime. In the meanwhile the political landscape is divided between four different categories: the first category is the old opposition under Mubarak, like the Wafd and the Tagamo parties, which have initially been part of the ruling bargain. They were (are) there on the political scene; however, they do not cross certain red lines, and do not expect to govern. The second group is composed of the new political parties and movements that were established after the January 2011 uprising like the Free Egyptians, the Egyptian Social Democratic Party and the Tamarrod youth movement. These parties and movements were in staunch opposition to the Islamists; however, since the 30 June demonstrations, they have been co-opted by the regime. They do not oppose the current regime, and their major concern is to develop a coalition with other secular parties to win some seats in the upcoming parliamentary elections. They have already started to form electoral coalitions for the September 2014 parliamentary elections. The likelihood that these parties become like the old parties is very high. The third group is the secular opposition, which are either newly established parties like al-Adl party or protest movements, like the Revolutionary Socialists and the Youth for Change movements who were present prior to or after the ousting of Mubarak. These were and still are in opposition to the ruling regime. Their major concern is the protection of civil, political and economic rights of citizens and a real democratization process. This group has been at the heart of regime opposition, some of the activists therein have been sentenced to jail during the rule of Mubarak, Morsi, Mansour and Sisi, like Alaa Abdel Fattah for instance. This group has also established a new coalition entitled the "Third Path," meaning that they are against both the Brotherhood and the military-backed regime. The fourth group is the political Islamist group, which is divided into two blocks, the Brotherhood and the Salafi adherents. The majority of the Brotherhood adherents are opposed to the military-backed regime, while the majority of Salafis are pro the newly established status quo. Some of the Brotherhood have defected from the opposition camp and have started some talks with the government to have some slice in the parliamentary cake. The Salafis on the other hand, are in favour of the military-backed regime. Initially the Salafis were in favour of the Mubarak regime, and some scholars argue that they were essentially a creation of Sadat to counterbalance the power of the Brotherhood on the street.[32]

So far there is no dominant political party, since Sisi was in the military ranks prior to his political role and did not belong to any party prior to his presidency. According to some Egyptian analysts, he is "above" the political quagmire. According to Mohamed Salmawy, an Egyptian novelist, Sisi is in no need to chair a political party, "since political parties are a means for communication between the citizens and the political leadership. Today's political leadership has direct communication with the grassroots. This direct relationship exceeds what political parties can accomplish. Moreover, despite some political and economic difficulties which the country has experienced, the political leadership still has a positive image in Egyptian society."[33] However, Sisi has a tendencyto support the second and third group of the political elite, with some co-optation strategies to the Salafis, since this movement is widely popular amongst the poor and uneducated citizens.

Provided that the political elite in Egypt have rather been out of touch with the citizens, it is important to analyse how the citizens perceive the current regime. There is scarcity of public opinion surveys, which analyse the perception of the citizens toward the Sisi regime. Few surveys show that the acceptance level of the interim government and of Sisi is rather high, more than 50 per cent. However, these same surveys have also shown the high acceptance rate of Morsi at the beginning of his tenure in office; however, his acceptance rates have rather decreased from 70 per cent to 35 at the end of his rule in office.[34] These trends show that the majority of citizens prefer "stability" in governance, with whoever would provide such. After the ousting of Morsi a new constitution was written by a non-elected Constituent Assembly and was passed with a landslide in January 2014. Sisi, who masterminded the overthrow of Morsi with popular support, is perceived as a strongman who later won presidential elections with more than 95 per cent of popular vote in fairly free elections. Sisi has used his and the military's high acceptance rates to venture on new economic reform policies. He introduced a schlock therapy to the Egyptian economy in July 2014 through eliminating gas and electricity subsidies. In a public speech, he argued that Egypt is on the verge of bankruptcy and all Egyptian citizens need to make some sacrifices. He implied that he wished he would not enact such a harsh policy on Egyptians. Nevertheless the need for this policy is imminent to bring the country back on the right economic track.[35] These new economic policies 63 are in accordance with the World Bank and the IMF's structural readjustment programmes, which might open the door for new negotiations for some loans. These policies are also in accordance with the neoliberal economic policies, which precipitate the importance of a balanced budget. Nevertheless, these policies will have dire impacts on the standards of living of the middle and poor classes of Egypt. So far, no mass demonstrations have taken place, except for sporadic demonstrations by taxi and bus drivers. Whether the regime will maintain its high legitimacy levels with these dire economic policies is still questionable. Countries that have enacted shock economic therapies like Poland in the 1990s have also introduced political democratization, to include previously excluded groups from politics. Egypt, on the other hand, is introducing major economic austerity measures while at the same time, increasing political autocracy.

The constitution provides extra judicial powers to the military, with no judicial oversight. The military held and still holds a "hidden economy,"[36] which is the part of the Egyptian economy that is controlled by the military. Estimates for the role of the military in the economy vary from 20 to 40 per cent of the economy. "The broad margin given to this estimate reflects the dearth of knowledge and lack of transparency surrounding the issue. As it stands now, military firms enjoy favourable tax treatment and are subsidized through the financial assistance they receive from the government defence budget."[37] Since Mubarak's ouster from 66 power, the military has had had an increased presence in civilian and bureaucratic positions. According to Zeinab Aboul Magd, "Retried generals manage two types of fields: upper bureaucratic positions and economic enterprises owned by the military. In order to keep a civilian face for the state in Cairo, only a few officers are hired as ministers. Outside the cabinet they prefer certain spots where influence and wealth are concentrated. In the north and south, 18 out of 27 province governors are retired army generals. This includes key locations, such as touristic provinces, sometimes Alexandria and major Delta areas. Additionally they serve as governors' chiefs of staff, directors of small towns, and heads of both wealthy and poor highly populated districts in Cairo."[38] The Sisi regime will certain ly not change these military privileges. On the contrary, it will most probably increase both retired and non-retired military personnel's privileges. Provided that the military is the backbone of Sisi's presidency, Sisi increased the military's pensions, only days after the initiation of the forceful economic austerity measures of July 2014.

Conclusion

Coercion and co-optation have been important political strategies enacted by the different regimes and policy makers in both pre and post Mubarak eras. During Mubarak's era, co-optation of political opposition and businessmen was essential in sustaining his grip on power. Coercion, on the other hand, was important in eliminating mounting political pressures from different human rights and protest movements. Mubarak increased the powers of the coercive apparatus, especially that of the police, to curb any political demonstrations. In introducing different structural readjustment programmes, from the 1990s onward, Mubarak tried to sustain his legitimacy through maintaining food and gas subsidies, in the hope of eliminating public discontent against his rule. Nevertheless, his diminishing legitimacy, especially through the increasing corruption associated with his presidency were important catalysts in the uprisings against him.

Morsi, on the other hand, was less adept at using co-optation and coercion strategies. He tried at the beginning of his tenure to co-opt different segments of society; nevertheless, his exclusionary policies of secular youth movements and of secular opposition were essential in bringing about mounting opposition against his rule. The coercive apparatus, essentially the military and the police, were not cooperative with Morsi, and hence, instead of depending on state institutions, he depended on thugs and militia associated with the Brotherhood to curb demonstrations, which affected his diminishing legitimacy. For that matter, his economic policies of maintaining food and oil subsidies did not add to his legitimacy, since the political elite had already been in opposition to his rule.

Abdel Fattah el Sisi is in a stronger position than his predecessors today, since he enjoys the three variables of autocratic sustenance. He has high legitimacy levels amongst the majority of the political opposition, and the citizens at large. Hence, his co-optation of different secular and religious political elites is sustained. He has the support of the state coercive apparatus, especially the military. His staunch opposition, mainly leftist and youth movements or the "third path" as it is called, are being eliminated through the state security apparatus through forceful measures. Nevertheless, these do not have much public sympathy, since they have been associated with much tumult and demonstrations on the street. It is clear today, especially after the presidential elections and the constitutional referendum that Egyptians at large prefer stability and a strongman, rather than demonstrations and youth movements. The extent to which Sisi will maintain his legitimacy after the initiation of the austerity measures is still early to estimate. There shall be some demonstrations of different stakeholders like labour movements and bus and taxi drivers, whose standards of livings would be highly affected by these measures. Mass demonstrations like the 25 January uprisings are not likely to take place any time soon. However, the increased use of force against the opposition by the coercive state apparatus is more likely to continue and to increase.

Notes

1. J. Gerschewski, "The three pillars of stability: legitimation, repression and co-optation in autocratic regimes," *Democratization* 20, no. 1, 2013: 14.
2. E. Krogstad, "The Post-Washington Consensus: Brand New Agenda or Old Wine in New Bottle?" *Challenge* 50, 2007: 67-85.
3. A. Joya, "The Egyptian Revolution: Crisis of Neoliberalism and Potential for Democratization," *Journal of African Political Economy* 38, 2011: 367-86.
4. See for instance the World Bank Country Study, *Egypt: Alleviating Poverty during Structural Adjustment*, Washington DC, The World Bank: 1991; African Development Bank Group, *Egypt: Economic Reform and Structural Adjustment Programme: Project Performance Evaluation Report*, Operation Evaluation African Development Bank Group, 2000.
5. See also WTO trade profile Egypt, at: http:/www.wto.org
6. A. Adly, *al-'ossul al-siyassiyya le al-tanmiyya*, Cairo: Sefsafa Publishing, 2013, p. 95.
7. S. Soliman, *The Autumn of dictatorship: Fiscal Crisis and Political Change in Egypt under Mubarak.* Stanford: Stanford University Press, 2011; Adly, *al-'ossul al-siyassiyya le al-tanmiyya* .
8. R. El Mahdy, "Egypt: A Decade of Ruptures," in *Taking to the Streets: The Transformation of ARab Activism*, L. Khatib and E. Lust (eds.). Baltimore: Johns Hopkins University Press, 2014.
9. N. Farah, *Egypt's Political Economy: Power Relations in Development*, Cairo: AUC Press, 2009.
10. Farah, *Egypt's Political Economy*, p. 49.
11. G. Sfakianakis, "The whales of the Nile: Networks, Businessmen and Bureaucrats during the era of Privatization in Egypt," in *Network of*

Privilege in the Middle East: the Politics of Economic Reform Revisited, S. Heydeman (ed.). New York: Palgrave Macmillan, 2004.
12. UNDP, *Arab Human Development Report: Challenges to Human Security in the Arab Countries*, New York: UNDP, 2009.
13. World Bank, *Egypt* online at: http://www.worldbank.org/en/country/egypt, 2015.
14. Soliman, *The Autumn of Dictatorship.*
15. For instance the survey conducted by Partners in Development, an independent think tank in 2008, and a survey conducted by the Danish Institute with the Ahram Center for Strategic Studies in May 2011.
16. UNDP, http://hdr.undp.org, 2011.
17. Soliman, *The Autumn of Dictatorship.*
18. El Mahdy, "Egypt: A Decade of Ruptures."
19. F. Vairel, "Protesting in Authoritarian Situations: Egypt and Morocco in Comparative Perspective," in *Social Movements, Mobilization and Contestation in the Middle East*, J. B. Vairel (ed.), 2nd edition, Standford: Stanford University Press, 2013.
20. M.Duboc, "Egyptian Lefitist Intellectuals' Activism from the Margins: Overcoming the Mobilization/Demobilization Dichotomy," in eds. Joel Beinin and Frederic Vairel, *Social Movements, Mobilization, and Contestation in the Middle East and North Africa 2nd Edition*.Stanford: Standford University Press, 2013.
21. S. Fawzy, "Demand Movements and Political Movements: A Comparative Critical Reading," in *'audat al-siyassa: al-harakat al-ihtijajjiya fi misr* [*Return of Politics: Protest Movements in Egypt*], D. Shehata (ed.). Cairo: Ahram Center for Political and Strategic Studies, 2010.
22. R. El Mahdy, "The Workers of Mahala: The Emergence of a New Labor Movement," in *'audat al-siyassa*, D. Shehata (ed.). Cairo: Al Ahram Center for Strategic Studies, 2010.
23. Jason Brownlee, *Authoritarianism in an Age of Democratization*, Cambridge University Press, 2007, p. 38.
24. Brownlee, *Authoritarianism*, p. 38.
25. Al Ahram Online, 6 December 2010, www.ahram.org.egy/NewsContent/1/5/1321/Egypt/Egypt-Elections, accessed on 10 July 2014.
26. A. Adly, *The Economics of Egypt's Rising Authoritarian System*, Beirut: Carnegie Middle East Center, 2014.
27. See for instance al-Shorouk and al-Masry al Youm's coverage of the IMF's visit in January 2012.
28. N. Sika, "Youth Political Engagement in Egypt: From Abstention to Uprising," *British Journal of Middle Eastern Studies, 39* (2012): 181-199.
29. N. Sika, "Youth Political Engagement in Egypt: From Abstention to Uprising."
30. Amnesty International, 3 July 2014, http://www.amnesty.org/en/news/egypt-anniversarymorsi-ousting-2014. Accessed on16 July 2014.

31. J. Charbel, *Mada Masr*, 10 July 2014. http://wwww.madamasr.com/content/year-legal-setbacks. Accssed on 17 July 2014.
32. I. Al- Hudaiby, "Islamism in and after Egypt's Revolution," in eds. Bahgat Korany and Rabab el Mahdy, *Arab Spring in Egypt: Revolution and Beyond,* Cairo: American University in Cairo Press, 2012.
33. M. Salmawy, "Hizb al-Ra'iss" [The President's Political Party], Al Masry al-Youm Online. 13 July 2014. http://wwww.almasryalyoum.com/news/details/481942. Accessed on 20 July 2014.
34. See for instance the Egyptian Center for Public Opinion Research (Baseera) at: http://www.baseera.com.eg/recentpolls_en.aspx
35. Abdel Fattah el Sisi Speech on 24 June 2014, at: http://www.youtube.com/watch?v=6br7AiSc4Kk.
36. I. Seif and Ahmed Ghoneim, *The Private Sector in Postrevolutionary Egypt.* Carnegie International For Interantional Peace, Beirut: Carnegie Middle East Center, 2013, p. 19.
37. Seif and Ghoneim, *The Private Sector*, p. 19.
38. Z. Abul-Magd, "The Middle East Channel: Foreign Policy," *Foreign Policy*, 8 May 2012. http://mideastafrica.foreignpolicy.com/posts/2012/05/08the_egyptian_republic_of_retired_generals.

References

Abul-Magd, Z. "The Middle East Channel: Foreign Policy," *Foreign Policy*. 8 May 2012. http://mideastafrica.foreignpolicy.com/posts/2012/05/08the_egyptian_republic_of_retired_generals.

Adly, A. *al-'ossul al-siyassiyya le al-tanmiyya.* Cairo: Sefsafa Publishing, 2013.

Adly, A. *The Economics of Egypt's rising Authoritarian System.* Beirut: Carnegie Middle East Center, 2014.

Al Ahram Online. 6 December 2010. www.ahram.org.egy/NewsContent/1/5/1321/Egypt/Egypt-Elections. Accessed on 10 July 2014.

Al-Hudaiby, I. "Islmaism in and after Egypt's Revolution," in eds. Bahgat Korany and Rabab el Mahdy, *Arab Spring in Egypt: Revolution and Beyond,* Cairo: American University in Cairo Press, 2012.

Amnesty International. 3 July 2014. http://www.amnesty.org/en/news/egypt-anniversarymorsi-ousting-2014. Accessed on 16 July 2014.

Brownlee, Jason. *Authoritarianism in an Age of Democratization.* Cambridge University Press, 2007.

Charbel, J. *Mada Masr.* 10 July 2014. from http://wwww.madamasr.com/content/year-legal-setbacks. Accessed on 17 July 2014.

Duboc, Marie. "Egyptian lefitist Intellectuals' Activism from the Margins: Overcoming the Mobilization/Demobilization Dichotomy," in eds. Joel Beinin and Frederic Vairel, *Social Movements, Mobilization, and Contestation in the Middle East and North Africa 2nd Edition* Stanford: Standford University Press, 2013.

El Mahdy, R. "The Workers of Mahala: The Emergence of a New Labour Movement." In *'audat al-siyassa*, D. Shehata (ed.). Cairo: Al Ahram Center for Strategic Studies, 2010.

El Mahdy, R. "Egypt: A Decade of Ruptures." In *Taking to the Streets: The Transformation of ARab Activism*, L. Khatib and E. Lust (eds.). Baltimore: Johns Hopkins University Press, 2014.

Farah, N. *Egypt's Political Economy: Power Relations in Development.* Cairo: AUC Press, 2009.

Fawzy, S. "Demand Movements and Political Movements: A Comparative Critical Reading." In *'audat al-siyassa: al-harakat al-ihtijajjiya fi misr* [*Return of Politics: Protest Movements in Egypt*], D. Shehata (ed.). Cairo: Ahram Center for Political and Strategic Studies, 2010.

Gerschewski, J. "The three pillars of stability: legitimation, repression and co-optation in autocratic regimes," *Democratization* 20, No. 1, 2013: 13-38.

Joya, A. "The Egyptian Revolution: Crisis of Neoliberalism and Potential for Democratization," *Journal of African Political Economy* 38, 2011: 367-86.

Krogstad, E. "The Post-Washington Consensus: Brand New Agenda or Old Wine in New Bottle?" *Challenge* 50, 2007: 67-85.

Salmawy, M. "Hizb al-Ra'iss" [The President's Political Party]. Al Masry al-Youm Online. 13 July 2014. http://wwww.almasryalyoum.com/news/details/481942. Accessed on 20 July 2014.

Seif, I. and Ahmed Ghoneim. *The Private Sector in Postrevolutionary Egypt.* Carnegie International For Interantional Peace. Beirut: Carnegie Middle East Center, 2013.

Sfakianakis, G. (2004). "The whales of the Nile: Networks, businessmen and bureaucrats during the era of privatization in Egypt." In *Network of privilege in the Middle East: The politics of economic reform revisited*, S. Heydeman (ed.). New York: Palgrave Macmillan, 2004.

Sika, N. "Youth Political Engagement in Egypt: From Abstention to Uprising," *British Journal of Middle Eastern Studies, 39* (2012): 181-199

Soliman, S. *The Autumn of Dictatorship: Fiscal Crisis and Political Change in Egypt under Mubarak.* Stanford: Stanford University Press, 2011.

UNDP. *Arab Human Development Report: Challenges to Human Security in the Arab Countries.* New York: UNDP, 2009.

UNDP. 201). http://hdr.undp.org.

Vairel, F. "Protesting in Authoritarian Situations: Egypt and Morocco in Comparative Perspective." In *Social Movements, Mobilization and Contestation in the Middle East 2nd Edition*, J.B. Vairel (ed.). Standford: Stanford University Press, 2013.

World Bank, *Egypt* online at: http://www.worldbank.org/en/country/egypt, 2015

13

Political Islam in Egypt after Morsi

Konrad Pêdziwiatr

The taking of oath of office by Mohammad Morsi on 30 June 2012 and thus becoming the first fully democratically elected president of Egypt, bore all the hallmarks of a surreal phenomenon. Here was a representative of the movement operating in Egypt for 85 years in an atmosphere of constant danger, threats of banning and confrontation with the authoritarian regime becoming the head of the very apparatus that for decades repressed the Muslim Brotherhood. At that moment Egyptian Islamism had clearly celebrated its most remarkable success ever.

Political Islam emerged without a doubt as one of the biggest winners of the political transformation initiated by the Arab Spring, not only in Egypt but also in the wider region of the Middle East and North Africa. Its activists and members having up till now fairly restricted access to the political scene took full advantage of the change in political opportunity and began to play a key role not only in politics at the local, but also national and regional levels.

In the case of Egypt this was true till 3 July 2013 when the army relying on supposed broad social discontent and with blessing of some opposition groups (e.g. Tamarod) and key figures of social and religious authority including the Grand Imam of al-Azhar (Ahmed el-Tayeb), the Coptic Pope (Tawadros II), and Mohamed El-Baradei removed President Mohammad from power, arrested the leaders of the Muslim Brotherhood and installed as new interim leader the head of the Supreme Constitutional Court, Adly Mansour.

From that moment the thesis of "failure" or even the "end" of political Islam in the country, and even more broadly in the region, has been gaining increasing popularity. The article will review the validity of this type of claims. It will shed light on the key successes and failures of political Islam in Egypt after the Arab Spring, the repercussions of the political decapitation of Muslim Brotherhood and possible scenarios for the future.

Death of Political Islam or Premature Obituaries

Since the end of the 1990s there has been an increasing number of researchers and scholars of Islam who have been predicting the end of the era of identity politics as practised by Islamists. *The Failure of Political Islam* by Olivier Roy[1] and *Jihad: the Expansion* and *Collapse of Islamism* by Gilles Kepel[2] are just two of a series of[4] books written in this spirit. The French scholars as well as many other analysts have argued *inter alia* that a particular type of Islamist programme has failed and been replaced, not by a non-Islamic mode of thought, but by different Islamic approaches. They have pointed out that Islamists have failed to deliver on their promise of a just government, a prosperous society and a flourishing culture. Moreover they have suggested that if the Islamist were to come to power they would resemble the repressive, one-party regimes that they want to replace.

At the same time, in contrast to the aforementioned assessments and predictions, Islamists have been achieving important political and social victories not only in the Middle East, but also in other parts of the Muslim world. Islamism has been very much alive both in the Muslim majority countries as well in the places where Muslims live as minorities, for example in the West. Some of the most dynamic Muslim organizations in Europe are those directly or indirectly linked with Muslim Brotherhood (e.g. Muslim Association of Britain playing a key role during the anti-Second-Iraq war movement).[3]

Its founding blocks are not made up of political parties that perform better or worse during elections but are based on support from broad social masses for which Islam is more than just a religion confined to the private sphere. They want to claim some public space for their religion and expressions of religiosity. Islamism functions within a dense network of dynamically operating institutions which make up important part of civil societies. Many of these institutions provide also basic elements of social welfare which is of particular importance in the countries that often lack even rudimentary social protections. The success of the Muslim Brotherhood not only in Egypt but also in other countries (e.g. Hamas in the Occupied Palestinian Territories) can be partially explained by social, economic, medical and other care the organization is providing to various communities (often the most unprivileged ones) through the wide range of its institutions. The Ikhwani clinics, community centres and other institutions became important mobilization areas in the absence of sufficient number of dedicated state institutions.[4]

The renaissance of polit ical Islam in recent years might be understood also as part of the process of de-privatization of religions which can be observed not only in the Muslim world but also outside of it. This process is particularly clearly visible when religion enters the public sphere of civil society to raise normative issues, participating in ongoing processes of normative contestation.[5] As Jose Casanova, one of the leading contemporary sociologists of religion, pointed out, these processes most frequently take one of the following forms: religions are de-privatized in defence of traditional life-worlds against state and market penetration (e.g. mobilization against abortion); or in defence of traditional moral norms against the absolutist clams of states and markets to function according to their own intrinsic functionalist norms; or last but not the least in defence of the principle of 'common good' against individualist modern liberal theories that would reduce the common good to the aggregated sum of individualist rational choices.[6]

Decapitation of the Muslim Brotherhood through the imprisonment of President Morsi and most of the leaders of the Ikhwan Muslimin, the closure of the mass media and many institutions affiliated with the movement, naming the Brotherhood a terrorist organization (December 2013) and outlawing its political arm, that is Freedom and Justice Party (August 2014), does not necessarily mean that the movement will cease to exist. As one of the *Al-Jazeera* journalists rightly pointed out, "Despite being drastically weakened by a campaign of arrests and detentions, they (Muslim Brotherhood activists and sympathizers–KP) have vowed to oppose courtroom proceedings by continuing their weekly street protests. Like a Nile River mosquito buzzing through the officers' mess, the Brotherhood has become a nuisance to the military that refuses to go away, however hard the authorities try to swat it."[7]

Similarly compared to other social movements, Muslim Brotherhood is essentially a collective action of individuals seeking to initiate, speed up or stop certain social changes. This collective action is carried out by a group formed as a network based on a set of shared ideas, values and identity.[8] If organizations that are part of this network can be quite easily dissolved and their leaders might be locked up or imprisoned, it is much harder to do so with values, ideas and identities. They cannot be so easily suppressed. The vast network of organizations linked with Muslim Brotherhood and their activities are relatively easily identifiable but individuals who sympathize with their ideas and values not necessarily so.

On the other hand, the nature of the activity that takes place in the context of social movements is in many respects different from professional politics. Social movements, even the best organized ones, are not the world of state bureaucracy and party politics. The lack of preparation to govern and to be part of this world was clearly visible with respect to many Ikhwani activists who entered parliament or held key posts in the government or in the local authorities. In contrast to, for example, Turkish Islamists who have first succeeded in securing some key posts in the local authorities[9] and only then went to challe18nge the political establishment and take active part in the parliamentary elections, members of the Muslim Brotherhood decided to profit from the revolutionary mood and contest all possible positions. They did so even in spite of their hesitations and reservations based on historic experiences.

Egyptian Salafists as Political Players

Before the key successes and failures of the Ikhwan Muslimin after the Arab Spring and repercussions of its ousting from power are analysed, it is worth noting that the whole organized political Islam has not been repressed since 3 July 2013. Some elements of it, namely the Salafi party Hizb an-Nour backed the military in July 2013 and continue to be part of the political process. In order to comprehend what many saw as an unexpected development and Egyptian Salafists' political strategy and post-July 2013 stand, it is essential to briefly shed light on their involvement in politics in the decades preceding these events.

Salafism had started to rapidly develop in Egypt already in the first half of the twentieth century and was initially dominated by Ansar al-Sunna al-Muhammadijja (then renamed as Ansar al-Sunna) created by Hamid al-Fiqqi, a student of Rashid Rida. Under strong influence from Saudi Arabia, the followers of Ansar al-Sunna were not much interested in hitherto Egyptian politics and were above all preoccupied with promoting correct practice of rituals and morals as well as discussing issues of appropriate clothing.[10] Already from that time, however, the key areas of popularity of Salafism included North Egyptian cities of Alexandria, Mansoura and Damanhur and the poorest parts of Cairo. Key Salafi institutions—major mosques and bookshops selling approved literature—function in these places till now.[11]

The 1970s saw the fastest growth of Salafism in Egypt when the Salafi School of Alexandria or the Salafi Call emerged. The group known also as Scientific Salafism was established in response to the perceived doctrinal laxness of Muslim Brotherhood, as well as, in opposition to their friendly relationship with the revolutionary regime in Iran and thus with a Shiite leadership in Tehran considered heretical by Salafists.

The Salafists were by and large tolerated under Hosni Mubarak, as long as they did not openly criticize the political establishment. The regime even supported certain Salafist organizations hoping that they will attract some of the politically driven members and supporters of the Muslim Brotherhood and restrain the growth of its popularity. The Salafists at the same time were expected not to interfere in the political sphere.

Under Mubarak, the Salafists recorded a dynamic growth in their organizational structures. At the same time these structures remained quite decentralized which helped to further spread Salafism. The Salafists reduced the need for material resources to the minimum and put the threshold for affiliation at a very low level. In practice all it took to become a Salafi was to follow the Salafi sheikh. This was in contrast to the highly hierarchical structures of Muslim Brotherhood, where new members had to undergo a challenging screening process.

The growth of Salafism in the decades prior to the Arab Spring revolutions was also linked with the economic reforms which have produced high rates of unemployment, increasing economic divisions and rising cost of living. These kinds of reforms greatly increased the appeal of Salafi sheikhs, who focused on social justice and led prayers and charitable projects in disadvantaged areas. According to some analysts to a smaller degree these reforms have popularized Muslim Brotherhood that has been also running a wide range of charitable projects but whose leadership has been strongly in favour of private property rights and entrepreneurship.[12]

Clearly this spectacular growth of Salafism in the last decades has been also a fruit of private and public funding, mainly from Gulf monarchies that helped the dissemination of Salafi ideas not only in Egypt but more broadly in North Africa. Up till the 25 January Revolution, the Salafi call advocated refraining from politics and proposed a gradual transformation of society rather than adopting models of institutional politics. Interestingly many Salafi sheikhs almost till the end of the revolutionary demonstrations advised their followers not to join public protests that led to removal of Hosni Mubarak.[13]

Less than two months af25 ter the revolution, however, the Salafi leaders decided to abandon the hitherto strategy of political disengagement and announced the establishment of a political party. The decision to create the Nour Party was taken already in March 2011 under pressure from the Salafi social base that did not want to mobilize electoral support for the party affiliated with the Muslim Brotherhood and out of the concern over the possibility of abolition of Article 2 of the Constitution stating that Sharia is the main source of law.

Many years of building its social base (*inter alia* through charitable projects) and significant organizational efforts after the revolution paid their dividend during the post-revolutionary elections. The Hizb An-Nour, capitalizing on widespread grassroots support for the Da'wa of Alexandria, achieved a spectacular victory in the 2011-12 parliamentary elections gaining second-largest number of votes after the Muslim Brotherhood's Freedom and Justice Party. The Islamist block led by the an-Nour received more than 7.5 million votes (out of 27 million votes) winning nearly 28 per cent of the votes. 111 seats out of 127 won by the Islamist Block went to members of An-Nour.[14]

While before the elections and immediately after them the Salafists cooperated with the Muslim Brotherhood, they started to progressively side more with the opposition (even with secularists, e.g. on the issue of prospective loan from the IMF). Since the 2012 constitutional referendum an-Nour started to play an active role in the opposition. It joined 2012-13 street protests against President Morsi that resulted in coup d'état and consequent ouster of President Morsi.

Not only to surprise of many external observers but also numerous people who voted for the party during the elections during the military coup in July 2013 an-Nour stood behind the army. Thus, it provided an Islamist fig leaf to the generals who wanted to at least partially mask their abrupt intrusion into the country's political processes. Such behaviour of the Salafists can be understood only knowing the minimal commitment of their leaders to democracy and the desire to achieve limited goals in political activity (above all, ensuring the safety for Salafists/protections from police brutality and locking Egypt's legal regime into a Sharia framework). Yet, some other analysts have argued that being a responsible player of the democratic processes and reliable political partner were too high expectations from the party which was conceived, founded and directed with significant influence of Saudi intelligence services. From such external perspective, the ideal is a situation when the military with ancient regime runs the country and when the Salafists run the mosques and preach an apolitical, Saudi-friendly message.[15]

Clearly joining the coup and standing behind Sisi especially after the violent clearance of Muslim Brotherhood sit-ins has cost An-Nour substantial part of its electorate. As El Ashwal points out An-Nour will most probably lose part of its support to other Islamist parties, such as the Asala Party, the Watan Party, and the Construction and Development Party (the political arm of Gamaa Islamiyya). Not only are the aforementioned parties closer to the Muslim Brotherhood, but they also take a more uncompromising position vis-à-vis liberal forces and criticize the political role of the Coptic church (especially after statements by the Coptic Patriarch were construed as supporting violence against Brotherhood supporters: 2013). On the other hand, it is rather unlikely that the support for the military would gain many voters for the Nour Party amongst the liberal Egyptians.

After July 2013 An-Nour is still part of the political game but for how long? Most probably as long as the Salafists remain useful to the generals in their efforts to create an illusion of democracy in Egypt. The same courts that banned Muslim Brotherhood and outlawed their political arm Freedom and Justice Party might be used to outlaw An-

Nour. In fact the trial on dissolving the Nour Party is already ongoing and the verdict has been adjourned till 18 October 2014.[16]

Successes and Failures of the Muslim Brotherhood in Power

If one wants to sum up the year of Islamists in power and analyse their most important successes and failures, it is essential to start with recalling their spectacular electoral victories. Although the Muslim Brotherhood had successfully participated in the parliamentary elections in the past when "victory was not an option"—to use the poetics of Nathan Brown[17]—since elections were not fully democratic (they achieved particularly good result in 2005 when 88 seats or 20 per cent of the Assembly went to their members)[18] they never achieved such a significant victory. Decades of preparations and building grassroots support coupled with significant organizational efforts in the wake of the 2011 revolutions (e.g., funding the Freedom and Justice Party) have produced for the Brothers very satisfactory results. They have not only achieved the best result in the parliamentary elections (37.5 per cent were in their favour) but also in the presidential ones (51.7 per cent of voters were cast for Mohammad Morsi).

At the same time one of their electoral successes can be viewed also one of the biggest mistakes that they committed after the revolution. While initially the Muslim Brotherhood announced that it would not file a candidate for the presidency, its political appetite grew considerably after the victorious parliamentary elections and contrary to the inner logic of self-restrain the movement decided to rally behind their own candidate. The need for self-restrain was clear in the opinion of Khairat al-Shater, the Brotherhood's deputy leader in 2011. He argued in one of the interviews immediately after the parliamentary elections that "the world's not ready for president from the Muslim Brotherhood; Egypt's not ready for it …the burdens of Egypt are too big for any one political actor."[19] His words turned out to be very sound judgements, but the leadership of the Muslim Brotherhood did not listen to them. Their key failure in this respect meant difficulty to restrict growing political ambitions and the tendency to act according to the logic "winner takes all." The army lost a battle when its favourite candidate, Ahmed Shafik, Mubarak's last Prime Minister, came second during the presidential elections, but at the end it won a war when a year later with the assistance of the opposition forces it ousted Mohammad Morsi from power. If the Brothers had decided to support the former MB member, Abdel Fotouh who was also running for the office (the candidate *inter alia* supported by An-Nour Party) they could have kept their promise and yet have their former member from the reformist wing at the top post in the country. Fotouh would be most predictably much more reconciliatory candidate and more persistently searching for alliances across the political scene. In this way the Muslim Brotherhood could have been still active, the political player.

In spite of the objections from the opposition, the Brothers have managed to successfully pass through the parliament limited legal changes, including voting on a new constitution. These limited successes have also a negative side, as they revealed the inability of the Brotherhood to build wide coalitions and to include the opposition forces in the processes of decision-making. As Alfred Stepan has rightly noted, one of the key elements that was missing in the Egyptian transition (in contrast to Tunisian one) was the "twin tolerations" that is two types of tolerations. The first one is that of religious citizens toward the state which requires that they accord democratically elected officials the freedom to legislate and govern without having to confront denials of their authority based on religious claims, such as the claim that "Only God, not man, can make laws." The second toleration is that of the state toward religious citizens, which requires that laws and officials must permit religious citizens, as a matter of right, to freely express their views and values within civil society, and to freely take part in politics, as long as religious activists and organizations respect other citizens' constitutional rights and the law.[20] Above all, it seems that Egypt has run out of mutual respect and understanding between the secular and religious elites. Their representatives instead of working together for the common good of the country and its citizens were involved primarily in the search of opportunities to show citizens how different they were, thus leading to further polarization of society. The military tried to above all show that the new leadership is incompetent to lead the country, while the Islamists argued that all their actions are only directed at "protecting" the nation from the Mubarak-era power structure or "the remnants of the old regime" (Arabic – *fulūl*).

Limited success in international politics including normalization of relations with the United States of America or successful mediation in the Israeli-Palestinian conflict after the Israeli operation Pillar of Defence in November 2012 in the Gaza Strip, have failed to minimize social discontent caused by failures in national politics. One of the most important one was the failure to meet economic and social demands from the Tahrir Square and an overall deterioration of the economic situation of the country. The high expectations aroused by the revolution were surely not easy to meet, but the Muslim Brotherhood as key member of the civil society had a good record of tackling some of social and economic problems at the local level. The scale of problems that members of the Ikhwan Muslimin faced at the national level was surely much more complicated and more difficult to tackle. This was one of the reasons why the Islamists sought some international financial aid and a loan from the International Monetary Fund (IMF). Almost $5 billion loan solicited from the IMF was aimed not only at improving the country's economic situation but also to initiate reforms that would put Egypt on the path of sustainable and sustained development and growth.[21] Many sectors of the economy were hit hard during the revolution and needed some boost. This was not so much the outcome of the revolution but rather problems accumulated over decades. One of the hardest hit was probably foreign investment and tourism that experienced unprecedented decline of the number of tourists coming to Egypt.[22] Not surprisingly, the actions taken by the government and president were not bringing about immediate improvements. In addition, President Morsi by placing himself over the law in November 2012[23] and the appointment of a group member responsible for the massacre of tourists in Luxor in 1997 as the province governor only deepened social grievances and gave additional arguments to the opposition to attack the head of state.

It has to be stressed that some of the aforementioned failures of and the Muslim Brotherhood while being in power were not so much the results of their incompetent management of state affairs but rather an outcome of their unsuccessful attempt to include the opposition forces in decision-making processes and building of the above-mentioned "twin toleration." The consequence of this was torpedoing of even the constructive initiatives of the Brotherhood by key state actors such as the military, security forces, the judiciary and part of the administration. The best evidence of the hostility of parts of the state administration towards the new Islamist leadership were widespread problems with the supply of electricity and fuel that seriously affected lives of ordinary Egyptians during the Islamist rule, and almost immediate solution of these problems after the removal from power of President Morsi on 3 July 2013.

The Repercussions of the Decapitation of the Muslim Brotherhood

As far as the consequences of political decapitation of Ikhwan Muslimin are concerned one of the most important ones is the petrification of the current position of the military in the governance structure of the country. It means maintenance of a situation in which the military remains a key political force in Egypt free from any civilian control. The victory of general Abd al-Fattah as-Sisi, who de facto removed President Morsi from office, in the hastily prepared presidential elections means that the power of generals and their involvement in Egyptian politics has only grown after the Arab Spring. The Egyptian democracy now, even more then before the 25 January Revolution, resembles a militocracy, i.e. a military dictatorship disguised as a democracy. With Sisi as a president, not only the main political powers but also substantial amount of economic powers reside with the military. Some experts point out that even up to 60 per cent of Egyptian companies are directly or indirectly controlled by the people in the uniforms.[24] Thus, one may argue that Egy42 pt is not a country that has an army, but rather an army that has a country. Morsi has been clumsily trying to limit the influence of generals at least in politics but he failed to do so.

Another equally important consequence of the military coup of July in Egypt is strengthening of the very popular belief amongst some Islamists that "democracy is not for Muslims." In Egypt many believe that Ikhwan Muslimin was the victim of a grand conspiracy. Despite many obstacles, the Muslim Brotherhood and other mainstream Islamist organizations for several decades have been consistently pursuing a strategy of action within the existing political frameworks. They manage as much political space as the semi-authoritarian regimes in the region are ready to give them.[25] When their power expands beyond the precisely marked borderlines (as it was the case, for example, in Algeria in 1991 or in the Occupied Palestinian Territories in 2006) then the rules of the political game are changed and attempts are made to re-marginalize political Islam. This type of situation in which "political victory is not an option,"[26] does not encourage Islamists to fully engage in the political process, but rather enhances the environment in which they want to pursue extra-political and frequently less peaceful strategies. Forced removal from power of the Muslim Brotherhood may contribute to the radicalization of some members of the group as well as various other Islamist groups sympathising with them not only in the country but also more broadly across the region or even around the world. Egypt becomes for Muslim radicals and their spin-doctors another "model example" of dashed and unfulfilled hopes and the alleged incompatibility of Islam with liberal democracy. It popularizes the idea that strategy of working within the system has failed. On the other hand, Asef Bayat for example argues in the recent article that if Mohamed Morsi had remained to end his presidential term in defeat, it would have had more serious implications for the future of Islamism. He claims that Morsi's ouster may in a sense have rescued the Muslim Brothers because it has revived in them the discourse of victimhood and the disruption of an unfinished project.[27]

Polarization of the society and disturbance of the temporarily regained individual agency are yet other results of the July coup. In Egypt, one may observe the deepening divisions between secularists monopolizing the posts of authority and Islamists gaining support amongst the religious masses. The Islamists can quite easily gain the votes of the masses with their grassroots projects but cannot convince the secular elites. The latter with the support of the army can maintain power but their leadership is increasingly lacking social mandate. Sometimes in order to obtain this mandate they have to strongly bend democratic principles. For example, President Sisi in order to obtain a satisfactory turnout in the presidential elections extended voting for additional third day. After removal from power of Hosni Mubarak, Egyptians have temporarily regained their sense of agency and felt again that they were able to make a difference in their country. In this they have falsified the opinion of Samir Kassir, a Lebanese journalist and thinker who was murdered during the Cedar Revolution in Lebanon in 2005; he wrote in one of his books that "The Arabs' misfortune is in their incapacity to be after they have been."[28] He did not live to see the time when a large number of people in the region decided to live in a new way and were ready to pay even the highest price for their decision. The times of great Arab civilizational achievements belong largely to the past. But as shown by the Arab Spring, the residents of the region have not yet said their last word. They will try once again to re-invent themselves, regain their agency and find a new place for their region on the geopolitical map of the world.

From the geopolitical point of view, the removal from power of the first fully democratically elected president of Egypt means strengthening of the semi-authoritarian regimes in the region, above all, Saudi Arabia and the United Arab Emirates. Indirectly it means also victory of the aforementioned countries in the regional battle for influence with Qatar supporting Ikhwani government.[29] This victory, however, came at quite substantial cost. After the coup the Egyptian leadership abandoned plans to seek a loan from the IMF. Instead it received urgently needed billions of dollars from allies in the Persian Gulf, in particular Saudi Arabia, United Arab Emirates and Kuwait. This funding came with no strict terms or pressure to initiate painful economic reforms. However, it does not mean that it comes at no cost at all. While Morsi and his government as part of the economic "renaissance project" planned to develop the Suez Canal, Egypt's biggest money-maker, with Qatari support, the generals have a different plan. Under military supervision the project is being developed with different allies from the Persian Gulf: Saudis, Emiratis and Kuwaitis.[30] Some analysts sympathizing with Muslim Brotherhood argue that this source of funding will also dry up since "the Saudis cannot pay for ever" (unpublished author's interview with Dr. Sabri from the Cordoba Foundation, London, February 2014).

One of the features of new Egyptian political reality is restrictions on freedom of expression and repressions of journalists and activists who do not speak and write enthusiastically about the new leadership. One of the television stations that faced the most severe repressions and hence most painfully experienced the sudden change of political opportunity structures in July 2013 was the Qatari owned Al-Jazeera. Its offices were closed, the equipment confiscated and most journalists were forced to broadcast from hiding. Those who were collecting information in less secretive way like Peter Greste, Mohammad Fahmy and Baher Mohammed were imprisoned and have been kept in jail for many months without much hope for a fair trial. On the other hand, in the micro scale one of the biggest losers of the sudden change of Egyptian political opportunity structures are the rulers of Gaza. Hamas was happy with the new partners in Cairo who were much more sympathetic to their ideas and goals. That is also why it enthusiastically loosened its relations with Syria and Iran. The military coup has significantly weakened the position of Hamas in the Occupied Palestinian Territories and in the Gaza Strip in particular and allowed Israel to strengthen its control over Palestinian territory.

In Lieu of Conclusions

The overthrow of President Morsi on 3 July 2013 meant the end of a certain chapter in the Egyptian history and termination of the political experiment that could take place only with the consent of the army. The fear of limiting its powers was one of the reasons that the generals decided not to experiment any more with the democratically elected Islamist leadership but to take the key positions of power into their own hands. They used dissatisfaction of various opposition forces with the Muslim Brotherhood government to justify their return from the back stage of politics into the front stage. However, a year later, none of those who supported 30 June demonstrations and demanded early elections have celebrated the first anniversary. On the contrary, many opposition figures expressed remorse for playing into the hands of Tamarud and the army. Moreover, the first anniversary of the coup came with many iconic figures of the 25 January revolution in prison. With the counter-revolution in power, it seems that the military regime is making sure to severely punish not only the Muslim Brotherhood but also everyone who participated in the 25 January revolution. Alaa Abdel Fattah, Ahmed Maher, Mohamed Adel, Mahienour El Masry, Sanaa Seif and many others' true offense is that they once dreamt of a democratic and free Egypt and of a better future. Those who participated in the 6 April movement and the 30 June demonstrations but opposed the coup found them legally banned in April 2014. The leftist Front Thuwar established in September 2013, after the Rabaa Massacre to carve an alternative path, strongly opposed to the military and at the same time was critical of the Muslim Brotherhood's rule, and shifted focus from a revolutionary path to mere survival. With more than 40,000 people detained, the front's main activity now is defending political prisoners, organizing media campaigns to raise awareness about their cases, and providing them with legal and financial support.[31]

After the brutal suppression of the Muslim Brotherhood peaceful protests and the imprisonment of the leadership, the conflict between Islamists and the army has been only deepening. All sides have reinforced their positions that resulted in the further polarization of the society. At present it is difficult to imagine any political compromise between the two sides without external pressures. In this sense, the international community with continued promotion of democracy in the region has an important role to play also in the Egyptian internal affairs.[32] Any political compromise has to involve also the participation of the Muslim Brotherhood. As 85-year history of the movement shows it is able to survive even the most severe repressions. Thus, the key question remains not if the Ikhwan Muslimin survives these repressions, but rather in what form and strength, and what will be the future ideological framework of the movement? As a model organization for all kind of Islamists what path the Muslim Brotherhood will take will be crucial for the whole Muslim world and even non-Muslim ones. Even though dubbed as "a reformist movement," the Muslim Brotherhood has had serious problems of reforming itself. Its members have quite easily criticized other political parties but found it very difficult to express any critical views on their own movement and continue to remain its members. This will surely need to change if Ikhwan Muslimin is to become again an important political player. The process of Muslim Brotherhood's reinvention will not be easy one with main leaders of the movement in prison. One suggestion of the former member, Abdel Fotouh is that the movement should in the coming months and years seriously concentrate on the level of civil society and trade unions and only from there, similarly to the Solidarity Movement in Poland, try to progressively alter political scene.

Although it is difficult to imagine any serious reconciliation process taking place with President Morsi in prison, a popular view that the Brotherhood will turn into violence is also not very likely.

First and foremost because it is contradictory to its ideological framework and political identity built since 1960s, as the movement that totally rejects violence. Moreover, the leaders of the Ikhwan Muslimin are well aware of the fact that embracing violence would mean erasing decades of efforts of "working within the system." It would prospectively endanger losing the rest of the popular support they have. Last, the Brotherhood does not embrace violence since it knows that doing so would mean losing the moral high ground, which up until now they bravely hold.

References

1. Olivier Roy, *The Failure of Political Islam*, Cambridge, Massachusets: Harvard University Press, 1994.
2. Gilles Kepel, *Jihad: Expansion et déclin de l'islamisme,* Paris: Gallimard, 2001.
3. Y. Birt, "Between Nation and Ummah: Muslim Loyalty in a Globalizing World," *Islam* 21, no. 40, 2006: 6–11; B. Marechal, *Les Freres musulmans en Europe. Racine et discours*, Presses Universitaires de France, 2009; X. Ternisien, *Les frères musulmans*, Paris: Fayard, 2005.
4. B. O. Utvik, "The Modernizing Force of Islam," in *Modernizing Islam: Religion in the Public Sphere in the Middle East and in Europe*, J. Esposito (ed.), London: Hurst & Company, 2003.
5. J. Casanova, *Public Religions in the Modern World*, Chicago: Chicago University Press, 1994.
6. J. Casanova, "Civil society and religion: retrospective reflections on Catholicism and prospective reflections on Islam," *Social Research* 68, no. 4, 2001:1041–1080.
7. A. Beach, "Brotherhood trials stoke security fears," 2013, at http://www.aljazeera.com/indepth/features/2013/11/brotherhood-trials-stoke-security-fears-201311472424333970.html.Accessed on 28.08.2014.
8. S. Mandes, "Ruchy społeczne w Polsce," in *Wymiary życia społecznego. Polska na przełomie XX i XXI wieku*, S. Marody (ed.), Warszawa: Scholar, 2007, pp. 439–66.
9. For example, Erdoğan as a Major of Istanbul from 1994.
10. Richard Gauvain, *Salafi Ritual Purity: In the Presence of God* , New York: Routledge, 2013.
11. J. Brown, *Salafis and Sufism in Egypt*, The Carnegie Papers, Carnegie Endowment For International Peace, December 2011.
12. N.EL Ashwal, *Egyptian Salafism between Religious Movement and Realpolitik,* Stiftung Wissenschaft and Politik,German Institute for International and Security Affairs, SWP Comments, August 201).

13. EL Ashwal, *Egyptian Salafism between Religious Movement and Realpolitik.*
14. J. Brown, *Salafis and Sufism in Egypt.*
15. Abdullah Al-Arian, Asef Bayat, Nathan Brown, Peter Mandaville, Jillian Schwedler, and John Voll, "Roundtable on The Future of Islamism: A Starting Point," *Jadaliyya*, 14 November 2013, http://www.jadaliyya.com/pages/index/15112/roundtable-on-the-future-of-islamism_a-starting-po.
16. *The Cairo Post* 2014.
17. Nathan J. Brown, *When Victory is Not an Option: Islamist Movements in Arab Politics* (Ithaca, NY: Cornell University Press, 2012).
18. Jerzy Zdanowski, "The Arab Uprisings in Historical Perspective, HEMISPHERES, Vol. 29, No. 1, 2014.
19. Peter Beaumont, "After Mubarak, the Brotherhood was triumphant. Now it is in crisis," *The Guardian* 27 July 2013, see: http://www.theguardian.com/world/2013/jul/27/muslim-brotherhood-egypt-libya-tunisia
20. Alfred Stefan, "Tunisia's Transition and the Twin Tolerations," *Journal of Democracy* 23, no. 2, April 2012.
21. Kinda Mohamadieh, "Egypt & the IMF: Conditions As Usual," *Middle East Institute*, 27 June 2013, see: http://www.mei.edu/content/egypt-imf-conditions-usual.
22. *Al Ahram*, 2014.
23. Mursi's constitutional decree declaring himself immune from Egypt's Mubarak-era judiciary and then withdrawal from this action.
24. Abigail Hauslohner, "Egypt's 'Military Inc' expands its control of the economy," *The Washington Post*, March 2014.
25. Nathan. J. Brown, *When Victory becomes an Option: Egypt's Muslim Brotherhood Confronts Success,* The Carnegie Papers, Middle East, January 2012.
26. Nathan. J. Brown, *When Victory is Not an Option: Islamist Movements in Arab Politics*
27. Abdullah Al-Arian et al, "Roundtable on The Future of Islamism."
28. Samir Kassir, *Consideration on the Arab Misfortune,* (in French) Sindbad Publications, 2004.
29. J. Dorsey, *Wahhabism vs. Wahhabism: Qatar Challenges Saudi Arabia*, Working Paper no. 262, Middle East Institute, Singapore, July 2014.
30. Hauslohner, "Egypt's 'Military Inc' expands its control of the economy."
31. Emad Shahin, "A Bitter Year: Egypt after the Coup," *Middle East Eye*, 3 July 2014, see http://www.middleeasteye.net/columns/bitter-year-egypt-after-coup-1375218562.
32. At the same time it seems that new status quo has become a political reality not only nationally but also internationally. The hope that people will rise up in defence of Muslim Brotherhood and the international community will back them up has failed.

14

Russia and the Middle East after the Arab Spring

Nikolay A. Kozhanov

The Russian government had, initially, tried to keep aside from the intra-Arab conflict and limited its reaction to the events in Egypt, Libya, Tunisia, and Yemen by the statements on the necessity of the peaceful settlement of conflicts. However, it suddenly found out that the new Middle East is not that friendly to Moscow as it was before. By 2012, the old regimes had already fallen, and the new authorities did not determine their attitude to Russia: the Russian neutral position prevented them from attributing to Moscow either the status of a friend or an enemy. When the authorities of the Russian Federations changed their tactics and started clearly voicing their preferences this new strategy also appeared to bring controversial results. The support of the regime of Bashar Assad shocked the large part of the Arab street: the understanding that Moscow supports the old dictatorial regime substantially contradicted with the image of the Russians as supporters of liberation movements in the Middle East that emerged during the 1960s and 1970s. Subsequently, this led to the cooling of Russian relations with the large part of the Arab world.[1]

Losing the Grip

Economic Losses

First of all, Moscow sustained heavy economic losses whose real volume is still to be determined. Thus, the fall of Qaddafi in Libya immediately led to the fleeing of Russian companies from this country whose consumer and investment markets were closed for them due to the controversial behaviour of the authorities of the RF during the civil conflict in this country. Although the leaders of new Libya periodically declare their intention to retain a certain level of economic contact with Moscow, experts in Russia are sure that the situation will repeat the experience of post-Saddam Iraq where it took Russian companies about six years to return.[2] The main Russian arms exporter Rosoboronexport estimates its financial losses in Libya to be between 2 and 6.5 billion dollars. For some companies of the Russian military-industrial complex, these losses are non-recoverable: in certain cases, Tripoli was the main buyer of their products.[3] Russian Railway Corporation RZD is another victim of the Arab Spring in Libya: its current losses are estimated in 2.2 billion dollars. Taking into account the fact that the management of this company planned to work with Qaddafi's government for many decades to come the amount of lost profit could be even higher. Russian oil and gas companies should not also be forgotten. Before 2011, such giants as Gazprom, Lukoil Overseas and Tatneft either were involved or planned to invest in the energy sector of Libya. However, their cooperation with Tripoli was seized.[4]

Finally, in April 2008, Moscow forgot about 4.5 billion dollars of Qaddafi's debts to the USSR in exchange for the involvement of Russian companies in new joint projects in Libya. After the fall of the Qaddafi and the freeze of economic relations between Tripoli and the RF, this sum also could be considered an irrecoverable loss of Moscow. Under these conditions, Russian experts are not very optimistic about the future of the assets of the RF in Syria: Moscow's active support of Bashar Assad leaves no illusion about the presence of Russia in this country after his fall. Since the early 2000s, the volume of trade between the two countries has gradually been growing. By 2012, it almost achieved two billion dollars. Traditionally, the trade balance was in favour of Russia and this, subsequently, made Syria an appealing market for Russian companies. In 2005, Moscow agreed to restructure the Syrian Government's debt to the former Soviet Union, literally forgetting about three quarters (according to other sources—only half) of the sum, in exchange for new contracts for Russian businesses. This has led to a substantial increase in Russian investments in the economy of the country (mostly in energy and infrastructural projects) which are currently estimated in USD 20 billion.[5] Russian sales of military equipment to Syria are quite impressive: if, in 2006, Moscow and Damascus signed military contracts for USD 4 billion, by 2010, this sum had allegedly increased to nearly USD 20 billion.[6]

Although, Libya and Syria represent the two most problematic cases for Moscow, Russian economic positions were generally undermined by the outbreak of the Arab Spring across the whole region. Thus, some experts speak about the problems with Russian arms sales in the region. The continuing political turmoil in Egypt harmed the incomes of Russian grain exporters who considered this country as one of the main buyers of their product in the Middle East.[7] The growing confrontation between Moscow and the Gulf Arabs caused by the Russian position on Syria tangibly limited Russian options to strengthen cooperation with the members of the Gulf Cooperation Council. For instance, during 2010-11, the Russian Federation offered Qatar a number of investment projects cost USD 10-12 billion in different fields of Russian economy (oil and gas, construction as well as gold mining sectors). However, all these proposals were ignored by Doha. As argued by some analysts, the political factor was not the last to determine the Qatari approach.[8] Even in the UAE, where the Russian presence in the Arab part of the Persian Gulf is probably the strongest, the Russians are considered an unreliable partner since the beginning of the Arab Spring. As stated Eldar Kasaev, by one of the leading Russian experts on the economy of the Middle East, "the UAE is a member of the GCC whose main ideologists Saudi Arabia and Qatar are famous for anti-Russian feelings. … [As a result,] it should not be assumed that the Emirates will continue to develop relations with Moscow if the Qataris and Saudis start waging an [undeclared] war against Russia."[9]

It is necessary to say that Qatar is also supposed to be one of the main Russian rivals in the gas market. After the beginning of the Arab Spring, this unofficial confrontation received an ideological base. Additional troubles are created by the fact that both the RF and Qatar are members of the Gas Exporting Countries Forum (GECF). Subsequently, political confrontation often influences the behaviour of these players within the framework of this structure. Thus, in 2011, Russia deliberately sent to the summit of the leaders of the GECF countries in Qatar a delegation whose level was far lower than that required by the protocol. In 2013, the Qataris responded in the same way when the meeting was held in Moscow.[10] Taking into account that the two other members of the Forum, Libya and Egypt, are busy with the domestic situation, such behaviour of Moscow and Doha does not make the GECF an effective organisation. This, in turn, harms the interests of all participants.

Losing Face

The troubles in the Russian economic relations with the members of the GCC are the results of changes in the perception of the RF in the Middle East. Probably the US invasion of Iraq in 2003 and the outbreak of the Arab Spring in 2011 were the most important tests for the image of Russia in the region. In the first occasion Moscow managed to come out victorious: its negative diplomatic reaction on the war in Iraq and voiced concerns that the Saddam's Weapons of Mass Destruction threat was just a pretext for the Americans to change the disliked regime in the foreign country found positive feedback in the Middle East. However, the very modest reaction on the events of the Arab Spring bewildered the Arab street and even caused certain disappointment in Moscow. The attempts of some Russian officials and analysts to present these events as another possibly outside-inspired movement which will not bring many changes in the political structure of the region only strengthened further criticism of the authorities of the RF.[11] Subsequently, the support of the central government by Moscow in the Syrian conflict was the last straw to break the camel's back. When, in 2012, the Russian diplomats first vetoed the UN SC resolution on Syria, the Russian Federation became closely associated with all things the Arab Spring was supposed to fight against: violence, dictatorship and bloodshed. As stated by Irina Mokhova, an expert on Russian-Arab relations, "almost all media resources from Morocco to Lebanon (with the exception of Algeria and Syria) became moderately critical on Russian efforts in the Middle East."[12]

The crucial role in this process was played by the newspapers and TV channels of Qatar and Saudi Arabia whose public opinion on Russia was and still is far from being positive. Taking into account the influence which *the Asharq Al-Awsat, Al-Hayat* and *Al-Jazeera* have on public opinion in the region and outside of it, Moscow was doomed to lose the information war for the Middle East. Thus, on 29 September 2012, *the Asharq Al-Awsat* published an editorial article by Tariq Alhomayed which accused Lavrov of fabricating the facts about the situation in the region. Moreover, the stance of Moscow on Syria was just an invitation for the discussion on other topics sensitive for the RF such as the state of democracy and Muslim minorities in Russia. For instance, in July 2012, *Al-Jazeera* voiced concerns about the domestic policy of Putin and called him "the dictator of the twenty-first century." The active polemics on these issues in the Arab press led to the further demonizing of the image of Russia. Subsequently, on 12 October 2012, in his interview to state channel Qatar TV one of the leading religious figures of the Middle East, Yusuf al-Qaradawi, called Russia "enemy number one" of Islam and Muslims.[13]

Political Defeat

The negative changes in the perception of Russia in the Middle East are closely related with another challenge to Moscow's interests in the region posed by the Arab Spring: the shrinking of the number of countries ready for the dialogue with the RF. First of all, the fall of the old partners of Moscow such as Qaddafi substantially questioned the future of Russian relations with the countries previously headed by these dictators with Russia. As assumed by Russian analysts, the US, EU and even China have much more chances to become the partners or even allies of new regimes than Moscow. According to them, the approaches of these non-regional states to the Arab Spring appeared to be more intricate. Thus, the US and EU openly supported the revolutionary movements whereas the Chinese created a reliable safe network by establishing close economic contacts with local private business whose interests are independent of the type of domestic political regime. Russia had none of these advantages.[14]

As it has been already mentioned, the Arab Spring hampered the development of Russian relations with those countries whose governments became interested in the establishment of closer political and economic ties with Moscow in the 2000s. The members of the GCC represent the most notorious example. The Russian support of Basher Assad diverted them from Moscow. After 2011, it took about two years before the RF could finally resume the effective discussion of bilateral, regional and international issues with Saudi Arabia.

Finally, the Arab Spring put a serious threat to the dialogue between the Russian authorities and the religious leaders of the Middle

East. The positive development of these relations are traditionally seen by Moscow as one of the factors directly influencing the political stability of the country: until the majority of Muslim religious leaders consider the situation with the rights of the Russian Muslim community normal, this, as believed by the authorities of the RF, seriously limits moral and financial assistance to radical Islamists acting in the south of Russia from abroad. Thus, in May 2012, the Russian authorities supported the organization of the international meeting of Islamic theologians from 23 countries in Moscow. The event was held under slogan "Islamic doctrine against radicalism." The list of invited participants included such prominent figures as Secretary General of the World Council of Muslim Scholars, Ali al-Qaradagi and vice-president of this organization, Abdallah Bin Bayyah. The meeting ended with the adoption of the declaration condemning religious radicalism. It also called upon Muslim theologians to be very careful when using such terms as caliphate (*khilãfã*), jihad (*ğihãd*) and takfeer (*takfir*) since they could justify the activities of religious extremists. This document was considered to be a serious diplomatic success of Moscow. However, the impact of this achievement was undermined when, a year after, the similar meeting was held in Cairo. That time, the gathering blessed the activities of the Syrian opposition and called the civil war in this country 'a jihad'. This statement indirectly affected Russia by logically posing it as a country supporting the side against which the holy war is waged. It could be hardly called a coincidence that the organizing committee of the Cairo meeting did its best to maximally include the participants of the Moscow meeting in the list of invited people.[15]

The Reasons for Failure

There are several reasons explaining why the Arab Spring appeared extremely harmful for Moscow's ties with the region. First of all, this was determined by the general ill approach of the Russian authorities to the Middle East. Seeing the region as a play ground for their games with the West, they did not pay attention to what was happening in the Middle Eastern countries. As opposed to the Soviet or Imperial times, Moscow's foreign policy towards the Middle East lacked direction and credibility. Policy priorities towards individual states and the region as a whole were contradictory and ill-defined. Russia refrained from diplomatic initiatives, while its links with regional governments were not used constructively. Thus, since 1991 and until recently, Russia neglected such factor as soft power. The creation of the Arabic service of the state Russia Today Channel in 2007 and the creation of the Russian cultural centres in the Middle Eastern countries during the 2000s were bold, but insufficient moves.

While the US and Europe were busy with the creation of the pro-western groupings within cultural, economic and political elites of the region through different cultural, humanitarian and educational programmes, Moscow minimized its cooperation with the Middle East in this field. Moreover, it literally cut relations with those pro-Russian groupings formed during the Soviet times. Subsequently, during the two decades after the fall of the USSR, these pro-Russian elements either perished or lost their influence without the support of Kremlin. For instance, this was the case of Syria where as stated by some analysts, the pro-Russian grouping was almost completely eliminated in the struggle for power after the rise of Bashar Assad in 2000. However, Moscow realized this only in 2011 when it tried to re-establish connections with people previously loyal to Moscow. As a result, in the events of the Arab Spring there were few people both on the side of the regime and on the side of revolutionaries who could lobby the interests of the RF.[16]

Moreover, before the Arab Spring, the Russian authorities developed the dialogue with the Middle Eastern countries primarily on the governmental level neglecting ties with non-state economic and political actors who could have created the safe-net for Russia during the Arab Spring. Subsequently, after the fall of the ruling regimes in Egypt, Libya and other countries, Moscow was compelled to start its relations with new authorities of the Arab states from the scratch.[17] The existing close connections of Kremlin with major Russian governmental and semi-governmental corporations also played the negative role. It is not a mere coincidence that the majority of the success stories of Russian business in the Middle East are related to corporations affiliated with the government. The Russian Government spares no effort to support its economic behemoth. On the contrary, medium and smaller businesses (as well as Russian industries which are considered to be of secondary importance for the economic elite) usually do not enjoy this level of support. As a result they are doomed to encounter numerous problems with Iranian realities on their own. After the outbreak of the Arab Spring, this situation had negative implications for Russian interests in the Middle East. The close support of the business interests at the government level led to the association of the Russian business with the Russian state, and, thus, made it dependent on the fluctuations of the political situation. Subsequently, the loss of political positions in the Middle Eastern countries caused the loss of economic position. The ties of medium and smaller business with the private sector would have preserved Russian presence in the region. However, the creation of these ties was never encouraged by the authorities of the RF.

By 2011, Russian foreign policy-making on the Middle East was fragmented as it involved several policy-making actors with sometime conflicting agendas—the Presidential Administration, the Ministry of Foreign Affairs, the Ministry of Trade and Economic Development, the Russian Chamber of Commerce and Industry, NGOs, as well as governmental, semi-governmental and private commercial companies and even the Russian Orthodox Church. In the absence of long-term policy goals and priorities, Moscow took a case-by-case approach sticking to the principle of momentary profit and balancing between all regional forces.

The Russian attempts to follow the principle of open doors and be friends for all were relatively incompetent even before the Arab Spring. Thus, during the 2000s, the periodical efforts of the Russian authorities to maintain equally good relations with Saudi Arabia, Iran and Israel without acknowledging problems existing in the relations of Riyadh, Tehran and Tel-Aviv with each other only irritated Moscow's partners. For instance, Moscow attempt to upgrade the Russo-Israeli relations during the visit of Putin to Tel-Aviv in 2012 without admitting the threat caused by Tehran's nuclear programme was, from the very beginning, doomed to be futile. In addition to this, since the 1990s, the Middle Easterners have been keeping somewhere in the back of their minds the thought that post-Soviet Russia is more oriented to the West. This, in turn, did not add much trust to Russia.

The events of the Arab Spring only confirmed an old wisdom that it is hard to be a friend for all. This was proven by the civil conflict in Libya. In 2011, the attempts of Moscow to play a shuttle diplomacy between the rebels and the government of Qaddafi raised a lot of questions in both camps. On one hand, the leader of the Libyan Jamahiriya was confused by the fact that Russia which, in 2008-10, was actively developing relations with Tripoli suddenly started to persuade him to start negotiations with his enemies and, possibly, to leave the throne. This could not be considered other than treachery. On the other hand, the opposition wanted an end to the dictatorial regime with the moral and military support of the West. Under these conditions, any attempts to persuade them to start the dialogue with the opponent could probably only give rise to questions about whether the authorities of the RF wanted the peace or tried to postpone the final blow to Qaddafi.[18]

Finally, the attitude of Moscow to the Middle East as a trading partner in the Russian relations with the West also played its role. Thus, as it had happened previously, in 2011, Moscow decided to use Libya as a trading item in order to bargain preferences in its relations with the US and EU. On 17 March 2011 the Russian Government did not veto UN SC resolution 1973 which paved the way for the US and EU to intervene in the Libyan conflict. Subsequently, the RF imposed sanctions on Libya and it was the first to stop arms exports to the regime of Qaddafi. In the eyes of the pro-western grouping of Russian ruling elite, these steps were worth making: in 2011, Moscow still hoped to reset relations with Washington, and the military contracts with France also played their role. Nevertheless, this time, the losses did not justify gains. The situation itself had changed: if, for instance, the Gore-Chernomyrdin agreement of 1995 when Russia agreed to stop military assistance to Iran had significant, but not crucially negative effect on Tehran, Moscow decisions on Libya probably determined the destiny of Qaddafi. In other words, in 1995, Russia only cheated Iran whereas in 2011, it betrayed the regime of Qaddafi. Under these conditions, the image of the RF in the Middle East suffered heavy losses: according to the traditions of the region, a treachery (no matter who is a betrayed person) is never forgotten.[19]

Treachery is also considered a sign of weakness (as well as the strategy of balancing between different forces: a strong player can afford to clearly demonstrate his preferences). This, in turn, assured the opponents of Russia in the region that in other cases the opinion of Moscow could be ignored. For instance, since the very beginning of the Arab Spring, the Qataris have been periodically repeating the idea that the RF has long lost its status of the centre of power in the international politics, but it still tries to return it by playing the role of a minor troublemaker and supporting the dictatorial regimes.[20] The representatives of the Syrian opposition went even further: when persuading the American and European policymakers to intervene in the civil conflict in Syria, they argued that Moscow has no real leverages on the West. As an example, they referred to the situation with Yugoslavia in 1999, Iraq in 2003 and Libya in 2011. According to them, in all cases the Russian Government was compelled to deal with the US and NATO behaviour as granted.[21]

End of the Game?

However, it is still early to say that, after the beginning of the Arab Spring, Russia completely lost its position in the Middle East. On the contrary, if the period 2011-2012 was the time of a serious stress-test for Moscow, the events of 2013 demonstrated that Moscow still has all chances to preserve its presence in the region. As stated by some experts, by 2013, the negative implications of the Arab Spring for the RF had been finally counterbalanced by positive trends.

Rethinking Approaches

First and foremost, by 2013, Moscow reconsidered its approaches towards the Middle East. The Russian foreign policy on the region became tougher in defending its red lines and, at the same time, cleverer. Thus, Moscow started to look at the domestic situation in the region more carefully. Currently, Russia does not conceal its interest in a dialogue with almost all forces in the Middle Eastern arena. For instance, over the past two years, Russia has established contacts with the different groups of the Syrian opposition.[22] Thus, if until the summer of 2012 the Russian authorities were dealing mostly with semi-legal and moderate opposition forces, such as members of the National Coordination Council, by autumn 2012, the Russians were looking for contacts with members of the Syrian National Council. And in 2013, these contacts were established at different levels. Finally, on 10 February 2013, in his interview on the Russian television channel Rossiya 1, Russian Foreign Minister Sergey Lavrov acknowledged that Moscow has links with "all groupings inside the Syrian opposition without any exceptions" and uses them for the periodic exchanges of views. As an example of such dialogue, the foreign minister referred to his recent meeting with the head of the National Coalition for Syrian Revolutionary and Opposition Forces, Sheikh Ahmed Moaz Khatib, on the sidelines of the Munich Security Conference on 1-3 February 2013.[23]

The agenda of such meetings has never been made public. However, information leaks allow analysts to assume that the Russian authorities are talking about ways of not only to bring about a ceasefire between the Syrian Government and the opposition, but also to start negotiations. Moscow is probably trying to demonstrate that, under certain conditions, it will be ready to deal with the new Syrian authorities after Assad's fall or resignation.

These declarations are supported by the examples of Russia's relations with the other Arab countries where authoritarian regimes have recently fallen, namely, post-Mubarak Egypt and post-Qaddafi Libya. Moscow was one of the first to start a dialogue with the Egyptian Government after the fall of Mubarak's regime. In November 2012, Lavrov visited the country and confirmed the Russian Government's readiness to pursue political and economic cooperation with Egypt, regardless of the Islamist background of Egyptian president, Mohamed Morsi. The same thesis was probably used by Lavrov during his meeting with the head of one of the largest Libyan parties–National Forces Alliance–Mahmoud Jibril in Moscow on 27 February 2013. As noted by some analysts, both in the case of Egypt and Libya, Russia tried to play on existing mistrust of the US and EU among political groupings in the above-mentioned countries. The signal sent from Moscow was simple: close ties only with American and European leaders did not save Hosni Mubarak and Muammar Qaddafi from their fate (i.e. there is a necessity to rely on alternative force which could be represented by Moscow). It is highly probable that the same thesis is (or will be) used by the Russian authorities in their contacts with the members of the Syrian opposition.[24]

Meanwhile, it is not the same tactics of open doors which Russia used before the Arab Spring. Russia is ready for the dialogue with many regional groupings but not with all of them: any connections with the radical Islamic groupings are not an option for the authorities of the RF. This Russian principle brightly contrasted with the behaviour of some western countries which could apply radically different labels to the Islamists fighting in Afghanistan, Iraq, Mali, Libya or Syria.

With the return of Putin, the role of the Middle East as a trading item in Russo-American and Russo-European relations became less obvious. On the contrary, Moscow set certain red lines (such as the unacceptability of foreign military intervention in Syria) whose crossing by the West could cause the retaliatory measures of the Russian Government. This Russian stubbornness was accompanied by the success of the Kremlin's diplomacy in 2013. Thus, Moscow received the support of its stance on Syria from China, India and a number of other countries. In September 2013, it undermined the US attempts to form the coalition for the military intervention in Syria and stepped up the initiative on the termination of the Syrian chemical arsenal. The latter proposal (at least, temporary) allowed Moscow to neutralize American efforts to use the WMD of Assad's regime as a pretext for the military operation against Damascus. Finally, whenever Putin raised the Syrian issue on the sidelines of the meetings of the leading world powers such as the G8 Summit in Loch-Erne (17-18 June 2013) and G-20 Summit in St. Petersburg (5-6 September 2013) he was always more persuasive and eloquent than his opponents. This was not left unnoticed by the public opinion in the Middle East. On one hand, in the eyes of those regional states which managed to preserve positive or neutral attitude to Moscow the Russian authorities managed to rehabilitate themselves after the ambivalent foreign policy on the region during the period 2011–early 2012. The authorities of the RF proved that they are able to keep a given word. On the other hand, the regional opponents of Russia such as Qatar and Saudi Arabia were compelled to recognize Kremlin as an important player whose opinion should be taken into account. Thus, such influential newspapers as the *Asharq Al-Awsat* and *al-Hayat* considered the failure of Obama to persuade Putin to change the Russian stance on Syria during the G-8 summit in Loch-Erne as a pure victory of Russia whereas the US administration was accused of "opportunism and weakness."[25]

Putin in Charge

The depth of the transformation of Russian foreign policy in the Middle East was also determined by the domestic situation in Russia and the personality of the Russian leader. Putin's agenda, aimed at the creation of a multi-polar world and greater Russian interaction with non-western players, inevitably drags the Middle East in the zone of Moscow's interests. However, his vision strongly contrasts with the Russian vision of the Middle East under Boris Yeltsin (1991-99) and Medvedev (2008-12). Both of them considered this region of secondary importance. This difference in Putin and Medvedev's perception of the Middle East was clearly demonstrated by their controversy over the Libyan crisis of 2011. While Putin labelled the US and EU as "new crusaders" Medvedev expressed his satisfaction over the news about the captivity of the Libyan leader. Subsequently, this different reaction on the Libyan events nearly led to a split in the Putin-Medvedev tandem.

There was no surprise that immediately after his return to the office of the President in 2012, Putin began to restore Russian relations with the Middle East that was seriously damaged under Medvedev. Thus, only two months after his election Putin met his Iranian counterpart Ahmadinejad. The meeting was held on 7 June 2012 on the sidelines of the SCO (Shanghai Cooperation Organization) summit in Shanghai. Putin clearly stated the Russian interest in the further development of relations with Tehran and called Iran "an old traditional partner" of Russia.

The Putin of 2012 was also different from the Putin of 2000 and 2004: more authoritarian, decisive and anti-western. He was seriously disappointed by the failure of change in Russian-US relations and existing tensions with the West. This could not but affect Moscow's stance on the Middle East. To a certain extent, the active Russian support provided to the Assad regime was Kremlin's revenge on the Americans and Europeans for Moscow's political and economic losses in Libya and Iraq. The Russian leadership was apparently offended that Russia's silent support for the western military operation did not receive any acknowledgement from the US and EU. This, in turn, impelled the Russian authorities to demonstrate that they can be serious troublemaker if their position on regional affairs is not taken into consideration by western players.

The general domestic situation in Russia also favoured changes in Moscow's foreign policy on the Middle East. The public discontent with Medvedev's cabinet and controversial reaction of the population to Putin's re-election in 2012 compelled the country's leadership to shore up the social base of the regime support. After 2012, the official propaganda started to appeal to the nationalistic sentiments of the

Russian population more actively. Their appeals found positive feedback. The large part of the mid- and low-layers of the Russian population would like to see Medvedev's successor more active in protecting their national interests and cementing relations with the non-western part of the world. Putin gave them what they wanted. Russian support for Damascus, close relations with Tehran and rapprochement with Egypt were supposed to symbolize for this section of the Russian population that was missing the "imperial." glory of the USSR, the return to old traditions of the Soviet Empire. Prior to its fall in 1991, the USSR had good political and economic relations with these countries.

Brave New World

The Arab Spring has changed the political map of the region. Its outbreak caused the formation of a new system of regional relations which roughly divided the Middle Eastern countries in the following three groupings:

1. Countries aspiring to the role of the architects of the Arab revolutions and leaders of the new Middle East (for example, the GCC members which were and still are actively involved in the process of the overthrowing of dictatorial regimes in Libya and Syria);
2. New regimes emerged as the outcome of the Arab Spring which are trying to find their own way of political development (such as Tunisia, Libya, Egypt, Yemen);
3. "Fragments of the old world" or countries which lived through the turbulence of regional uprisings and managed to preserve their old regimes (such as Algeria).

As it appeared by 2013, all these three groupings have their own interests in establishing the certain level of good relations with Russia. Thus, for such countries as Algeria whose governments are concerned with the growing influence of the Gulf monarchies in the region as well as scared to repeat the destiny of the Qaddafi or Mubarak regimes Russia is seen as a reliable partner and protector. The Syrian experience shows that the RF under Putin is capable of outbalancing the western influence and can guarantee the certain level of security for its partners.

For instance, approximately since 2012, analysts argue about the intensification of Algerian dialogue with Moscow. In spite of certain setback in military cooperation (which, however, is of temporary nature and, to a certain extent, determined by the decision of the Algerian authorities to diversify the sources of military supplies), Algiers could be called one of the closest partners of Moscow in the North African region. By 2013 the volume of trade between the two countries achieved the level of USD 2.7 billion and continued its growth. After the beginning of the Arab Spring, Algeria and Russia have been confirming their decision to strengthen multidimensional cooperation within the framework of the declaration on strategic partnership signed by the authorities of these states in 2001. To a large extent, this behaviour of Algiers and Moscow is determined by common threats and challenges posed in the aftermath of the Arab Spring. They are equally concerned with the rise of Islamism in the region, intense western interference in the Middle Eastern affairs and the growing influence of Qatar and Saudi Arabia. Both countries are also worried about the perspectives of their presence in the European gas market as well as with the attempts of the EU to diversify the sources of hydrocarbon imports.[26]

During 2012-13, in order to have a constant opportunity to exchange opinions on these issues, Algeria and Russia substantially increased the number of working meetings at different levels. Thus, in September 2012, Lavrov met with his Algerian colleague Mourad Medelci on the sidelines of the UN General Assembly in New York. In November 2012, deputy minister for Maghreb and African Affairs Abdelkader Messahel visited Moscow. In February 2013, Lavrov made Algiers a part of his North African trip. During his stay in this country, the Russian foreign minister had consultations with Algerian president Abdelaziz Bouteflika and Medelci. In return, the latter visited Moscow on 25 June 2013. Finally, during 1-2 July 2013, minister of energy and mines Youcef Yousfi and the head of the Council of the Nation, Abdelkader Bensalah, represented Algeria at the GECF summit in the Russian capital.[27] The results of this meeting demonstrated that this country remains the reliable partner of Russia within the framework of the Gas Forum, thus, outbalancing the uncooperative behaviour of Qatar. On the bilateral level, the Algerian authorities do their best to coordinate the efforts of the two countries on the European hydrocarbon market (as reported by some analysts, the issues of Russo-Algerian energy cooperation in Europe are coordinated by special president envoy to the GECF, chairman of the board of the directors of Gazprom, Viktor Zubkov). In response, the Kremlin provides Algiers with moral support and expert assistance in its negotiations with the EU on energy issues. The Russian oil and gas companies such as Gazprom, Rosneft and Stroytransgaz are also actively involved in the development of the hydrocarbon reserves of Algeria. In the spring 2013, for the support of the activities of Russian companies in this country, Moscow and Algiers held the meeting of the bilateral commission on the trade, economic, scientific and technological cooperation.[28]

However, not only old partners decided to strengthen their relations with Moscow. New regimes also did not intend to cut ties with RF. Their decision was determined by the two following groups of factors. On one hand, even though in the majority of cases it is difficult to call Moscow as the main political and economic partner of the Middle Eastern countries, the level of relations with the RF achieved by the beginning of the Arab Spring could not be immediately downgraded. Thus, in the case of Egypt, Cairo was dependent on the imports of Russian grain. By 2011, the Arab republic bought about 4.8 billion tonnes of this product from the RF and, thus, it turned Moscow to one of the guarantors of Egyptian food security. Given the dependence of the budget incomes of this Middle Eastern country on tourism, it was also the unaffordable luxury for the Egyptians to lose 2.5-3 million Russian tourists annually visiting Egypt by 2012. Apart from this, since the early-2000s Cairo demonstrated certain amount of interest in cooperating with Russia in the field of oil, gas and nuclear energy as well as mining, tourism infrastructure, high technologies and space. By 2012, the subsidiary of Russian oil company Lukoil, Lukoil Egypt, was conducting geological exploration in the Gulf of Suez whereas another Russian company Novatek was going to make the geological survey of the el-Arish gas block in the Mediterranean Sea. Finally, Russian companies SMV Engineering and Verteks took the decision to invest their money in gold mining and complex ore extraction.[29]

On the other hand, as it was mentioned above, the Arab Spring proved to the Middle Eastern countries that the dependence on one political and economic partner (no matter, the US, the UK, France or Russia) is dangerous. According to some analysts, the fall of Mubarak left the Arab street with a bitter aftertaste: the neutrality of Washington was considered as certain treachery of its fallen ally.[30] Under these conditions, new regimes tried to diversify the range of their main trading and political partners. Thus, both Morsi and post-Morsi administrations were very fast in confirming their loyalty to the Russo-Egyptian friendship and the treaty on strategic partnership signed by Medvedev and Mubarak in 2009. As a result, in 2012, Lavrov visited the Arab republic twice (on 9-10 March and 4-5 November). This provided the ground for the two meetings of Putin with Morsi. One of these took place on the sidelines of the BRICS meeting in Durban on 27 March 2013. The next time, the Egyptian president visited his Russian colleague on 17-19 April 2013. The meeting took place at the presidential residence in Sochi. The range of discussed questions included possibilities of Russian assistance in the development of the nuclear programme of Egypt, the continuation of Russian exports of fuel and grain to the Arab republic as well as options for providing Cairo with the loan of USD 2 billion.[31] After the fall of Morsi government, the Egyptian minister of foreign affairs, Nabil Fahmi, visited Moscow in order to confirm that the political turmoil did not affect the bilateral relations.[32]

The restoration of Russo-Libyan dialogue is also possible. Although the political situation in this country is far from being stable, Moscow tries to support a certain level of the dialogue with the Libyan political groupings. The first sign that these contacts may potentially lead to the resumption of economic cooperation was received in September 2013. As reported by Russian media sources, on 24 September 2013, Russia delivered to Libya a military consignment consisted of 10 infantry fighting vehicles (IFV) BMP-3 (according to other sources, antitank missile complexes Khrizantema-S developed on the base of BMP-3) as a symbol of the new era in the military ties of the two countries. The high ranking military officials, General Abdel-Salam Jadallah Obeidi and Brigadier General Yousef Abu-Hajar, were sent to take part in the official ceremony of the transfer of these IFVs to the Libyan side. According to some analysts, it could not be a mere coincidence that the arrival of this military equipment was preceded by the visit of the Algerian minister of international cooperation and foreign affairs, Mohamed Abdelaziz to Moscow in September 2013.[33]

The fall of regimes in the countries previously friendly to Russia does not mean the end of partnership between the RF and these states have the experience of Russian-Iraqi relations. Thus, after the US invasion of Iraq in 2003, arms and energy markets of this Middle Eastern state were considered to be lost for Moscow. Kremlin analysts believed in the inevitable political and economic reorientation of Baghdad to Washington. However, the late 2000s were marked with the massive return of Russian oil and gas companies to Iraq. As it appeared, Baghdad was interested in this: the Russians were ready to work in difficult conditions for less money (as compared with western companies). They were and still are actively cooperating with the authorities of the regions where their companies have projects by employing the locals, donating money for charity needs, developing social infrastructure and establishing good relations with local warlords. Subsequently, by 2013, Baghdad started signing agreements on the development of oil and gas fields with Russian companies on more favourable conditions than usually offered to foreigners. Moreover, the Iraqi authorities closed their eyes on the active penetration of the energy giants from the RF to the part of the country controlled by the Kurdish regional government.

In 2012, Russia and Iraq signed the package of military contracts whose overall volume is estimated to be USD 4.2 billion. According to these contracts, Moscow was supposed to sell to Baghdad anti-aircraft complexes Pantscir and attack helicopters Mi-28. As it was argued by some military sources, Russian military contracts with Iraq signed in 2012 were not limited by the above-mentioned vehicles. According to them, the main reason for the Iraqi interest in Russian arms is the mistrust of Baghdad to the western partners and the wish to diversify the range of the suppliers of military equipment.[34] It is notable that even the corruption scandal (Moscow was accused in bribing some Iraqi officials in Baghdad in order to have these contract signed) which emerged around these military deals shortly after the sides reached the agreement upon them did not lead to the cancellation of the contracts.[35]

In general, by 2014, even the toughest opponents of Russia among the Middle Eastern countries demonstrated their intention to talk to the RF. Probably this was determined by the firm position of Kremlin on Syria and its persistence in the preserving contacts with the region after the return of Putin. In all these cases, Moscow demonstrated that its opinion should be taken into account. Under these circumstances, the members of the GCC states were compelled to maintain dialogue with Russia. The visit of prince Bandar Bin Sultan, Secretary General of the National Security Council and head of the Saudi Intelligence Agency, to Moscow on 31 July 2013 and the meeting of Putin with General Sheikh Mohammad Bin Zayed Al Nahyan, Crown Prince of Abu Dhabi and Deputy Supreme Commander of the UAE Armed Forces on 16-17 September 2013 are, probably, the most notorious examples of this. In the first case, the details of the talks between Putin and Prince Bandar are still not official. Putting speculations aside, analysts argue that this was an unofficial attempt to bridge relations between the RF and the Saudi kingdom previously tangibly undermined by the Syrian crisis. As noticed by expert on regional affairs Naser al-Tamimi, in spite of existing contradictions, Moscow and Riyadh have certain topics for constructive dialogue including regional political stability and bilateral cooperation in the fields of energy and space.[36] For instance, in 2004, Lukoil Overseas signed the contract with Saudi Arabia. According to the document, this company was granted a 40-year long concession on the exploration and development of the gas field in the Rub-al-Khali desert. For the implementation of this project, Lukoil Overseas and Saudi Aramco established the joint company Lukoil Saudi Arabia Energy Ltd. (LUKSAR). The share of the Russian company is 80 per cent. In 2006, the exploration works of LUKSAR resulted in the discovery of a new hydrocarbon field whose estimated resources will yield 85 million tonnes in equivalent fuel. Currently LUKSAR is making an assessment of discovered reserves in order to begin the development of the field. By August 2011, the accumulated investments of the Russian company had achieved 300 million dollars.[37]

As believed by some analysts, during the visit of Prince Bandar, the Saudis decided to use the energy leverage to influence the behaviour of Moscow. Thus, as reported, they allegedly guaranteed that the GCC countries will not create obstacles for Russian gas exports to the EU in exchange for the refusal of Kremlin to support Assad. Apart from that Riyadh promised to start the full-scale imports of Russian arms. However, this information has never been officially confirmed.[38] The visit of Mohammad Nahyan to Moscow was more transparent. The sides openly confirmed their interest in the development of bilateral economic relations. Being from the point of the Gulf Arabs quite an often visitor to Moscow (the previous visit of Mohammad Nahyan to Russia took place in October 2012), the sheikh declared the intention of the UAE to invest up to USD 5 billion in Russian transport infrastructure. Putin and Nahyan were satisfied with the growth of the trade volume between the two countries which hit the level in USD 2 billion. Subsequently, they expressed hopes that the positive trend in the bilateral trade will continue.[39]

Russian Relations with the Middle East after the Ukrainian Crisis of 2014

In 2014, the beginning of the serious confrontation between Russia and the West in the wake of the annexation of Crimea by Moscow brought substantial changes in Kremlin‘s policy towards the Middle East. First of all, Moscow’s contacts with the countries of the region became a part of Russian strategy aimed at an avoidance of complete international isolation. Russia obviously welcomes any intention demonstrated by the regional players to talk to Moscow and, on its own end, it also tries to involve the Middle Eastern powers in active discussion on a wide range of issues. Thus, the attempt of Cairo to diversify its foreign policy vectors through the intensification of relations with Russia in 2014 found positive reaction in Moscow and resulted in Putin’s trip to Egypt on 9-10 February 2015. Special attention is paid by the Russian authorities towards the development of contacts with the regional organizations and to the creation of additional ground for the dialogue between Moscow and the countries of the region. Thus, apart from the “Russia-GCC Strategic Dialogue” initiative the Kremlin also launched the Arab-Russian Cooperation Forum where Russian officials and high-ranking representatives (usually at the level of foreign ministers) of the Arab countries could discuss existing political and economic problems So far, the Forum has held two meetings: in Moscow (February 2013) and in Khartoum (December 2014).

Moscow has actively developed its contacts with the Organization of Islamic Conference (OIC) and the League of the Arab States (LAS). The Russian authorities are seriously concerned with the attempts of some forces in the Middle East to present Moscow as the main enemy of Islam and provoke conservative political groupings within the OIC and LAS countries to support the activities of radical Islamists in the Caucasus and Central Asia. Currently, Moscow is trying to use the areas of common interest in order to demonstrate to the OIC and LAS members that Russia is not an enemy of the Muslim world. Thus, in February 2015, Moscow hosted the OIC delegation headed by Egyptian foreign minister Sameh Hassan Shukri to discuss the current situation in Palestine and East Jerusalem. On 29 March 2015, Putin sent his message to the LAS summit that stated Moscow's intention to develop relations with the Arab countries and support the peaceful settlement of all existing regional conflicts. Among other, the Kremlin expressed its support for the two-state solution in Palestine.

Through its active Middle Eastern policy, Russia also seeks to demonstrate to the US and the EU that they should not move further in their confrontation with Kremlin over Ukraine as Moscow's assistance may play a crucial role in the settlement of existing international issues. From this point of view, conflicts existing in the Middle East provide ample opportunities for the Russian authorities. On 30 December 2014, Moscow was among the eight UN SC members who supported the resolution that was supposed to set the timeframe for the establishment of an independent Palestinian state. Moscow provided important support to the negotiation process between P5+1 and Iran. In January 2015, it conducted what was positioned as the global meeting of the Syrian opposition members with the representatives of Assad regime. Later on, the modest results of these negotiations were positioned as substantial achievements of Russian mediators aimed at the stabilization of the situation in a war-torn country. The same trick was repeated by the Russians in April 2015 when they organized the second meeting of the Syrian opposition with the representatives of official authorities (so-called Moscow-2 meeting). Its results (modest as in the case of Moscow-1 meeting) were again portrayed by the moderator of negotiations, Vitaly Naumkin, as another important positive achievement.

To a certain extent, Moscow managed to convince the West of its importance. Thus, the active Russian role in the multilateral negotiations on the Iran's nuclear issue is considered by American analysts as one of the main factors that, so far, guaranteed the success of the negotiations process. In March 2014, it was enough for Russian deputy minister of foreign affairs Sergey Ryabkov only to mention that in the wake of the Ukrainian crises the Kremlin can reconsider its participation in the work of the P5+1 group on Iran to keep people in Washington concerned about this possibility during the remaining part of 2014. High-ranking officials of the EU also view the Kremlin as a significant player in the Middle Eastern quartet on Palestine. On 5 March 2015, UN special envoy for Syria, Staffan de Mistura, during his speech at the Royal Institute of Foreign Affairs argued that Russia can be helpful as a part of negotiation process on Syria because only Moscow (and Tehran) can directly speak to Bashar Assad and its regime. He also gave a positive feedback on Russian efforts to arrange a separate forum for dialogue between the Syrian opposition and Damascus in Moscow. Literally the same statements were made in April 2015 by the high-ranking representative of a leading US think-tank directly involved in the track-two diplomacy in Syria: in spite of the fact that he recognized the failure of the Moscow-1 and Moscow-2 meetings, he stressed that Russia was the only country successful in creating the ground for negotiations between the regime and the opposition. Finally, it could not be a coincidence that, after the success of the nuclear negotiations in Lausanne, the US diplomats in Moscow started to test the ground regarding the possibilities to cooperate with the Kremlin on other regional issues including the situation in Yemen and Libya.

Conclusion

The events of the Arab Spring and their aftermath were a serious stress-test for Russian foreign policy on the Middle East. The fall of old dictatorial regimes compelled Moscow to adjust its approaches to a brand new political vista which was not always friendly to the Kremlin. If before 2011 the Russian authorities considered the region to be of the secondary importance within the framework of their global diplomatic doctrine, the Arab Spring lucidly demonstrated that in order to secure Russian national interests Moscow needs to be more active in developing its relations with the regional countries. In other words, it was high time to restore, at least, part of Russian influence in the Middle East lost after the fall of the Soviet Union. Moreover, the revolutionary events changed the general Russian perception of the Middle Eastern countries. By 2013, they were not seen as just another trading item in the relations of Moscow with the US and the EU or a chessboard where Russia and the West were playing their games: the Arab spring made Kremlin regard them as independent players on the international arena with their own task and priorities and deal with them as equals.

On the other hand, the Arab Spring gave the answer to the countries of the region concerning the place of modern Russia within the system of the international relations of the Middle East. Moscow's stubbornness in defending its interests in Syria as well as readiness to continue the dialogue with new regimes proved that the RF is an important player in the region which should neither neglected nor underestimated. Although the Russian authorities are still periodically making short-sighted and hasty steps (such as the demonstrative evacuation of the Russian embassy from Tripoli on 3 October 2013 in response to the provocation of unknown militias), there are hopes that the diplomacy of Moscow become more coherent and subtle.

References

1. Interview with an analyst on the Middle East Politics, St. Andrews, June 2013.
2. Igor Naumov, "Rossiyskiye Ubytki ot Arabskoy Vesny," *Nezavisimaya Gazeta,* 29 February 2012. *http*://www.ng.ru/economics/2012-02-29/1_arab_vesna.html. Accessed on 4 October 2013.
3. Naumov, "Rossiyskiye Ubytki ot Arabskoy Vesny."
4. Eldar Kasaev, "Rossiysko-liviyskie Ekonomicheskiye Otnosheniya," in http://iimes.ru/rus/stat/2010/08-06-10.htm. Accessed on 4 October 2013.
5. Vladimir Evseev, "Nikotoryie aspekty rossiysko-siriyskogo sotrudnichestva," http://www.iimes.ru/rus/stat/2008/04-03-08b.htm. Accessed on 31 May 2013; Ministerstvo Ekonomicheskogo Razvitiya Rossii, "Torgovo-ekonomicheskiye otnosheniya Rossiyskoy Federatscii I Siriyskoy Arabskoy Respubliki," http://www.economy.gov.ru/minec/pressnewsdoc1227277900147?presentationtemplate=docHTMLTemplate1&presentationtemplateid=2dd7bc8044687de796f0f7af753c8a7e&WCM_Page. ResetAll=TRUE&CACHE=NONE&CONTENTCACHE=NONE& CONNECTORCACHE=NONE. Accessed on 31 May 2013.
6. Evseev, "Nikotoryie aspekty rossiysko-siriyskogo sotrudnichestva"; Aleksey Sarabyev, "Rossiysko-Siriyskoye 'nastoyaschee-budushchee': voenno-morskoy aspect," *Rossiyskiy Sovet po Mezhdunarodnym Delam,* 10 October 2011. http://russiancouncil.ru/inner/?id_4=35#top. Accessed on 31 May 2013.

7. Ekaterina Kats, "Arabskiy Shchet," *Kompaniya*, No. 33, 2011 http://ko.ru/articles/23468. Accessed on 4 October 2013.
8. Eldar Kasaev, "Rossiya i Katar: Prichiny Ekonomicheskoy Stagnatcii," http://www.iimes.ru/?p=17847. Accessed on 4 October 2013.
9. Eldar Kasaev, "Ekonomicheskoye Partnerstvo Rossii I OAE: Tekushchee Sostoyaniye i Politicheskiye Riski," in http://www.iimes.ru/?p=18069. 4 October 2013.
10. Kasaev, "Rossiya i Katar."
11. Irena Mokhova, "Obraz Rossii v Arabskom Mire."
12. Mokhova, "Obraz Rossii v Arabskom Mire."
13. Mokhova, "Obraz Rossii v Arabskom Mire."
14. Aleksandr Shumilin, *Rossiya i "Novye Elity" Stran "Arabskoy Vesny": Vozmozhnosti i Perspektivy Vzaimodeystviya*, Moscow: Rossiyskiy Sovet po Mezhdunarodnym Delam, 2013, p. 34.
15. Dmitriy Nechitaylo, "Severokavkaztcsy v Grazhdanskoy Voyne v Sirii," in http://www.iimes.ru/?p=18111. Accessed on 4 October 2013.
16. Vladimir Akhmetov, "'Russkaya Komanda' v Sirii?" in http://www.iimes.ru/?p=17868. Accessed on 5 October 2013.
17. Shumilin, *Rossiya i "Novye Elity" Stran "Arabskoy Vesny."*
18. "Margelov: RF Aktiviziruyet Kontakty s Oppozitcsiey i Vlastyami Livii," *RIA Novosti*, 27 May 2011. http://ria.ru/arab_ly/20110527/380644465.html. Accessed on 5 October 2013.
19. "Medvedev Podpsal Ukaz o Sanktcsiyah protiv Livii," *VoA*, 12 August 2011. http://www.golos-ameriki.ru/content/russia-lybia-medvedev-sanctions-2011-08-12-127578108/241893.html. Accessed on 5 October 2013; "Rossiya Sklonyaetsya k Uzhestocheniyu Sanktcsiy protiv Livii," *Zhenmin Zhibao*, 15 August 2011. http://russian.people.com.cn/31519/7568885.html. Accessed on 5 October 2013; "Bastrykina Poprosili Proverit Deyatelnost Medvedeva na Fakt Izmeny," *Nakanune*, 4 February 2013. http://www.nakanune.ru/news/2013/2/4/22299398/ Last accessed on 5 October 2013
20. Kasaev, "Ekonomicheskoye Partnerstvo Rossii I OAE."
21. Interview with an expert on Syria, Washington DC, May 2012; interview with an expert on the Middle East, St. Andrews, June 2013.
22. Ministerstvo Inostrannikh del Rossiyskoy Federatcsii, "Intervyu minisra inostrannikh del Rossii S.V. Lavrova v programme 'Voskresniy vecher s Vladimirom Solovevim' na telekanale 'Rossiya-1'," Moskva, 10 fevralya 2013 goda'. http://mid.ru/bdomp/brp_4.nsf 2fee282eb6df40e643256999005e6e8c02ebc66354ef10e544257b0e0045ad41!OpenDocument. Accessed on 31 May 2013.
23. Ministerstvo Inostrannikh del Rossiyskoy Federatcsii, "Intervyu minisra inostrannikh del Rossii S.V. Lavrova v programme."
24. Interview with an expert on Russian foreign policy, Moscow, February 2013.

25. Grigoriy Kosach, "Pozitcsiya Rossii po Siriiskomu Krizisu v Arabskoy Presse posle Vstrechi G8," http://www.iimes.ru/?p=17779. Accessed on 5 October 2013.
26. Ministerstvo Inostrannikh Del Rossiyskoy Federatcsii, "Intervyu Ministra Inostrannikh Del Rossii S.V. Lavrova Alzhirskoy Gazete 'Al-Khabar', 3 Iyulya 2013," in http://www.mid.ru/bdomp/BRP_4.nsf/fa711a859c4b939643256999005bcbbc/c48f6a5826b92fc544257b9d003f674f!OpenDocument. Accessed on 5 October 2013.
27. Ministerstvo Inostrannikh Del Rossiyskoy Federatcsii, "Intervyu Ministra Inostrannikh Del Rossii S.V. Lavrova Alzhirskoy Gazete 'Al-Khabar'."
28. Eldar Kasaev, "Alzhir: Ekonomicheskiye Svyazi s Rossiey i Sostoyaniye Energeticheskogo Sektora," in http://www.iimes.ru/?p=18101. Accessed on 5 October 2013
29. Eldar Kasaev, "K Voprosu o Torgovo-Ekonomicheskikh Svyazyakh Rossii I Egipta," in http://www.iimes.ru/?p=16844. Accessed on 5 October 2013.
30. Interview with an analyst on the modern Middle East, Moscow, August 2013.
31. Vitaliy Bilan, "Vizit Presidenta ARE M. Morsi v Rossiyu I Egipetskaya Yadernaya Programma," in http://www.iimes.ru/?p=17374. Accessed on 5 October 2013.
32. Ministerstvo Inostrannikh Del Rossiyskoy Federatcsii, "O Peregovorakh Ministra Inostrannikh Del Rossii S.V. Lavrova s Ministrom inostrannikh Del Egipta N. Fakhmi," in http://mid.ru/brp_4.nsf/newsline/ECF7E11312785DD644257BE8004A55AB. Accessed on 5 October 2013.
33. Igor Korotchenko, "Liviya Poluchila Pervuyu Partiyu Novikh Rossiyskikh Vooruzheniy Posle Sverzheniya Kaddafi," in *VestiFM,* 30 September 2013. http://radiovesti.ru/blogs/post/80001. Accessed on 5 October 2013.
34. Viktor Nekhezin, "Rossiya Prodala Iraku Nedodelanniye Vertolety MI-28," BBC, 28 June 2013. http://www.bbc.co.uk/russian/international/2013/06/130628_iraq_russia_helicopters.shtml. Accessed on 5 October 2013.
35. "Irak: Kontrakty na Pokupku Oruzhiya v Rossii ne Otmenyalis," BBC, 13 February 2013. http://www.bbc.co.uk/russian/russia/2013/02/130213_iraq_contracts_russia.shtml. Accessed on 5 October 2013.
36. Naser al-Tamimi, "Saudi-Russian Relations: Between Assad and Sisi," *Al-Arabiya*, 18 August 2013. http://english.alarabiya.net/en/views/news/middle-east/2013/08/18/Saudi-Russian-relations-between-Assad-and-Sisi.html. Accessed on 5 October 2013.
37. Ludmila Shkvarya, "Rossiya i Strany Zaliva: Investitsionnoye Sotrudnichestvo," *Aziya i Afrika Segodnya*, no. 5, 2011: 18-23.
38. "Saudovskaya Araviya Obeshchayet i Ugrozhayet Rossii po Sirii," *Vesti,* 27 August 2013. http://www.vestifinance.ru/articles/31671. Accessed on 5 October 2013.
39. Aleksey Chesnokov, "OAE Vlozhat Milliardy Dollarov v Infrastrukturu Rossii," *VestiFM,* 12 September 2013. http://radiovesti.ru/article/show/article_id/105871. Accessed on 5 October 2013.

Contributors

Deen Sharp, Doctoral student, Earth and Environmental Science Department, The Graduate Center, City University of New York, New York, USA.

Harel Chorev, Fellow, Moshe Dayan Center for Middle Eastern and African Studies at Tel Aviv University, Tel Aviv, Israel.

Priya Singh, Former Fellow, Maulana Abul Kalam Azad Institute of Asian Studies, Kolkata, India.

Deepika Saraswat, Doctoral student, Political Geography Division, Center for International Politics, Organisation and Disarmament, School of International Studies, Jawaharlal Nehru University, New Delhi, India.

Kingshuk Chatterjee, Associate Professor, Department of History, Calcutta University, Kolkata, India.

Sujata Ashwarya Cheema, Assistant Professor, Centre for West Asian Studies, Jamia Millia Islamia, New Delhi, India.

Alper Y. Dede, Assistant Professor of International Relations, Zirve University, Gaziantep, Turkey.

Mujib Alam, Assistant Professor, Academy of International Studies, Jamia Millia Islamia, New Delhi, India.

Joseph Alagha, Professor of Political Science, Haigazian University, Beirut, Lebanon.

Mustapha Kamel Al-Sayyid, Professor, Department of Economics and Political Science, Cairo University, Cairo, Egypt.

Paul Rivlin, Senior Fellow, Moshe Dayan Centre for Middle Eastern and African Studies, Tel Aviv University, Tel Aviv, Israel.

Nadine Sika, Assistant Professor, Department of Political Science, American University of Cairo, Cairo, Egypt.

Konrad Pêdziwiatr, Assistant Professor, Krakow University of Economics, Krakow, Poland.

Nikolay A. Kozhanov, Senior Lecturer in Political Economy of the Middle East, St. Petersburg State University, St. Petersburg, Russia.

Index